1988

Red Guard Factionalism and the Cultural Revolution in Guangzhou (Canton)

Westview Replica Editions

This book is a Westview Replica Edition. The concept of
Replica Editions is a response to the crisis in academic and
informational publishing. Library budgets for books have been
severely curtailed; economic pressures on the university presses
and the few private publishing companies primarily interested in
scholarly manuscripts have severely limited the capacity of the
industry to properly serve the academic and research communities.
Many manuscripts dealing with important subjects, often representing the highest level of scholarship, are today not econom-
ically viable publishing projects. Or, if they are accepted for
publication, they are often subject to lead times ranging from
one to three years. Scholars are understandably frustrated when
they realize that their first-class research cannot be published
within a reasonable time frame, if at all.

Westview Replica Editions are our practical solution to the
problem. The concept is simple. We accept a manuscript in camera-
ready form and move it immediately into the production process.
The responsibility for textual and copy editing lies with the
author or sponsoring organization. If necessary we will advise
the author on proper preparation of footnotes and bibliography.
We prefer that the manuscript be typed according to our speci-
fications, though it may be acceptable as typed for a dissertation or prepared in some other clearly organized and readable
way. The end result is a book produced by lithography and bound
in hard covers. Initial edition sizes range from 400 to 800
copies, and a number of recent Replicas are already in second
printings. We include ámong Westview Replica Editions only works
of outstanding scholarly quality or of great informational value,
and we will continue to exercise our usual editorial standards
and quality control.

About the Book and Author

Red Guard Factionalism
and the Cultural Revolution in Guangzhou (Canton)
Stanley Rosen

This study examines the causes of factionalism within China's
Red Guard during the Great Proletarian Cultural Revolution. Professor Rosen explores the reasons behind the division of students
into two large, antagonistic factions--conservative and rebel. He
then analyzes internal divisions within the rebel faction, showing
the social bases for membership in the various subfactions. Focusing
primarily on middle-school students in Guangzhou, but looking also
at university students, he reaches two primary conclusions: (1) the
class origin of middle-school students tended to determine whether
they joined forces with the rebel or the conservative faction, and
(2) the Cultural Revolution was contested most fiercely at those secondary schools that contained significant numbers of students of
cadre and intellectual family origin--the "good" schools. Professor
Rosen examines the interests of each of the factions; their constit-
uencies and sources of support; and the issues that divided rebels
and conservatives, as viewed in light of post-Mao politics.

Stanley Rosen is assistant professor of political science at the
University of Southern California. He also has taught at the Univer-
sity of California, San Diego, and at the United College of the Chinese
University of Hong Kong.

Red Guard Factionalism and the Cultural Revolution in Guangzhou (Canton)

Stanley Rosen

Westview Press / Boulder, Colorado

A Westview Replica Edition

Published in 1982 in the United States of America by
     Westview Press, Inc.
     5500 Central Avenue
     Boulder, Colorado 80301
     Frederick A. Praeger, Publisher

Library of Congress Cataloging in Publication Data
Rosen, Stanley, 1942-
     Red Guard factionalism and the Cultural Revolution in Guangzhou (Canton)
     (A Westview replica edition)
     Bibliography: p.
     Includes index.
     1. China--History--Cultural Revolution, 1966-1969. 2. Education--China--
History--1949-1976. 3. Hung wei ping. 4. Canton (China)--Politics and
government. I. Title. II. Series.
DS778.7.R67   951'.27   81-16386
ISBN 0-86531-222-2   AACR2

Printed and bound in the United States of America

For my parents

Al Rosen
and
Frances Rosen

Contents

Abbreviations

BJRB	Beijing Ribao [Beijing Daily]
BR	Beijing Review
BTZB	Bingtuan Zhanbao [Regiment Combat News]
CB	Current Background
CCP	Chinese Communist Party
CCRG	Central Cultural Revolution Group
CMAC	Central Military Affairs Commission
CNIFP	China News Items From the Press
CNS	China News Summary
CQ	The China Quarterly
DSJP	Daily Summary of the Japanese Press
FBIS	Foreign Broadcast Information Service
GLF	Great Leap Forward
GMRB	Guangming Ribao [Bright Daily]
GPCR	Great Proletarian Cultural Revolution
JPRS	Joint Publications Research Service
JYGM	Jiaoyu Geming [Educational Revolution]
LAD	Liberation Army Daily
MCC	Military Control Commission
MTG	Military Training Group
NCNA	New China News Agency
NFRB	Nanfang Ribao [Southern Daily]
PLA	People's Liberation Army
RMRB	Renmin Ribao [People's Daily]
SCMM	Selections from China Mainland Magazines
SCMP	Survey of the China Mainland Press
SCMP(S)	Survey of the China Mainland Press (Supplement)
SEM	Socialist Education Movement
SGL	Shenggelian [Provincial Revolutionary Alliance]
URS	Union Research Service
WHB	Wenhui Bao [Literary News]
YCL	Young Communist League
YCWB	Yangcheng Wanbao [Guangzhou Evening News]
ZGQN	Zhongguo Qingnian [China Youth]
ZGQNB	Zhongguo Qingnian Bao [China Youth Daily]

Tables, Figures, and Maps

FIGURES

MAPS

Acknowledgments

First and foremost, I must express my debt to all those former Red Guards who unselfishly sacrificed their time and energy so that I might understand a bit better the meaning of the Cultural Revolution. Without their assistance this book could never have been written.

The Facilities provided by the Universities Service Centre in Hong Kong likewise were invaluable. I would like to thank B. Michael Frolic, Martin Whyte and John Dolfin, the directors of the Centre during my stay there from 1972-1976, and during the summer of 1980.

I also wish to acknowledge the aid and the unstinting hospitality of C. P. Ch'en and the staff of the Center for Chinese Studies of the University of California, Berkeley on my frequent visits there.

The University of Paris VII provided me with Red Guard newspapers from Beijing that were unavailable in the United States or Hong Kong.

Financial aid enabling me to work on this project has come from a variety of sources over the years. While at the University of California, Los Angeles, such aid came in the form of National Defense Foreign Language fellowships, Education Abroad teaching fellowships, and the President's Pilot Work-Study Internship. While at the University of Southern California, I have received financial aid from the Haynes Foundation and the East Asian Studies Center.

Helpful comments on the dissertation from which this book derives were made by Richard Baum and Ezra Vogel. Editorial advice and assistance was provided by Mervyn Seldon. Richard Gunde read the completed manuscript and made many useful suggestions. Typing aid was provided primarily by Rose Cruz, with important additional help from Calvin Chan and Anne Avzaradel.

Introduction

When the Chinese Great Proletarian Cultural Revolution (GPCR) of the middle and late 1960s burst forth, the
initial response both in China and the West seemed primarily to be one of mystification. The spectacle of
severe splits among leaders long thought to be compati-
ble, of armed struggles between factional units whose
uniform pledges to Chairman Mao and the Party Center appeared to make their similarities greater than their differences, and of destructive Red Guards who were bent on
"tearing down the old world to build a new one" was at
first difficult to explain.

When explanations did begin to emerge, following the
revelations in the Chinese press, they centered most often on intra-elite differences that were traced back at
least to the 1950s. Outside observers seldom subjected
the organizations formed by the Chinese masses to the
same scrutiny they reserved for the Chinese leadership.
It is clear, however, that the ambitious goals of the
GPCR could be achieved only through the mobilization of
China's masses in support of these goals. Therefore the
organizations formed by these mobilized masses, rather
than conflicts dividing the elite, are the concern of
this book. More specifically, the behavior of China's
youths is examined. The actors include both middle
school and university students in Guangzhou, with primary emphasis on middle school students.

The focus on secondary school students stems from
the analysis of the educational structure as the most
important determinant of upward mobility for Chinese
students and an evaluation of the differing positions
within this structure of three main classes of students
and other youths. Expressed simply, youths who had been
sent to the countryside (sent-down youths) had already
lost, university students had to a large extent succeeded, and middle school students were still contending.
This assessment of middle school students as "contenders"
forms the prime backdrop of this book.

This analysis of factionalism among secondary school students seeks to demonstrate that the pattern of factional formation and factional participation grew directly out of the contradictions and conflicts - some manifest, some latent - which had already divided the students before the GPCR. Thus, Part One presents an examination of the Chinese educational system and classroom relationships at the middle school level over the 1960-66 period, and Part Two is devoted to the GPCR.

Upon beginning the research for this book, I felt that a detailed analysis of pre-Cultural Revolution conditions in Chinese schools would be unnecessary; indeed, along with many observers of the GPCR, I assumed that the factionalism that was so prominent a feature of the movement was a response primarily to issues that had surfaced only _after_ the movement had begun. Some students were simply ideologically more attuned to the appeals of the "Maoist" radicals in Beijing and thus became "Rebels" determined to overthrow "those in the Party taking the capitalist road." Other students were inclined to become "Conservatives" and thus more circumspect in launching attacks on leading Party and military figures.

As I began reading the Red Guard press and, especially, as I began to interview former Rebel and Conservative Red Guards, it quickly became clear to me that, at least in the case of middle school students, an understanding of GPCR participation patterns required the detailed study of the educational system and student relationships in the 1960s. My initial results revealed, for example, that the two large factions were class-based. Secondary school students of "middle" and "bad class" origin were much more likely to become Rebels while those of revolutionary cadre and military origin joined the Conservatives in large numbers. Moreover, GPCR patterns of participation varied from school to school. As interviewees repeatedly brought up these class origin and school differences, it became clear that I would have to seek explanations for these phenomena by increasingly centering my interviews and my reading on the 1960-66 period. This new focus revealed that by the eve of the GPCR a surprising number of cleavages had developed within China's secondary schools and, moreover, that the roots of Red Guard factionalism were to be found in these cleavages. It is to these "roots" that I now turn.

This analysis takes as its starting point several inherent contradictions in the structure of China's educational system. This system was responsible for accomplishing a number of state priorities which were often incompatible. For example, the educational system was required speedily to produce the competent personnel necessary for a country seeking to modernize rapidly; the same educational system was expected to further the opportunities of children of workers and peasants. In like manner, the educational system was programmed to instill socialist values of cooperation and collectivization at the same time as it sorted out those individuals who were qualified to further their education from those who were expected to join the urban labor force or to rusticate. The attempts of national policy makers to balance these often contradictory priorities led to alternations in policy from year to year, and the shifting criteria by which these policy decisions were made were of great importance in explaining the cleavages that developed.

The three criteria used in recruiting and promoting students were academic achievement, class origin, and political performance. Students could be characterized by the advantages and disadvantages they possessed with regard to each of these criteria. Because the relative weight of these three criteria shifted over time, there was considerable variation in and uncertainty over the recruitment process. Thus, students who would be favored when the state stressed the class origin of applicants might be disadvantaged if academic achievement were to become of prime importance, and vice versa. As "contenders" still competing for the prize of higher education, students in middle schools were most directly affected by these shifts in national policy. These policy alternations were much less of a factor in explaining the GPCR behavior of university students.

It is important to realize that these student recruitment decisions were being made at a time - the mid-1960s - in which urban students faced declining opportunities for upward mobility. Compared to the 1950s, middle school graduates began finding it increasingly difficult to move on to the university or to obtain an urban factory job. This was certainly true of Guangzhou, the city with which this book is most concerned.

On the eve of the GPCR, middle school students found themselves embedded in an educational structure marked by the following prominent features, each of which intruded upon the cooperative environment the state was attempting to foster:

(1) The importance of a university education for qualified students was repeatedly stressed by the official media. At the same time, students were also being told that it was equally glorious to depart for the countryside and devote their lives to aiding China's peasants. However, students were discouraged from opting for the second road if they could qualify for the first by their performance on the university entrance examination.

(2) China's middle school administrators also emphasized to their students the importance of a university education. Secondary school officials competed with

each other to garner the best students and, through their recruitment, sought to raise their school's promotion rate to the university. "Success" for a school had become linked to a high promotion rate.

(3) The increasing competition among secondary school officials led more and more to a hierarchically structured secondary school system. In one sense the "regular" middle school system had always been bifurcated, with the main division coming between junior and senior high. Upon graduating from junior high, students had several options, among which was a continuation on to senior high. The primary function of senior high, however, was to prepare students for the university. As all schools intensified their efforts to recruit those most likely to gain university entrance, the gap between the schools, represented by promotion rate, generally became wider and wider.

(4) Concurrent with an increasing rigidity in informal school "rankings" (in terms of promotion rate), as the good schools got better and the poor schools became worse, was a general tightening in senior high enrollment. Expansion in the educational system was taking place primarily at the lower levels, in primary school and junior high. Good senior highs, and good junior highs as well, could afford to become much more selective in their enrollment decisions by 1964 and 1965.

Student relationships must be understood in the context of this picture of the educational structure. By the eve of the GPCR, a series of cleavages divided China's secondary school students. Most prominent perhaps was the cleavage separating those of high academic achievement and less-than-good class origin from those whose attributes were just the reverse. This particular cleavage was the most obvious and most important among those in the same classrooms.

Students could also be divided on the basis of the school they attended; those who went to keypoint schools (zhongdian xuexiao) with high university promotion rates were likely to be much more politically active than those who attended less favored schools. Within the same school as well, junior and senior high students had differing characteristics. Students in senior high tended to have superior academic achievement and inferior class background as compared to their counterparts in junior high.

A precise distinction between those of "good class origin" and those of "less-than-good class origin" is crucial to this analysis. Among those of good class origin, the increased importance accorded to class origin by the mid-1960s benefitted those from revolutionary cadre and military families much more than it did those from working class and peasant homes. At the same time, among those students whose class origin was "less-than-good," those of bad class origin were singled out and disadvantaged much more than those from "middle class" origins (such as intellectuals, middle peasants, peddlers, and so forth).

As the GPCR drew near, there were thus two groups of students who were most favored by the educational policies and the educational system as they existed in the mid-1960s: students of revolutionary cadre (including military) origin and students of middle class origin who had high academic achievement.

In spite of the advantages possessed by these two groups vis-a-vis other students, however, each of the two favored groups had reason to feel disgruntled as a result of the educational policies of the mid-1960s. While students of cadre and military backgrounds had begun to benefit from the new "class line" policies of the Party, the lingering importance accorded to entrance examination scores by the better universities continued to militate against their success. At the same time, within the middle schools, policies visibly aided those of good class origin, particularly children of cadres. Examples of such policies would include special tutorial sessions for those of good class origin, favoritism in recruitment to the Young Communist League (YCL), and so forth. Most unsettling to some was the fact that the very best of the secondary schools began, in 1964, to recruit children of cadres almost exclusively. Thus, even as those of middle class origin remained competitive at the highest levels of schooling, there was at the least some uneasiness about what the future might hold.

The arrival of the GPCR in one sense prevented a resolution of these contradictions dividing China's students; in another sense, however, the GPCR provided a lighted stage upon which these contradictions could be publicly played out. In effect, the criticisms levelled against the educational system during the GPCR gave middle school students the opportunity to display the types of political activism that had become progressively trivialized in the pre-GPCR period. Each of the two contesting forces was able to seize upon the pre-GPCR faults and GPCR missteps of the other to demand a cleansing of China's "revisionist" system of education.

Compared to middle school students, the behavior of university students in the GPCR has been dealt with somewhat less directly in this study. The treatment of university students has for several reasons most often been in the context of overall factional developments. First, whereas it proved to be relatively easy to account for GPCR factional participation by middle school students on the basis of social background characteristics such as class origin, it was much more difficult to do so for university students. Although class origin was of some importance in explaining factional participation by uni-

versity students, it does not seem to have been the major
factor it was for secondary school students. In fact,
none of the university students I interviewed thought it
was the key determinant. The crucial factor, rather,
seems to have been ideological acceptance of the "Maoist"
position, based on a more sophisticated understanding of
Chinese society. Many of those successfully mobilized
as "Rebels" by the Maoists at the Party Center appear to
have been from good class backgrounds. In Guangzhou the
overwhelming majority of university students who participated did so on the Rebel side. Whereas middle school
students formed their various Red Guard units primarily
on the basis of their response to the "class line" issue,
university students were more concerned with such questions as cadre assessment.

Second, an important theme in this study is that a
fuller understanding of the GPCR must take into account
the divisions within factions as well as between them.
Thus, particularly in our discussion of the Rebels in
Guangzhou, we disaggregate this large organization to
reveal the subfactional splits that periodically threatened to tear such large units apart. Because these
powerful subfactional forces -often aligned around a
"headquarters" - were led by Red Guard units and individuals from the various universities, our analysis of the
factionalism of university students has often been included within our discussion of these subfactional
splits.

A Word On Sources

The material presented derives from three main
sources. The first is the official press. Since I am
concerned with a local area, much of the most useful information has come from local newspapers such as Yangcheng Wanbao and Nanfang Ribao, both published in Guangzhou. Throughout the period covered, but particularly
during the GPCR when local newspapers were looked upon
suspiciously as provincial leadership came to be questioned by Red Guards, were taken over by one or another
faction, or ceased publication altogether, I have relied
on such national organs as People's Daily (Renmin Ribao),
Red Flag (Hongqi), Liberation Army Daily, Guangming
Ribao, China Youth Daily (Zhongguo Qingnian Bao), and
so forth. One looks to these newspapers and magazines
with nationwide circulation for early signs of policy
shifts.

The second source I have used extensively is the
newspapers published by the Red Guards. The official
media were extremely reluctant to detail the differences
between Red Guard groupings, particularly in the early
period when the GPCR leadership was intent on mobilizing
as many students as possible. Invidiously comparing one

group to another would have dampened the enthusiasm of
the lesser group. It was thus to the Red Guard press
and their "little newspapers" (xiaobao) that one turned
to discover the differences existing among student
groups. Fortunately for this study, xiaobao from both
Beijing and Guangzhou are available in some quantity.
In addition, the coverage provided is to a certain extent
complementary in that the newspapers from Beijing are
rich for the early GPCR period (until mid-1967) whereas
the Guangzhou papers cover mostly late 1967 and most of
1968. The papers, however, tend to be from university
groups. Those put out by middle school students are
much less numerous. Still, some extremely useful data,
including some pre-GPCR educational statistics, can be
gotten from the Red Guard press.

My final source consists of interview data, gathered
primarily in Hong Kong during the years 1971-76, and the
summer of 1980. This, not coincidentally, was a period
in which vast numbers of people left China. The largest
number, particularly those who left illegally, were very
different from those who had left during the previous
major exodus in 1962. Post-GPCR arrivals consisted mostly of youths who had experienced the GPCR firsthand; many
had been active participants. During my five years
there, I was able to meet and interview in depth a great
many of these youths, several of whom had been Red Guard
leaders not just at their own schools, but at the municipal level as well. Since some had been members of the
editorial boards of the very Red Guard papers I was reading, I was able to gain particular insights into an occ-
asional article that at first glance appeared to be con-
fusing. Most importantly, details learned in interview-
ing approximately 100 former students and Red Guards,
from a wide variety of Guangzhou schools, provided insights on the relationship between the pre-GPCR educational system and the basis of factions. Interviews also
helped explain why factionalism developed at different
speeds and took somewhat different forms at the different schools. The elaboration of these school differences
forms an important segment in several of the chapters,
including the early pre-GPCR chapters. Most of the students I interviewed had been members of the "Rebel" faction, called the "Flag" faction. This was especially
the case of those who had been leaders. In addition,
the majority of those interviewed were of ordinary or bad
class background. Those I interviewed of worker-peasant
background tended, at best, to be active in the GPCR at
classroom or school level rather than at citywide level.
This was also the case for those I interviewed from cadre backgrounds.

Part 1:
Students and Schools,
1960–1966

By the eve of the GPCR, several cleavages had developed within China's student population. Even more fundamental, there was a contradiction between the two primary aims the state was attempting to achieve through its educational system: 1) the creation of a "new Socialist man" who would be both "red and expert"; who would emphasize cooperation and collective values over competition and individual self-aggrandizement; and 2) the use of the educational system to determine future job assignments for Chinese students. Additionally, by the mid-1960s, these contradictions were being fueled by students' narrowing prospects for upward mobility.

In laying the groundwork for an explanation of the causes of GPCR factionalism, Chapter One argues that, given the structure of the educational system and the behavior of central leaders and local officials working in the field of education, the second aim ultimately was accorded more importance than the first. Chapter Two then examines the effect of the structure described in Chapter One on classroom relationships and student behavior.

1
Mission and Structure of the Educational System

As a first step to understanding the Chinese educational system of the 1960s, it is necessary to realize that a broad consensus regarding the importance of a university education prevailed among students, middle school officials and the central leadership. Nearly all Chinese students in urban areas who had managed to reach higher middle school sought to extend their education into the university. As will be shown, there really were few other viable alternatives once one had chosen to attend a "regular" senior high.[1]

The aspirations of these students were strongly reinforced by middle school officials who, in their own interests, sought a high promotion rate to the university. Moreover, official policy as transmitted through the official press, in consistently pointing out China's need for those with a higher education and strongly encouraging all eligible students to sit for the entrance examinations, sanctioned the prevailing values among students and educational administrators.

Although these features were constant, throughout the 1960s there were important changes in China's educational system. While the basic educational structure remained unchanged, over the 1960-66 period the state did at times alter its priorities and some of its policies, to conform to changing conceptions of the mission of the educational system. Shifts in state policy required adjustments by secondary school administrators eager to maintain or increase their school's success in promoting students to the university. Finally, these official policy shifts and the behavioral modifications they induced in administrators affected different categories of students in dissimilar ways.

The early 1960s witnessed the high tide of academic achievement as the main criterion for university enrollment in China. Beginning in 1964, however, a student's class origin became of great importance for university admission. These shifts in national policy regarding

11

recruitment criteria emphasis seem to have exerted a
major influence on both students and administrators.

CRITERIA FOR UNIVERSITY RECRUITMENT

University selection in China has, since 1949, been
a function of the changing relationships among three
major criteria, geared to three priorities the government
held paramount.
One priority was the desire to build a strong and
modern state. There was a great demand for skilled
personnel to occupy the key positions required for an
industrializing state with a rapidly expanding economy.
Thus, the expert emerged, the person whose academic
achievement (chengji) had shown him/her to be best suited
to filling the strategic posts in an advanced nation.
At the same time there was a commitment from the
beginning to create an educational system which would no
longer exclude the children of the workers, peasants, and
other laboring people. The revolution had been made in
their name and it was strongly felt that they were entitled to its fruits. In addition, it was understood
that they would be most likely to defend the revolution.
Children of those whose social position had fallen as a
result of the success of the revolution might have to be
relied on for a transitional period, but in the long view
it was clear that the offspring of workers and peasants
would have a natural inclination to be red, and therefore reliable. So the second criterion for university
entrance was family background (jiating chengfen),
frequently called family chengfen.2
The "red" and the "expert" ideally would be combined
in one person, a proletarianized intellectual of good
academic achievement who would be committed to serving
the proletariat. While those who were born in the homes
of the laboring masses were assumed to have a head start
through family socialization and gratitude to the Party,
the road was open to all youths to achieve proletariani-
zation and redness. Those of petty bourgeois or even
exploiting class background could not choose their family
chengfen, it was constantly repeated, but they could
choose their behavior. By "integrating with the workers
and peasants" and, particularly in the case of youths
from bad family backgrounds, by drawing a clear line
between themselves and their families, they too could
achieve redness. While the road was acknowledged to be
a difficult one, no one was theoretically beyond the
pale. Those of good class background, too, were expected
by their deeds to live up to the Party's expectations.
An individual's commitment to socialism could thus be
measured through the third criterion, his individual
performance (geren biaoxian).

Admission to any level of schooling beyond primary school took account of all three factors. Furthermore, the relative weight given to each criterion varied considerably over time. The balance could be and was adjusted in accordance with shifting emphasis on one or another of the state's priorities. As will be shown, the modulations in national policy regarding the relative weight of these criteria energized the entire structure of relationships among students, administrators and university enrollment.

As for the criteria themselves, the easiest to determine was academic achievement. The student's score on the examination for middle school (tongkao) set by the province or the unified national university entrance exam (gaokao) set in Beijing was the sole academic criterion considered.

Class origin was slightly more complicated in spite of, or perhaps because of, the many chengfen categories which existed. While each student had a fixed class designation based on his/her father's employment and source of income three years prior to Liberation in his locality, and while this designation was in his dossier, a person's class status could change, particularly during movements. This ongoing process of readjustment in a parent's class status could theoretically cause serious problems to a son or daughter, especially one who sought to become an activist and a member of the YCL. Although in most cases and during non-movement periods chengfen could be considered fixed and permanent, there was just enough ambiguity in the formulation to cause a limited number of students some uncertainty about their official class designation (see Chapter Two).

Basically, a person's class background was either good, ordinary, or bad. Those with good class background would include pre-Liberation workers (further subdivided into industrial and non-industrial, etc.), poor and lower-middle peasants, revolutionary cadres and revolutionary military, and revolutionary martyrs (the so-called five red categories).

Within the designation "good class background," revolutionary cadre and revolutionary military had the highest social status. After all, their "redness" had come from active participation in the revolution at a time of uncertain success. They had been the vanguard who had struggled on behalf of the workers and peasants. Thus, children of cadres could point with some pride to the accomplishments of their parents, while children of workers and peasants could merely be grateful to the latter for liberation from the previous system of exploitation under which their parents had suffered.

The ordinary or "middle" classes would include the petty bourgeoisie such as shop assistants (dianyuan), urban paupers (chengshi pinmin), peddlers (xiaofan),

clerks (<u>zhiyuan</u>), free professionals (<u>ziyou zhiye</u>),
middle peasants, and higher intellectuals. Distinctions
within this class were taken into consideration both in
middle school and university enrollment and continued to
be important in factional formation during the GPCR.[3]
Those designated as having bad class background
(including the former exploiting classes) comprised such
categories as overseas merchant, capitalist (of several
types such as compradore capitalist, national capitalist,
etc.), landlords, rich peasants, and those of whatever
original class background whose behavior led to their
being labelled as "old Guomindang official," bad
element, counterrevolutionary element, and so forth.
The most difficult of the criteria to measure was
individual performance. To be sure, the student's desire
to be "progressive," to seek and actually become a Youth
League member, to be enthusiastic about labor, to serve
as a student cadre all tended to reflect well on the
student's "activism"; however, to a large extent, activism seems to have been caught in a squeeze between
the other two criteria. During periods in which academic
achievement was most valued, a student's "redness" could
be demonstrated by studying well. During periods in
which good class background was a student's most important asset, activism again was superseded.

The Selection Process

Although there is no space to enumerate the steps
taken by the students in applying to the university, it
is helpful to look generally at how the criteria already
discussed were taken into account in choosing among
applicants.[4]
Each university or institute had its own minimum
score required on the nationwide unified entrance examination; in general, the better and more prestigious the
school, the higher its minimum standard. In fact, the
schools at the tertiary level were divided into three
categories (<u>biao</u>). The best schools were in category
one. They generally recruited nationwide, and required
the highest examination scores. Those in category two
were easier to enter and those in category three still
easier. Schools like Beijing University or Qinghua
University might consider only those students with a
minimum average entrance exam grade of 75%.[5] Lesser
schools in category one (but still considered very good
schools) - such as Guangzhou's South China Engineering
Institute - might require a minimum of 65% (depending on
the department applied to), and so on.
First, the student listed his choices in order by
category. Second category schools might require a minimum standard of only around 40-50% and third category
schools would be even lower. Thus, to get into a good

first category school, it was necessary to qualify academically. Second, each student was given a classification (leibie) based on family origin. There were three
possible classifications: good, signified by the number
1; ordinary, signified by the number 2; and bad, signified by the number 3. This classification was arrived
at after a complex procedure, requiring the filling out
of an extensive family history on the part of the student, followed by an investigation on the part of the
school. Third, the middle school gave its opinion on
what the disposition of the student's case should be,
based on the student's family background, his social and
overseas relationships, and his behavior. Based on these
three criteria the school stamped a 1 (can be guaranteed
to be put into a secretive or restrictive course of
study); a 2 (can be guaranteed to be put into an ordinary, less sensitive field of study); or a 3 (not permitted to enter university under any circumstances).

After the entrance examination the representatives
of the different universities picked out the files of
those students who had reached the minimum grade required
by the university they represented, based on the student's sequence of choices. For example, if a student
listed the physics department of Zhongshan University
(say, 60% minimum standard required) as his first choice
in category one and the physics department of Qinghua
University (say, 75% minimum standard) as his second
choice, the student would be considered first by Zhongshan University. If Zhongshan University accepted him,
Qinghua University would never, in fact, get to see his
file, even if his examination grade were over 80%. On
the other hand, if he listed Qinghua first and his grade
were between 60% and 75%, he would also have a possible
problem. Since he did not meet the standard for Qinghua
they would not inspect his file further. Assuming his
second choice were Zhongshan and he met their standard,
he would now be competing against students who had listed
Zhongshan as their first choice, and this would hurt him.
Particularly vulnerable were those students who might be
able to meet the academic standards of schools like
Qinghua or Zhongshan, but who might be rejected on other
grounds, such as family background. By the time the best
schools had rejected them and had returned their file
(one school at a time had access to a student's file) the
lesser schools might well be filled up. This was particularly true of the second and third category schools.
Therefore, the order in which choices were listed, as
well as the number of schools listed in each category,
was a matter of careful planning based on estimation of
entrance exam score, class origin, YCL membership, and
so forth.[6]

For this reason, it was not unusual for students to
apply to schools and for subjects for which they may not

have been overly enthusiastic. With the largest number
of university openings in engineering and hard sciences,[7]
good strategy often dictated that the student who wanted
to maximize his chances should apply to one of these
departments rather than to a department of liberal arts.
Students not of good class background knew, too, that it
would be foolish to apply to such well known schools as
Beijing Aviation Institute or Harbin Military Engineering
Institute, which emphasized a student's family origin as
much as a student's grades. On the other hand, the poor
student of good class background, particularly cadre
background, was usually able to find a school to accept
him, since some of the third category schools required
only a 20-30% minimum exam score to be considered. For
example, there was the Institute for Training Political
Cadres (Zhengzhi Ganbu Xueyuan) for children of cadres
or others of good background whose grades were not particularly good. Those trained in schools of this type
were likely to be sent to organs such as the Central-
South Bureau to do sensitive political-legal work.[8] Another example of a "special" school was the People's
Education Institute (Renmin Jiaoyu Xueyuan). According
to a knowledgeable informant, students attending this
school tended to be those who had good grades in school
but did not perform well on the all-important unified
university entrance examination. In cases such as this
a recommendation from the student's school was very
important, while class origin was relatively unimportant.[9]
     Some of the better but lesser-known schools tried
to make sure they would get a good yearly harvest by
making personal contact with the prospective middle
school graduate. For example, one interviewee reported
that a representative of the Central Finance Institute
in Beijing came to her Guangzhou middle school and, after
reading through the dosiers of the graduating seniors,
approached several of the most promising, gave them a
twenty page form to fill out, including such items as
family history, general attitude, understanding of previous political movements and their significance, and so
forth. Most of the students sought out tended to be
children of cadres and/or politically active YCL members
of reasonably good background. The interviewee, as the
branch secretary for the YCL in her class, was one of
those so sought out. She was told to list the Central
Finance Institute as one of her top choices and, if her
exam grade were high enough, she would be chosen.[10]
     The middle schools, on their part, tried to aid
their students by going over sample exams and giving
practice exams to the students. This gave the student
a pretty good idea where he stood academically and advice
from his teachers helped him to decide what his choices
should be.

THE MIDDLE SCHOOL STRUCTURE IN GUANGZHOU

China's middle school system, before the GPCR, consisted of junior and senior sections of three years each.
In discussing middle schools, junior and senior middle
will at times be treated as one unit rather than spoken
of separately. This will be done for several reasons.
First, since there was in fact a six-year program, a
student who had begun junior middle in 1960, assuming
regular progress, would have been a third-year student
in senior high at the time of the GPCR. Thus, in looking
at shifts in official policy over these six years and
their effects on students, it will be helpful to bear in
mind that in many instances - when comparing, for example, how the classroom atmosphere in 1965 was different
from that of 1962 - the students being examined are those
whose middle school experiences encompassed both of those
periods.

Second, although some middle schools had only junior
middle sections, the better middle schools supplied education at both junior and senior levels. A student who
entered middle school in 1965 could therefore be at the
same school as one who had entered in 1960. This "generational difference" was to prove to be of no small importance when it came to factional behavior later.

Third, the better middle schools tended to keep
their best students on after completion of junior middle.
There were very few openings for "outsiders" in senior
middle school, particularly at the keypoint schools.

On the other hand, there were significant differences between the two levels. Senior middle schools, as
the primary suppliers of university students, maintained
much stricter admission standards than those set for entrance to junior middle sections. When a student was
accepted for the higher level, it was assumed that he
was being prepared for university entrance. In fact,
the schools developed a vested interest in serving a
"gatekeeper" function, keeping out all those who seemingly had no chance to compete successfully. In terms
of junior high enrollment, however, we are dealing with
students of the ages of 12 or 13; assessments of their
future university prospects could only be speculative.
Because of the great expansion of schools on this level
in the 1950s and 1960s, it was possible for them to
enroll almost all primary school graduates who applied.
Furthermore, the stated aim was to expand the system to
encompass those working class areas which had suffered
through lack of school facilities in the past. Not
surprisingly, then, there were always many more students
in junior middle than in senior middle.

Another crucial reason accounting for the large
number of students in junior high was that a student's

decision as to his future could be delayed until after his graduation from junior high at age sixteen. Options available included, by 1964, entrance to various technical, teacher training or work-study vocational schools, continuation into a "regular" senior middle preparatory to the university, the pursuit of an urban factory job, or volunteering to "take root" in the countryside as a "sent-down, educated youth." Only by continuing on to senior middle did the student resolve to go for the brass ring of higher education; all other choices were essentially decisions to opt for less glamorous, but more secure, employment opportunities. Therefore, the major competition between aspirants for university education at this stage was not whether they could obtain entrance to junior high but whether they could get into a good junior high or, failing that, be one of the relatively few who were able to move from a poor or average junior high into a good senior high.

The selection process for middle school worked in the following way: the student, whether applying for junior or senior middle school, would list four choices, usually after advice from both parents and teachers. He then took the citywide examination and, depending on his result, his class background and his individual performance, he would be allocated to his first, second, third, or fourth choice school. It was not uncommon, however, for students to be allocated to schools they had not applied for, particularly by 1964 and 1965 when, with the increasing emphasis on class background as a factor in selection, students whose older siblings had previously been able to enter first-rate schools because of academic achievement now found themselves barred from these same schools because of unacceptable family origin. In making their choices, students were not unaware of the differing quality of the schools. If there had been any doubts, a ranking system had been set up in Guangzhou in 1962, dividing the middle schools into three categories, largely on the basis of promotion rate to the next higher level school - in effect, on the basis of university promotion rate. Even though this ranking system for choosing schools was officially abandoned after one year, it retained its influence in following years. All students I interviewed, for example, compared schools on the basis of these rankings and, when choosing schools, in any year up to the GPCR, the student's general knowledge of a school's ranking was an important consideration in his choice.[11]

In applying for middle school in 1962, a student first listed the school he wished to attend in category one. There were three things that could happen: a) he could pass the citywide unified examination and be accepted to the school of his choice; b) he could pass the examination but with too low a score for acceptance at the first category school he had listed. In this case, he would be allocated to a lesser first category school; or c) he could fail the examination. In the last event, he would then take the citywide exam for a second category school, again listing his first choice. Once again, the same three outcomes were possible. A failure of this second examination meant he would now take the exam for third category schools, which included "public" schools (minban xuexiao) as well as agricultural middle schools. Finally, unsuccessful candidates could enter a middle school for children of factory workers, although even then an examination was required.[12]

Table 1.1 below provides a list of Guangzhou's regular middle schools (technical schools, work-study schools, minban schools, etc., are excluded) and their rankings, in part based on the original rankings, but brought up-to-date (1966) through interviews with many former students from these schools.

Table 1.1

Ranking of the Regular Middle Schools in Guangzhou

School Number or Name	Ranking
1	I^1 +
2	I^1 +
3	I^3 +
4	I^3 +
5	I^2 +
6	I^2 +
7	I^2 +
8	I^3 +
9	II^1 +
10	II^2 +
11	II^3 +
12	II^2 +
13	I^3 +
14	II^2 +
15	II^2 +
16	I^2 +
17	$II(I^2)$* +
18	II^2 +
19 (Municipal Experimental School)	I^2 +
20	II^3
21	I^2 +
22	I^3
23	II^3
24	II^2
25	II^3 +
26	II^3
27	II^3

School Number or Name	Ranking
28	II^1 +
29	II^1 +
30	II^1 +
31	II^3
32	II^3
33	II^3
34	II^3
35	II^3
36	II^3
37	II^3
38	II^3
39	II^3
40	II^3
41	II^3
42	II^3
43	II^3
44	II^3
45	II^3
46	II^3
47	II^3
48	II^3
49	II^3
50	II^3
51	II^3
52	II^3
Guangya	I^s +
Huafu (middle school attached to South China Normal Institute)	I^s +
Provincial Experimental (Shengshi)	I^1 +
South China Normal Institute Experimental (Huashi)	I^2 +
Girls' Middle School	I^2 +
August 1 Middle School	** +
Railroad Middle School	I^3 +
Qiaoguang (set up mainly for overseas Chinese students)	II^{2*} +
Overseas Chinese middle school (Huaqiao Zhongxue)	I^2 +

+ indicates that the school contained both a junior and senior middle section

* Number 17 Middle School originally was in category II according to the 1962 rankings, but most students seemed to feel it had risen in prestige since then. Qiaoguang Middle School, on the other hand, was a first category school in decline.

** The August 1 Middle School is a special case in that

it was a school limited to children of cadres at
regimental level or above. But although it was the
center for the Conservative "Doctrine Guards" during
the Cultural Revolution, I found very few students
who knew much about this school. For example, most
students, even Rebel leaders during the Cultural
Revolution who were knowledgeable about almost all
the important middle schools in Guangzhou, were unclear on some basic points about the August 1 Middle
School, such as whether or not the school had a senior
middle section.

Note 1: School categories (I, II, III) are based on 1962
rankings from Yangcheng Wanbao, July 10, 1962;
Wenhui Bao (Hong Kong), July 16, 1962; Yangcheng
Wanbao, August 15, 1962. Category III would be
for minban schools, so no school in this table
has a category three ranking. The rankings
within categories come from interviews with
former students from many of these schools. In
addition to asking the students to rank the
schools, I have made use of their own prefer-
ences when applying to junior and senior middle
school to compile this table.

Note 2: Schools 44-52 were set up in 1963 or later and
thus their ranking comes solely from interviews.

Note 3: I^S refers to schools I have called "true elite"
schools; there was general, almost universal
agreement among those I interviewed, that Huafu
and Guangya were in a class by themselves.

Note 4: At the time of the 1962 rankings, #6 Middle
School was attached to Zhongshan University; #7
Middle School was the experimental school of
Guangdong Normal Institute; #16 was the attached
middle school of Zhongshan Medical Institute;
#21 was the attached middle school of Guangdong
Normal Institute. At the time of the Cultural
Revolution, these affiliations no longer existed.

Note 5: Although I refer to four categories (true elite;
good; ordinary; poor) in the book, there was a
wider variation between the schools. Category
I^2 generally corresponds to what I have called
good schools. Category I^1 would be closer to
"very good schools." Category I^3-II^2 contains
schools I have referred to as ordinary, ranging
from "good-ordinary" to "mediocre-ordinary."
Schools in the II^3 range are poor.

Two maps at the end of Chapter One provide a fuller,
more detailed picture of the Guangzhou middle school
system. One shows the location of the regular middle
schools, the other divides Guangzhou into broad "neighborhoods" on the basis of residential patterns. While

the official press only rarely refers to the location of
a school, or the district in which the school is found
(usually when a school is first set up, is expanded, in-
creases the number of students of worker-peasant background, etc.), former students from many of these schools
have helped me draw these maps which may contain minor
inaccuracies.
    Certain geographic points are worth a brief mention.
First, the importance of the Eastern District, which contained many of Guangzhou's better schools, and which was
to become the key battleground for middle school Red
Guards during the GPCR, can be seen more clearly from
these maps. Second, the newer schools, as distinguished
by the higher numbers, were generally set up in outlying
areas and factory districts. Third, older parts of the
city such as Central Guangzhou were overcrowded, had poor
schools, and had a population which included few of cadre
or higher intellectual origin.

Types of Schools

    Because this and subsequent chapters will frequently
discuss one or another of Guangzhou's middle schools, an
examination of the differences between them, particularly
with regard to their student bodies is useful. Generally,
the situation at 1) the true elite middle schools (where
promotion rate to the university could run as high as 70-
90% in some years), of which there were two in Guangzhou;
2) the good middle schools (promotion rate to the university was generally between 30-40%; 3) the ordinary
schools (promotion rate generally 15-30%); and 4) the
poor schools can be compared.

    1. A True Elite Middle School: Guangya Middle
School prior to the GPCR (considered the second best
middle school in Guangzhou).[13] As an acknowledged key-
point school with a history tracing back to 1888, Guangya
had always been able to attract both students of high
intellectual ability and students from politically prominent families. Thus, by 1966, on the eve of the GPCR,
its student body was of mixed social background. Of
particular interest was the way in which the students
were distributed by year (nianji). Middle school in
China, prior to the GPCR, was a six-year program. Students who entered in 1960, assuming they went all the
way through, would have been in third year senior middle
school by 1966. Those who had entered in 1965, on the
other hand, would have been in first year junior middle
school. What makes this interesting is the fact that
admissions standards underwent a major change in 1964
when class background came to rival academic achievement
as the major criterion for enrollment, particularly at
the better schools. Thus, 75% of the 1964 and 1965

entering classes at Guangya were of revolutionary cadre
(including revolutionary military) background. On the
other hand, because enrollment prior to 1964, especially
in the 1960-62 period, tended to emphasize academic
achievement, the number of students of intellectual background in senior middle school at Guangya was fairly
substantial. Compounding the division was the fact that
several of Guangzhou's best schools, like Guangya, had
in 1960 initiated an experimental program, derived from
Soviet experience, to allow the students to complete six
years of middle school in five years.[14] Although in many
schools the program ended in 1962, in Guangya the decision was made to discontinue the program for newly entering students, but to allow those who had entered in
the 1960-62 period to finish up. At Guangya all students
who began in the 1960-62 period started out on the as-
sumption that they would finish at the end of five years.
It was later decided, however, that an examination should
be given at the end of the third year to determine which
students were academically qualified to finish up in two
more years and which would still need three more years.
On the eve of the GPCR, of those students taking the
screening examination in 1965 (in other words those who
had entered in 1962), the majority had passed and could
finish up in two more years. They were divided into
five classes (ban). Those who did not pass, however,
were lumped together in one class and were required to
take a regular three year senior middle program. Over
90% of those scoring poorly on the examination and thus
constituting this latter class were of revolutionary
cadre background. When the GPCR began, students such as
these, along with those of good class background who had
entered in increasing numbers in 1964 and 1965, overwhelmingly became "Conservative" Red Guards and launched
ferocious attacks on "bourgeois academic authorities"
and the "bourgeois educational system." Ironically,
because of a particularly lenient promotion policy, the
cadre children with poor grades at Guangya were more
concentrated than might otherwise have been the case.
At other schools in Guangzhou, students were required to
take a citywide examination after junior middle to determine which school they would attend for senior middle.
It was by no means certain that they would remain at the
same school for all six years. At most schools, therefore, students of cadre background but with poor grades
had difficulty advancing from junior to senior middle
at the same school.[15]

2. A Good Middle School: Number 21 Middle School.[16]
The situation at the good middle schools was a bit different from that of the true elite schools. On the one
hand, these schools had trouble getting the very best of
the children of cadre background, particularly after

1964; they also had difficulty getting those students
with the very best grades. But, while students of high-
level cadre background (13-level or above) and students
with outstanding academic achievement tended to congre-
gate at the few extraordinary schools, the fact that
there were so few schools of this type enabled schools
like Number 21 to enroll quite a large number of cadre
children and an even larger number of students whose
parents were intellectuals. In several of the very good
schools, including Number 21, geography played an important part as well. A rather high percentage of these
schools were located in Guangzhou's Eastern District, a
district which had begun to become the chosen residential
area for Guangzhou's intellectual elite as far back as
the 1930s.[17] After 1949 it was the area in which most
of the army personnel and revolutionary cadres had their
residences, and many of the children of these officials
chose to attend nearby schools; this was particularly
true of many military officers who had come down from
North China.

At Number 21, then, in a somewhat similar way to
Guangya, were both children of cadres who had entered
primarily because of good class background and connections,[18] and children of intellectual background who
were accepted as students because of their grades. There
were some differences between these two types of schools,
however. First, the number of cadre children at the true
elite schools was always much higher than at the good
schools. Both Guangya and Huafu, the two best schools
in Guangzhou, recruited citywide (sometimes also from
other provinces) and their students thus tended to come
from outside the immediate neighborhood. Schools such
as Number 21, however, while generally acknowledged as
"very good" schools, were not as prestigious as the
aforementioned two schools, so their students more often
were from the locality. Second, while schools like
Guangya and Huafu tended to recruit very few students of
worker-peasant background, schools like Number 21 accepted greater numbers of these students, particularly
starting in 1964. This is not to argue that a large
percentage of a class would be made up of students of
worker-peasant background; quite the contrary, these students were underrepresented in all the better schools.
Nevertheless, relative to Guangya and Huafu, their numbers tended to be larger.[19]

3. <u>An Ordinary School</u>.[20] The ordinary schools
tended to be even more "neighborhood-oriented" than the
good schools. Many of them did not possess boarding
facilities. Being unable to boast of a high promotion
rate, they had difficulty drawing either high-level cadre
children or children with outstanding grades. Before the
class line policy began to be strongly implemented in

1964, their student bodies were heavily weighted toward students of ordinary family background. A significant portion of a class might be students of exploiting class background as well. Entering classes of 1964 and 1965, on the other hand, would contain a higher percentage of students of working class background, as well as more students of shop assistant and peddler background, since the latter two categories were considered at the top of the ordinary background classification.

4. A Poor School.[21] Poor schools tended to be newer schools, especially those with only junior middle sections. Those in industrial districts, such as those in Southern Guangzhou, tended to have a high proportion of students of working class background. Those in Central Guangzhou had more of a mixed group. It was relatively difficult for graduates from these poor schools to get into a good senior middle school, much less an elite school; those who were able to continue their education generally found themselves at an average senior middle school or at a work-study school. I interviewed a fair number of students who, having attended average or poor schools for junior middle, and seeing no chance to gain acceptance to a good school for senior middle, opted out of the university sweepstakes by applying to work-study schools, in several cases at the insistence of their parents.

CHANGING TRENDS IN "CLASS COMPOSITION" IN THE 1960s

In an attempt to determine the "class composition" of Guangzhou's secondary schools in the 1960s, a formal survey questionnaire was distributed to more than 80 individuals who had attended middle schools in Guangzhou during the 1960s and are now in Hong Kong. Since this questionnaire, which was jointly administered by Jonathan Unger of University of Kansas and myself, sought also to discover relationships among such variables as class background, Youth League membership, Cultural Revolution participation and post-Cultural Revolution allocation (who was allowed to remain in Guangzhou, who was sent to the countryside, etc.), tables representing our results will appear in several chapters of this book. Because each student was expected to report on all students in his/her classroom, data on approximately 3,000 students were obtained.

Several points are apparent from Table 1.2 below. First, there is a significant difference between the junior and senior high figures. To begin with, it is clear that students of worker-peasant origin were present in much larger numbers at junior high than at senior

Table 1.2

The "Class Composition" of Guangzhou Secondary Schools, 1962-66

The Prestige Schools

Official Pre-Liberation Class Backgrounds of Fathers	The Top 4 Schools*	The Next-Best 8 Schools*	The Middle Range of 18 Schools*	The Neighborhood Jr. Highs*
Senior High School				
Revolutionary cadre	27%	16%	7%	
Good-class worker and peasant	12%	16%	16%	
Non-intelligentsia middle class	16%	11%	17%	(None in sample)
Intelligentsia middle class	34%	43%	27%	
Overseas Merchants	2%	3%	6%	
Bad Class	9%	11%	27%	
	100%	100%	100%	
No. of classrooms surveyed	5	8	18	
No. of students in sample	223	251	813	
Junior High School				
Revolutionary cadre	48%	17%	9%	8%
Good-class worker and peasant	11%	24%	34%	42%
Non-intelligentsia middle class	3%	14%	19%	16%
Intelligentsia middle class	32%	30%	19%	20%
Overseas merchants	2%	4%	8%	3%
Bad class	4%	11%	11%	11%
	100%	100%	100%	100%
No. of classrooms surveyed	5	12	12	14
No. of students in sample	234	603	570	722

*The top 4 schools include Huafu, Guangya, Numbers 1 and 2. Huafu and Guangya have been designated "True Elite" middle schools elsewhere in this book. Numbers 1 and 2 were the best of Guangzhou's "Good" schools.

The next-best 8 schools include numbers 5, 6, 7, 16, 17, 21, Girls' Middle and Overseas Chinese Middles. They have been designated "Good" schools elsewhere in this book.

The middle range of 18 schools corresponds to what have been called "Ordinary" schools elsewhere in this book.

The Neighborhood Junior Highs have been called "Poor" schools elsewhere in this book.

Source: Questionnaire remembrances of Hong Kong interviewees.

high. This is particularly true at the average and poor
schools which show a rather consistent percentage of 34-
42% of students of worker-peasant origin at junior high
as against 15-17% at senior high. Separate interview
data seem to indicate that students of worker-peasant
background were generally both less able to compete and
less inclined to continue on to regular senior highs,
often opting for immediate urban factory jobs or vocational, technical schools which would lead to such jobs.
In addition, the increasing emphasis on class origin as
a criterion for middle school enrollment had the greatest
impact at the level of junior high. This finding is
entirely consistent with what is known from documentary
as well as interview data. The great expansion in the
educational system in the 1960s was in primary and lower
middle school. The issue was increasingly becoming not
whether urban students would be able to attend junior
high, but which students should attend the best of the
junior highs. In this regard, it is interesting to note
the figure of 48% revolutionary cadre (and revolutionary
military) at the top four junior highs and the figure of
42% worker-peasant background at the neighborhood junior
highs, i.e., those junior high schools which had been
recently established and contained no senior high sections. This, too, is consistent with both interviews
and Red Guard newspapers, the latter often decrying the
easy access to the best middle schools possessed by those
of revolutionary cadre origin once the class line policy
began to be implemented.22

    The figures for children of intellectual middle
class background are also very revealing. First, these
students were most heavily represented at the best
schools, the very good schools, and the best of the ordinary schools. For example, whereas those of revolutionary cadre origin show a marked decrease in percentages when one compares senior high to junior high enrollment at the better schools, the percentage of students
of intellectual background increased from junior to
senior high at every type of school, in some cases sharply, such as at the very good schools. What we find then
is that even on the eve of the GPCR, students of intellectual family background were, in spite of the accelerated emphasis on class line starting in 1964, still
extremely competitive for senior high positions.

    Another interesting facet is provided by the figures
for those of bad class origin. Their strongest presence
was in the senior high sections of the ordinary schools
which, as can be seen from the figures, were unable to
recruit significant numbers from those of cadre origin
and hence had to rely to some extent on students of bad
class origin because of their grades and students of
working class and non-intellectual middle class (e.g.,
peddler and shop assistant) origin because of their

origin. They simply took whatever was left after the more fashionable schools had made their choices. Finally, it is clear from interviews that the high percentage of bad class youths in senior high, particularly at the ordinary schools, is due to their entrance prior to 1964. Many were either in senior high three at the time of the GPCR or, in some cases, had already graduated.

Table 1.2, of course, makes no pretense to absolute standards of accuracy depending, as it does, on student memories. Issues such as class background, however, had become so salient, particularly during the GPCR, that most students were able, after careful thought, to remember rather clearly. The questionnaires of those who were unsure or who, after a check was made with other students from the same school or, in some cases, the same class, proved to be unreliable, were discounted (around 10%). The results, offered in conjunction with other data, seem, however, to be suggestive indeed.

Because it proved to be impossible by means of a questionnaire to get an accurate sample of quantitative enrollment figures by year (1960-66), I have endeavored, based on separate in-depth interviews with approximately 100 former students (including many, but by no means all, who had filled out the questionnaire) to provide a general picture of the changing student population at Guangzhou's middle schools in the 1960s (see Table 1.3).

Several broad trends emerge. Most clearly, children of cadre background were the main recipients of the benefits from the 1964-65 emphasis on family background. Although children from working class backgrounds tended to increase their presence at poor, ordinary, and good schools, children of revolutionary cadre origin were becoming more and more concentrated at the elite schools, as well as increasing their presence at the good schools.

Since the majority of university students came from these two types of schools, the possible influence the new class line policy would have on future university enrollment patterns was not lost on the students.[23]

The Red Guard press, too, confirms the trend at the best schools. Consider the following two reports, the first from a newspaper printed at Guangya; the second from a Huafu newspaper:

> In 1964 our school took in 6 classes, totalling 240 new students, more than 170 of whom were children of cadres, approximately 75% of the class. In 1965 in junior middle one, this phenomenon was even more typical. Lu Zhihui [the principal of Guangya] recently explained: the higher authorities have directed that we manage Guangya, Number 2 Middle and Huafu as similar schools for children of cadres gradually within the next several years.[24]

Table 1.3

Changing Student Population at Guangzhou's
Middle Schools in the 1960's

Type of School	Senior Middle 3 and Junior Middle 3 (Those who entered in 1960 or 1963) Predominant Family Origin of Students	Senior Middle 1 and Junior Middle 1 or 2 (Those who entered in 1964 or 1965) Predominant Family Origin of Students
True Elite	Cadre and Higher-Level Intellectual Origin	Higher-Level Cadre Origin
Good	All Origins, with Heaviest Concentration on Those of Intellectual Origin	Cadre, Intellectual and Worker Origin
Ordinary	Predominantly Middle Class (both Intellectual and Non-intellectual) Origin and Exploiting Class Origin	Working Class and Middle Class (both Intellectual and Non-intellectual) Origin
Poor	Middle Class Origin (both Intellectual and Non-intellectual); Working Class Origin; Exploiting Class Origin	Working Class Origin (in working class sections of Guangzhou); Middle Class Origin (primarily Non-intellectual in non-industrial areas)

Note 1: Middle Class Origin can be divided into three sub-categories: Higher-level Intellectual, Intellectual, and Non-Intellectual. Higher-level Intellectual Origin students were in largest proportions at the True Elite schools and to a lesser extent at the Good schools. Non-intellectual Middle Class Origin students predominated at the poorer (Ordinary and Poor) schools, although one did find many children of office clerks and teachers at the Ordinary schools.

Note 2: The pattern for Senior Middle Two is more complex.

Source: In-depth interviews with former students. The table represents general trends as pointed out by interviewees; it is not a statistical compilation.

Table 1.4

The Class Backgrounds of the First-Year Class
in Guangya Middle School, 1965

Workers	Poor and Lower-Middle Peasants	Cadres	Office Workers	Landlords
44 (16.3%)	10 (3.7%)	202 (73.3%)	19 (6.7%)	0

Source: Guangya 831, March, 1968.

> Wang Bingshan [Huafu's principal] said:
> "...attached middle is a key-point school,
> study comes first, we don't accept children
> of workers and peasants with poor academic
> achievement. We have many children of pro-
> fessors with fine academic achievement; if
> we didn't accept them, it wouldn't be good."
> Afterwards, to meet a need, slowly the direc-
> tion began to change and the door was opened
> wide for the convenience of the children of
> high-level cadres on the Provincial Party
> Committee.[25]

Perhaps more subtly, another Huafu newspaper report
showed how children of cadres were replacing children of
workers and peasants at their school as the GPCR drew
near (Table 1.5).

Table 1.5

Class Backgrounds of Students Held Back at Huafu in the 1960s

	Students Held Back		Students of Good Class Origin Held Back	
1961-62	10	7	70%	(Worker-Peasant Origin
1962-63	70	40	56%	as % of Total)
1963-64	10	8	80%	(Revolutionary Cadre
1964-65	2	2	100%	Origin as % of Total)

Source: Xiaobing, December 24, 1967, pg. 2.

Since the primary reason students were held back a
grade was poor academic achievement, Table 1.5 reveals
two things: First, it shows that emphasis on academic
performance was at its peak in 1962-63, a period in which

a rather large number of students were being held back in school. Second, the figures for 1963-65, showing the significant increase in the percentage of children of cadres among those being held back may, in conjunction with other data being presented, be a further indicator of the increasing recruitment of children of cadre background by the best of the middle schools by the middle 1960s. The above source also refers to a report given at the school by an important leader (shouzhang) who urged additional recruitment of children of revolutionary cadres, as well as those of worker-peasant background. The report was given in July 1964 yet, at the time of the GPCR, Huafu, a school in a suburban area with much farmland, had only eight students out of 860 in lower middle school of poor or lower-middle peasant background. The paper declined to inform its readers of the number of children of cadre or military background among the 860. Interviews with students who were in lower middle school at Huafu at the time suggest this missing figure would be very high.[26]

Although I interviewed many people from poor schools in Guangzhou, perhaps the best comparison between the keypoint schools and the poor schools was provided by a Beijing Red Guard group comparing their elite school, Beijing Number 4 Middle School, to a poor school:

> We visited XX Middle School. This school was set up in 1963 and only had a junior middle school section. Of the more than 1,200 students, children of workers and peasants occupied 50% of the places. Because of the revisionist system of ranks used in running schools, this school-which mainly had children of workers and peasants-suffered discrimination in all ways and was treated as of no interest!
>
> Let's bring up a few examples: Of the 59 teachers in the whole school, none were first grade (yiji) or second grade teachers, and only one was third grade. Our school has 123 teachers. Of these, two are special grade (teji), three are first grade, six are second grade and fourteen are third grade....
>
> As to going to the Education Bureau to hear reports on the situation (xingshi baogao), ordinary teachers from "high-level schools" all can attend, but none of the politics teachers from this school are qualified to attend....
>
> In Beijing there are other schools of this kind. Students who attend this kind of school haven't passed the examination to attend "the school of their choice," thus they are

allocated to this kind of school.[27]

The Effect of the Change in Selection Criteria on Students and Schools

If we take the period from 1960 to 1966 as a whole, we can readily look upon 1961-63 and 1964-66 as polar opposites with regard to selection criteria both for recruitment to middle schools and universities. In 1961, as the full force of the economic depression was beginning to settle over China, the policies of educational expansion which had been a feature of the Great Leap Forward (GLF) began to be rescinded, sometimes with as little fanfare as possible. Middle schools felt the impact of these retrenchment policies. Generally, unlike the primary schools in Guangzhou, the cutback in middle school education was not drastic although, as can be seen in Table 1.6, the number of middle school students did decline over the 1960-62 period.

Table 1.6
New Students at Guangzhou Middle Schools, 1960 and 1962

	Senior High	Junior High
1960[a]	6,500	24,000+
1962[b]	5,070	23,500+

Source: [a] Yangcheng Wanbao, September 1, 1960; [b] Nanfang Ribao, August 26, 1962, p. 1.

The major change, however, was not so much in numbers as it was in the renewed emphasis on "educational quality" (jiaoxue zhiliang) which was appearing in the press. What this meant was that in both 1961-62 and 1962-63 the better senior middle schools were accepting students largely on the basis of their academic achievement. The best of the junior middle schools, which of course were those which had senior middle sections, were to a certain extent doing likewise. By 1964-65, however, educational quality was no longer prominently featured in the press, having been replaced by a renewed emphasis, harking back to some of the aims of the GLF, on increasing the representation of children of good class background in senior middle schools and universities. Because middle schools had come to judge their quality on the basis of how many students they could produce for the universities, these changes, instead of benefitting the children of workers and peasants, worked to the advantage of the children of revolutionary cadres and revolutionary armymen who were now able to compete successfully with those of intellectual background for university places.

Judging from interviewees, the new stress on class line seems to have affected children of intellectuals in another way as well. Before 1964 children whose parents were state cadres with responsible positions and the perquisites that went with such positions quite often would list their class origins as "cadre" when filling out forms. Before the emphasis on class line this self-designation was seldom questioned. With class origin becoming increasingly important as a criterion for educational mobility, however, considerable attention began to be given to this self-designation, particularly at the better schools and in senior high. Several interviewees who had transferred from ordinary neighborhood junior highs into good schools in the Eastern District for senior high reported on this phenomenon. In the neighborhood schools they had been surrounded by students from "non-distinguished" class backgrounds and so they felt perfectly secure and, indeed, accurate when listing "cadre" as their own background. Upon entering schools like Number 7, Number 21, or Girls' Middle, however, it quickly became very clear to them, particularly by 1964, that designating oneself as "cadre origin" was reserved to those who were of "revolutionary" cadre origin (those whose parents were Party members and had joined the revolution three years prior to Liberation in the area in which they joined). In the far different atmosphere of a classroom at, say, Number 21 Middle School, most students whose parents were state cadres (primarily working in intellectual endeavors) began to use the designation "office worker" (zhiyuan) to describe their class origin. Those who were less politically sophisticated or were slow to realize the changed circumstances were derided by students whose parents were, as they put it, really cadres. Before 1964 one's class origin usually had been checked closely only when one was being considered for membership in the YCL and, in the atmosphere of the early 1960s, even when a person was told that their self-designation was inaccurate, it made little difference.[28]

MIDDLE SCHOOL ADMINISTRATORS AND UNIVERSITY PROMOTION RATES

Originally, many of Guangzhou's best schools predated the People's Republic, being either missionary schools such as Middle School Number 7 or state schools such as Middle School Number 1. Having formidable reputations, outstanding facilities, good teachers, and so forth, it was natural that these schools should become key-point schools, particularly since the goal in the 1950s was to produce an adequate number of senior middle graduates to meet the needs of the expanding universities.

Educational quality came to be, as a matter of course, synonomous with a high promotion rate to the university. As Table 1.7 shows, before 1957 expansion of senior

Table 1.7

Annual Growth in Admission of New Students Nationally

Year	Number of Senior High Grads	Number of New Students to be Admitted to Colleges and Universities	Number of Candidates to Take Exam
1952	36,000	65,900	-
1953	54,700	71,500	-
1954	70,000	90,000	110,000
1955	(86,000)*	90,000	-
1956	156,000	164,000	-
1957	180,000	107,000	250,000

*Assumes an identical rate of increase between 1954-55 as between 1953-54.

Source: Joseph C. Kun, "Higher Education: Some Problems of Selection and Enrollment," The China Quarterly Number 8. October-December, 1961, p. 138.

highs outstripped expansion in higher education. In that year, however, a sharp cutback in university admissions led, for the first time, to a surplus of senior high graduates. Although open enrollment policies during the GLF temporarily reversed this trend, the economic depression after the Leap led to a closing down of many schools and a dismissal of many students. This decline in the percentage of senior high graduates who could be accommodated in the universities led, not surprisingly, to increased competition among the middle schools and to a declining promotion rate for many of them. Nevertheless, educators were reluctant to abandon the 1:1 relationship between educational quality and promotion rate. For example, a 1963 report about the proper behavior for a middle school teacher, which was intended for foreign audiences, quoted an older teacher from the elite Beijing Number 4 Middle School who proudly stressed his school's typical university promotion rate of 80 percent.[29] By 1965 numerous articles in the press were opposing this particular method of judging academic quality, with the blame often placed on teachers.[30]

Still, given the reluctance to set up alternative criteria, even when criticizing the prevailing attitude

toward promotion rates, there were often attempts to
"balance" the criticism. For example, in one article
from a provincial education journal in late 1964 the
following sentence appears: "The level of the rate of
students proceeding to higher studies can be considered
one of the standards for the evaluation of the quality
of the work of a school."[31] Several months later, the
insidious danger in such viewpoints was pointed out in
the same journal:

> Today, in the schools, the struggle between
> the two educational ideologies is consider-
> ably sharp. Though we have initially crit-
> icized the bourgeois educational ideology
> of the one-sided quest after the rate of
> students proceeding to higher studies, the
> problem has not yet been thoroughly solved.
> Some people seem to understand the truth
> but really they do not. Some are waiting
> and watching for further development. And
> some even overtly conform with requirements
> but covertly violate them. If we bring for-
> ward the proposition that the level of the
> rate of students proceeding to higher stu-
> dies can be made a standard for the evalua-
> tion of the quality of school work, we shall
> possibly provide a retreat for such people.
> They may say, "Even if the rate of students
> proceeding to higher studies is not a stan-
> dard for the evaluation of school work, at
> least we can say that it is a good thing and
> not a bad thing, for more students to proceed
> to higher studies." And they will exploit
> this to carry out the stubborn resistance
> against the Party's educational policy, and
> continue to use overt or covert measures in
> the one-sided quest after the higher rate
> of students proceeding to higher studies.[32]

Nevertheless, even this rather uncompromising article
found it necessary to conclude that schools which correctly implemented the Party's educational policy might
indeed succeed in having a high promotion rate to the
university.[33]

Nor could objections to undue concern with high
promotion rates be expected to be taken seriously so long
as the press continued to praise elite schools. As late
as the end of 1964, Guangming Ribao was enthusiastically
publicizing and disseminating the experiences of Harbin's
Number 12 Middle School, whose vital statistics, as
proudly detailed in the newspaper, show it to be very
elite indeed:

Supplied Educational Institutions at a
Higher Level with 3,076 qualified new
students.
Supplied 1,426 Reserve Laborers, 122 of
whom have gone to the countryside.
Thus, 68.3% of the students went on to
the university; 2.7% went to the
countryside.[34]

In the same month as the above report, Beijing Ribao
was trumpeting the achievements of one of China's most
famous elite schools, Number 101 Middle School. According to the Beijing Ribao report, 80% of this school's
junior and senior high graduates had gone on to a higher
school over the three previous years.[35]
Some schools in cities where urban employment was
more of a problem did go so far as to attempt to use a
different standard, to fit their own particular needs.
The following example from a Red Guard newspaper reveals
the draconian methods used:

In 1964, "capitalist roaders" of the Jiangmen
Educational Bureau, Resettlement Office, and
other units proposed a criterion for evalua-
ting the success or failure of a school. It
was that a school could be rated as being
first-class not only when its students gained
the highest marks but also when the number of
its students going to the countryside was the
largest. As a result, the various middle
schools left no stone unturned in "mobilizing"
their students to go to the countryside.
In 1965, such middle schools as the
First and Second Middle Schools of Jiangmen
invented a new "mobilization" method: After
they had sat for the senior middle school
entrance examination and before notices about
the results were issued, all graduates must
surrender their residential cards. It was
stated that if they refused to do so, no
notices would be issued to them, and that
they would not be given jobs if they failed
to pass the examination.[36]

Still, this was a rarity. School officials had
strong interests in maintaining the existing situation.
Maintenance of a high promotion rate assured a school of
remaining a key-point school with close connections to
the provincial or municipal Party committee, which in
turn guaranteed the school the continued allocation of
the best teachers, highest rates of funding, new equipment, and so forth. And, of course, these advantages
led to the continued enrollment of the best students,

thus perpetuating the high promotion rates which had made
everything possible in the first place.

The newspapers did their part as well. The majority
of articles in the Guangzhou newspapers dealing with high
schools report the situation at the better schools, with
Guangya and Huafu getting the most space. When Guangya
celebrated an anniversary of its founding, top provincial
leaders would show up at the school to take part in the
celebration, leading of course to newspaper coverage.[37]
Beijing schools with long histories competed with each
other in their celebrations.[38] Outside the large cities,
promotion for education officials may have been related
to the promotion rates of their schools. One 1965 graduate of Kaiping county Number One Middle School reported
that when his school set a county record for promotion
rate to the university in 1965, the school principal was
promoted to work at the special district level.[39]

The needs of the state, as well, seemed to preclude
a major reorientation. During the Socialist Education
Movement (SEM), when there was a strong emphasis on
politics and ideological transformation, there was a
surge in the level of student activism, one manifestation
being a refusal on the part of some students to take the
university entrance examination. With most students at
the better middle schools swearing to follow the Party
forever after they participated in the university matriculation exams, those who wanted to distinguish themselves
as "real activists" vowed to go straight to the countryside.

Chinese schools had, after all, always stressed
political values along with academic coursework. Social
action in the form of "serving the people" was a constant
theme not only in primary school texts, but also in the
official press and in small group discussions. Serving
agriculture and "integrating with the peasants" had been
key themes in the official press even in the early 1960s
albeit there had been relatively few volunteers eager to
participate in the rustication movement launced at that
time. The enhanced political-ideological environment in
middle schools by 1964, however, had contributed to a
reorientation of priorities on the part of a fair number
of students. In fact, Chinese officials were finding
that their appeals to youth to leave the city for the
countryside were, if anything, being heeded too well.
The official response is perhaps best gauged by a statement allegedly made in 1964 by the then vice-major of
Shanghai:

> If this year's senior middle school graduates
> who are good in politics and good in study
> don't want to take the exam for university,
> but want to respond to the call to participate
> in agricultural production, we cannot say they

are incorrect...if it becomes a common
phenomenon, then it will be a big problem.
This is a kind of deviation...worth paying
great attention to.[40]

In Guangzhou in 1964 great attention was already
being paid to this "phenomenon." At a representative
conference for 1964 graduates of Guangzhou middle schools,
there was the following situation:

Some representatives originally thought that
being promoted was not as glorious as direct
participation in agricultural production and
so they were prepared not to sit for the
promotion examination but instead wanted to
go straight down to the village. Now, they
recognize that the state needs both a large
group of youth with revolutionary consciousness to participate in productive labor or
other work, and also needs a part of the
youth with revolutionary consciousness to
be promoted to study at the next higher
level school to continue studying .... Weng
Zhaoyang ... said: "In the past I onesided-
ly considered ... one should not take the
exam for university, but should go directly
to the countryside; only after participating
in this conference have I now changed this
one-sided viewpoint." ...She would prepare
to grasp the time to review her lessons and
welcome the examination for promotion.[41]

The national press also was emphatic in urging
senior middle graduates to study assiduously and sit for
the university entrance examinations, calling on the YCL
to exhort students, especially those who were outstanding,
to take the exams.[42] Accordingly, in this atmosphere, it
became difficult to do more than mildly object to those
middle school officials who perhaps exceeded the limits
in preparing their students for the exams.

Strategies of Middle School Officials

While the key-point schools generally were able to
retain their importance over time, there were cases of
upward or downward movement, and many more instances of
attempts at upward movement which recorded only partial
success or even total failure for those in authority
making the attempts.

1. A Successful Case: Number 21 Middle School.
Number 21 was established in 1955, with a rather low
standard. Because it was located near the Overseas

Chinese New Village, many of its early students were of this background. In 1959, a Guangdong Normal Institute was set up and Number 21 became its attached middle school. With the help of this new connection, Number 21 was quickly able to expand its teaching faculty, its area, and its teaching facilities, leading to an improved reputation. But in order to elevate significantly a school's status, it was necessary to raise the school's promotion rate to the university. The surest way to do this was to absorb those with good class backgrounds and good academic achievement at the same time. This proved unrealistic because students of this type were at a premium and generally went to the very best schools. Thus, the educational authorities at Number 21 adopted a compromise measure. As a former student of this school related:

> The school accepted two kinds of students. One type was those with low achievement, but outstanding class background. The other type was those with rather high academic achievement, but who were reluctant to apply to the very best schools because their backgrounds were not impeccable. Many of this latter group were from intellectual backgrounds. Generally speaking, worker-peasant children could not compete; although they belonged to the category of those of good class background, they were nevertheless still a notch below those of revolutionary cadre origin.[43]

Even after the closing down of the Normal Institute to which the school was attached, the location of Number 21 in the Eastern District, coupled with the school's rather high standing at the time of the 1962 rankings, allowed the school to remain competitive. The increasing emphasis on family background as a criterion was not a deterrent because of the school's location.

2. A School in Decline: Number 6 Middle School.[44] At the time of the 1962 rankings Number 6 Middle School was already facing some problems. Although the school had never been in the class of Guangya, Huafu, Number 1 or Number 2 Middle Schools, as the attached middle school of Zhongshan University, it was considered one of the top two schools in Southern Guangzhou. It had several advantages which helped attract students. For example, it was a boarding school and, among its other fine athletic teams, the swimming team was considered the best in the city among high schools. Several potential problems, however, hindered attempts at raising its promotion rate. One was its location (see map). Because it was in an area bounded by both factory districts and people's

communes, as many as one-third of its students might be
of worker-peasant background at a given time. On the
other hand, the area had many organizations engaged in
cultural work, such as Zhongshan University, the Ocean-
ographic Research Institute, the Guangdong Education
Institute and the Pearl River Film Studio, thus guaranteeing some students of intellectual background. Also,
the presence of the large Shidanggang Naval base, home
of the South Seas Fleet (Nanhai Jiandui) nearby, insured
the presence of children of military cadres. The reputation of the school, however, was due as much to its relatively spacious grounds and boarding facilities, its
sports teams, its affiliation to Zhongshan University
and its more or less captive student body which included
children of intellectual and cadre background who wanted
a school near home, as to its promotion rate, which fluctuated and was not much better than some of the schools
ranked below it. According to several informants from
the school, in the years prior to the 1962 rankings, the
school's general attractiveness had led many students
from overseas Chinese families to choose to attend, which
had deleterious effects on the promotion rate. Furthermore, according to a Red Guard newspaper, the school had
already been criticized in print in late 1959 when the
municipal committee and the Education Department decided
to give an unexpected examination as a way of checking
up on the quality of the better schools. Because the
leadership of Number 6 Middle School had not organized
a crash review program for its students, the school fin-
ished last among those tested. This, according to the
newspaper, left its reputation in something of a shambles
(shengming langjie).[45] Sometime after the 1963 graduating class, Zhongshan University dropped it as its attached school and the school name reverted to Number 6
Middle School. Some, though not all, of my interviewees
from that school felt that the low promotion rate of the
school had contributed to the university's decision. By
the eve of the GPCR, the school's promotion rate had
fallen below 20%. Interestingly enough, Number 6 Middle
School still maintained a rather good reputation among
those who went to other schools, but the interviewees
who were there in the years after the severance of its
affiliation with Zhongshan University were aware of the
school's decline, perhaps indicating a good public relations effort on the part of the school authorities.

    3. Temporary Success: Number 28 Middle School.[46]
Number 28 Middle School in North-Central Guangzhou, a
second category school, was able to set a new record for
promotion rate to the university in 1963 (over 30%).
How and why were they able to do it? In 1962, when the
schools were ranked, Number 28 was put into category two.
On the other hand, Number 13 was put into category one.

This was done, the officials at Number 28 felt, solely because Number 13 had a higher promotion rate to the university. Number 28 viewed Number 13 as the worst of the category one schools. Its facilities, grounds, history, general reputation and so forth were no match for Number 28; only its promotion rate was a bit higher. This irritated the authorities at Number 28 and they set out to surpass Number 13 and become a first category school. At that time Number 28, along with Numbers 29 and 17, was considered at the top of category two. The method they adopted to improve their promotion rate was to take all the students moving from second to third year senior middle school and rearrange the original classes. They took all the students who wanted to apply for humanities and social science college courses and put them in one class. They took all those who wanted to study science and engineering in college and put them into the two remaining classes. They then assigned the top humanities and social science teachers to the first class and the top natural science teachers to the other two classes. The teachers were expected to devote extra time to preparing their students for the university entrance examination. Those courses not considered "useful" (because they would not be tested) were neglected. In other words, students who were to be tested on social science subjects were not expected to worry about physics. This policy led to their unprecedented promotion rate in 1963. The extremes of this policy were stopped after one year, however, because of criticism from the Education Bureau.[47]

The following year, Number 28 tried to avoid too severe a slippage by using another method of reorganization, one for which they had not yet been criticized. After consolidating the four classes moving from senior middle two into three classes, they made class one into a key-point class, putting those with good or ordinary background and good grades into this class and everyone else into classes two and three. In other words, those with poor grades and/or bad class background, among others, were relegated to classes two and three. It was an obvious attempt to maximize promotion rate by concentrating the school's resources on those whose chances were most favorable. As expected, the key-point class easily outdistanced the other two by getting 12 of its members into the university.[48]

4. High-cost Short-term Success: Number 5 Middle School.[49] Middle School Number 5, in Southern Guangzhou, was already a well-known first category school with a university promotion rate well over 30% on the average. In 1964, according to an interviewee from that school, the promotion rate fell to 26%. In an attempt to reverse this slide, a well-known mathematics teacher who had been an important official under the Guomindang and had also

been attacked during the 1957 antirightist movement was brought in. His job was to teach mathematics to the graduating seniors so as to raise their promotion rate. Apparently he was successful; the informant reports the promotion rate to the university for the school went over 40% in 1965.

This should be considered only a short-term success because, when the GPCR arrived, Number 5 Middle School and its personnel were treated very harshly indeed. Even earlier, in fact, Number 5 Middle School had been so flagrant in using teachers of bad class background and questionable historical associations that it had been made the key-point for the Socialist Education Movement among Guangzhou middle schools prior to the arrival of the GPCR.[50]

5. <u>Total Disaster for All Concerned</u>: <u>Number 14 Middle School</u>.[51] This particular case gives a very clear, albeit extreme, example of the lengths to which some middle school officials went in their jockeying for success. Number 14 was only an average second category school in Central Guangzhou, with a lower rate of promotion than, say, Number 28. My interviewees and the Red Guard press referred to it as one of those "schools for the common people" (xiaoshimin xuexiao). This type of school, particularly given its location, had almost no possibility of attracting students of either cadre or intellectual background through normal channels. One informant related that it was best known to outsiders by the nickname "the school which watches the cowboys" (kan niuzai zhongxue) because it was located just across the way from the Overseas Chinese Middle School,[52] with the behavior and Western-imitated dress of the latter's students attracting much attention in Guangzhou. Originally, Number 14 Middle School was not going to accept any more senior middle students after those that entered in 1963. It was felt that the school was too small and the facilities too limited. But with the class line issue heating up in 1964 there were suddenly many excellent students who were unable to gain entrance to a good senior high. The principal, Li Qiu, went to the Education Bureau and discovered the files of all those students who had been turned down by the schools of their choice because of bad family origin. He chose the best of the "leftovers" for his school and assigned all of these students to one class.

None of them had listed Number 14 among their four choices and all were disappointed at being at such a mediocre school (one informant told me she cried on learning that she had been allocated to Number 14). Their class teacher told them they were being relied on to bring Number 14 up to the first rank of middle schools. Thus, on the eve of the GPCR, in senior middle two at

this school there were two classes. One class was composed of those who had gone to lower middle school at
places other than, and better than, Number 14. The other
class consisted of students who had been at Number 14 for
lower middle school. The first class had a large majority of students of bad class background to whom the
school authorities were particularly partial because of
their grades; the other class contained mostly students
of ordinary class background with no particular academic
talent. The former class received special treatment.
For example, Number 14 was a school which taught English.
Because these newly recruited students had previously
studied Russian, the school had to find some Russian
teachers for them, which they did, making it the only
class in the school in which Russian was taught. As
might be surmised, the early focal point of the GPCR in
Number 14 Middle School was this class and the role of
the school principal in putting it together.

While the above case is both tragic and pathetic,
most, if not all, senior middle schools seem to have
been obsessed with the problem of keeping or making their
schools competitive with others. It has been shown that
by 1964 Guangya was recruiting children of cadres for 75%
of its openings. A school like Number 1 Middle School,
one of the oldest and best in Guangzhou, had the geographical misfortune to be in the western suburbs of the
city, an area primarily distinguished by few cadre residences and overflowing with residents of bad class background. As the principal, Chen Ping, was reported to
have said in 1964, "It looks like we'll have to start
recruiting children of cadres from the Eastern
District."[53]

The situation in Beijing seems to have been similar,
with some variations. For example, because of the large
number of what I have called "true elite" middle schools
in Beijing (one scholar has estimated that boarding
schools for children of cadres alone numbered around
30),[54] there was developed a formula for guaranteeing
which schools were "elite." As described by a Red Guard
newspaper, this formula became known as the "6:6 system."
Basically, it meant that a school had to provide six
years (junior and senior middle) of education and had to
have six classes (ban) per year. As the newspaper put
it, this caused some schools which only had 23 classrooms
to recruit 33 classrooms of students and go to a "three
shift system" in an effort to qualify as a "high-level
school."[55]

In Guangzhou this was not feasible. There was, more
commonly, a reverse trend of keeping the school small in
order to increase the promotion rate percentage-wise.
The principal of Number 2 Middle School, generally considered to be the third best school in Guangzhou, according to the Red Guard newspaper:

...formulated a three-year promotion (to
university) norm: in 1963 promote 60%, in
1964 70%, in 1965 reach 80%. In 1963 he
raised the slogan "pass Guangya and catch
up to Huafu," then folded his arms across
his chest and took an oath: "If we don't
catch up to Guangya, I won't be at rest even
after I die." He said even more candidly:
"key-point schools should have a high promotion rate; if the promotion rate is low, and
the number of people participating in agricultural production is higher, then we (administrators) should be spanked."[56]

According to a 1965 graduate from this school, instead of maintaining six classes at the senior middle level as Huafu and Guangya did, Number 2 pruned their original four lower middle classes so that by senior high
there were only two classes left.[57] They discouraged
their good students from transferring to other schools
after junior middle and accepted very few transfers themselves. In this way they were able to sustain a high
promotion rate right up to the GPCR.
While it seems easy to understand the motivation of
officials at schools such as Number 2, which already had
achieved "keypoint" status and sought to maintain the
steady flow of funds which went with such status, at first
glance it is harder to fathom the rationale of officials
at mediocre schools like Number 14. Perhaps they held
out the hope - however flimsy - that their schools, as a
reward for success, might somehow be anointed in the future as a keypoint. Indeed, the transformation of neighborhood ugly ducklings into keypoint swans, while rare,
was not unprecedented. The example of Number 21 previously given was duplicated in other cities:

Take the instance of our Beijing University's
Attached Middle School. Its predecessor was
the 104th. Middle School, a common school that
admitted students from the vicinity. In 1957,
there were 142 workers' and peasants' children
but only two cadres' children. In 1960, Lu
Ping's shady gang, after consultation with the
shady Education Bureau, converted it into the
Beijing University's Attached Middle School,
with a view to promoting high-standard graduates of the school direct to the Beijing
University. Ever since then, there had been
a sharp decline in the proportion of workers'
and peasants' children but an abrupt rise in
the proportion of children of high-ranking
intellectuals and high-ranking cadres. By

1965, workers' and peasants' children formed
only 9% of the student population in this
school whereas cadres' children had jumped
from 0.5% to 33.7% and was continuing to
rise. In some junior middle classes, cadres'
children occupied more than half of the
places.[58]

While non-key point schools and those in small towns
generally were having difficulty successfully competing
with the best of the urban schools for scarce university
places, for those studying in suburban areas the pyram-
idal structure of China's educational system precluded
all but a few from going on to senior high:

In 1963 a kind of meaningless cliche became
even more widespread [than the 1962 emphasis
on dividing students into those to be cultivated for labor], saying that schools in
the municipality have as their major task
"the cultivation of new students for schools
at the next higher level," and suburban
village schools have as their main task "the
cultivation of labor reserve strength." Because of this the thoughts of the broad masses of teachers and students at our suburban
school became even more confused. In that
year (1963), there were more than 80 students
in the two graduating classes at the school,
but because they felt there was no hope of
being promoted, the absolute majority of the
children of workers and peasants gave up
their studying, so that only one person got
into senior high.[59]

UNIVERSITY ENROLLMENT, 1960-1966: CHANGING PATTERNS

There is ample evidence that the percentage of students of working class and cadre backgrounds increased
steadily from the early 1950s until 1960.[60] By 1961,
however, the policy of a continually increasing proletarian representation in higher education was suddenly relegated to the back burner. The Red Guard press - both
from Beijing and Guangzhou - reveals how different the
1961 and 1962 university enrollment policy was in comparison to earlier as well as later years. For example, we
are told that the attack on the progressive education
policies of the Great Leap Forward, which had opened wide
the university doors to workers and peasants, began in
November, 1960 with the National Cultural and Educational
Work Conference, at which the "elevation of teaching

quality" was stressed in contrast to the Leap's emphasis
on "quantity" and "size." Higher schools that had been
newly built were expected to "undergo readjustment...some
among them really fall far short in many respects, and
they should be differentially maintained, improved,
merged with others, or abolished altogether...."[61] As
this conference took place after the 1960 enrollment process had been completed, it was in 1961 that the new emphasis on "controlling enrollment" began to make itself
felt. By 1962 candidates were divided into sections
solely on the basis of exam grades; only after the candidates in the high-grade sections were chosen were those
in the low-grade sections inspected.[62] Apparently the
officials doing the selecting were slow to grasp the full
impact of the emphasis on grades. As one Red Guard paper
points out:

> In 1961 in the Beijing Special District's
> higher education entrance exam there were
> 367 students whose exam score was 80% or
> above, but because of their complicated
> political situation, they hadn't yet been
> accepted. Counterrevolutionary revision-
> ists Song Shuo and Wu Zimu paid no heed
> to the strong protests from the schools,
> but grasped the neck of each school under
> the municipality, forcing them to take
> these students. In 1962, those students
> in the Beijing Special District scoring
> 80% or above, no matter what their poli-
> tical conditions, were all accepted.[63]

The paper also reported that, among the new students, the
matriculation rate of students of worker-peasant background in 1962 fell 13% in comparison to 1961 while
children of exploiting class origin increased their representation by 4.6%.
      In Guangzhou the situation seemingly was comparable.
One interviewee of working class background reported that
20 students in his graduating class at Number 2 Middle
School were successful in getting accepted to the university in 1961. Of those who were unsuccessful, after
repeating the examination in 1962, eight more were
successful. All eight were students from bad class backgrounds.[64]
      Statistics from Zhongshan University confirm the
change in 1962 (Table 1.8).
      Within the universities at this time, there was a
heavy emphasis on academic achievement. Students of
worker-peasant background and transferred cadres (diao-
gansheng) felt the pressure most. For example, at
Beijing University, 242 students were held back in 1962,

Table 1.8

Class Origins of Students at Zhongshan University, 1960 to 1962

	% of Students From Good Class Backgrounds	% From Exploiters' Families	% From Middle Class Families	% Total	% of YCL Members
1960	69%	8%	23%	100%	60%
1961	73%	8%	19%	100%	-
1962	40%	30%	30%	100%	30%

Source: John and Elsie Collier, China's Socialist Revolution (New York, 1973), p. 130.

of whom 155 were worker-peasant students (64%). Of the 42 students who dropped out that year, 33 were children of worker-peasant background (79%).[65] From June, 1960 to January, 1962, 60 rightist elements were recalled to the school and allowed to return to their studies. They were also given university subsidies and were permitted to skip classes in politics.[66]

Another Red Guard paper offered the following statistics for Beijing University as a whole:

Table 1.9

Class Origins of Students at Beijing University, 1960 and 1962

	Students of Worker-Peasant Background (Including Revolutionary Cadre Background)	Students of Middle Class Background	Students of Exploiting Class Background and Children of Shaguanguan[67] Counterrevolutionary Elements
1960	66.8%	21%	12.2%
1962	37.7%	33%	29.3%

Source: Bingtuan Zhanbao, August 18, 1967, p. 3.

As was pointed out during the GPCR:

> In this kind of situation, it is not surprising that in 1962, after the university entrance examinations, some capitalists, in order to celebrate the entrance of their children into university, put on a big spread and praised the promotion policy of 1962 as relying on real ability, as the fairest and most reasonable. Moreover, a few counterrevolutionary revisionist

elements also shamelessly exclaimed:
"1962 is the year in which the class
line has been carried out most
completely..."68

Moreover, beginning in 1961, high-level investigation teams visited a number of key universities, such as
Beijing University and Zhongshan University, to make sure
the new line was being enforced. At Zhongshan University,
for example, the vice-secretary of the Party committee
was found guilty of neglecting teaching, putting too much
emphasis on physical labor, neglecting the welfare of the
old intellectuals, placing too much emphasis on class
analysis, trying to get rid of old scholars on the
grounds that they were highly reactionary, and so forth.69
An interesting sidelight to the 1960-62 figures is
provided by a table in China Youth Daily, August 16, 1966,
which was later reprinted in the Red Guard press (Table
1.10).

Table 1.10

Class Origins of Students in the Department of
Geophysics, Beijing University, 1960-1963

	Revolutionary Cadre Origin	Worker and Poor Peasant Origin	Middle Class Origin	Bad Class Origin
1960	21%	41%	30%	8%
1961	10%	30%	48%	12%
1962	13%	27%	37%	23%
1963		18%		

Source: China Youth Daily (Zhongguo Qingnian Bao), August 16, 1966.

Interestingly, one can see that the increase in the number of students of bad class origin from 1961 to 1962 was
at the expense of those of middle class background rather
than those of good class background.
The point being made in all the figures given above
is that students of worker-peasant background were being
kept out of higher education by students of exploiting
class background in the pre-GPCR period. More significant, however, is the fact that the emphasis is always
on the 1961-63 period. The enrollment figures for 1964
and 1965, a period in which the trend had changed completely and children of exploiting class background were
being increasingly barred both from universities and
elite middle schools while children of army personnel and
revolutionary cadre background began to be recruited in
large numbers, are universally avoided.70
Somewhat surprisingly, this tendency to ignore the

1964-1965 period seems to have been perpetuated into the post-GPCR period. Consider the figures provided in Table 1.11.

Table 1.11

Class Origins of Students at the Institute for
Foreign Languages, Beijing, 1960-1962 and 1971-1975

1960-1962

Students of Worker-Peasant Origin = 45%
Students of Army Personnel and Revolutionary Cadre Origin = 25.5%
Students of Exploiting Class Origin = 17%
Students of Middle Class Origin = 12.5%

1971-1975

Students of Worker-Peasant Origin = 63%
Students of Army Personnel and Revolutionary Cadre Origin = 25.5%
Students of Exploiting Class Origin = 0%
Students of Middle Class Origin = 11.5%

Source: David Crook, "Who Goes to College in China Now?," Eastern Horizon, Vol. 15, No. 3, 1976.

There unfortunately is only some limited data for the period after 1962-63 which is indicative of the new trends. For example, in 1964 Beijing University, Beijing Normal University, and China People's University all reported a record number of incoming freshmen from families of working people.[71] Interviewees report that children of shaguanguan counterrevolutionary elements were barred from higher education in 1964. Those fortunate students of bad family origin who were able to enter universities in 1961 or 1962 seem to have become quite as embarrassing to their universities as the students of worker-peasant origin had several years earlier. One interviewee of bad-class origin who had entered South China Engineering Institute in 1963 discovered within the space of a year that the school's Party branch was transferring him and a dozen of the other bad class and politically backward students to the less prestigious Guangdong Engineering Institute.[72]

Finally, a Japanese source reports that 52% of the students at Beijing University on the eve of the GPCR were of proletarian family origin.[73] Since the Fall 1962 figure was 37.7% (see Table 1.9) and since the May, 1962 figure had been 48%,[74] this shows that students of proletarian origin (which would include those of revolutionary cadre and military origin as well) had once again begun to displace those of non-good background (almost certainly those of bad class background, given the figure of

29.3% cited in Table 1.9) as the GPCR drew near.

Concurrent with the changes in enrollment figures was the pressure, which began to build up against the Ministry of Education beginning in 1964, following Mao Zedong's remarks on education in February at the Spring Festival.[75] When the Ministry called a conference on Natural Science and Engineering later in the year it found its "rightist tendencies," represented by the "Sixty Points" on education which had been drafted in 1961, under strong attack.[76]

Furthermore, the 1964 entrance examinations were becoming geared more toward students of good class background than those of high academic achievement. The exam format was changing. In 1959 there had been three exam groups covering: (1) science and engineering; (2) medicine, agriculture and forestry; (3) social sciences and humanities.[77]

The politics exam, a required subject in each examination group, generally tested a student's awareness of the political line as presented in the national media rather than probing for deeper understanding. In 1963, in fact, before the emphasis on class line, a politics exam was not administered at all.

Other changes grew out of the deemphasis on academic achievement. In 1964 exam groups one and two were merged into an overall sciences category by dropping biology and requiring mathematics for the group two students.[78] In 1965 physics was eliminated as well. This left only chemistry as an examination subject in science, presumably aiding those students from non-elite schools. It was no longer necessary to spread their smaller teaching staffs and laboratory funds over three subjects.

Foreign language exams also followed the political line. A foreign language was not listed as a requirement for the years 1955-1958, although it had been required for university entrance until 1955. The requirement was reintroduced in 1959 and continued until the GPCR, although various exemptions were allowed. For example, worker-peasant students were exempt from the foreign language exam in 1964 and 1965.[79]

University and Middle School Students in Guangzhou, 1960-66: Increasing or Decreasing in Number?

Another important question concerns the number of students competing for higher education and the number accepted. Were the numbers of graduates of senior middle schools increasing, decreasing, or remaining about the same?

Despite incomplete and somewhat contradictory statistics, certain trends can be discerned. As Table 1.12 shows, enrollment in higher education in Guangzhou seems to have taken a big dip following the Great Leap Forward, then to have started up again.

Table 1.12

Higher Education in Guangzhou: New Students, 1959-1965

Year	New Students (Higher Education in Guangzhou)
1959[a]	9,500 students (22 Institutions)
1962[b]	3,000+ students
1965[c]	6,000+ students

Source: a Da Gong Bao, Hongkong, September 9, 1959.
       b Yangcheng Wanbao, September 3, 1962, p. 1 (translated in JPRS No. 16,433, November 30, 1962, p. 1.
       c Da Gong Bao, September 6, 1965. The 1965 figure is for the Guangzhou district (qu) rather than the municipality (shi).

Some elaboration of these figures is necessary. First, one would expect the 1959 figure to be a high one because of the needs generated by the enthusiasm of the Great Leap Forward. On the other hand, 1962 was clearly the low point in university enrollment. One successful applicant told me that the promotion rate from Guangzhou as a whole that year was 13.3%. He obtained the figure from classmates whose parents were officials in the Education Bureau. The best middle school in Guangzhou - Huafu - had a promotion rate of only 66% that year. The next best - Guangya and Number 2 Middle School - reached only 33%.[80] Still, these schools were satisfied, the Huafu principal actually inviting the school's teachers out for a meal to celebrate their "success."[81] Finally, the 1965 figure may be a bit inflated if it includes students at some "non-regular" universities (those of a work-study nature); the report is not specific on this point.

Fortuitously, a more recent report from China comparing educational growth during the 1960s confirms these trends:

Owing to serious natural disasters in the three subsequent years (following the Great Leap Forward) and interference from Liu Shaoqi's revisionist line, the development in education slowed down and it was not until after 1964 that it started to make steady advances again. By 1965, the number of students in primary schools, secondary schools, and colleges had jumped to 116 million, 14,418,000 and 674,000 respectively....[82]

The lack of expansion at the tertiary level was reflected at the senior high level as well. As Tables 1.13 and 1.14 suggest, although there was a steady increase in the expansion of junior high education, there was a leveling off and even a decrease in "regular" senior high enrollment. Students graduating in increasing numbers from junior high had, starting in 1964, greater flexibility in deciding which road to travel. One increasingly popular route was to opt for terminal mid-level education.

Table 1.13

Graduating Students in Guangzhou Middle Schools, 1959-1965

Graduating Seniors

Year	Senior High	Junior and Senior High Combined	Junior High
1959-60a	5,400		12,000+
1962-63b	4,000+		15,000+
1963-64c		15,000+	
1964-65d	4,000+	26,000+*	15,000+
1965-66e		28,000**	

* Although the number of junior and senior middle graduates as reported in the press in 1965 add up to less than the combined total as reported, there appears to be a reasonable explanation. By 1965, as can be seen from the table on middle school entering students given below, students were beginning to be listed not necessarily as "regular" senior or junior middle students but as students at the senior or junior "level." Thus, the number of senior high entering students in 1964 included those who entered teacher training, technical and vocational schools as well. Presumably, this was also being done with the figures on graduating students. The rationale for recording the statistics this way related most likely to the desire to overcome criticism, particularly with regard to the vocational schools, that ridiculed these schools as "irregular" in that they were not really schools, but work-training places.

** Although the 28,000 figure is not broken down further, we are told that as of April, 1965 there were over 89,000 students in lower middle school in Guangzhou. Thus, it is reasonable to assume that the overwhelming percentage of the 28,000 figure a year later would be made up of lower middle school graduates.[83]

Source: a. Yangcheng Wanbao, September 1, 1960
b. Ibid., July 28, 1963; Guangzhou radio, August 12, 1963
c. Yangcheng Wanbao, June 19, 1964
d. Ibid., July 14, 1965 and May 6, 1965
e. Guangzhou radio, April 8, 1966

Table 1.14

Middle School Entering Students in Guangzhou

Year	Senior High	Junior and Senior High Combined	Junior High
1959a		30,000+	
1960b	6,500		24,000+
1962c	5,070		23,500+
1963d	ca. 5,700+		ca. 24,000*
1964e	10,000+**		30,000+***
1965f	(Not available)	(Increased over the previous year when combining junior and senior high)	35,000+

* The 1963 figure is gotten by computation from data supplied in
  1964. The figure for 1964 is large because starting in 1964
  mid-level technical schools, teacher training schools, and
  vocational schools began being included in published enrollment
  figures as part of the larger total. Thus, the 1963 figure is
  derived from the statistic that the 10,000+ figure of 1964 is
  a 76% increase in the number of places at the same level (tongji)
  the year before.
** Since there were over 5,700 entering students in vocational
   schools alone in 1964 (see below), the number of regular senior
   high students entering in this year actually probably dropped.
*** This figure includes results from 149 schools. There were 13
    junior high schools that gave entrance exams at a later date,
    so their numbers were not available at the time of this newspa-
    per report. Again, the 1963 figure is derived from the 1964
    data.

Source: a. Wenhui Bao (Hong Kong), June 25, 1959
        b. Yangcheng Wanbao, September 1, 1960
        c. Nanfang Ribao, August 26, 1962, p. 1
        d. Yangcheng Wanbao, August 22, 1964
        e. Ibid.
        f. Da Gong Bao, September 6, 1965; Wenhui Bao, April 2,
           1965

In 1963, in Guangzhou, there were 1) 15 Technical or
                                      Specialist (jishu)
                                      Schools
                                   2) 4 Schools to Train
                                      Skilled Workers
                                      (jigong)
                                   3) 3 Teacher-Training
                                      Schools[84]

In 1964, 25 vocational schools (primarily of the
half-work half-study variety) with 5,700 students were
added.[85] In 1965 six more vocational schools were added

with the total number of students now in vocational
schools said to be more than 11,000.[86]

According to interviewees, these vocational schools
started drawing off large numbers of students who in
previous years would have expected to move from junior
to senior high. Although many had qualms when the half/
half schools were set up in 1964, by 1965 they were being
seen by the students, and more importantly, by the parents of the students, as a safe guarantee of urban work
after one to three years.[87] Even the least favored of
these schools, such as the ones operated by the Commercial Bureau (Shangye ju) and the Service Bureau (Fuwu ju),
were having little trouble recruiting students. In 1964,
for example, vocational schools affiliated to the above
two bureaus had difficulty finding suitable students
because they trained people for jobs such as barbering,
restaurant work, and cake making. Thus, they were more
or less forced to accept a number of students of bad
class background and/or relatively advanced age, including "social youths" who had taken the university entrance exam two or three times without success and were
now resisting the call to strike roots in the countryside.[88] By 1965, as the class line policy intensified,
and as it became easier to find applicants of good class
background for these schools, six hundred of the original
students selected in 1964 were suddenly expelled.[89]

The Two Beneficiaries

Which students, then, were still opting for senior
middle schools leading, hopefully, to university education? In general, two groups were most strategically
placed to benefit from the selection process in 1965.
The first group comprised students of high academic
achievement whose class backgrounds were generally petit-
bourgeois. The second group included those of good class
background; in Guangzhou, this meant students of revolutionary cadre or working class background.

For several reasons, the benefits of the post-1964
emphasis on class origin favored those from cadre families rather than those from working class homes. First,
it was only relatively late that even junior middle
schools started to be built in many of Guangzhou's working class areas. For example, in a 1964 report on 60
newly built or enlarged middle and primary schools,
Guangzhou radio stressed that:

> ...most of these schools are situated in the
> new industrial areas, in workers' residential
> areas, and suburban villages. Children of
> workers and poor and lower-middle peasants
> will thus be able to go to school near their
> homes.[90]

There was a similar report at the end of 1965. The aim, as was pointed out in the case of Number 33 Middle School, was to recruit more and more students of worker-peasant background, especially those who were first generation students from their families.[91] But the new middle schools being built had no senior middle sections. In fact, there was no expansion at all in the senior high system after 1961-62.

Also, there was the ever-present problem of cost. One researcher has estimated secondary school costs as follows:[92]

> Junior High School Tuition = 5 yuan per term
>   (2 terms a year)
> Senior High School Tuition = 7 yuan per term
> Notebook and Stationery Fees = 4 yuan per term
> Book Fees = 4 yuan per term
> Activities Fee = ca. .5 yuan per term
> Additional Boarding School Expenses
> Dormitory Fees = Varied with the respondent, but
>   between 3 and 10 yuan per term
> 3 Meals Per Day = 9-10 yuan per month

Considering that the average male worker earned between 40-50 yuan a month, these expenses for schooling were not inconsiderable. Commuting or boarding would have been necessary for most since the better schools, with rare exceptions, were not in the industrial areas of Guangzhou. The parents, themselves usually not very well educated, might reason that a factory job for their child, obtainable directly upon graduation from junior high, made good sense financially. This was especially likely to be the case if the parents had reasonably good "connections" at their own or in other factories.

The lingering importance attached to entrance examination results right up to the GPCR also continued to militate against the success of those of working class origin. Since universities were divided into three categories, roughly corresponding to level of administrative control (from Central to District level), with schools in category one requiring higher examination scores than those in category two and so on, students of worker-peasant origin were most competitive for entrance to category three schools, which tended to be local, vocational institutes.

Indeed, the continuing importance of academic achievement as a criterion for university entrance was clearly stated by a department director of the Ministry of Higher Education who told a foreign visitor in 1965: "...we cannot sacrifice quality for quantity by admitting to our universities students who do not meet the standards." As to students of worker-peasant background, the same official replied: "When there is a tie in marks

the candidate of proletarian origin is given priority."93
     For children of revolutionary cadres and armymen it
was a far different picture. Aside from their far better
financial situation, they generally felt that they were
best qualified to maintain the momentum of the revolution
and take over from their parents. Concluding from remarks of interviewees, as well as articles in the Red
Guard press, it seems roughly true that children of workers sought to replace their fathers in factory jobs while
children of cadres set their aspirations much higher. As
shall be seen in the next chapter, middle school officials and teachers, perhaps with this in mind, treated
children of workers and children of cadres very differ-
ently. One Red Guard newspaper is very explicit in discussing the fate of children of worker-peasant background,
even after 1964:

> In recruiting for Beijing middle schools,
> children of workers and peasants also had
> layer upon layer of restrictions. They
> were squeezed out of keypoint schools, but
> children of those of the exploiting class
> could rely on their high marks to enter
> keypoint schools. Children of those taking
> the capitalist road, even more, as objects
> of "consideration" went to "elite" (jianzi)
> schools. Beijing X middle school is a key-
> point school. In 1964 and 1965, of all the
> new students recruited by that school, not
> one was the son or daughter of a worker or
> peasant. 50-80% of the sons and daughters
> of workers and peasants were sent to "melon-
> vegetable"* schools under the two-shift
> system.**94

Of the group whose academic achievement was high,
the most favored were those of intellectual background.
There were several reasons for this. To begin with,
there was of course the family situation. The traditional value attached to schooling remained strong,
particularly considering the options open to children of

---

* The Chinese expression used is "gua cai dai" (melon and
  vegetable substitutes). The expression comes from the
  "three bad years" of 1959-61 when there was a shortage
  of grain; the Chinese press at the time urged the popu-
  lace to substitute melons and vegetables for the unavailable grain. Thus, students of worker-peasant
  background are being told to substitute poor schools
  because good schools have no place for them.
** Statistics demonstrating the advantages of those of
  exploiting class origin all derive from 1961 and 1962.

intellectuals. To compete with children of workers for
factory jobs would have been difficult indeed; other
options, such as jobs in the service trades, agricultural work, or primary school teaching were disdained by
students from all class backgrounds. In a certain sense,
the emphasis on family background helped the students of
middle class background as well. In 1961 and 1962 their
prime competition had come from students of exploiting
class origin. The new stress on origin practically eliminated the latter from consideration except in rare cases, while the continuing emphasis on minimum exam scores
still gave the former an entree to the best schools. One
former student, with most of his relatives in education
work, put it this way:

> By the middle sixties, universities were
> looking for kids from very good family ori-
> gin (high or mid-level cadre) or else kids
> of higher intellectual background. Children
> of worker-peasant background, and even those
> of lower-level cadre background were discrim-
> inated against unless they were especially
> recommended by their schools. Given the
> following three applicants: 1. Intellectual
> background (father a university professor);
> 2. Working class background (father a wor-
> ker); 3. Intellectual background (father a
> primary or middle school teacher), a good
> university would most likely choose the can-
> didates in the order 1., 2., 3., if all fac-
> tors were constant (i.e., grades, perfor-
> mance).[95]

Judging from other interviews, as well as Red Guard
newspapers, children of academics, especially professors,
were very much overrepresented in the elite senior middle
schools as well. As one angry group of Red Guards wrote:

> In 1960, when the Middle School Attached to
> South China Normal Institute [Huafu] carried
> out a five-year experimental program for
> lower and senior middle school, the absolute
> majority of students recruited were children
> of professors, lecturers, engineers, and
> those of exploiting class background. The
> principle was to recruit the "cream" (jianzi)
> of those studying. These students in the
> experimental classes shut themselves behind
> closed doors to study; using the language
> of their parents, they became "bookworms"....[96]

Indeed, as one Huafu student who was there recalled it:

> When the time came to choose students for the
> experimental classes, the school tried to
> mobilize students who were good academically,
> like children of professors or other intell-
> ectuals. Although they also sought out
> some average students as a sort of "con-
> trol," the whole point of the experiment was
> to see how hard they could push the students,
> how much they could learn. Thus, getting
> the brightest students was a sine qua non.
> Of the 300 advancing from lower middle, 80
> were chosen for the two experimental clas-
> ses.[97]

By 1964 and 1965, children of exploiting class background were finding it almost impossible to gain admittance to schools like Huafu. Except for those already
locked into a senior high program which they had entered
in 1963, most of those of bad background I interviewed
were either already in work-study schools or intending to
enter them after graduation from junior high.
    The only students capable of entering the best uni-
versities without the proper academic credentials were
the children of cadres with appropriate connections, and
even then some deviousness was required. The Red Guard
press provides several examples of this phenomenon. For
example, the son of He Long, upon graduation from senior
middle school, applied to Qinghua University but lacked
the grades required for admission. He therefore first
transferred to Qinghua's attached middle school to repeat
third year senior high and then was able to "rise directly" to the parent university.[98]

CONCLUSION

    On the eve of the GPCR, there were several salient
factors in the mission and the structure of the Chinese
educational system at the middle school level. First,
there was the congruence of student desires, middle
school administrators and both national and local officials in stressing the importance of university education, although for somewhat different reasons. The
officials wanted to guarantee that senior middle schools
would continue to produce outstanding students who would
contribute to the continuing economic development of the
country. The middle school administrators focused their
concern on raising the promotion rate of their students
to the university. As for the students, both Chinese
tradition and the present attitudes of those administer-
ing education policy encouraged them to seek higher
education. Using the official press and the comments of
their teachers as a basis, most students had no difficul-

ty rationalizing their desire to go on to the university as equivalent to serving their country in the most meaningful way.

Second, the figures for Guangzhou cited above seem to indicate a decline in the number of students at the "regular" senior middle schools by the eve of the GPCR. In effect, given the expansion of university places vis-a-vis 1962 when many schools had been forced to close down,[99] entrance to the good senior high schools was becoming almost as difficult as entrance to the university.[100] One report, by Barry Richman, based in part on figures the Chinese had given to foreign visitors at different times, shows the junior/senior high enrollment pattern to be possibly even more striking when looked at nationally (Table 1.15).

In all fairness, Richman questions the junior/senior middle ratios for 1959-1960 as against the figures for 1964. Also, we now know that the overall figure quoted by Richman for total middle school enrollment in 1964-1965 is too high (see p. 51). Nevertheless, both figures were provided by officials from China's Education Ministry and, at the very least, seem to reflect the enormous expansion in junior high enrollment without a corresponding increase in senior high enrollment.[101]

Third, the declining enrollment at the senior high level was in large part due to conscious decisions made both by the state and the individual. The state was concentrating its resources on expanding education at the junior middle and primary level; the expansion at the senior high level was exclusively in the form of work-study vocational schools. The effect was to bifurcate the educational system even more than previously. On the one hand, the division in function between junior and senior high which had always existed was becoming more clear-cut as educational options for junior middle graduates opened up after 1964. On the other hand, the differences between the senior highs became even more pronounced as a result of the same phenomenon. Unless one went to one of the top senior highs, one's prospects for university entrance were not very promising. By 1964, the two Guangzhou schools with the highest promotion rates to the university, Huafu and Guangya, were producing at least 10 percent of Guangzhou's senior high graduates.[102] According to one Red Guard's account, middle schools in Fujian seemed even more hierarchically structured. In that province, fully 80 percent of the university students came from just three schools.[103]

The implications for this study are immense. With the continuing emphasis on academic achievement combined with the more recent stress given to family origin, there developed several important cleavages in Guangzhou's middle schools on the eve of the GPCR. These can

Table 1.15

National Statistics on General Secondary Education

	Enrollment (In Thousands)			Number of Graduates (In Thousands)		
Year	Junior	Senior	Total	Junior	Senior	Total
1949-50	831.8	207.2	1,039	250	46	296
1957-58	4,340	780.0	5,120	1,091	221.7	1,313
1958-59	7,340	1,180	8,520	*	242	*
1959-60	7,740	5,160	12,900	*	*	*
1964-65	21,000	2,100	23,100	*	*	*

* Not available

Source: Barry Richman, Industrial Society in Communist China (New York: Random House, 1969), p. 140.

be summarized as:

1. Junior high vs. senior high (in different schools).
2. "Good" senior high vs. mediocre or poor senior high.
3. Junior high vs. senior high in the same school.
4. Students of high academic achievement vs. students of good class background.
4a. Students of intellectual background vs. students of worker-peasant or cadre background.
4b. Students who entered middle school before vs. after 1964 (the year the class line policy began to be strongly enforced in enrollment).

China's secondary school students were embedded in an educational structure marked by increasing competition among those who sought to climb the educational ladder. The main arena of competition was the classroom, with the competition centering increasingly on that most visible sign of success for secondary school students: entrance to the Young Communist League. It is to this competition that we now turn.

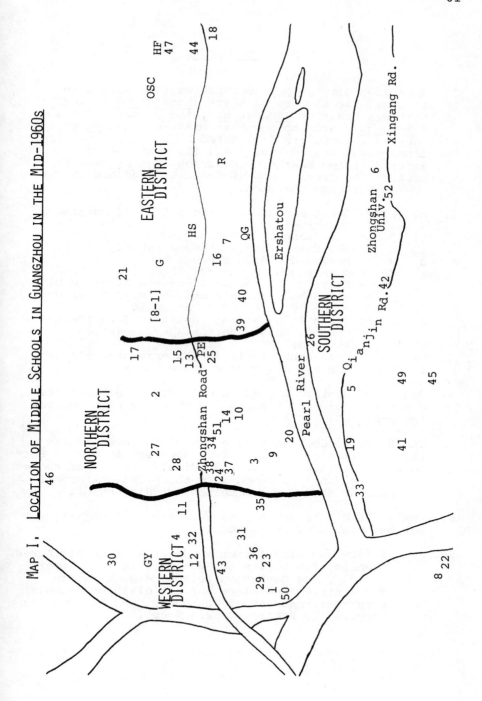

MAP I. LOCATION OF MIDDLE SCHOOLS IN GUANGZHOU IN THE MID-1960s

Notes to Map I

1. Guangzhou city proper encompasses four main districts: the Eastern District (Dongshan qu), the
   Northern District (Yuexiu qu), the Western District
   (Liwan qu), and the Southern District (Haizhu qu).
   These districts are delineated by the broad vertical
   lines appearing on Maps I and II, with the Pearl
   River dividing Southern Guangzhou (Henan) from the
   rest of the city. Much of Central Guangzhou is part
   of the Northern District.

2. a. OSC = Overseas Chinese Middle School (Huaqiao
              Zhongxue)
   b. QG = Qiaoguang Middle School
   c. G   = Zhu Zhixin Girls' Middle School
   d. R   = Railroad Middle School
   e. GY = Guangya Middle School
   f. HF = South China Normal Institute Attached Mid-
              dle School (Huanan Shifan Xueyuan Fuzhong),
              commonly referred to as Huafu
   g. HS = South China Normal Institute Experimental
              School (Huanan Shifan Xueyuan Shiyan
              Xuexiao)
   h. PE = Guangdong Provincial Experimental School
   i. [8-1] = August 1st. Middle School

3. Huafu and Numbers 18, 44, and 47 Middle Schools are
   a bit further into the suburbs than can be shown on
   the map.

4. The Overseas Chinese Middle School is shown in the
   Eastern District; before 1965, however, it was in the
   Northern District. Number 51 Middle School, as shown
   on the map, in 1965 moved into the premises formerly
   occupied by the Overseas Chinese Middle School.

5. Number 48 Middle School, in suburban Shuijungang, has
   not been included on the map.

Source: Interviews with former students at many of these
        schools, two visits to Guangzhou in the summer
        of 1980, the Guangzhou telephone book (which
        lists street addresses for all of these schools),
        a current resident of Guangzhou, and information
        supplied by Professor Ezra Vogel.

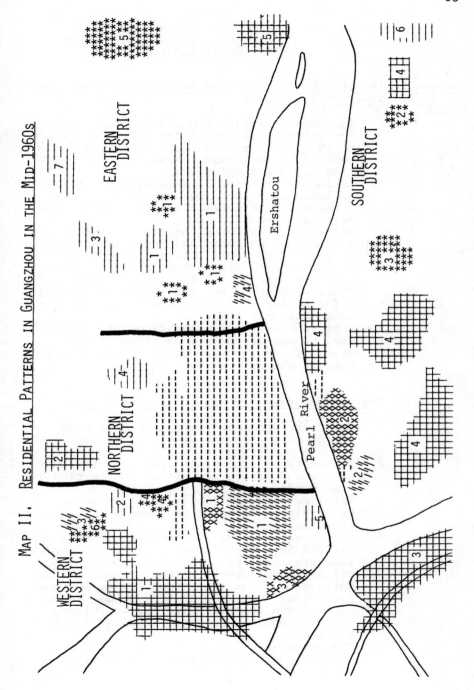

MAP II. RESIDENTIAL PATTERNS IN GUANGZHOU IN THE MID-1960s

64

Notes to Map II

(Revolutionary Cadre and Revolutionary Military
Areas of Residence)

1. Guangzhou military region, residence area
   for cadres in organs under the jurisdiction
   of the province, the municipality, and the
   Central-South bureau, as well as for other
   high and mid-level cadres.
2. Residence area for high-level military affiliated with the army hospital.
3. Guangdong provincial military district and
   garrison command.
4. Residence area for high-level cadres of the
   provincial and municipal Party committees,
   as well as for some military cadres.
5. Residence area for some high and mid-level
   cadres at the provincial level (particularly
   those working in the foreign trade, foreign
   affairs, agricultural reclamation and customs (haiguan) fields).
6. Residence area for military cadres affiliated to the Southern Seas fleet (Nanhai
   Jiandui) and its rear services department.
7. Same as Number 3 above.

(Residence Areas for Higher Intellectuals)

1. Residence area for a proportion of those
   personnel in the fields of literature, drama
   and other artistic circles.
2. Dormitory and residence area for directors,
   actors and office workers of the Pearl River
   Film Studio.
3. Intellectuals affiliated with Zhongshan
   University, including professors, lecturers
   and other staff.
4. Residence area for a proportion of those in
   various artistic circles as well as doctors,
   teachers, and news media personnel.
5. University district, including South China
   Engineering Institute, South China Agricultural Institute, South China Normal Institute, Jinan University, Overseas Chinese
   Remedial School, Foreign Languages Institute, etc.
6. Residence area for a number of those in
   artistic circles, as well as teachers.

(Working Class Districts)

1. Xicun Industrial District
2. Sanyuanli Industrial District
3. Fangcun Industrial District
4. Henan Industrial District (includes Xiaogang District, Industrial Road District, Textile Road District, and Zhigang District)
5. Yuancun Industrial District

(Areas Occupied Primarily by Those of Exploiting Class Chengfen, Primarily Capitalist Class)

1. "Xiguan," traditional residence district of capitalists in Guangzhou.
2. "Henan" residence district of capitalists in Guangzhou.
3. "Xizeng road Huaye lane" residence district of capitalists in Guangzhou (mixed residential area in that there is also a good sampling of those working in literary and art circles residing there).
4. "Dongshan" district formerly occupied by those well-off financially (including capitalists as well as overseas Chinese). (There was some difference of opinion among my informants with regard to this district. While there was no question about the pre-1949 residence pattern there, several knowledgeable informants thought that most of the formerly wealthy families living in this area before Liberation had moved to the Western District of Guangzhou when the Eastern District had become the favored area for revolutionary cadre and military personnel).

These areas of the map contain Guangzhou residents of all class backgrounds except those of high-level revolutionary cadre or military background. Very few higher intellectuals, as well, would reside in this area. On the other hand, there were teachers (of primary and secondary school), workers, non-intellectual middle class, etc., scattered throughout this Central Guangzhou area. Administratively, most of this area was part of the Northern District.

66

 (Areas 1, 2, and 3)

These areas of the map indicate concentrations
of non-proletarian laboring people and non-intellectual "middle class." For example, peddlers (xiaofan), those who bought things second-
hand to sell to others (shoumai lao), coolies,
lumpenproletariat, etc., were relatively concentrated in these areas.

Source: Interviews with former residents from different
areas of Guangzhou. While there is obviously no
claim to complete accuracy, the map does give a
reasonably accurate picture of residence patterns in Guangzhou as of 1966. I first decided
to prepare this map when it became apparent that
most of my Red Guard interviewees thought of
Guangzhou, its middle schools, and even the development of the Cultural Revolution at least as
much in terms of districts and their differences
as in terms of the city as a whole.
In addition to many former Red Guards, I would
like to thank Yang Shizhang of the University
of Michigan for checking the accuracy of the
completed map. Two visits to Guangzhou and
interviews with a current resident also proved
helpful.

2
Student Relationships
Prior to the Cultural Revolution

Classroom relations among Chinese middle school students in the 1960s were a direct result of the tension between two contradictory, and seemingly irreconcilable, ideals. On the one hand, the system sought to produce intellectuals who would be both red and expert, willing to serve the revolution joyfully in whatever capacity the state deemed necessary, and with a strong sense of shared interests and unity rather than of competition and individual benefit. With this goal in mind, many student activities such as labor cooperation, mutual help, small group meetings and so forth were fostered.[1] On the other hand, the decision as to who would continue his/her schooling and who would join the labor force had to be made at the middle school level. As described in Chapter One, this latter role of the middle schools assumed overwhelming importance by the 1960s, defining the structure of the educational system in such a way that all other goals were rendered subordinate. Students, too, taking their cues from the priorities of their elders in the educational field and from the official press, tended to emphasize cooperation when it was not likely to interfere with their opportunities for upward mobility through the educational system. In short, state policy itself, perhaps unwittingly, guaranteed that the striving for educational mobility would become the key to student relationships. Furthermore, the manipulation by educational authorities of the three main criteria for mobility - academic achievement, class origin, and individual performance - turned the classroom atmosphere into one more characterized by apprehensive rivalry than comradely friendship.

The key to understanding the divergence between student relationships as the Party would have preferred them to be and as they actually were is the notion of individual performance (biaoxian) and its somewhat amorphous character. Biaoxian was the link between the red (good family origin) and the expert (good academic achivement). In order to become a suitable revolutionary successor (jieban ren) a student of questionable background had to perform well; to quote the Chinese press, "one cannot choose one's class origin, but one can choose one's future road." The person of good family origin, already predisposed by his parentage to have the appropriate "class feelings," was expected to avoid any infection from the remnant bourgeois and petty bourgeois values still existing in China's transitional society; at the same time he/she needed to perform well in study so as to become the proletarian intellectual China required to insure both modernization and directed social change.

Thus, in deciding the merits of candidates for scarce senior middle and even scarcer university places, biaoxian and even more so, "activism" (jiji xing) was, at least theoretically, of crucial importance. The other two criteria (family origin and academic achievement) were to a greater or lesser extent objective; a student's behavior, however, could be individually determined. More problematic, though, was the measurement of this behavior. Both origin and academic achievement were fairly straightforward and measurable; both the individual student and the school were aware of the student's standing with regard to these criteria. But how did the student know where he stood politically or, more directly, in the overall competition? How did he know when his "activism" was being duly noted and if it would be rewarded? The surest objective indication of such subjective status was membership in the YCL.

Because membership in the YCL was generally limited to less than one-half of the students in a given class, it was sought by the large majority of those who aspired to a college education. Because membership was taken both by the CCP and the students as a sign of the student's ideological progressiveness, a close look at the changing standards for YCL membership may suggest overall trends in CCP policy toward youth in the 1960-66 period.

BEFORE AND AFTER THE CLASS LINE POLICY

In the early 1960s, in keeping with the general emphasis on academic achievement, a student's political progressiveness could be judged primarily by his/her success in becoming a technical specialist. Chen Yi's much-reprinted 1961 speech was unambiguous:

> It is the political duty of the student to
> learn his specialized subject. It is the
> political duty of the school to bring up
> large numbers of experts. The student who
> has higher political consciousness should
> know better the importance of learning his

specialized subject and should learn it
harder. The school which turns out better
students owes this success to better political leadership. Hence, the student of an
ordinary school should spend most of his
time and energy on the study of his specialized subject.[2]

Tao Zhu in Guangzhou echoed the new line when he
said, "The landmark of whether a school is good or not is
good teaching, good grades of the students. . . . Our
mission is teaching, not other things."[3]

The effect on both the general classroom atmosphere
and YCL recruitment policies can be gauged from the
situation at Huafu in the early 1960s, as reported in a
Red Guard newspaper:

Wang Bingshan with all his strength promoted
"the exam for entering the institutes of higher
education has primacy," "teaching knowledge has
primacy," opposed putting politics to the forefront, luring young students to take the road
of "white experts." Wang . . . confessed:
"Everyone listen, I myself only grasp professional matters. I do not involve myself with
politics." He also said "putting politics to
the forefront and reforming thought in reality
means to do your studies; if your studies are
no good, then you are a second-class fellow
who's not paying attention to your affairs."
. . . .A student whose political consciousness
is high should be good in his studies. It
should be reflected in his studies. He moreover tried to change the character of the
League saying "if his study grades are not
good, if failing in exams, even if he enters
the League, he cannot affect very much. In
this way, the prestige of the League branch
will be adversely affected." He was attempting to make the League serve as the subservient
tool of the revisionist educational line he was
promoting.[4]

During these years (primarily 1961-63) the YCL took
in many students of mediocre or even poor backgrounds
because they had outstanding futures as scientists,
engineers, and technicians. Only by 1964 was a definition of politics more favorable to those of good class
background - one similar to what had been emphasized
during the GLF - again put forth.

Hu Yaobang's report at the 9th YCL Congress in June
1964 stood Chen Yi's speech on its head:

The important question of on whom one should
rely in carrying out the socialist revolution
and socialist construction is not understood
ideologically by everybody. For example,
certain people consider that experts, technicians and intellectuals should be mainly
relied on in the development of industry and
carrying out of construction. Such a viewpoint is erroneous. Socialist construction
does need intellectuals, but intellectuals
always belong to certain social classes and
serve the interests of these classes. Only
by accepting the leadership of the working
class and serving and linking up with the
masses of workers and peasants will the
intellectuals be able to play a positive
role in the revolution and construction.[5]

The YCL's recruitment policy likewise underwent a
change as youths from good class backgrounds were now the
main targets for recruitment.[6] Just as the Fall 1964
school term was beginning, China Youth reported on the
previous erroneous YCL policy which needed changing:

At present, some secondary schools use examination grades to determine whether or not a
youth meets the conditions to enter the
League, even to the point of having as a
regulation that only with an average academic achievement above 90% could a student
enter the League. There was a child of cadre
origin at a middle school in Xian whose grades
in all courses were very good, except that he
didn't pass mathematics. However, his study
attitude was extremely good, serious and
sincere. Everyone acknowledged this. The
main reason for his poor performance in math
was his poor basis, not his lack of diligence.
Recently, in accord with this situation and
this student's behavior in other aspects, the
YCL branch felt that he already possessed the
conditions to be a YCL member and accepted him
into the League. This affair led to a discussion in the school. Not a small number of
students thought that now the requirements for
being a League member had been lowered. As we
see it, the League branch was correct. To
enter the League is to devote yourself to
revolution; one cannot only look at grades,
one also has to look at politics, at the
purpose for studying and at the attitude toward
study. As to youth from laboring families who
are good in politics, try very hard in studies,

and in other aspects possess the conditions
for League members, even if their study results are somewhat lacking, they still should
be accepted into the League; as to youth from
exploiting class families whose political
manifestation is not good, even if their study achievements are very high, they cannot be
accepted into the League. In accepting new
League members in schools, if we only look at
grades and not politics, this violates the
Party's class line.[7]

The new line continued into early 1965, with the
blame for the previous preference for academics over ideology beginning to fall on teaching personnel:

Why was it that certain school teachers were
so indifferent to children of worker families
and even went so far as to discriminate against
them? Why did some teachers try one way and
another to reject Zhu's application for League
membership? Why did they accept as League
members those students from bourgeois families
and even allow them to become secretaries of
League branches so long as they did well in
their classwork, regardless of their ideological consciousness, and no matter whether or
not they had drawn a clear dividing line with
families of exploiting classes? What problem
after all did this reflect? For whom after all
were we training successors?[8]

Although these reports do treat "political activism"
as of great importance, what appeared to have been actually happening, according to interviewees, was a perver-
sion of the concept of political performance. In the
early 1960s there was a dire need for "experts"; thus, expertise was acceptable as a political standard. With the
implementation of the class line policy, it became necessary to redress this imbalance and give preference to those
of good class background. The swing of the pendulum again
led to the tendency to view political performance largely
in terms of one of the other criteria: family origin.
    Needless to say, a person's family origin was not
sufficient to guarantee his reliability. Revolutionary
successors were expected to meet five requirements:

1. They must be genuine Marxist-Leninists.
2. They must be revolutionaries who whole-heartedly
serve the overwhelming majority of the people of China
and the whole world.
3. They must be proletarian statesmen capable of

uniting and working together with the overwhelming
majority.

    4. They must be models in applying the Party's
democratic centralism, must master the method of leadership based on the principle of "from the masses, to the
masses," and must cultivate a democratic style and be
good at listening to the masses.

    5. They must be modest and prudent and guard
against arrogance and impetuosity; they must be imbued
with the spirit of self-criticism and have the courage
to correct mistakes and shortcomings in their work.[9]

While these five criteria, which are drawn from a
People's Daily editorial of August 1964, seem to slight
the importance of family origin, the following passage
in the same editorial shows that this was not the
intention:

> To select successors to the nucleus of leader-
> ship at all levels in strict conformity with
> the five conditions, special attention must
> be paid to implementing the Party's class line.
> The focus of selecting and training the succes-
> sors should be on advanced cadres of worker,
> poor peasant and lower-middle peasant origin.
> With their history of severe exploitation and
> oppression these people from the proletariat
> and semi-proletariat have the most revolution-
> ary political attitude and thus most readily
> accept Marxism-Leninism and Mao Zedong's
> thinking. They can work most resolutely for
> the overwhelming majority of the people in
> China and the rest of the world, rally the
> overwhelming majority of the people for the
> revolutionary cause, consciously carry out the
> mass line and have the courage to carry out
> self-criticism. Of course, successors to the
> revolutionary cause should not be selected and
> cultivated only from the viewpoint of class
> origin. A few persons of good class origin
> who are subject to corruption by the ideology
> of the exploiting classes will not be able to
> carry the socialist revolution through to the
> end. On the other hand, some persons who do
> not come from families of laboring people can,
> through education by the Party, forsake their
> original class and be tempered through revolu-
> tionary struggles into proletarian revolution-
> aries. But attention must be paid to ensure
> that people of good class and family origin,
> who have been tempered for a long period
> through class struggles, account for the great
> majority of the nucleus of the leadership in

the revolutionary ranks of the proletariat.[10]

The schools responded quickly to these "instructions" and students of good class background began to be "cultivated" in a manner somewhat reminiscent of the treatment those of high academic achievement had received in the previous period. Emphasis on academic achievement as a criterion for student recognition and prestige within the classroom of necessity also declined. To give one example, to be selected as a "Five Good Student" a student had to be outstanding in both study and politics. Nevertheless, school authorities tended to emphasize either one or the other of these two standards in making their choices, depending on national policy at the time. In the 1960-63 period academic achievement was stressed; from 1963-66, however, to be so chosen was merely a recognition that a student had already become a political activist.[11]

The tension between academic achievers who tended to be of ordinary or bad background and political activists who were more likely to be of good class background was also exacerbated by the possessiveness with which some students clung to their "assets." One former Huafu student reported on the dissatisfaction among many of those of good class origin in her class when, in 1965, the three highest grades in politics were scored by three students of exploiting class background. Those who saw politics as inseparable from family origin felt such a result was inconceivable and grumbled that this was a betrayal of the Party's class line.[12]

On their part, students with good grades were often assigned to aid those less gifted. These exchanges did not always engender feelings of mutual satisfaction, as can be seen by the complaints of some tutees early in the Cultural Revolution against teachers who favored "seven black elements" just because of their grades,[13] and against the tutors for conceit.[14]

The arrogance of the academic achievers met its mirror-image when it came to politics. The Red Pairs campaign (yi bang yi, yidui hong), in which an activist was paired with a non-activist in an attempt to produce a pair of activists, foundered because activists were primarily concerned with distinguishing themselves from their fellow classmates and the more backward members of the pairs in turn resented the patronizing airs of some of their tutors.[15] Some pairings seemed conceived in tragicomedy. One excellent student, the son of a Guomindang regimental commander, was paired with a poor student whose father was a regimental commander in the People's Liberation Army. This particular arrangement worked out relatively well until the early period of the GPCR, when one became a Red Guard and the other a struggle object.[16]

As to the shift in YCL recruitment, interviews I

carried out in Hong Kong from 1972-76 with approximately
100 emigres who had been in middle schools in Guangzhou
during the 1960s verify the trends discussed above.
Former students reported that, prior to 1964, "activism"
and "individual behavior," somewhat amorphous and ambiguous concepts, were the most important criteria for YCL
membership, thus allowing a person of ordinary, or even
bad class origin, to demonstrate his or her activism/
behavior by enthusiastic participation in labor, by
aiding other students who were poor in study, by observ-
ing discipline in class, and even by merely studying hard
and making good grades. The situation, however, became
suddenly and dramatically reversed in 1964 and 1965.
Before 1964, at least in Guangzhou, a near majority of
YCL members seem to have been students of "non-good backgrounds." After the class line policy was implemented,
those who were not of "five red" background suddenly
found it much more difficult to get into the YCL.[17]
Table 2.1 below offers a rather similar picture.

Table 2.1

The Changing Patterns of New League Enrollments, 1962-65*

New Enrollees, By Year	1962-63	1963-64	1964-65
Revolutionary cadre	30%	32%	38%
Working-class	24%	26%	38%
Middle class	37%	34%	21%
Bad class and overseas Chinese	9%	8%	3%
	100%	100%	100%

*The figures for the 1965-66 school year are incomplete,
since the term was thrown into chaos by the Cultural
Revolution. The figures we gathered suggest, though,
that higher percentages of middle and bad-class students
were getting into the League in 1965-66.

Source: Questionnaire remembrances of Hong Kong
Interviewees.

     In 1965 there was a reverse shift in emphasis in the
official press so that a person's behavior (biaoxian) was
explicitly stated to be the most important criterion for
YCL membership. Many articles appeared, stressing the
point that children of exploiting class origin could draw
a clear line with their families (huaqing jiexian) and be
judged on their merits.[18] While there is mixed evidence
as to whether students of bad class background were able
to benefit from this policy and increase their represen-

tation in the League, there are several mitigating factors which indicate that, regardless of the situation in the League, their access to <u>educational opportunities</u> had actually declined.

In the first place, the models of exploiting class youths, several of whom had attained Party or League membership and who were being cited for emulation, ranged from Yu Shanling, who insisted on emigrating to Xinjiang against her parents' wishes[19] and Zhuo Ailing, who went to Xinjiang from Shanghai[20] to Sun Yunjie who, during the Socialist Education Movement, collected and revealed counterrevolutionary statements and acts made by her elder brother, thus aiding her to enter the Party.[21] This was indeed a far cry from the halcyon days of 1962 when approximately 30% of Beijing University's students were from exploiting class background and "politics" meant becoming a specialist.

In the second place, increasing overall numbers in 1965 concealed the pattern of implementation. Based on my interviews, in the majority of cases one student of bad class origin was able to enter the YCL per class, even after the emphasis on behavior had become official policy. Of the many who might be vying for League membership, one was generally chosen as a model and recruited. Another pattern consistently pointed out by interviewees was that the selection of students of bad class background, or even ordinary class background, for the YCL - and this was especially true in 1965 - was accompanied by the admission of students of worker, peasant, or cadre background. There was a conscious attempt not to recruit <u>only</u> non-good background students. What this meant, in practice, was that if the League branch in a particular class recruited no students of good background that year (because they were all already in the League, the ones outside the League had no interest in joining, and so forth), then it was unlikely anyone would join that year and, indeed, some classes on which I have data support this point. In certain cases I have even found that YCL members of bad class origin were criticized by the school YCL committee for sponsoring other students of similar origin at this time.

Another factor inhibiting the recruitment of students of bad class background in 1965 was that a fair number of those in senior middle two and three had already entered the YCL in the pre-1964 period, some even being considered "veteran League members"; as for those in senior middle one, there already were fewer students from bad family backgrounds because of the increasing inability of these students to continue on from junior middle school. Thus, by the time of the Cultural Revolution, the YCL was divided in that many of the veteran YCL members were of ordinary or bad class background whereas the more recent members tended to be

of cadre background (in the best schools) or worker background (in the ordinary schools). In addition, because
of the heavy recruitment of those of good family origin
in the two years immediately prior to the Cultural Revolution, most schools had a situation in both junior and
senior middle sections in which the higher years (especially senior middle three) contained many of ordinary or
bad class background who had "proved" themselves and
joined the League before 1964 while the lower years
(especially senior middle one and junior middle one and
two) were dominated by students of good class background
who were becoming aware of the enhanced importance
attached to this background, and hence gradually began
to assert themselves as the GPCR approached. Although
grades were clearly still a major source of prestige,
the class line policy altered the atmosphere in the
classroom. This changed classroom environment (see
below) was to reach its peak in the early stages of the
GPCR, when those of good class background were able to
take "revenge" on any student or teacher deemed guilty
of failing to enforce the class line policies of the
preceding period.

I interviewed some students of working class background who had entered middle school in 1964 and exhibited such tendencies. One became a "Doctrine Guard" (a
conservative Red Guard organization) and delighted in
"pushing around" bookworms (shudaizi) and teachers during
the Cultural Revolution. Another, at a different school,
traced his unhappiness to the fact that his school, which
had taught only Russian until 1963, changed to half-
English and half-Russian. He entered in 1964 and by that
time it was clear to all students that English was the
preferable language, the one that would aid them most if
they continued their studies, whereas Russian was the
language of the 1950s. When they divided up the nine
classes, the first four classes were to study English,
the last five to study Russian. He said the first four
classes clearly were better academically whereas classes
5 to 9 had a much higher proportion of students of good
class background. He fought to get transferred into an
English section but was unsuccessful.[22] Many of these
younger, disgruntled students were active early in the
Cultural Revolution, for example during the "Destroy Four
Olds" movement.

Those of good class background were being favored in
other ways, too. The favoritism considered potentially
most threatening by students of ordinary or bad class
background was the extra help being supplied to those of
impeccable family origin, particularly in the period
before the university and senior high entrance examinations. Since these review classes were limited to those
of good class origin, other students had no way of
knowing what the extra help consisted of. Because

articles in the press specifically referred to these tutorials as necessary in order to raise the promotion rate
of those of good class origin, there was a widespread
belief and concern that the extra help, in addition to
various study aids, included examination hints.[23]

THE ADVANTAGES OF CHILDREN OF CADRES

Even before the explicit emphasis on class background became an important component of student life,
discussions in the press concerning the relationship between family origin and behavior were to be found.[24]
With the arrival of the Socialist Education Movement (SEM)
and its attendant stress on class struggle, there was a
more determined effort to deal with the origin/behavior
question. For example, Liberation Army Daily (LAD) in
1964 ran a series of articles dealing with this question.
Interestingly enough, in light of later splits during the
GPCR on this point, the LAD symposium divided the three
erroneous viewpoints by class origin:

> Comrades who think that one is "red by nature"
> are generally of three types. 1) Those who
> think that, being of good class origin, they
> are susceptible to revolutionary ideas and can
> naturally be revolutionized. 2) Those who
> think that being children of revolutionary
> cadres, eating revolutionary food and wearing
> revolutionary garments, they can be naturally
> revolutionized. 3) Those who think that "born
> in the new society and brought up under the
> red banner," they are less affected by the
> influence of the old society and can naturally
> be revolutionized.[25]

Although all students were being told that revolutionization could only come through constant effort, it
was also frequently pointed out that, because of the
primary influence of the family, those of good class
background in effect had a head start in achieving revolutionization. The division between students of worker-
peasant background and revolutionary cadre background
was also one stressed in the press. In Guangzhou this
sometimes took the form of different schools mobilizing
different groups of students, as in the following 1963
report:

> This semester each school will continue to
> strengthen the class education of the stu-
> dents about the current situation. Each
> school's YCL and Young Pioneers organization
> is at present investigating how to make this

> education deeper and more prevalent. At
> Number 17 Middle School where there are
> comparatively many children of cadre back-
> ground, early in the term it is planned to
> call a forum of children of veteran cadres
> to encourage these students to inherit the
> revolutionary aspirations of their fathers
> and older brothers. . . . Some primary
> schools in the municipality and district
> and Guangzhou's Experimental School plan
> to mobilize students from worker-peasant
> families to investigate their own "family
> histories" and afterward to carry out
> meetings to "compare the bitter with the
> sweet."[26]

The key difference between children of revolutionary cadres (including military and martyrs) and those of
ordinary worker-peasant background was their parents'
role in the liberation of China. In a real sense, those
who suffered most before 1949 (the workers and peasants)
owed a debt of gratitude to the revolutionaries who liberated them. As the passive recipients who gained most
from the efforts of revolutionary cadres, workers and
peasants were not in a strong position to provide class
education to the children of their liberators. During
the SEM, when classrooms were mobilized to go to factories or villages to hear stories of past sufferings at
the hands of exploiters, children of cadres were not the
most attentive of listeners. As one Red Guard newspaper
put it:

> Last April some classes in our school went
> to a factory attached to Qinghua University
> to participate in labor. They were extremely
> respectful towards the master workers; when
> the old worker told his family history, our
> classmates all strained to hear, some shedding
> tears. However, one classmate of cadre family
> origin said to someone in a low voice: "This
> worker certainly isn't a Party member." When
> the summing-up meeting was held, some class-
> mates spoke about the education they had re-
> ceived from the master (worker); they (cadre
> children) said: "What's the point of talking
> about this." In addition, while they were
> installing the original parts board of the
> transistorized electronic calculator in the
> workshop, some cadre children played volleyball.
> The master went to stop them, but they didn't
> listen. When they returned, they said that
> the master wasn't putting politics in command,
> so they didn't pay attention to him. Let's

look at another example. When we went. down
to the countryside to labor, some cadre
children lived for a week at the home of a
poor peasant without uttering a word. The
poor peasant said: "Several of these schoolmates really have airs." The commune members
have decreed that every Saturday afternoon
is the period for the study of Mao's works.
At this time all the commune members very
solemnly change into clean clothes, put on
Chairman Mao badges and gather together to
listen to an advisor explain Mao's works.
(Cadre children) didn't participate, saying
"it's of no interest; what's so interesting
about (peasants) studying Mao's works."[27]

It was difficult to forestall such feelings of superiority. References to family origin had begun to per-
meate all areas of student life. For example, the procedure for entering the YCL included as an important step
the recitation of one's biography at a meeting. Often
these meetings were expanded to become "YCL education
meetings" (tuanke jiaoyu dahui). As young students,
their biographies of necessity mostly concerned their
families. When cadre children delivered their accounts,
they stressed the number of years their fathers had made
revolution. Children of worker-peasant background emphasized how poor their families had been before Liberation and how much their present situation was due to Mao
and the Party. For those of exploiting class backgrounds, a denunciation of the crimes of their family
was de rigeur, complete with tears if possible. It is
therefore not surprising that children of cadres should
view themselves as a separate group. In some classes the
YCL was informally divided into two groups, the first
group being those of cadre background, the second group
containing everyone else.[28]
Middle school teachers and administrators reinforced
these feelings of superiority. In elite schools like
Guangya, the school organized meetings limited only to
cadre children, encouraging them to follow in the foot-
steps of their parents. Because of the desire of school
officials to increase promotion rates into the university,
coupled with the subtle pressure parents applied by
monitoring the progress of their children, there was an
attempt to guarantee that all children of cadres had
gotten into the YCL before graduation.[29] One Red Guard
paper described the situation at Guangya:

. . .the son of counterrevolutionary revisionist element Zhao Ziyang reached senior
middle two and still had not entered the
YCL. This caused a great deal of anxiety

to our school's powerholders. Principal
X on the one hand reproachfully questioned
the YCL committee: "How is it Secretary
Zhao's son has not been recruited to enter
the YCL?" On the other hand, he personally
went to (Zhao's) class to involve himself
and said to the YCL branch secretary: "You
people should consider the question of Zhao
XX's entry into the League; is it possible
that secretary Zhao's son is still not safe!"
The family heads of some cadre children also
wondered what problem their children had; if
they didn't get into the League, who should
get into the League! They repeatedly questioned the school in an urgent manner, "How
is it my child still cannot enter the League?"
The school then would quickly pull the child
into the League.[30]

At Guangya such an atmosphere was perhaps to be
expected. But it seemed to be prevalent at somewhat less
fashionable schools as well. One interviewee, of
ordinary-level cadre background, described to me the way
he was "rushed" for the YCL in 1965, when he was in
senior middle three:

They put YCL members in seats next to me in
class, etc. But I always ended up arguing
with them. They tried to talk about any
subject I might be interested in and made
all sorts of concessions to me. Previously,
they hadn't been close to me and in fact I
hadn't been able to get along with them.
In senior middle three, however, all the
YCLers (not just one or two) sought me out
deliberately to talk to me. Since I was
the captain of the basketball team, some
used sports to try to win me over, seeking
me out to discuss basketball, soccer and so
forth. Others tried different approaches.
But they never directly brought up my class
background as a reason for joining. However,
it was quite clear that they sought me out
because of my good class origin and they did
hint at this.[31]

The interviewee was one of only two children of revolutionary cadre background in the class and the only one of
the seven students of good class background still not in
the League. He had felt his grades and class origin
would be sufficient for university entrance.[32]
    This emphasis on the recruitment of those of good
class background - particularly children of cadres - into

the YCL before graduation from senior high is shown rather clearly in Table 2.2 below.

Table 2.2

League Membership by Class Origins (Graduating Class of 1966 only)

	Size of Sample	% in League
Revolutionary Cadre	64	89%
Working Class	101	60%
Intellectual Middle Class	242	23%
Non-intellectual Middle Class	121	19%
Bad Class and Overseas Chinese	189	11%
Percentage of Graduating Students Who Were League Members		30%

Total Size of Sample: 717 Students; 16 Senior High Classrooms

Source: Questionnaire remembrances of Hong Kong interviewees.

POLITICAL MOVEMENTS

Although the alteration of middle school and university recruitment policies to give added weight to class origin had become pronounced by 1964, there were clear signs of the coming trend by late 1962 and 1963. One of the first events to affect middle school students directly was the campaign to emulate Lei Feng. As the first of several emulation movements of this type, the Lei Feng campaign enjoyed considerable support. As a perhaps unintended side effect, however, the campaign demoralized some youth of non-five red background. For example, an article early in the campaign which argued that a good family background was not sufficient to guarantee a person's redness, also emphasized:

> Generally speaking, comrades from families of the working class or poor peasants are in a better position than those from families of the exploiting class so far as ideological remolding is concerned. A good class origin can play an active role in enhancing one's consciousness. This point should be affirmed in the first place. Comrade Lei Feng's deep class consciousness and his ordinary but great communist spirit were inseparable from the fact that he came from a family of hired peasants and had suffered great hardships at the hands of the landlord class and from

the exploitation and oppression by the rul-
ing class in the old society. Such bitter
experiences intensified his hatred for the
old society and helped him considerably to
make progress after joining the revolution.
Therefore, it is not right to deny the
definite role a good class origin plays in
one's ideological remolding.[33] (emphasis
added)

Quickly recognizing how discouraging the Lei Feng
model had become to large numbers of students, one
People's Daily article began in the following manner:

In learning from Comrade Lei Feng, some
people think that without having suffered
exploitation and oppression and without
having tasted the bitter cup as Comrade
Lei Feng had in the old society, it would
be impossible for anyone to reach the same
degree of class consciousness and possess
the same lofty character as he had. There
are even some who deplore that, instead of
having been born in a poor and suffering
family, they were born unfortunately in
exploiting class families, so that they
were contaminated with bad thought. This
way of thinking is in essence none other
than the following: First, Comrade Lei
Feng's high degree of ideological consciousness and excellent moral qualities were
entirely attributable to his humble origin;
and second, no one whose family origin is
not good or who has never suffered hardship
since one's childhood can have a communist
ideological consciousness. Such an idea is
of course not right.[34]

But the article then went on:

When one who belongs to an exploiting class
family leaves that family and takes instead
the road of revolution, the exploiting class
thought and consciousness with which one is
originally imbued will not vanish immediately,
but will vanish only after a prolonged and
difficult process of reform. However, provided one humbly accepts the Party's education,
makes subjective efforts, and strengthens one's
own tempering and cultivation, one may reform
oneself radically so that one is completely
changed into a new thing. Of course, compared
with those who belong to working class families,

one will have to have greater determination
and must have a spirit of stubborn perse-
verence if one is to achieve satisfactory
results.[35]

Even though this article and others went on to argue
that loyalty to the Party and awareness that one needed
ideological remolding were even more important factors
than class origin, some students reached what to them was
an inescapable conclusion: there was no possibility for
them to develop the class consciousness reached by a Lei
Feng. In effect, students of good class background possessed a necessary, if not sufficient, condition for
revolutionization. The increasing emphasis on class
origin from this point on did nothing to contradict these
beliefs.

Widely differing responses to this movement exacerbated the existing contradictions between students, as
well as turning those which were latent into manifest
ones. There is general agreement among interviewees that
the movement to study Lei Feng led to increased activism
on the part of high school students. The difficulty,
however, was in how to go about reforming one's thought
and what actions would constitute progressive behavior.
Since Lei Feng's outstanding quality was his selfless
service to others, students started competing with each
other in performing this or that unpleasant task. The
potential for opportunistic, feigned activism was high.
When it became the fashion for students to wash out the
clothes of some fellow student without seeking credit,
some students managed to choose very carefully whose
clothes they washed - YCL aspirants would choose clothes
belonging to those already in the League - and then have
their good deed "accidentally" discovered. The more
unsubtle would burst out with quotations from Chairman
Mao in the middle of the night and later claim they had
been talking in their sleep. This kind of activism led
to debates over the standard by which one judged a
revolutionary. Some - the minority - argued that this
emphasis on petty details (xiaojie) was not what revolution was all about; to judge a person one should look at
the larger issues (dajie). The majority, including most
of the YCL members, bristled at this criticism and took
it as an attack on Lei Feng and Party policy. Their
position was that the so-called large issues came out
and revealed themselves in the small details. As they
put it, "the rays of the sun, after all, can be seen on
a drop of water." It developed into a question of who
the YCL should aim at in its recruiting policy: those
more creative and independent-minded or those more docile
and obedient. The Lei Feng model was used as a club
against those arguing the former position. The majority
averred that to be the "docile tool" of the Party was not

to be a slave and that those implying otherwise were in effect saying that Lei Feng was the greatest slave in history rather than a great revolutionary.

An interesting coalition of forces developed on this issue. In what was to be a pattern at some schools early in the Cultural Revolution, many children of cadre origin joined non-YCL members of intellectual background in supporting the minority view. Cadre children, particularly those of high-level cadre background, tended to object to any restraints on their behavior and their privileged upbringing had produced a lack of fear about speaking out. Since they were presumed to have the reddest of red family backgrounds, strong "class feelings," and a firm stand, an emphasis on a person's main aspect rather than any "petty details" would serve them very well indeed. Although those of ordinary class background had no trouble participating in this debate, those of bad class background were much more circumspect and tended to take the orthodox position if they participated at all.

The Lei Feng campaign, then, had at least two visible effects: it stimulated both real and feigned activism, and it disheartened students of non-good background. The first effect was to lead more and more to attempts by students to prove that their activism was indeed real. The pressure was mounting particularly on students from ordinary and bad class backgrounds. In this regard the phenomenon of students - in some cases entire classrooms - refusing to sit for university entrance examinations, which has been noted in Chapter One, began to appear.

In 1965 there were several attempts to deal with the uncontrollable genie from the Lei Feng/class line bottle. One movement which had started previously was the "study for the revolution" (wei geming er xuexi) campaign. This movement was basically an attempt to distinguish the bourgeois concept of studying for individual success from the proletarian one of studying for the revolution. However, while in general the concept of studying for the revolution was unexceptionable, the movement, like classroom relationships generally, got sucked into the maelstrom of the class origin/academic achievement disputation. With politics and ideological transformation being daily emphasized in the press and in class, with the school curriculum undergoing reform, when there were strong pressures on urban students to volunteer to go the countryside if they were unable to qualify for promotion to the next higher grade, it quickly developed that many students, for one reason or another, felt that studying was impractical and wasteful.[36] In this atmosphere, the impact on students who still felt that academic study was very important was particularly harsh. Although the official press tried to restore the political/academic

balance by criticizing such slogans as "now the primary
question is one of revolution, not of studying"; "the
more you study, the deeper the influence of capitalist
ideology"; "if you study poorly, then and only then are
you red"; it was not an easy task.[37]
    Since this was a period when students of good
class background, especially graduating seniors, were
being given special study help, including examination
hints, in an attempt to raise their rate of promotion,
there developed in the classroom an atmosphere of mutual
suspicion and hostility between those of good class background and those of ordinary or bad class background.[38]
Students of good class background and, say the interviewees, some teachers as well, would look upon any student
who was not of worker, peasant or cadre background, and
who spent a fair amount of time on his/her studies,
as undoubtedly studying for individual glory and the
university entrance examination. For their part, students who were not of good class background and were thus
not permitted to sit in on the tutorial sessions and
forums devoted to raising the study achievements and
promotion rates for good background students, felt that
they were being treated unfairly and might be severely
disadvantaged when the university entrance exam had to
be taken. In a situation in which the criteria for
recruiting university students, entering the YCL, and
becoming a YCL cadre were all shifting in favor of
political factors, students who felt perhaps their only
chance to attend the university would be through study
achievement feared that they might be squeezed out
entirely.
    Another attempt to redress the new imbalance of
forces set in motion by the class line policy was the
emphasis on a person's performance, rather than only
his class origin. First raised directly in a speech by
Peng Zhen in January 1965[39] and expressed most forcefully in a September editorial,[40] the new stress on
performance (it was not a replacement for the class line
policy) sought to encourage those who, due to the
vagaries of birth, found themselves rather suddenly
disadvantaged by the shifting sands in 1963 and 1964.
The entire tone of the September editorial indicates the
prevalent attitude towards children of exploiting class
background after the emphasis on class line:

> Children of exploiting class families may
> generally be asked to take part in some
> study, recreational, and sports activities,
> provided they want to make progress. Those
> who conduct themselves well may be assigned
> suitable social work. Those who are truly
> qualified for YCL or Party membership may
> also be admitted into the YCL or the Party.

> Some comrades, afraid that others may
> call them "unsteady in stand" if they make
> friends with the children of exploiting
> class families, dare not get close to these
> children. Such fears are unnecessary.
> Can the deeds of young people of bad
> family background be a "false appearance?"
> That is possible. However, false appear-
> ances can be distinguished from true ones.
> Emphasis on deeds does not amount to em-
> phasis on appearances. ...feigned activism
> cannot remain undetected, but will sooner
> or later be brought to light.[41]

Indeed, other articles in the press strongly imply
that most people sought to avoid contact with those of
bad family origin for fear of contamination.[42] That the
emphasis on behavior did not lead to a flood of new YCL
members of exploiting class background can be seen from
statistics published at the time. For example, a Zhengzhou factory in which those in charge of YCL work had
become afraid of contamination by youths of bad class
background, was written up, in part because it started
"implementing the Party policy of attaching importance
to the performance of individual workers."[43] The figures
produced for new League members in the first half of 1965
are provided in Table 2.3.

Table 2.3

New League Members at a Factory in Zhengzhou, 1965

Worker and Poor and Lower-Middle Peasant Origin	260	(81.3%)
Middling Backgrounds	54	(16.9%)
Exploiting Class Origin	6	(1.8%)
Total	320	

Source: Zhongguo Qingnian Bao, October 5, 1965.

Although the total distribution by class origin of
the factory's total labor force was not reported, the
figures do seem to suggest that the number of youths of
exploiting class origin benefiting from the new policy
was not great.
This seems consistent with other reports. In Shanghai, of the 200,000 youths entering the League between
May 1965 and May 1966, about 80% came from families of
workers and poor and lower-middle peasants.[44] Of the
400,000 recruited in 1965 in Sichuan, Liaoning, Gansu
and Shanghai, again about 80% were children of workers
and poor and lower-middle peasants.[45] In announcing
these figures, the NCNA report seemed to hint broadly
that the successful youths of bad origin were more a

symbol to others of like background not to lose heart
than an example of successful ideological remolding:

> In the course of recruiting new YCL members,
> an all-out effort was made to implement the
> mass line advanced by the Party, so that
> close attention was paid to the family back-
> ground of the new recruits as well as their
> behavior. Not only a large number of youths
> born of families of workers, poor and lower
> middle peasants, or laboring people of other
> trades, but also some youths born of exploit-
> ing class families but eligible for YCL member-
> ship, were admitted into the YCL. Having
> gained admission into the YCL, these youths
> said that they would obey the Party forever,
> draw a clear dividing line between themselves
> and their exploiting class families, and
> prove themselves revolutionary successors
> of the proletariat. This played an active
> role in urging still greater numbers of youths
> born of exploiting class families to remold
> their thinking diligently and follow the
> revolutionary road.[46]

In fact, there was something of a "Catch-22" about
the whole "emphasis on performance" campaign, at least
in terms of the more traditional rewards given for
success. To "prove" one's activism and betrayal of
family origin, one ideally had to take the lead in such
ways as volunteering to go the borderlands or to the
frontline of agricultural production. It was difficult
otherwise to truly demonstrate one's sincerity and
strength of purpose. The "rewards" of a university
education or a factory job could thus not be given to
those whose "emphasis on performance" required tempering
under conditions of hardship. If one therefore sought
either higher education or to remain in the city one was
subject to being viewed as insincere about one's ideological revolutionization and in breaking off with one's
exploiting class family; on the other hand, if one did
volunteer to devote one's life to furthering socialist
construction in a backward area, one would likely get
one's wish. In either instance, there was little chance
for those of bad class background to attend a university
or obtain a good urban allocation as of 1965-66.

As almost all interviewees reported, those among the
bad class youths who became "models" in 1965 were a
rather pathetic lot, looked upon suspiciously or at best
patronized by good class youths who were always on guard
against any deterioration in their behavior or hint of
feigned activism or family feeling, and despised by

ordinary class or other bad class youths who viewed the
entire "emphasis on performance" policy as it was implemented as primarily a series of humiliations for those
willing to be campaign "objects" (duixiang).

There was also the campaign to emulate Wang Jie,
commencing in November 1965. Although in a similar way
to the "Study Lei Feng Campaign" this new movement was
aimed at all youths, the clear focus seemed to be directed towards those of ordinary class backgrounds. Wang
Jie was a much more believable figure to most students,
especially those who felt their class background would
be held against them. In addition to raising such
mundane topics as marriage, home leave and demobilization
in his diary, Wang dealt directly with and wrote realis-
tically about his class background. Seeing comrades who
joined up with him and were less activist being promoted
over him and allowed to join the Party, he put the blame
on the fact that his family origin was middle peasant,
the same being true for all his relatives. For those
young people who did not get the message, the commentary
provided by the LAD made it crystal clear:

> Chairman Mao made a nationwide call in March
> 1963 asking the Chinese people to "learn from
> Comrade Lei Feng." This acted as a great new
> stimulus to Wang Jie, helping his progress
> along the revolutionary road. He set Lei Feng
> up as his model, measuring everything he did
> by his actions. But the more he compared him-
> self with Lei Feng, the greater the distance
> seemed between them. By studying Chairman
> Mao's teachings on class analysis he began to
> understand his own family background, and how
> he was still influenced by a lot of petty-
> bourgeois individualistic ideas. If he wanted
> to approach closer to his ideal - Lei Feng -
> he had to work really hard at getting rid of
> this "burden."[47] (emphasis in original)

There was now one hero for those of good background
and another for those who were number two and needed to
try harder. I found in my interviews that those of good
class background tended to identify more with Lei Feng
and those of non-good background with Wang Jie. I also
found that while many said that Wang Jie's class background was not emphasized during study sessions devoted
to his deeds, those who became leaders of the Rebel
faction during the Cultural Revolution felt that his
middle peasant origin was the most significant fact about
Wang Jie.[48] As one Rebel Red Guard group later wrote:
"Nobody can say that Wang Jie's glory was below that of
Lei Feng."[49]

The activism generated beginning with the Lei Feng

89

campaign continued unabated right up to the GPCR. By
late 1965, there seemed to be a policy of "something for
everyone." The class line policy and its impact on classroom relationships had strongly stimulated those of
worker-peasant background who were now starting to make
inroads into the better middle schools and universities.
The YCL was opening up to them in a way not possible when
grades were of most importance. Those of ordinary class
background were cushioned against the full effects of the
new policy by the existence of the much less fortunate
exploiting class origin students who were under more
pressure to demonstrate their progressiveness. Their
grades and continued access to the better middle schools
allowed them to remain competitive for university places,
but the rising tide of those of good class origin made
it more difficult for them to avoid activism or to be
merely "politically passable."[50] Those of bad class
background were most disadvantaged by the new line. At
first the shock of the new policy produced strong tremors.
One student who was in a senior middle one class in 1964
recalled the minor sensation caused at his school by the
university entrance results that year:

> One student was very famous in our school
> because of his grades. He was said to be
> the best student Number 28 had produced in
> recent memory. He was also a veteran YCL
> member and had been on the school YCL
> committee. He was very active in school
> politics and was outstanding in sports.
> Of course his class background was very
> bad, but he had long seemed to have over-
> come it. When this student was not able
> to gain entrance to any university, it
> caused something of an uproar among stu-
> dents of the school. Those of bad class
> background, and even some of middle class
> background, were stunned and went around
> saying to each other: "If he can't make
> it, what chance have I?" This particular
> case demoralized a lot of people.[51]

Official policy in 1965 sought to overcome this kind of
pessimistic attitude by appealing to those who had begun
to lose heart.
What this new emphasis on "performance" seems to
have produced is not necessarily an increase in the
chances for bad background students in their quest for
university education, but an almost frantic and belated
"activism" which led in many cases to their ostracism
from former friendship groups. One analyst calls this
"the insecure political activism strategy" and described
it as follows:

For some urban high school students becoming a political activist is a strategy
marked by desperation. ...their only
chance to avoid being sent to the countryside is to make a name as a political
activist. Their efforts to prove their
political zeal, which intensify in the
junior and senior years as graduation day
nears, create costs for their classmates.
The aspiring activist is more feared than
the established activist. Someone trying
to gain admission to the Youth League is
more dangerous than a member, and a bad
background activist is more of a threat
than an activist with good background
credentials. As one respondent described
bad background YCL aspirants, "These people were dangerous because they would do
anything to appear progressive."[52]

One of my interviewees, who had been the foremost
Red Guard leader at the middle school level in Guangzhou,
produced a long manuscript on the Cultural Revolution in
which he referred to the entire 1963-66 period as "the
crisis of the YCL." He and others had objected, at the
time, to what was becoming the current definition of a
"revolutionary." Speaking for those whose ordinary class
background and refusal to embrace the current interpretation of "activist behavior" made it impossible to join
the YCL, he wrote a poster in 1965 entitled "Those Who
Don't Enter the League Also Can Make Revolution," which
divided the class. This general dissatisfaction of many
with YCL standards was to become important when the GPCR
furnished students with the opportunity to display what
they considered "revolutionary" behavior.

SCHOOL DIFFERENCES

While the foregoing analysis is generally accurate
for urban middle schools in Guangzhou as a whole, important differences characterized different schools and
influenced the Cultural Revolution pattern in those
schools. The desire to be politically activist and to
join the YCL was much stronger among students at the
elite and good schools. The knowledge that they were
well placed to enter the university seemed to be a strong
motivating factor. Among those from average or poor
schools there was much less interest in engaging in
politics. Youth League branches at these schools tended
to be smaller than those at the better schools. There
seemed to be a fear, expressed to me by some, that too
much activism, especially Youth League membership, would

put heavy pressure on an unsuccessful university applicant to take the lead in volunteering to go to the
countryside. Generalizing broadly, while in the best
schools YCL membership was looked upon as a stepping-
stone to the university, in the inferior schools non-YCL
membership and non-prominence was looked upon as a way
to avoid the countryside.

Press reports of the time stress the activism and
desire for YCL membership which was characteristic of
China's key-point schools. To cite just two examples,
a 1959 report in Nanfang Daily showed that about 30% of
the students at Guangya were already in the YCL; in
addition, 85% of the non-YCL activists had applied to
join the YCL.[53] The figure of 30% is very high since the
total number of students would include those in lower-
middle school where the number of YCLers of necessity
would be very few. A more recent case was Number 12
Middle School of Harbin. Founded in 1953, this school
had become a model by the middle 1960s and was extensively written up in the press. A Guangming Daily report
from the late 1964 informed its readers that of the 780
students who had reached the age for YCL membership in
the previous term, more than 600 had participated in the
study of League lessons (over 77%). Again, the figure
may not seem overly high until one realizes that in many
schools the desire for League membership only becomes
strong when one has reached senior high and is thinking
of university education. At Guangya and Harbin Number 12
Middle School, students became politically active much
earlier.[54] Table 2.4 provides some confirmation that YCL
membership was more common at the better schools.

Table 2.4

The Percentage of League Membership in Guangzhou
Secondary Schools,1962-1966

| | Prestige Schools | | | |
	The "best" 4 schools	The next "best" 8 schools	The "average" 18 schools	The neighborhood jr. highs
Senior High	42%	42%	26%	--
Numbers of class- rooms surveyed	5	8	18	--
Junior High	19%	19%	10%	7%
Numbers of class- rooms surveyed	5	12	12	14

Source: Questionnaire remembrances of Hong Kong interviewees.

At schools such as these - which contained both students of high cadre origin and students of high academic achievement - wide-ranging debates on the issues of the day were most likely to occur. As an example, several respondents reported on the liveliness of the bulletin board newspaper at Huafu. One issue which generated much debate in the middle 1960s was the question of skipping grades (tiaoji). At Huafu some students with exceptional grades, particularly in physics and mathematics, had been able to go directly from senior high one to senior high three. Since the national press had publicized Shanghai's Yucai Middle School's system of allowing students to skip grades and even go straight to the university after second year senior high, the school authorities at Huafu, under the general heading of the relationship between red and expert, supervised a debate on the desirability of this policy. As might be expected, two viewpoints were set forth. One group, made up mostly of those of cadre origin who had poor grades, argued that the whole notion was bourgeois and that special treatment and emphasis should not be put on individual excellence, especially with regard to grades and exams. The other side, made up generally of those with intellectual backgrounds and outstanding grades, felt it would be a waste of time and damaging to the country's development to hold such gifted students back. The interviewees said there was no definitive conclusion to this debate.[55] In debates concerning academic issues, most students felt free to participate and the discussion was rather wide-ranging. On other issues debated at the school, such as the question of "natural redness," participants largely included only those of good class origin. The fact, however, that schools like Huafu routinely sponsored such discussions sets such schools off from those where wide-ranging debates were much rarer.

CONCLUSION

By the eve of the Cultural Revolution, students who had always been divided by their standing with regard to the three criteria used to determine the ladder of success in post-1949 China were ostensibly less united than ever before. Students of different class backgrounds and differing academic abilities in various types of schools had developed assorted approaches and strategies based on their assets and liabilities. Classrooms, particularly at the better schools from which the bulk of the future university students would be drawn, were divided along several lines of cleavage, some more manifest than others:

1. Class origin (ranging from revolutionary cadre and military background to exploiting class background).

2. YCL member vs. non-YCL member.
3. Aspirant YCL member vs. non-aspirant YCL member, i.e., activist vs. non-activist.
4. Academic achievement (ranging from excellent to poor).

In addition to these distinctions dividing individual students, student attitudes and behavior also differed depending on the quality of the middle school at which they were enrolled. Finally, even at the same school, for reasons already discussed, there were significant differences between those students enrolled in junior high and those in senior high.

Given these multiple points of cleavage, it is rather difficult to generalize about student behavior during the Cultural Revolution; nevertheless, the following chapters, in discussing the development of Red Guard factions among middle school students in Guangzhou, will attempt to do precisely that by examining just how the pre-Cultural Revolution differences we have been inspecting stimulated student participation (or lack of same) as the Cultural Revolution unfolded.

Part 2:
The Cultural Revolution

The conflicts and contradictions - some latent, some manifest - which were detailed in chapters one and two most probably would have continued to simmer beneath the surface had it not been for the larger issues dividing Mao from many of the CCP's leading figures. Once stirred, these larger issues, concerned ultimately with the nature and direction of the Chinese revolution, churned up and brought to the surface those questions which were of most concern to middle school students, namely university entrance criteria and the opportunity to demonstrate their activism in an important, rather than a petty, context.

Part Two examines the development during the GPCR of the fundamental contradictions discussed in Part One. In the clash of these contradictions many of the divisions that had tentatively separated students on the eve of the GPCR became yawning, and seemingly unbridgeable, chasms. The debates over appropriate criteria for university entrance, for example, not only continued, but became increasingly caustic and often degenerated into name-calling, recriminations, and physical abuse. Students became separated into groups, and then further separated into factions. On a grand scale some students became self-proclaimed "Rebels" and others were saddled with the label "Conservative". Still others tried, and some succeeded, in "non-participation" in the struggles which rent the schools of China. All this is the subject of Part Two.

"Rebels" and "Conservatives": Definition of Terms

The division of students into "Rebel" and "Conservative" factions was a basic phenomenon of the GPCR. In general, Rebels can be distinguished from Conservatives on the basis of ideology, social background characteristics, and issue orientation.[1] Most prominently, Conservatives sought to defend China's institutionalized power base - the Communist Party organization - while Rebels focused their attacks precisely upon this power base. The objects of Conservative venom were most often "bourgeois academic authorities" and others of questionable class origin, code-named "ghosts and monsters." When Conservatives did oppose leading Party members, it was often only after such people had become official targets and, even then, usually as individual miscreants rather than as typical representatives of the Party organization.

With regard to ideology, Conservatives and Rebels are most clearly distinguished by their differing interpretations of the nature of the class struggle which all acknowledged as central to the aims of the GPCR. The Conservatives, defining class solely in economic terms, felt justified in singling out the remnants of the bourgeoisie as the main targets of the movement; the Rebels, adopting a definition of class which took into account political consciousness and behavior, argued that the targets of class struggle could include anyone violating the thought of Mao Zedong, and that through proper study proletarian class consciousness could be obtained even by those of bad class origin. Given these perspectives, it is not surprising that the Conservative faction included more individuals who were satisfied with previous Party governance of China and with the current distribution of power in society; moreover, the majority of these individuals were of good class origin. The Rebels, on the other hand, attracted more support from a variety of dissatisfied elements, including many of less than impeccable class origins.

These general distinctions between the two factions, while extremely useful, unfortunately obscure some important qualifications. First, the generalization that the Conservatives included those more satisfied with the status quo than the Rebels needs to be qualified. Although this was probably true among workers and within cadre ranks, among middle school students this was not necessarily the case. It is important to realize that, regardless of objective conditions, both children of cadres and children of intellectuals - soon to become the major factional antagonists at the middle school level in the GPCR - felt discriminated against. Although a strong argument could be made that these two groups of students were the most highly favored in Chinese society, neither group perceived its situation as favorable enough. Since high academic achievement remained a key factor in entrance requirements at the better universities and thus continued to confer status on secondary school students, children of cadres felt that the increased emphasis on class line had not been thoroughgoing. Children of intellectuals, however, became more uneasy as the policies associated with the stress on class began to take shape.

The generalization that the Conservatives consisted primarily of those of good class origin while the Rebels contained those of less than good origins also needs to be elaborated further. In accepting this generalization, one must subdivide "less than good" into middle and bad class; one must also distinguish university students from middle school students. In particular, a distinction between those of middle and bad class origin is fundamental to an understanding of the rise of the Rebel faction. Evidence will be introduced in chapters four, five, and six to show that it was students of middle class origin who formed the backbone of Rebel strength. Those of bad class origin tended to be reluctant participants at best although, when they did join a faction, the large majority supported the Rebels.

The correlation between class origin and factional participation holds most clearly for middle school students. University students tended to divide into factions at the beginning of the activist phase of the GPCR - in June and July 1966 - over the assessment of Party committees and Party-sponsored work teams. Most especially, those responding to Maoist ideological appeals to oppose the work teams became the Rebels. Middle school students, while also affected by these early issues, remained from the first more concerned with the question of class   Given the salience of the class issue, the division of students into clearly identifiable factions at the middle school level did not begin until the formation of the Red Guards in late August 1966. The Red Guards were organized using the so-called "blood line theory" (xuetong lun) [placing extreme emphasis on a person's class origin] as the major criterion for membership. Children of cadres were able to use this theory to gain control over the middle schools at that time. It was only with the official repudiation of this theory early in 1967 that the middle class youths - until then suppressed - were able to "rebel." The earliest Red Guards, made up of those from the best class origins, became the Conservatives. Their opponents - those who objected most strenuously to these early Red Guards and had the temerity to stand in opposition to them - ultimately became the core of the Rebels. Thus, it is not surprising that as late as December 1966, according to the account of a Red Guard leader, although Rebels in Guangzhou's universities already outnumbered Conservatives by 20:1, middle school Conservatives still outnumbered Rebels by 3:2.[2]

Unlike many previous accounts of the GPCR, the emphasis in this book is not on the political relationships between the various actors at the elite level (army, government, Party, Mao, and Central Cultural Revolution Group). Nor is it primarily on the interactions of these elites with organizations at the mass level. The present study focuses less on the elite level and more on the

mass level; thus, discussions of elite politics are
stressed only when they can be shown to be directly relevant to events taking place at the mass level. Therefore, to treat the Rebel and Conservative mass organizations in Guangzhou as aggregate actors and to examine
their behavior in relation to elite level actors would
conceal the complexities which are at the heart of this
study. Because it is politics within the mass organizations that are frequently examined most closely, it is
often necessary to disaggregate the Rebel and Conservative mass organizations in order to bring out subfactional splits. When the overall factional split in
Guangzhou is discussed, the designation Rebels (the Red
Flag faction) and Conservatives (the East Wind or General
faction) is most applicable. When delineating divisions
within each of these factions, however, Rebels and Conservatives will be divided further, into radical and
moderate constituent units. For example, in treating
politics within the Red Flag faction it will be necessary
to trace the origins of the differing perspectives
adopted by the radical Red Headquarters and the more
moderate New First Headquarters and Third Headquarters.
Although all three headquarters were Rebel groupings and
in fact together constituted the citywide Red Flag
faction, they had diverse origins and diverse concerns
as well. At times they cooperated rather closely in
their opposition to the East Wind faction; more frequently, however, their alliance against the Conservatives was
necessarily loose. On certain occasions their internal
divisiveness threatened to overshadow the joint struggle
they were ostensibly waging against the common opponent.
This investigation of subfactional divisions will be
explored most fully when considering the organizations
formed by middle school students, as these students did
not give their allegiance directly to a faction, but
generally gave it to a subfactional headquarters within
the faction.

   Part Two is divided into four chapters. Chapter
Three traces the twists and turns in factional formation
in Guangzhou from the initial phase of the GPCR until
April 1967, at which point the factions had finally become stabilized. Although many of the "big events" of
the GPCR were still to come - including the well-publi-
cized incidents of armed struggle - all the major actors
in the drama had already appeared, so that the remainder
of the GPCR marked the waxing and waning of forces already in place rather than the appearance of new protagonists. Because this chapter is primarily descriptive
and rather general, Chapter Four will provide a closer
look at GPCR participation among Guangzhou's middle
school students. It will examine participation rates by
type of school, class origin, YCL membership, and so on,
testing the generalization regarding the relationship

between class origin and factional participation. Interview and survey questionnaire data will be introduced in
support of this and other hypotheses. Chapter Five will
investigate the variations in the GPCR process by focusing on a number of individual middle schools, presenting
a set of "models" of GPCR development and showing the
diversity which existed from school to school. In this
chapter, schools will be divided into "true elite,"
"good," "ordinary," and "poor," as they were in Chapter
One.

Chapter Six will resume the narrative of GPCR developments after April 1967. Having introduced the major
actors earlier, it will now be possible to look more
closely at intra-factional politics as familiar issues
such as educational reform begin to resurface and Party
leaders in Beijing attempt to effect "great alliances"
among the feuding mass organizations. It is also in
Chapter Six that the relationship between the elite level
and the mass level, and between events in Beijing and
Guangzhou, impinge upon the analysis most fully. As
national and local Party and military leaders begin to
move the GPCR toward demobilization and "construction"
after September 1967, the fate of Guangzhou's factions
becomes more than ever dependent on the outcome of the
triangular struggle between the Maoists in Beijing, with
their power base in the Central Cultural Revolution Group
(CCRG), Zhou Enlai and the moderate forces, and Guangzhou's military leadership, headed by military commander
Huang Yongsheng. Given the close ties between Guangzhou's Conservative mass organizations and the local PLA,
the Rebels find that their only hope of success lies in
maintaining the support of both the CCRG and Zhou Enlai.
As the moderate forces in Beijing begin to consolidate
their control, Guangzhou's Rebel leadership is compelled
in turn to moderate its policies to keep pace, putting a
great strain on the fragile balance of forces within the
Red Flag faction. Although Guangzhou's Rebels do achieve
a certain unity by 1968, the decision by those in control
at the Party Center to demobilize the Red Guards leads,
by summer 1968, to the victory of Guangzhou's Conservative forces.

3
The Cultural Revolution in Guangzhou: The Initial Division Into Factions (June 1966–April 1967)

The opening salvo of the Cultural Revolution is often said to have been Yao Wenyuan's November 1965 article on Wu Han's play Hai Rui Dismissed From Office.[1] Indeed, there are many reasons for considering it as such. Yao's article led to a crystallization in the debate over Wu Han (was it essentially a political or academic question) and foreshadowed the differences between Shanghai and Beijing and between the army's propaganda instruments and the Party's.[2] Moreover, in retrospect it is clear that the later, more visible contention over the very purposes and goals of the GPCR can be seen in embryo form at this time. From another perspective, however, the Wu Han debate was both too early and too late to be considered a starting point. Too late because the issues dividing students had already been defined by shifting educational policy throughout the 1960s, and too early because direct student participation in any independent way in the GPCR did not occur until late May-June 1966.

At the middle school level, especially in a city far from the center of the struggle, student life during the first five months of 1966 went on much as before. The official press did increasingly warn of the lack of experience of youth in class struggle and the need for ideological revolutionization,[3] but the abstract literary and philosophical issues raised in the press seemed remote to secondary school students, particularly those busy preparing for final examinations and matriculation examinations. Political activity was still being organized through normal channels, i.e., the YCL and student cadres. Indications of the importance of the burgeoning movement came only with the events of June 1966, including Nie Yuanzi's June 1 poster at Beijing University, the stress on educational reform, and the arrival of work teams in the schools.[4]

Nie's poster, coupled with the editorials in People's Daily in early June, revealed several lines of

direction both for attentive students as well as school
officials. First, Nie's poster opposing Party secretary
Lu Ping demonstrated that even Party committees might be
criticized, using the method of posting big character
posters. Second, the editorials starting with "Sweep
Away All Monsters" on June 1 developed the argument that
it was necessary to launch a revolution in the realm of
ideology and finally to eliminate the culture associated
with the exploiting classes. To quote briefly from two
of these editorials:

> The exploiting classes have been disarmed and
> deprived of their authority by the people, but
> their reactionary ideas remained rooted in
> their minds. We have overthrown their rule
> and confiscated their property, but this does
> not mean that we have rid their minds of re-
> actionary ideas as well.[5]

> The most fundamental task in the Great Social-
> ist Cultural Revolution in our country is to
> eliminate thoroughly the old ideology and cul-
> ture, the old customs and habits which were
> fostered by all the exploiting classes...and
> to create a new proletarian ideology.[6]

The strategy open to Party officials in schools was
clear. They could avoid the fate of Lu Ping only by
supplying representative models of "monsters" whose ideology still had not been transformed.

JUNE TO AUGUST IN GUANGZHOU: MIXED SIGNALS

But Guangzhou was not Beijing. In the capital, even
in the early stages of the GPCR, information on proper
revolutionary behavior was available from a variety of
sources, such as representatives of central leaders,
liaison stations established at Beijing and Qinghua
Universities, and so forth. In Guangzhou, there were
fewer authoritative sources. Responsible for the GPCR in
the middle schools, the Guangzhou Municipal Committee
sought to provide general guidelines for all of Guangzhou's schools. Appropriate behavior for Party committees at secondary schools was indicated by the early publication of one positive and one negative example in the
local press. The two cases reveal the municipal committee standard of proper GPCR conduct. Later, however, it
will become clear that many of the "leading" middle
schools in Guangzhou followed somewhat different scen-
arios.
The two schools contrasted were Number 10 and Number
45 Middle Schools, neither of them front rank schools.[7]

Briefly, the reports on Number 45 described how Liu Xiao-fang, a third-year junior high student of working class origin, had felt for a year or more that her school was lagging behind others in politics and was overly empha-sizing study achievements. Students of worker-peasant background were being held back or being forced to leave school. She felt that the GPCR would provide an opportu-nity to get rid of the "freaks and monsters" among the teachers. Seeing the GPCR developing at other schools, Liu and other students asked permission to make sugges-tions about certain teachers. The Party secretary, Cai Sanjian,[8] refused to permit this, arguing that the main enemy at present was Deng Tuo (an associate of Wu Han then being criticized in Beijing), and he must not be allowed to slip away. Dissatisfied, Liu and some class-mates went to the Guangzhou Municipal Bureau of Education to report on Cai's control over the movement, requesting that higher levels immediately send a work team to take over leadership of the school. When Liu returned to school, she was accused of "mistaking Number 45 Middle School for Beijing University" and a meeting was sched-uled to struggle against her. The timely arrival of the work team liberated her.

The positive model of Number 10 shows how a Party committee successfully dealt with the "freaks and monsters" threatening the educational system. First, the Party committee suspended such courses as politics, Chinese language, and history, substituting the study of Mao's works as the main course. Next, they took two com-positions dealing with farming and analyzed them. One, by a student of non-proletarian family origin, had re-ceived 90 marks from the teacher; the other, by the child of a cadre, had received 55 marks. Through an analysis of these two compositions, the students were shown how the educational position had been captured by the class enemy. By encouraging the students to put up big char-acter posters concerning this problem, it was discovered that there were people like Deng Tuo and Qin Mu hidden at Number 10 Middle School.[9] In fact, a "Petofi Club" led by the former acting secretary of the school's Party branch was allegedly uncovered. As in the case of Number 45, it was alleged that children of worker and peasant background were being squeezed out in favor of cultiva-ting bourgeois successors. One innovation for which the school was praised was the creation of a Cultural Revolu-tion Student Congress consisting of "328 students demo-cratically elected by various classes and grades, and of alumni graduated many years ago and students undertaking farming in mountainous and rural areas."

The juxtaposition of these two schools made several points clear to those taking part in the GPCR. First, it was evident that mere criticisms of Deng Tuo or other previously fallen and/or removed figures was not enough.

Party committees would have to feed living, local targets
to the increasingly restless students. Indeed, this was
precisely the case at the one Guangzhou middle school
about which there is a published account: Dai Hsiao-ai's
school.[10] Second, if a Party committee could not satisfy
student desires for "revolution," the student could go
directly to the higher levels to complain and request new
leadership (such as that supplied by a work team). Again,
this occurred at Dai's school.[11] Third, the discrimina-
tion suffered by children of worker-peasant-cadre background was becoming a key issue. In fact, the importance
of academic achievement was being called into question.
As one of the three criteria used to determine advancement up the educational ladder, this issue potentially
was most likely to divide the students. But at this
early stage in the movement, the emphasis on the wrongs
perpetrated on students of good class origin by the pre-
GPCR stress on grades had not changed the CCP's policy of
laying emphasis on deeds. As municipal Party secretary
Bo Huaiqi was reported to have said in a speech at Number
10 Middle School:

> Comrade Bo Huaiqi hopes classmates who come
> from exploiting class family origin will
> receive revolutionary tempering and testing
> in this great cultural revolution and will
> actively participate in the struggle to-
> gether with the broad masses of worker-
> peasant-soldiers and revolutionary intellec-
> tuals, and will actively study and use Mao's
> works, resolutely betraying their exploiting
> class families and drawing a clear line with
> them, firmly traveling the revolutionary
> road to be proletarian successors, so that
> the bourgeoisie will have no successors. He
> further said: the Party's class policy lays
> stress on deeds, classmates of exploiting
> class family origin will have a future if
> they firmly take the road of revolutionization.[12]

There were, however, other portents indicating an
alternate current to the stress on deeds: the increased
stress on "class line." On June 13 the Central Committee
of the CCP and the State Council strongly condemned the
Chinese educational system for placing "bourgeois politics in command." Drawing the most criticism was the
policy of enrolling students by examination. This was
cited as "a serious violation of the Party's class line"
because it "shut out many outstanding children of workers,
former poor and lower middle peasants, revolutionary
functionaries, revolutionary armymen, and revolutionary
martyrs...."[13] To effect a transformation in this system,
enrollment work was to be postponed for half a year.

The immediate consequence of these developments was an increase in participation in the GPCR. As interviewees reported, senior middle three students no longer needed to prepare for the university examinations.14 Moreover, the new provincial regulations for enrollment of senior high students also encouraged participation.15 Although class origin was explicitly included as an important criterion for enrollment, "a suitable number of children from families of the exploiting classes, who have given a good account of themselves ... and who give prominence to proletarian politics" were also to be selected. The regulations also called for the introduction of a system of selection by recommendation in place of the old examination system.

All indications up to this point portended an increasing role for biaoxian in determining a student's prospects for educational advancement. Children of intellectual class origin could take heart because "revolutionary intellectuals" were being bracketed with workers, peasants, soldiers, and revolutionary cadres as leaders of the GPCR.16 Students generally felt liberated from the confines of petty activism. Here, finally, was a national movement which called for heroic behavior reminiscent of the kind they had been reading about since primary school. A chance for direct participation in the struggle against the class enemy was heady wine indeed.

In this setting the work teams sent from the Guangzhou Municipal Committee made their appearance in the middle schools.17 Work team behavior varied from school to school, depending both on the team's prior instructions and the situation at the assigned school. In some cases, where the Education Bureau lacked confidence in the school leadership, as in the Number 45 Middle School example cited above, the work team took over control of the movement completely. In other cases, where confidence in the leadership was strong, as at Number 10 Middle School, the work team relied more on the existing leadership. Generally considered most reliable were those Party secretaries who had taken up their positions very recently, particularly in the 1963-65 period when the class line policy was being implemented. Thus the work teams strongly supported such recent transferees as Zhang Jian of Number 10, Zhang Ke of the Girls' Middle School, and Chen Ping of Number 1. In some cases the work team felt it necessary to try to prop up a Party secretary already under attack, as in the case of Wang Bingshan of Huafu.

Of greater importance to a study of student factionalism, however, was the attitude taken toward the students themselves. Here it is particularly important to separate universities from middle schools. University students, particularly those who had already participated in the Socialist Education Movement in the countryside,

were much more mature and politically aware than their
middle school counterparts. They were more likely to
pose a problem for Party committees and work teams seeking to control the GPCR. With this in mind, under the
direction of Tao Zhu, who had been the leading official
in the Central-South region until his promotion to Beijing in May 1966 to serve as an advisor to the Central
Cultural Revolution Group (CCRG), the Central-South
Bureau, in sending out work teams, decided to single out
one percent of the university students for struggle.[18]
   Work teams used both class origin and biaoxian in
determining upon whom to rely. In most schools for which
there is data, class origin seemed to be of more importance, but only if the good background students were
obedient to work team policy. One former university
student from Guangzhou has written about the basis for
categorization at his university:

> When the work team set up categories to decide
> who was reliable the five reds were put in the
> first category. In the second category were
> those who were comparatively reliable and had
> good biaoxian. The third category included
> those from bad backgrounds who had good biao-
> xian, and those of good background whose biao-
> xian was not very good, as well as those who
> had previously said some strange things, but
> were considered capable of reform and trans-
> formation. The fourth category included the
> five [bad] elements and those who had neither
> good backgrounds nor biaoxian. The work team
> especially attacked this fourth category.[19]

   The work teams, upon entering a school, often assumed all power. They would seek out students of good
class background, as well as those who were political
leaders in the school, such as members of the school's
YCL committee (tuanweihui). At Number 4 Middle School,
for example, they relied on the right, center, left
classification of each student the YCL committee had
secretly prepared just prior to June 1966.[20] While the
work teams remained at the schools they set up Preparatory Committees (chouweihui) composed of those of good
class background and/or obedient to their wishes. In
some schools, like Number 21 Middle School, class origin
was most important in determining membership on the
Preparatory Committee;[21] in other schools, like Number
24 Middle School, biaoxian seems to have been of at
least equal importance.[22] The work team at Dai Hsiao-
ai's school also used biaoxian as an important criterion,
allowing students who were not from good class backgrounds to sit on the committee.[23] A broad generalization (which would not hold for every single case, how-

ever) would be that work teams emphasized class origin more in the better schools, i.e., those with significant numbers of students from revolutionary cadre and military origin; in schools in which few students from cadre or military origin were to be found, biaoxian assumed more importance. Part of this was due to the fact that in these latter schools, where good class background re- ferred to working class background, political awareness and political activism was less pronounced and working class youth, often oriented more toward urban factory jobs than toward university entrance, displayed a greater interest in the free time afforded by the cancellation of classes than they did in the increased opportunities for activism.

While opposition to the work teams by a prominent minority of students was a salient feature at Guangzhou's universities, opposition at the middle school level was less widespread. Where such opposition did appear, it often came from those of high-level cadre background, who resented restrictions on their "right to rebel." Even obedient students, however, found the routinization of the movement that characterized the work team period a source of some frustration. Dissatisfaction, even on the part of those straining to display their activism, tended to be diffuse and rather sub rosa at this time.

The work teams were withdrawn in late July-early August, but in many cases left behind a liaison officer who continued to advise the students. Nevertheless, the withdrawal of the work teams left the students for the first time with an opportunity to organize free of the control either of school Party committees (which had fallen or, at a minimum, been forced to step aside) or the work teams. In this atmosphere, the students were compelled to examine the official press and important central documents to determine such major questions as how to organize, at whom to direct the spearhead, and so forth. Under these circumstances, students travelling from Beijing to Guangzhou on "exchange of experience" missions (chuanlian) began to play a crucial role in interpreting the developments in Beijing. Before exam- ining their role, however, a brief examination of the status of the GPCR as of late July-early August is necessary.

In the early part of the GPCR, much of the informa- tion regarding differences between Mao Zedong and his supporters in the newly established CCRG on one side, and the Party organization headed by Liu Shaoqi and Deng Xiaoping on the other, which was to become widely dis- seminated in late 1966 and 1967, was unavailable to Guangzhou middle school students.24 To give some idea of their isolation from the Center, here is how one Red Guard, who later was to become the leader of Guangzhou's most important middle school Rebel headquarters, described how he discovered the work teams were to be withdrawn:

> In August 1966 middle school students from all
> Guangzhou gathered at Yuexiushan sports field
> to listen to the broadcast report of the 8th
> Central Committee's 11th plenum, as well as
> to hear speeches which had been given by Jiang
> Qing, Liu Shaoqi, and Chen Boda. Because
> those giving the talks had unclear accents
> and the recording was not good, the students
> were not quite sure what was going on. The
> only thing that everyone heard clearly was
> that the work teams were to be withdrawn.
> This affair, as far as the broad numbers of
> middle school students were concerned, did
> not cause a great reaction.... No one could
> understand why the work teams had to withdraw,
> nor did anyone know about the situation with
> the work teams in Beijing and how they had
> been driven out, although our school did have
> a minority who opposed the work team.[25]

Most of what was available in the press up to this time concentrated on promoting the study of Mao Thought[26] or the role of the Party in the GPCR,[27] providing little concrete information of a practical nature to students eager to participate. The major guide as to the meaning of the GPCR was provided by the 11th Plenum in the form of the "16 Articles" and a communique, both of which were released on August 8.[28]

The "16 Articles" emphasized that at least two groups were to be targets of the movement:

1) "The main target of the present movement is those within the Party who are in authority and are taking the capitalist road." (Article 5)

2) "In this great cultural revolution, the phenomenon of our schools being dominated by bourgeois intellectuals must be completely changed." (Article 10 – Educational Reform)

Still, in the overall context, and given the fact that the CCP was still trusted to lead the movement, the major thrust at this time seemed to be against the "freaks and monsters" left over from the old society. Article 1 seemed to make clear that the danger of a comeback by the overthrown bourgeoisie was the major threat and that the struggle against "those persons in authority who are taking the capitalist road" should be seen in this context.

Article 5 was entitled "Firmly Apply the Class Line of the Party" and the Party leadership was enjoined to "be good at discovering the Left and developing and strengthening the ranks of the Left, and...firmly rely

on the revolutionary Left."[29]   Although there was no further attempt to delineate who the "Left" might be, given
the general understanding of the Party's class line at
that time, coupled with the attacks on bourgeois educational authorities, examinations, and so forth, the students of good class background initially benefitted most
from the appearance of this document.

While the emphasis on free debate and minority
rights (Article 6) offered some guarantees that those who
held unpopular views would be tolerated, these guarantees
were rather more effective in stimulating "rebels" in
Beijing universities who could already see the split at
the elite level between the CCRG and the Party organization than in stimulating Guangzhou middle school students
who were still groping for an understanding of what was
expected of them.[30]   Thus, while it is true that the
withdrawal of the work teams and the adoption of the "16
Articles" changed the whole dynamic of the movement by
shifting to an emphasis on free mobilization of the
masses and changing the pattern of communication between
elites and masses, at least in the short run the "lifting
of the lid" led to the mobilization of those students
most likely to be conservative in support of the Party
organization - those of the five red categories.[31]   The
major student activities of mid-August - the Destroy the
Four Olds Campaign and the establishment of the Red
Guards - both favored students from good class
backgrounds.

The Emergence of the Red Guards

Since a major theme of this book is that the socio-
educational cleavages among middle school students that
led to the establishment of Red Guard organizations in
1966 remained constant throughout the GPCR, with new
issues that arose in the movement quickly becoming
associated with the existing factional split, it is
necessary to analyze in some detail the organization of
different Red Guard groups. In treating this question,
several points must be borne in mind. To begin with,
one of the most striking characteristics of the Red Guard
movement was its uneven development from school to
school. As an example one can compare the formation of
the first Red Guards in the two middle schools with which
Western readers are most familiar - Dai Hsiao-ai's school
in Guangzhou[32] and Ken Ling's school in Xiamen (Amoy).[33]

In Dai's school there was great enthusiasm when they
learned of the August 18 rally in Beijing at which Mao
Zedong accepted a Red Guard armband. However, since the
reports of this rally gave no hint of organizational
details, the students were at a loss as to how to
proceed. After much discussion and preparation, it was

decided that membership in the Red Guards was to be open
to all students whose political conduct had been "good,"
irrespective of class background. By August 20, however,
Song Xuemin, a Red Guard from Qinghua University, arrived
at Dai's school. He immediately informed the students
that the Red Guards should be drawn only from students of
the five red categories, with students of other social
classes forming separate organizations to be led and
trained by the Red Guards. Thus, the Red Guards were
reorganized according to these principles.[34]

Ken Ling's account is rather different. The first
"Red Guard" group in his school was set up as early as
July 16 and the ceremony was presided over by the first
secretary of the Xiamen Municipal Party Committee, Yuan
Gai. Only 56 students, including Ling himself, who was
of ordinary class background, were chosen for this honor.
Class origin was apparently one criterion considered in
choosing, but not the only one. Fewer than 10 percent
of the students at his school were of good class
background.[35]

Both of these schools, however, are extremely
atypical. Dai's school was provincially, rather than
municipally, controlled and was geared to training future
functionaries for the state rather than to cultivating
students for the university. Partially because of this,
coupled with the school's relative isolation in North
Guangzhou, there was very little contact between Dai's
school and the regular middle schools. Therefore, although the school could be said to have been progressive
politically, during the GPCR the students there were
perpetually lagging behind the regular middle schools
both in terms of the information they had and the activities they undertook. The formation of their Red Guard
organization on the basis of "good behavior" is a case
in point. Throughout the GPCR, Dai and his friends
seemed to depend for most of their outside information
on visits to universities, rather than on liaison with
other middle schools.

Ken Ling's school also had several unusual qualities.
Most prominently, as noted, only a small percentage of
the student body was from the five red categories. For
this reason, among others, the work team sent to Ling's
school exercised extremely tight control over the GPCR
seeking, rather unsuccessfully, to isolate the school
from outside events. (For further details on the pecu-
liar qualities of Ling's school, as well as some discrep-
ancies between his account and materials on his school
available in the Red Guard press, see footnote 30).

In many of Guangzhou's schools, the initial student
organizations began to be formed in late July-early
August. This was particularly the case at schools with
significant numbers of children of cadre or military
origin. Students of such impeccable backgrounds had

routinely been drawn together before the GPCR. Early
GPCR criticisms centering on "bourgeois academic authorities" and academic achievement had tended to unite them
further. The more activist-oriented among them had found
themselves colleagues on the Preparatory Committees set
up by the work teams.

It was only with the arrival of a couplet from
Beijing, however, that their ranks really solidified.
The couplet was a simple one:

> When the father's a hero, the son's a good fellow
> When the father's a reactionary, the son's a bastard

In Beijing the couplet had appeared in late July. The
effect, over the next several months, was the complete
repudiation of the last vestiges of the policy of emphasis on performance. It also solved the problem left over
from the somewhat murky work team policy which had
stressed both origin and performance. With this couplet,
the tricky problem of assessing performance - an inexact
process at best - no longer need be the major concern.36

From late July to mid-August, debates on the absolute validity, basic validity, or partial validity of the
couplet raged in Beijing. In Guangzhou as well, the
debates on the couplet at first were relatively open.
In some schools, even those of bad class origin, given
sufficient bravery, were free to speak their minds.37
The events of middle and late August soon pushed the
debates aside. The key event, of course, was Mao's first
reception of the Red Guards on August 18. Mao's approval
of the Red Guards, signified by his widely photographed
acceptance of a Red Guard armband, coupled with NCNA's
report of the rally at which the Red Guards were defined
as "an organization set up by middle school pupils from
families of workers, former poor and lower-middle peasants, revolutionary cadres and revolutionary armymen,"
effectively silenced any remaining opposition to the
"five red" concept.38 All outstanding issues on which
the students were still divided were relegated to a
secondary level. At the Girls' Middle School, for example, there had been criticism of both the work team and
the GPCR Preparatory Committee, with debates over whether
to rearrange the membership of the committee. The formation of the Red Guards and the subsequent exclusive
reliance on class origin as the criterion for revolutionary purity overwhelmed these other questions.39 At
Number 3 Middle School, those of five red origin used
this opportunity to expel all those of less pure chengfen
who, because of YCL leadership posts and obedience, had
shared power with them under work team auspices.40 At
Huafu, where two factions, each centered around children
of high-level cadre origins, had been battling over a
series of issues, the couplet and the August 18 reception

temporarily brought them closer together.[41]

The Red Guards from Beijing middle schools played the key role at this time. Arriving in Guangzhou on <u>chuanlian</u> missions, they visited many of Guangzhou's secondary schools, generally making their headquarters at those elite schools with significant numbers of children of cadre origin. They vigorously pushed the couplet, exhorting their counterparts in Guangzhou to spare no mercy for the class enemy. Up to this point, the GPCR had focused on criticism of and attack on teachers and administrators. Although impure class origin had been considered something of an encumbrance, all students had been able, if they so desired, to take part in besieging these authority figures. In fact, many had done just that. Lacking a good <u>chengfen</u>, it was incumbent upon those students who wished to demonstrate their revolutionary fervor to manifest the proper <u>biaoxian</u>. This was even more the case because of the fall of Peng Zhen, the major of Beijing, and one of China's top leaders. Peng had been associated with the 1965 policy of "emphasis on deeds" and among the charges now being levelled against him was the accusation that this policy, in effect, had been "emphasis on superficials" rather than on true revolutionary deeds. Now the situation had shifted dramatically. For the first time, students began to attack students. The mere possession of a bad <u>chengfen</u> subjected students, at a minimum, to isolation and humiliation. Beatings were not unusual, particularly for those in junior middle classes. Humiliations were many. Those from bad class origins were compelled to enter schools from a special gate. They were made to sit apart from others in the classroom and at meetings.

Students from middling origins fared somewhat better. The severe treatment meted out to the children of the seven black categories served as a buffer, allowing them to avoid physical punishment. There were some humiliations, however. Classrooms and meetings were divided physically into three sections, with seats assigned on the basis of good, middle, and bad class background. Students of middle class origin were not permitted the honor of joining the newly-formed Red Guard organizations. Still, the newly-formed Red Guards acknowledged a distinction between those from middle and bad origins. An addition to the sacrosanct couplet had enjoined:

...if the father is middling, the son sits on the fence.

Using the time-honored tradition of relying on the firm Leftists (those of five red categories), uniting with those who can be united with (the fence-sitters of middling origin) in order to isolate and destroy the enemy (those of seven black category origin), in many (but not all) schools, an auxiliary organization was set

up called the Red Outer Circle (Hongwaiwei). Those au-
thorized to join this organization were to be guided by
the parent organization of Red Guards. By their "deeds,"
they were expected to prove they were deserving of Red
Guard status. Biaoxian, although it had become of dwin-
dling importance with the establishment of Red Guard
organizations based solely on class origin, still had a
role to play. The Red Guards themselves, however, were
now in a position to distinguish the superficial from the
genuine. Moreover, given the tenor of the times, positions in the Red Outer Circle were much coveted. Despite
the second-class status it seemingly conferred on those
who joined, there were compelling reasons why many students sought to join this Circle. Primarily, it was a
chance to display one's activism and support for Mao in
the GPCR in what to all intents and purposes was an officially-sanctioned organization.

Although the YCL continued to limp along for several
more months, the birth of the Red Guards had sounded the
death knell of the League. Students accustomed to
China's system of officially-sponsored activism did not
find it difficult to shift their allegiances from the
increasingly moribund and suspect YCL to a fresh and un-
tainted organization. Moreover, the Outer Circle was
something of an elite organization in itself. As the
chosen Red Guards informed the Outer Circle aspirants,
membership was to be restricted to certain categories of
students. First, one had to be of middling background or
better. Second, one had to be firmly dedicated to the
revolution and the defense of Chairman Mao and to demonstrate the latter through one's actions, including the
firm support of one's parent Red Guard organization.
Under these conditions, many students rushed to join.
After all, the Red Guards, if not a creation of Chairman
Mao, had nonetheless been blessed by him. Moreover,
there was the possibility held out that a suitable performance in the auxiliary organization could lead to
promotion into the parent group. In some schools the
Outer Circle even included some of good class origin
whose bona fides were still being checked.

In this process, the Beijing Red Guards played a
particularly important role. In aiding a school's students to establish a Red Guard organization that would
emulate the Beijing model in its orthodoxy, these Red
Guards newly arrived "from the side of Chairman Mao" (as
they repeatedly put it to any who doubted their authority)
often treated Guangzhou as if it were Beijing. Thoroughly obsessed with the concept that the father's rank determined the son's qualifications, they scrupulously
examined the eligibility of all those claiming to be of
revolutionary cadre background. In a class at Number 21
Middle School, for example, Red Guards from the Middle
School Attached to Beijing Aviation Institute reclassi-

fied eight students who had declared themselves to be of cadre origin. Their more appropriate classification was office worker (zhiyuan) according to the visitors, since their parents were really high-level state cadres as distinct from "revolutionary" cadres.[42] Because of its concentration on elite schools and children of cadres, this type of reclassification tended to be more common in lower middle schools in Eastern Guangzhou than in other sections of the city.[43]

Even more prevalent, however, was the method used by the Beijing Red Guards and their Guangzhou counterparts to deny students of working class background their rightful places in the new organizations. Subjected to a strict definition of "worker" as employed by the Beijing Red Guards, a fair number of students who had previously carried this class designation suddenly found themselves being viewed as "children of the laboring people," but not of the proletariat. Increasingly rigidifying their belief in the blood line theory, the visitors from Beijing argued that, as everyone knew, "worker" really meant "industrial worker" (chanye gongren); those whose parents had been coolies or artisans were not really entitled to the designation "working class origin." Had these restrictions been instituted in Wuhan or Shanghai, perhaps they could have been justified. In a city like Guangzhou, which historically had been a commercial city and hence had relatively few who qualified as children of industrial workers, such restrictions appeared arbitrary and opportunistic, and were soon to cost the early Red Guards dearly the support of children who had all along proudly proclaimed their working class origins.

Nor was this the only measurement the visitors used to determine working class origin. In some schools the Red Guards demanded a check on the occupation of a student's grandfather as well, before they were convinced the person in question was of true working class origin. This latter ploy could be especially effective in maintaining control over an organization. Even after becoming Red Guards, those who posed a threat to the leadership of children of cadre origin might find their class status reclassified, albeit unofficially. Once again, such policies were by no means universal in all Guangzhou middle schools, but varied from school to school and even, to a certain extent, from classroom to classroom. What was standard, however, was the usurpation of the leadership role in the new Red Guard organizations by those of cadre and military origin. The Beijing Red Guards went further and sought out those students whose parents were Northerners as the purest of the pure. These were most often those from military origins and, indeed, in the best schools there were strong tensions between those of military and those of revolutionary cadre background.

Nevertheless, the vast majority of good class origin students initially supported the blood line theory which stemmed from the couplet. Most students, perhaps especially those of working class origin, recognized leadership by the children of cadres as a somewhat natural tendency. As was seen in Chapter Two, before the GPCR the school authorities seemed to encourage such sentiments, motivating children of cadres by comparing their behavior, often invidiously, to the glorious deeds of their parents. There were differences, of course, in the implementation of the couplet. Generally speaking, students of working class origin were much milder than those of cadre origin in their criticisms of those of bad class origin; those of cadre origin were milder than those of military origin; finally, those from Guangzhou were milder than those local students whose parents were Northerners.

At first, there was minimal opposition to the newly established Red Guard organizations. These organizations, in addition to the official support they had received, were in a position to dispense rewards and punishments to friend and foe alike. For example, concurrent with the establishment of the Red Guards, was the movement to "Destroy Four Olds." At first, students of middling origin joined those of good class origin in enthusiastically participating. The aim of the movement was to destroy old ideology, culture, habits, and customs, which in urban areas usually meant the invasion of the homes of those suspected of possessing "bourgeois" objects.[44] Quickly, however, the movement became more organized and those of middling origin were ordered to desist. They were permitted, instead, to engage in the movement under Red Guard auspices. Students of middle background, in fact, were sent out on Destroy Four Olds missions with a Red Guard as mission leader. Of course, one had to be an Outer Circle member to take part and, in fact, enthusiastic participation in these missions was an important measure of one's biaoxian and possible suitability as a future Red Guard. Even to those of intellectual family origin who did participate, the irony must have been inescapable. The bourgeois objects they were confiscating were rather similar to items in their own homes; the more successful they were in uncovering bourgeois manifestations in the homes they raided, the more they became tainted by virtue of having grown up in a rather similar environment, and the further they thus had to go in proving themselves worthy revolutionary successors.[45]

The denial of the right to participate in Destroy Four Olds missions was just one manifestation of the monopolization of activist undertaking enjoyed by the Red Guards. Recognizing the potential strength of the Red Guard movement, the Guangzhou Municipal Committee and the Guangzhou Military Region had moved quickly to unify the

newly emerging forces under a single rubric. Middle
school units were united in September into a General
Headquarters called "Guangzhou Mao Zedongism Red Guards"
(hereinafter called "Doctrine Guards"), with individual
units at most of Guangzhou's secondary schools.[46] This
close association with official circles guaranteed the
Doctrine Guards such material support as large sums of
money, railway tickets, vehicles, and printing facilities.[47] All distribution from official circles went to
a school through its Cultural Revolution Preparatory
Committee which, after readjustments, had come under the
complete control of the Red Guards. Therefore, this
latter group was able to decide the allocation of these
goods among the student body. Distribution of these
resources was another way in which the first Red Guards
could command obedience. For instance, at one school,
when students were issued little red books of Mao quotations, the Preparatory Committee limited the recipients
to those of good class origin who supported them.[48]

Even more important than these denials of the fruits
of symbolic output was the attempt to prevent dissidents
from communicating with each other, particularly through
the medium of chuanlian. Chuanlian had begun in mid-
August; as a matter of fact, at Mao's first reception of
the Red Guards on August 18, there already were student
representatives from Guangzhou middle schools in attendance.[49] At the second rally on August 31, Zhou Enlai
announced that "all college students and representatives
of middle school students from other parts of the country
should come to Beijing, group after group, at different
times."[50] It was the Red Guard organization in the
school, however, that determined which students were
worthy of representing the school in Beijing. Even after
chuanlian was expanded, the Preparatory Committees in the
schools had the power to determine which students might
take part. Free travel tickets issued by the municipal
committee to the schools went directly to the Preparatory
Committees, which in turn distributed them to those supporting their authority.[51]

Some students attempted to engage in unauthorized
travel to Beijing at this time; however, they had to
contend with Doctrine Guards actively policing the railway stations and checking travel documents and chengfen.
Moreover, these "inspectors" could claim official backing
for their activities. With the help of the provincial
and municipal Party committees, the Guangzhou Red Guards
had set up a "provost team" on September 17, with provincial leaders issuing certificates and armbands to members.[52] In addition, those trying to travel independently were reviled at school as "without organization and
without discipline," a label most students still sought
to avoid.[53] Finally, each time Mao received the Red
Guards in Beijing, there were local celebrations in each

of Guangzhou's secondary schools. Organized by the Preparatory Committees and visiting Red Guards from Beijing,
these celebrations were off-limits to dissidents and
those of bad class background.

In early September, a period designated as the "Red
Terror" (hongsi kongbu) was proclaimed by the Red Guards.
Those disobedient to the Preparatory Committees and those
of seven black category background came under increased
pressure and control. It was in this period that the
emphasis on the family chengfen of both students and
teachers was carried to its most extreme form. Beatings,
along with indignities of varous types, became common-
place. Aside from teachers, the students of bad class
origin bore the brunt of physical abuse. In addition,
however, the Red Guards used the opportunity afforded at
this time to put pressure on dissidents generally. For
example, those not of impeccable five red background who
resisted the leadership of the Red Guards were not issued
meal tickets. Only after they had submitted a series of
detailed reports on their class origin were these tickets
restored.[54]

Because of the tight control exercised over the
movement by the Red Guards operating through the Preparatory Committees in each school, dissatisfaction in various forms manifested itself even during the height of the
Red Terror period. Significantly, the earliest open
opposition to the terror tactics and the extreme emphasis
on the blood line theory came from within the ranks of
the Red Guards. This was not surprising; given the summary manner in which those of non-five red origin were
treated at this time, opposition of an overt sort could
come only from those allowed to speak. The most important early manifestation of disagreement with the blood
line couplet among middle school students came from the
Middle School Attached to South China Normal Institute
(Huafu). Huafu was considered the best school in Guangzhou, containing a large number of students of revolutionary cadre and military background. In the early part of
the GPCR, Huafu became something of a focal point for
Guangzhou's secondary school students. Events at the
school attracted attention because of the presence of two
Red Guard organizations, each made up of children of high-
level cadre and/or military background. The disputing
factions at Huafu sponsored an open debate meeting on the
blood line couplet that was attended by many of Guangzhou's secondary school students, particularly those from
schools in which the tenets of the couplet had been implemented with a vengeance, i.e., those from Eastern
Guangzhou. Although both factions at Huafu argued in
favor of the couplet, one group felt it was correct absolutely, while the other group argued that raising the
issue in this way was not good tactically and, moreover,
some students of non-five red origin were capable of

revolutionary behavior, given proper leadership. The
form of this meeting was similar to debate meetings at
other middle schools at this time. All students mounting
the platform to speak stated their family origin and the
year their fathers had joined the revolution. Needless
to say, the large majority of the speakers at this meeting were children of high officials.[55]

This debate meeting was influential for several reasons. First, although both factions were made up primarily of children of cadre and military origin and although
neither opposed the couplet, the very fact that more than
one acceptable position could be taken with regard to the
question of the blood line theory made an impression on
those students from schools in which no overt dissent was
permitted. Second, the logic of the position argued by
the moderate side in the debate - that the blood line
theory was insufficient by itself in determining one's
capacity for revolution - led others to go a step further
and question the blood line theory itself. It is important to note that this early questioning of the blood
line theory coincided with the beginning of a general
malaise among the majority of middle school students. In
a somewhat similar manner to the work team period, students once again had very little to do.

The Influence of University Students on the Middle School Movement

As has been noted, in most schools the first Red
Guard organization had strict membership standards; being
of five red origin was a necessary but not sufficient
condition for membership. Even after the Doctrine Guards
had organized citywide in September, the emphasis on
organization and discipline among the Red Guards remained
as strong as the stress on class origin.[56] Given the
tightly controlled pattern into which the middle school
movement had fallen, it is not surprising that the break-
through against the power of the Doctrine Guards was
stimulated from the outside. The influence of both the
movement at Guangzhou's universities and then outside
university students arriving on chuanlian ultimately led
to the rise of Guangzhou's Rebel faction.

Although Guangzhou's middle school students had been
more visible in their early implementation of the GPCR,
as in their attacks on teachers and bourgeois life-styles,
the division into factions had occurred earliest at the
university level. At Zhongshan University (Zhongda), for
example, the first split developed over the Party committee's leadership of the movement. The Party secretary,
Li Jiaren, at first treated the GPCR as an extension of
the Socialist Education Movement, arguing that the most
important contradiction was in the cultural sphere and
the superstructure generally. He was opposed by a group
of students who had just returned from engaging in

Socialist Education work in the countryside and, heavily influenced by the "23 Points" of January, 1965 (which had emphasized that "the crux of the current movement is to purge the capitalist roaders in authority within the Party"), objected to Li's stress on the cultural sphere.[57] Two views of the Party committee quickly developed, with the majority in support and the minority in opposition. The arrival of two separate work teams in June was to no avail, nor were the Red Guards arriving from Beijing, who likewise were divided, thus intensifying the struggle.

The early split at Zhongda, however, exercised far less influence on Guangzhou's middle school students than the division at South China Engineering Institute. An event that became famous throughout the city as the "Letter from Beijing" incident was to have a great impact on those who later became Rebel leaders at Guangzhou's middle schools. Briefly, a student at Beijing Medical Institute, the sister of Gao Xiang, a student at South China Engineering Institute, sent a letter to her brother in June 1966, in which she stated that "except for Chairman Mao and the Party Center, the leadership of Party committees at any level can be doubted."[58] Gao posted this letter as well as an open letter to all students and Party members in the Institute. Not long after, some other students posted an appeal for the founding of a United Command in Guangzhou to be placed under the direct control of the Party Center and Chairman Mao.[59] The provincial Party committee, acting through the school's work team and its Party committee, immediately labeled the whole incident counterrevolutionary. Within two days, five of the students involved in the incident secretly set off for Beijing to win backing for their position. In the meantime, the Public Security Bureau and the provincial Party committee sought to prevent the spread of this incident by setting up an investigation center to cover the six universities located in Guangzhou's Shipai District for a three-month period, as well as investigating 200 students, teachers, and cadres at South China Engineering Institute. Gao Xiang himself was investigated most thoroughly. Although his father was a leading cadre (14-level) in the foreign trade field, attempts were made to find incriminating evidence in the latter's political background. Gao Xiang was constantly followed, denied participation in GPCR activities, and ostracized while efforts were made to prove him a counterrevolutionary. Six charges were filed against him; the two most interesting were that he opposed the school's work team and conspired with Party members in issuing his open letter to the college.

By September, the situation in Guangzhou had changed greatly. Work teams had been recalled by the Party Center; in fact, at some colleges the work teams had been chased away by Rebel groups. Rebels at the university

level were gaining in strength as it became increasingly
legitimate to call into question the leadership that had
been exercised by work teams, school Party committees,
and even the provincial Party committee.

In this altered atmosphere, Gao Xiang and his supporters convened a series of open meetings at South China
Engineering Institute to report on his trip to Beijing
and on the entire "Letter from Beijing" incident. The
meeting lasted several days and was attended by large
numbers of students from all over Guangzhou. One interviewee, who was to become a key Rebel leader of Guangzhou's secondary school students, commented on how "the
buses going out to Shipai (the location of the Institute)
were overflowing during those few days," as well as on
the number of students cycling to the site.[60] At the
meetings, Gao and others accused the provincial committee
of oppressing them and also reported on the favorable
reception given them in Beijing by the CCRG.

The value of these open meetings for those middle
school students who attended was in bringing home to them
the split at the Party Center, and the difficulties faced
by Mao and Lin Biao. In addition, such open criticism of
the provincial Party committee surprised them. They
began to understand more clearly the main thrust of the
16 Points. Whereas many had previously accepted the
argument that rectification of "those in the Party taking
the capitalist road" was primarily directed at those
Party members in intellectual and cultural circles, they
now realized that the cancer in the Party had spread much
further.[61]

Providing further enlightenment to nascent middle
school Rebels were the wall posters at the universities
they visited. For the first time in their experience,
the blood line couplet was being criticized. At a number
of universities, particularly at Zhongshan Medical Institute which housed liaison stations for Rebel Red Guard
groups from Beijing Aviation Institute and Beijing Industrial Institute, they could read detailed, well-written
criticisms of the blood line theory which had been copied
from Beijing's universities and colleges. Direct contact
with liaison personnel from these prestigious Beijing
universities aided them in learning how to read the national press intelligently and, perhaps even more important, how to achieve maximum utility from articles or
sections of articles that were favorable to their cause.

Perceptive students who had been frozen out of the
GPCR at their schools because of class origin deficien-
cies or lack of obedience were now returning from these
local chuanlian forays much more self-confident. Although it was still difficult as well as dangerous for
most to engage in criticism of their school's Preparatory
Committee, these visits with university students, especially those from Beijing, convinced them that the Red

Guards in their own schools were rather uninformed as to the true meaning of the GPCR and were able to exercise such local power only through their reliance on the provincial and municipal Party committees.

Nevertheless, the period before October was a transitional one for Guangzhou's middle school students. The work team withdrawals had meant a great deal at the university level because, as in Beijing, it had been seen as a victory for the minority faction. At the middle school level, work team withdrawals were much less significant. At some schools where work teams had been opposed, only the children of the highest-level cadre background dared stand openly against them. In other schools, where opposition had come from those with a less exalted status, the blood line couplet had quickly made the work team issue passe. Criticisms of work team behavior could indeed increase the confidence of such students who had been proved right in their opposition but (unlike the situation at the university level), since the control exercised by the middle school Red Guards was based primarily on their family origin and official favor, it would take further erosion of both the couplet and the provincial and municipal committees before their stranglehold on power could be broken. The criticisms that were being levelled at the blood line couplet at this time were still by and large limited to questioning its extreme form.

Given this situation, there developed in many schools a second Red Guard organization that had a broader membership base and was less directly tied to the official power structure. Interestingly, this phenomenon was much more common at "ordinary" than at "good" schools. For example, at Number 29 Middle School the earliest Red Guards had been limited to those students of good class origin who had been well-known personalities (hongren) in the school before the GPCR, and had maintained good relations with the school's Party committee. In late September, a second group of Red Guards was set up, made up mostly of others of five red origin, plus a smaller number who were of middle background.[62]

At Number 3 Middle School a second Red Guard organization rose in this period to challenge the monopoly exercised by the Doctrine Guards. Seeking a broader membership base, the organization expanded the original five red categories to encompass what it called "nine yellow categories." Lacking any clear signal from above on how to assess the relationship between revolutionary behavior and class origin, the new organization took Mao's "Analysis of the Classes in Chinese Society" as their criterion and allowed those whose origin Mao had classified as the semi-proletariat, such as shop assistant, peddlar, and handicraftsman, to enter.[63]

Summarizing the situation before October, we find

the following prominent features:
1. At many schools two Red Guard organizations
coexisted. The initial Red Guard unit consisted of a
minority of the school's students of five red origin.
In addition, the unit was usually controlled or led by
children of cadre or military background, and often had
supported the school's Party committee. The second Red
Guard unit had arisen as a result of dissatisfaction with
the original Red Guards. Adopting a broader membership
base, in some schools this second group was dominated by
children of ordinary cadre and working class origin (as at
Guangya); at other schools the ranks were enlarged to
include the best of the middle background students (Number 3), and even those of petty bourgeois origin (Number
29).
2. In many cases, those joining this second unit
had initially been sympathetic to the earliest Red Guards
but found their opportunities for activism and relatively
conformist revolutionary behavior severely restricted by
the rigid, hierarchical structure that marked the organizations established at the height of the blood line
couplet. It is not surprising that the majority who
joined this second group had been Red Outer Circle members of the first group, pre-GPCR YCL members or, in
some schools, actual members of the first Red Guards who
had chafed under the leadership monopoly of the children
of high-level cadre background.
3. The differences between the two Red Guard units
were, in retrospect, not as great as their similarities.
Both organizations were led by students of good class
origin, in the one case cadre-based, in the other worker-
based. Both had been set up before the criticism and
repudiation of the "bourgeois reactionary line" (zifanxian) and its middle school manifestation, the blood line
theory, which were to come at the end of the year.
4. The existence of these two Red Guard units still
left at least two categories of students unaccounted for:
the first group included those who were of good or middle
class origin, yet were left out of the Red Guards either
because they had refused to accept subordinate positions,
felt the policies of the early Red Guards to be erroneous,
or had been considered particularly vulnerable because of
special family problems; the second group consisted of
those of bad class background. Students in this latter
category, although most oppressed during the early period
of the GPCR, for the most part never successfully rebelled against their inferior status. Students in the
former category, however, particularly those of middle
class background, were later to become beneficiaries when
the GPCR, beginning in October, began to shift to a more
radical phase.
Moreover, as will be seen, it was in those we have
labelled as the "good" schools, particularly those in

Eastern Guangzhou, that these students of middle class background were to emerge as the leading Rebels, both in their own schools and in the municipality.

THE RISE OF THE REBELS IN GUANGZHOU'S MIDDLE SCHOOLS

October 1966 was a key month in the GPCR. In Beijing, the Rebel faction traced its "liberation" back to the early days of October, concentrating on Lin Biao's National Day speech (October 1), the editorial in Red Flag Number 11 (October 3), the Urgent Directive of the Central Military Affairs Commission and the General Political Department of the PLA (October 5), and the rally to "open fire on the reactionary bourgeois line," attended by 120,000 teachers and students, as well as by Zhou Enlai, Jiang Qing, and other central leaders (October 6).[64] These events soon transformed Beijing's Rebels from the minority faction (shaoshu pai) into the majority faction (duoshu pai).

It was not long before the fallout from these events in Beijing reached Guangzhou. Once again, it was the Red Guards coming south from Beijing universities who had the greatest impact on Guangzhou's middle schools. The first wave of outside Red Guards had reached Guangzhou in August. Secondary school Red Guards, hoisting the banner of blood line theory and exhorting their Guangzhou counterparts to demonstrate their "class feelings," had spurred the latter to ever greater displays of animosity toward the class enemy - those of bad class origin. Among the Red Guards from Beijing's universities, however, those representing the minority faction had offered some limited encouragement to the oppressed. Nevertheless, their emphasis at that time had been on questioning the leadership of the provincial and municipal Party committees, on reporting on the anti-work team movement in Beijing, and so forth. Still supporting the leadership of the GPCR by those from the five red categories, they had little immediate effect on power relations at the middle school level.

A good example of the above can be seen by examining the impact of Song Xuemin, a student from Qinghua University, on the Guangzhou situation. This was the same Song who was so important in the creation of the Red Guards at Dai Hsiao-ai's secondary school. Song's main effect was through a series of report meetings he gave at Guangzhou's universities. For example, addressing 10,000 students (including a fair number of middle school students) at South China Normal Institute in late August, Song passionately related the case of Kuai Dafu, a Qinghua student who had been persecuted by the school's work team but had recently been rehabilitated by Zhou Enlai.[65] Song broadened his defense of Kuai to a defense of all those who

had been denied their freedom by powerholders, whether in
the form of a work team, a Party committee, or by higher
levels. Still, because he did not criticize the blood
line theory, the newly formed Doctrine Guards were not
excessively threatened by his oratory. In fact, using
his acceptance of the five red formula, many Red Guards
continued to justify their monopoly over the movement and
their excesses by arguing that his defense of freedom was
of course not absolute but was class-based, applying only
to those of good class origin.[66]

By October, however, the early Red Guards still in
control of the Cultural Revolution Preparatory Committees
in the schools were beginning to lose their stranglehold
over the GPCR. Increasing attacks on the provincial and
municipal Party committees by outside Red Guards made it
difficult for these local officials to keep close liaison
with Preparatory Committees or to supply the funds and
equipment that enabled the latter to maintain the support
of the majority of the students. Within the Doctrine
Guards itself, a split had already developed in which a
minority favored an assault on leading local level Party
officials while a majority opposed it.[67]

The blood line couplet as well was beginning to be
openly attacked by bold Rebels in a number of Guangzhou's
"good" schools. Having begun to set up small-scale combat teams based primarily on classroom groups, these em-
bryonic units began, in a few selected schools, openly to
compete with the initial Red Guard groups for the sentiments of the masses. The second wave of Red Guards from
Beijing universities were bringing news of the growth of
that city's minority faction, of a speech given by CCRG
director Chen Boda in which he criticized the leadership
exercised by children of high-level cadres on the basis
of the now increasingly suspect blood line theory, of the
right of all students to engage in chuanlian. Minority
Rebel groups were consulting liaison personnel from Beijing, now ensconced at most of Guangzhou's universities,
on a regular basis to obtain insights into elite-level
politics and its relation to their own struggles.

All of the above developments were part of a larger
process - the expansion of the student movement from the
schools into society - that could only undermine the influence of the increasingly "conservative" middle school
Red Guards. Although, in one sense, the destruction of
the four olds had also been such an expansion, the tight
control exercised at that time by the Red Guards rendered
the experience perilously close to petty activism even
for the majority of those who were allowed to participate;
they were, after all, being subjected to a test (kaoyan)
to determine their suitability to join the parent organization. Chuanlian as well had been tightly controlled
through the issuance of travel tickets, funds, and equipment, and the presence of Red Guard inspectors at the

railway station. By late October-early November, the municipal committee was no longer issuing tickets or supplies to the Preparatory Committees, those students who had "illegally" taken part in chuanlian had gone unpunished and, in fact, had returned with fascinating tales of their experiences, and the Center had begun advocating chuanlian through the medium of long marches.[68]

Cut off from the resources of the now beleaguered municipal committee, no longer able to control behavior through monopolization of outlets for activism and selection of those deserving enough to participate in chuanlian, the Preparatory Committees began to lose their importance. The Rebel forces, although still weak, began to absorb isolated combat teams set up by those dissatisfied with the leadership of the Red Guards. Moreover, they appealed directly to members of the Red Outer Circle who, now that class origin was less of an obstacle, saw no need to remain in an organization that promised permanent subordinate status. Ironically, faced with large-scale defections, the Preparatory Committees reversed their policies and began "officially" to encourage everyone to leave on chuanlian, primarily to avoid the criticism building up against their leadership of the movement, and to prevent the Rebels from doing extensive mobilization work.

In most Guangzhou schools, the extended chuanlian experiences brought a large portion of the free-floating students into the Rebel camp. Returning to their schools in late December-early January, they were greeted by the New Year's editorial, providing them a powerful stick with which to subdue the remnants of the old Red Guards. Among other tactics the "capitalist-roaders" were said to have employed was the following:

> (They) organize students who are children of "revolutionary cadres, workers and peasants" into Red Guards and use these against those Red Guards who are Mao/Lin followers. They make adroit use of the slogan "if the father's a hero the son's a good fellow, if the father's reactionary, the son's a bastard" in order to rally cadres' sons and daughters who naturally protect their parents, who in their turn are "power-holders" or their supporters.[69]

Although it now became somewhat fashionable to be a Rebel, the dispersal of the student body into small groups during chuanlian had prevented a strong, united Rebel organization from developing in most schools. There were now many combat teams, based largely on political beliefs held in common. Nevertheless, in many schools there was a recognizable hard-core who commanded prestige because they had not been tainted by support for

the previous erroneous line. In a fair number of schools
there were some who had not only withheld their support,
but had actually united organizationally in opposition to
the control of the Red Guards at a time when the latter
were still able to inflict sanctions on free-thinkers.
Proudly calling themselves the Minority Faction, after
their counterparts in Beijing's universities, student
leaders opposed to the Red Guards began to meet like-
minded individuals at other schools beginning in December
while on chuanlian. Returning to their own schools in
January they sought to expand and consolidate their Rebel
organizations internally while continuing to develop an
inter-school Rebel force.

Vindicated by the radical twist the GPCR was now
taking, those who had been part of the Minority Faction
were now readily acknowledged by others as the logical
leaders of the Rebels. Generally, the credentials of a
Rebel were established by what his/her position had been
with regard to: 1) the school's Party committee; 2) the
school's work team; and 3) the blood line theory couplet.
By far the most important of these was the third. In a
number of schools the Party committee had either collapsed, been pushed aside and opposed by the work team,
or been defied by children of cadre origin right from the
start of the GPCR. The work teams, too, had in some notable cases been opposed by those whose impeccable class
backgrounds had made them fearless. However, it was on
the issue of the couplet that the majority of the schools
divided. Early splits over other issues were frequently
obscured by the division caused by the couplet. Even in
the most prominent case of division prior to the couplet,
that of Huafu, the debate meeting the two sides held on
the couplet offered minimum solace for those of non-good
background seeking an independent role.

The importance of the couplet as the crucial source
of division can be seen from the recollections of one
interviewee who not only had been the Rebel leader at his
own school, but had been an important leader in Guangzhou
as a whole, with responsibility for liaison work throughout the city. In a series of interviews, he profiled the
nature of the factional split at each school with which
he was familiar. Of the 31 schools he profiled, 19 (61%)
split into factions over the issue of the blood line
theory. In many of the additional 12 schools, this issue
exacerbated a split that had already developed. Most
important, this was particularly the case at the better
schools in which children of revolutionary cadres and
children of intellectuals were the main protagonists.
The issue of the couplet was of least enduring importance
at the poorer schools with only junior middle sections,
particularly those in which the majority were of working
class origin. In these latter schools the enduring
splits usually came later, over such issues as the

assessment of the work of the Military Training Groups sent into the schools in 1967 to restore order.[70]

Given the importance of the issue of blood line theory as a touchstone, it is not surprising that those who became Rebels tended to come from worse family backgrounds than those who remained loyal to the early Red Guards. As will later be shown, this was true both of the Rebel leadership as well as its rank and file.

Developments in Guangzhou's Universities

Up to this point, the middle school students and the university students in Guangzhou had primarily been involved in separate struggles. True, university students had, at various times, been influential in the middle school movement, but it was Beijing rather than Guangzhou university students who had sustained those in secondary schools oppressed by the couplet. Aside from the "Letter from Beijing" incident, the visits secondary school students made to universities were primarily for the purpose of reading wall posters, many of which were reprints of Beijing posters; of visiting liaison stations set up by Beijing students; and of listening to speeches by Beijing Red Guards who had arrived on chuanlian. To a great extent, Guangzhou's university students had also been busy learning from their Beijing counterparts.

The events of Janaury were to change all this. Over the next few months Guangzhou's university and middle school students were to draw closer together, much more so than was the case in Beijing. Before dealing with the key issues of these months, however, an examination of developments at Guangzhou's universities is necessary.

By October 1966, Guangzhou's university students had become clustered around three large headquarters. The key distinction that separated these headquarters was the assessment of the work teams sent out in June 1966 to supervise the GPCR in each school. The First Headquarters was originally centered in Guangzhou's Eastern District and was led by Rebels at Guangzhou Engineering Institute and Zhongshan Medical Institute. Although the First Headquarters had been organized in October by Red Guard units opposed to the work teams, an early split had developed between the Engineering Institute Rebels and Rebels from Zhongshan Medical Institute and the Institute of Chinese Medicine. The latter two schools argued that the source of the work team mistakes should be pursued to a conclusion, while those at the Engineering Institute felt that the issue had already been resolved when the work teams had acknowledged their errors.

The Third Headquarters, also set up in October, was led by the Rebels from South China Engineering Institute, specifically those who had become prominent because of their participation in the "Letter from Beijing" incident.

Although also favoring the continued criticism of the
work teams, the disagreement within the First Headquarters and their own prominence led them to establish a
separate headquarters. The only headquarters to defend
the work teams had been the Second Headquarters, although
its varied membership seemed to make this headquarters
something of a hodgepodge. For example, in addition to
such staunch work team defenders as the Zhongshan University Regiment, some middle school students of cadre
origin who had not been accepted into the Doctrine Guards
also participated in this headquarters; in some cases the
groups they led had actually been Rebels in their own
schools. The Second Headquarters, in part because of its
support for the work teams, in part because of its internal contradictions, was the first to collapse. It had
already disappeared by the end of 1966. The Zhongshan
University Rebels, who were to become so prominent in
1967, were much less so in 1966. Zhongshan University Red
Flag was not formally set up until November 24, although
a prior Rebel organization had been loosely affiliated
with the First Headquarters.[71]

The first major incident bringing Guangzhou's Rebels
together was the closing of Red Guard News (Hongwei Bao),
known as Yangcheng Wanbao until September 1, 1966. This
incident, which took place on December 13, was important
for several reasons. First, it formalized the alliance
between Guangzhou's Rebels and those from other cities.
Participating in the newspaper's closure were twenty-four
units, including Beijing Aviation Red Flag, Harbin Military Engineering College Red Rebel Corps, Mao Zedong
Thought Red Guard Guangzhou Liaison Center of Wuhan
Universities and Colleges, Zhongshan University Red Flag,
Guangzhou Medical College Red Flag, and South China
Engineering Institute Red Flag.[72]

Second, according to one eyewitness source, it
brought the CCRG more clearly into the picture in support
of the Rebels. Initially, guards from the PLA in front
of the newspaper's offices rejected student demands to
seal the paper. After discussion among the Rebels, contact was made with representatives of the CCRG; Jiang
Qing, although not mentioning the newspaper in particular,
was quoted as saying that she supported all activities
of the Red Guards. The Rebels took this as tacit support
for their action and felt emboldened to challenge the PLA
guards.[73]

Third, it brought the workers into the GPCR for the
first time. In the debate over whether or not the newspaper should be closed down, both the Rebels and the provincial Party committee mobilized working class support,
with the latter more successful because of its control of
the labor union and hence the large factories. Conservative worker organizations, soon to play a major role in
the GPCR, really date from this period.

Fourth, it revealed more clearly a pattern provincial and municipal officials had begun to follow after October, that of bending to rather than resisting the demands of the Rebels. Tao Zhu, for example, acquiesced in the closure of Red Guard News and instructed officials in Guangdong to support the minority who had succeeded in closing it down.[74] In addition, the municipal committee issued a notice to each office unit in Guangzhou requesting cadres not to hinder the activities of the Red Guards in closing the newspaper which, according to the notice, had committed serious mistakes in carrying out the Party's line in art and literature. The notice called the closing a "revolutionary, correct action."[75] This tactic of non-resistance was to be followed during the power seizure as well, causing the Rebels taking power to appear somewhat less than radical.

Fifth, it brought the question of Tao Zhu to the forefront and, in so doing, revealed divisions among the Rebels that would reappear during the January "power seizure" period. In late December some of the Rebels supporting the closure of the newspaper wanted to repudiate Tao Zhu as well, since those in defense of the paper had claimed that, given Tao Zhu's well-known support of the paper, such a closure would be an attack on him. Those supporting an attack at this time included Zhongshan University Red Flag, Pearl River Film Studio East is Red, Harbin Military Engineering Red Rebel Corps, and Beijing Aviation Red Flag; these, in fact, were the same organizations which soon took the lead in seizing power.[76]

Divisions Among Middle School Rebels

During this December-January period of ferment in which the university students were involved in the Red Guard News incident and the criticism of Tao Zhu, middle school Rebels were in the process of setting up their own unified citywide organizations. The two organizations that were to contain the large majority of the city's secondary school students were the Guangzhou Regiment (Guangzhou Bingtuan) and the New First Headquarters Middle School Department (Xinyisi Zhongxuebu). Although these organizations were to collaborate on many issues at a later date, they developed different perspectives based on their different origins. The latter organization had its strongest support in the Western and Central areas of Guangzhou and was led by the Rebels from Number 1 Middle School. The Regiment, on the other hand, was almost exclusively centered in Eastern Guangzhou and was led by a steering committee composed of seven individuals, one each from seven schools with strong Rebel organizations.[77]

The different postures developed by the organiza-

tions stemmed in part from their geographical bases.
Western Guangzhou, as was shown in Chapter One, contained
few cadre or military residences, and in fact had remained an area in which those of bad class background were
overrepresented. Eastern Guangzhou was the district
which contained many of Guangzhou's best schools and was
the location of most of the residences for revolutionary
cadres and military. It was from here that the Doctrine
Guards drew their strength. Their headquarters was
located at August 1 Middle School, but they were also
strong at many of the other Eastern District schools.
The Guangzhou Regiment traced its origin to the chuanlian
work engaged in by small Rebel groups seeking to maintain
contact in the face of strong pressure from the Doctrine
Guards during the "Red Terror" period. Initially, the
Guangzhou Regiment's main task was to thoroughly destroy
the "bourgeois reactionary line" which, in Eastern Guangzhou, had taken the form of blood line theory as carried
out by the Doctrine Guards.
     In the West the issues were different. Although the
blood line theory had been carried out - as indeed it had
all through China - its ferocity had been extremely
limited. Aside from the isolated case of Guangya Middle
School, the Doctrine Guards were not strong in the West;
in fact, even Guangya's Doctrine Guards were equally
active in the East, where the action was. At Number 1
Middle School, the earliest school in the West to rebel,
the issue at first had focused on the Party committee.
Because the municipal committee had taken an active interest in the struggle there, the key issue soon became
one's assessment of the role of that committee in the
GPCR. This concern with cadre assessment was to remain
the major feature of the movement at that school and to
draw it much closer to the university movement. Because
of this concern, Number 1 Middle School very early had
set up relations with Guangzhou's First Headquarters and
had become the founders of that organization's middle
school section. Once the precedent was established,
other schools in the area influenced by the situation at
Number 1 and/or attracted by the prestige of Number 1
Middle School or an affiliation with a university headquarters followed suit and joined the organization.
     Schools in the East at first remained independent of
the various headquarters. In fact, the Guangzhou Regiment tried to maintain its independence throughout the
movement and, because of its ability to mobilize large
numbers of followers in a short time, when it finally
decided in April to affiliate with a larger headquarters,
it was able to exert a great influence on its parent
organization.

THE POWER SEIZURE PERIOD AND ITS ROLE IN THE DEVELOPMENT OF FACTIONALISM

The next, and in retrospect most important, stage in the development of factionalism in Guangzhou was initiated by the "power seizure" which occurred on January 22. Although there is no space to delineate the details of the power seizure, some aspects of it are of relevance to this study.[78] To begin with, the power seizure was discussed and carried out by units which had been involved in the closure of Red Guard News. The defenders of that newspaper made no move to prevent its implementation. Conservative worker organizations which had arisen early in January as a result of the struggle over the newspaper were almost immediately put on the defensive by the fall from power of Tao Zhu on January 4, as the CCRG in Beijing took advantage of the GPCR's radical thrust to purge itself of its more moderate members. Amid rumors that Jiang Qing was personally coming to Guangzhou to struggle against Tao, a criticism rally, sponsored by the provincial committee and the organizations that had previously supported Tao, was held on January 18. Those who had opposed Tao earlier, such as Zhongshan University Red Flag, ridiculed this rally and denounced its participants.[79] When the power seizure came, only a few days later, the Conservative groups were still nursing their wounds and were completely uninvolved.

Second, power was seized by a minority of the Rebel groups, basically the same minority that had in December pushed for a repudiation of Tao but had backed down when some important Rebel organizations felt it was premature. In this instance, however, the more radical wing of the Rebels, led by Zhongshan University Red Flag and outside groups from Beijing, Harbin, and Wuhan had sufficient reason to believe their power seizure was sanctioned by CCRG leaders in Beijing. Lin Jie, a member of the CCRG, on January 19 had given the Beijing liaison station of Zhongshan University Red Flag instructions on seizing power in Guangzhou, urging them, through chuanlian work, to unite with other groups to seize power and to rely on working class participation and leadership. Finding themselves faced with the same reluctance exhibited by the First and the Third Headquarters as had been the case in December, on this occasion they decided to act first and, after accomplishing a fait accompli, seek to bring about broader support after their action had proved successful. The role of the outside Red Guards in this action was extremely important. They had become closely aligned with Zhongshan University Red Flag in December and provided important information on CCRG attitudes, power seizure preparations in the rest of the country and, what was to become perhaps most important, access to and information about the Guangzhou Military Region leadership.[80]

Third, the power seizure proved to be a failure for
several reasons. The provincial and municipal committees
readily gave up their power, so the expected "struggle"
which, it had been hoped, would unite the Rebels by
bringing in those who had initially been reluctant to
participate, never materialized. Those disinclined to
take part felt themselves vindicated by the results of
the seizure. The number of participating units was small
- around 20 - and many of the important ones were from
outside Guangzhou. In fact, both the First and Third
Headquarters accused the outside Red Guards of "befriend-
ing some organizations while dealing blows at others," to
complain about the close ties of these organizations to
Zhongshan University Red Flag. On January 30 several
Rebel organizations, led by South China Engineering Institute Red Flag, went so far as to ransack the liaison
stations of Beijing Aviation Red Flag, Harbin Military
Engineering Institute Red Rebels, and Wuhan Third Headquarters.[81]

The PLA, ostensibly neutral, did nothing to help
those who had seized power. One interviewee from "Zhongshan University August 31" who took part in the power
seizure described how the PLA sent representatives who
"stood in the doorway and watched the proceedings without
saying a word." To the enthusiastic students who were
looking for some encouragement, this kind of PLA discipline and non-intervention was somewhat unsettling.[82]
Officially, the PLA took a wait-and-see attitude; nevertheless, they clashed with the "power seizure faction"
(now known as the Provincial Revolutionary Alliance or
Shenggelian) over several issues. The first clash occurred when the Rebels tried to take over the Guangzhou
Broadcasting Station. The PLA, guarding the station,
supported the station's Conservative majority while resisting the Rebels. Second, the Rebels in their initial
power seizure had declared a takeover of Guangdong's Public Security Bureau. Three days later, Conservative
forces in the Bureau staged a counter power seizure, and
were supported by the PLA. Third, leading Shenggelian
(SGL) units raided the Guangzhou Military Region on
February 8 in a coordinated action taken with Rebels inside the PLA.[83] The origins of the attack actually go
back to the earliest period of the GPCR, when Rebels within the military had been suppressed. It was this February attack that was to prove most costly to the SGL
forces, one they were later to acknowledge as a "mistake."[84]

By February, in fact, the SGL forces were effectively beaten. Erstwhile Rebels, staunch Conservatives, and
the PLA were all arrayed against them. The First Headquarters became so divided over issues related to the
power seizure that they split into three separate parts:

the New First Headquarters, which took a mixed position on the power seizure, recognizing the serious mistakes that had been made; the Red First Headquarters, which firmly opposed the power seizure and became a staunch ' defender of the PLA; and a third group that maintained neutrality. The Third Headquarters continued its animosity toward SGL, even to the point of accepting into its fold the Conservative policemen who had staged the counter power seizure at the Public Security Bureau.

As for the PLA, the February 8 raid provided Huang Yongsheng, Commander of the Guangzhou Military Region, the opportunity to abandon his public neutrality and start taking actions against SGL.[85] In addition, the entrance of the army as an opponent to SGL allowed the dormant Conservative forces that had supported the provincial and municipal Party committees to shift their allegiance to the PLA. February saw the return of Conservative organizations to prominence. The District General Headquarters (dizong) and the Red General Headquarters (hongzong)-worker organizations which had arisen during the struggle to defend Red Guard News, and had later been declared Conservative organizations by SGL - were rehabilitated by an investigation report published in Nanfang Daily on February 25.[86] The Guangzhou liaison station of Nie Yuanzi's New Beijing University Commune put up a wall poster attacking SGL, claiming that the latter's analysis of the GPCR was "upside down" in its assessment of revolutionary and conservative forces.[87] According to informants, the poster further defended the Conservative worker organizations. After its publication in Nanfang Daily in March, six million copies were reprinted for circulation throughout the province.

Ties between Conservative workers, cadres, and the PLA were consolidated during February because of a worsening economic situation. While SGL organizations were still trying to convince other "Rebel" units to join them, the PLA set about reorganizing an orderly and effective system of administration, production, and distribution. Ignoring all forces involved in the SGL imbroglio - including such opponents as the Third Headquarters - leading cadres and workers affiliated to such organizations as the District General Headquarters and the Red General Headquarters were mobilized and de facto power and influence passed to these groups.[88] By March 5 the leadership of the military was formalized when Guangdong was put under a Military Control Committee (MCC). They had even earlier moved swiftly against the remnant SGL forces, banning non-student organizations such as the August 1 Combat Corps and Pearl River East is Red. Because student organizations were protected by Regulation 7 in the 16 Articles, their units were not forcibly abolished, although they were pressured severely. Under PLA auspices the pressure increased throughout March.

Thousands were arrested and listed as members of reactionary organizations. What had perhaps been most damaging to SGL was the fact that the power seizure had never been recognized by the CCRG in Beijing. Without this support of the radicals in Beijing, SGL was denied the legitimacy that might have enabled it to mobilize support and postpone the suppression carried out by the military against its leading members in March.

Middle School Students During the Power Seizure and Its Aftermath

What of Guangzhou's middle school students? At the time of the power seizure, except for the relatively small number of schools having Rebel units belonging to the First Headquarters, middle school Rebels were still in the process of strengthening and expanding their organizations at school level. Although the Guangzhou Regiment had already been set up, it was still unknown; to maintain its independence, it had avoided participating in meetings and discussions with university Rebels.[89] In fact, a good example of the insularity and independence of the Regiment at this time is provided by the first public activity it engaged in. On January 21, a day before the power seizure, the middle school section of the First Headquarters was holding a meeting to criticize Bo Huaiqi and Li Zheng, municipal committee cadres who were responsible for the GPCR in its early stages, including the dispatch of the work teams. The command group of the Guangzhou Regiment, in an effort to become more widely known throughout the city and to strengthen its reputation among its own subordinate units, raided the hall and denounced the meeting for "interfering with the main orientation of the middle school movement, which should be the criticism of the bourgeois reactionary line (viz. the blood line theory) within the schools."[90] Meetings to criticize already fallen cadres, they argued, were a waste of time. Three days later, when SGL was trying to win over the First Headquarters, the latter pointed to this earlier event, to the surprise of the SGL forces:

> The meeting lasted from 2 p.m. till 8 p.m. during which quarrels were very violent. The Guangzhou 1st H.Q. accused "8/31" of Zhongshan University of having sabotaged their "January 21" conference, and said that whether "8/31" was a Rebel group was in doubt. (As a matter of fact "8/31" of Zhongshan University was not aware at all that there was a "January 21" conference, which was held by middle school Rebel groups.)[91]

The incident reveals several things about the relationship between middle school and university students. First, there was a difference of focus between the middle schools affiliated with the First Headquarters and those belonging to the Regiment. The concerns of the former schools - such as cadre assessment and, to some extent, criticism of the work teams - were similar to concerns expressed by university Rebels, where splits had come early; Rebels from schools affiliated with the Regiment, because of the strength of the blood line theory pushed by the children of cadres, were most concerned with this latter phenomenon and, as the GPCR developed, became more and more obsessed with the struggle against the social privileges of these children, and the struggle against their organization - the Doctrine Guards.

Second, given the generally similar concerns of the university and middle school students within the First Headquarters, the headquarters tended to act as a single unit in its ventures; in addition, the middle school section was not really strong enough or independent enough to put pressure on the parent organization. The Guangzhou Regiment, on the other hand, viewed the Doctrine Guards as its main enemy, sometimes setting it at odds with Guangzhou Rebel organizations concerned with larger GPCR issues. Relations between the Regiment and other Rebel forces thus became more a matter of compromises and trade-offs.

In the power seizure itself, the leading units of the Guangzhou Regiment divided over whether or not to support SGL. Favoring support were Number 7, Number 16, and the Railroad Middle School; opposing SGL were Number 21, the Girls' Middle School, and South China Experimental, thus effectively paralyzing the organization. Within each school as well, splits developed so that SGL received very little backing from middle school students.

The First Headquarters Middle School Section, following the parent organization, also split, with the large majority joining the New First Headquarters. The Third Headquarters had not devoted much energy to mobilizing middle school students so that those Rebels in the Guangzhou Regiment opposed to SGL remained unaffiliated. As to the Doctrine Guards, they of course were most vociferous in their opposition to SGL and, in fact, as military training groups moved into Guangzhou's middle schools in late February, the Doctrine Guards were able to use the opportunity to recoup their losses. Finally, the Red First Headquarters at the middle school level became a catch-all organization for those who opposed SGL, supported the military, had split off from the Doctrine Guards earlier or, to hear their opponents tell it, were opportunists who simply wanted to be on the winning side (see Figure 3.1, page 146).

The Key Role of the Military Training Group (MTG)

Military training had originally been scheduled for the students as early as late December 1966, but the order generally was not implemented at that time.[92] On February 19, 1967, however, an eight-point directive was issued by the CCP Central Committee calling on middle school teachers and students to go through a period of "short-term military and political training."[93] After experimental implementation, on March 7, Mao issued a further directive calling on the army to conduct military and political training in universities, middle schools, and higher classes of primary schools, for the purpose of "reopening school classes, strengthening organization, setting up leading bodies on the principle of 'three-in-one' combination and carrying out the task of 'struggle-criticism-transformation'."[94] Although the primary goal of the MTGs was the elimination of factionalism, in most cases they only succeeded in exacerbating the divisions already in existence. Perhaps this was inevitable given the situation they encountered upon entering the secondary schools and the tasks to which they were assigned.

It is important to realize that the MTGs entered the schools during a period of some confusion. Nationally - and in Guangzhou as well - the Rebels had been put on the defensive by the "February Adverse Current." The February 19 Directive had called for the "reorganization, consolidation and development" of the Red Guard organizations. It had emphasized that "Red Guards should be formed mainly of revolutionary students born of families of the laboring people (workers, peasants, soldiers, revolutionary cadres and laborers engaged in other fields)." Students not from these class backgrounds were allowed to join the Red Guards only if they "cherish deep feelings for Chairman Mao, have the proletarian revolutionary spirit and have consistently behaved themselves comparatively well politically and ideologically." This was a return to the July 1966 situation in which once again behavioral criteria were set up only for those of intellectual or bad class background. Nevertheless, because secondary school students were less directly affected by the SGL debate, when the MTGs arrived they often found the Rebels in control and the Conservatives in a passive state. For this reason, the two schools carefully chosen as keypoints for MTG work were marked by a relatively even distribution of power between Rebels and Conservatives and by the absence of any one dominant Red Guard organization. Moreover, the schools - Number 13 and Number 15 - were ordinary schools in terms of pre-Cultural Revolution ranking, and had relatively few children of cadre origin.

When the MTG arrived at Number 13 they found seven Red Guard organizations, ranging from the earliest Red

Guards - the Doctrine Guards - to those who were rather sympathetic to SGL.95 Because of the desire to eliminate factionalism as well as to take class origin into account, the MTG initially supported neither of the extremes - the Doctrine Guards who had propagated the blood line theory or the most vocal of the Rebel groups, which had arisen on the basis of opposition to blood line theory. They rather sought out a moderate organization, the large majority of whose members were children of working class origin. Finding it rather easy to convince this organization to dissolve itself, they next sought to convince the school's other organizations to dissolve as well, preparatory to realizing a great alliance on the basis of the Yanan Middle School in Tianjin, the national model for "great alliance" work.96

Reacting most negatively to the MTG calls for dissolution were those Red Guard organizations that had arisen in January and hence tended to be more sympathetic to SGL. In addition, the members of these units saw MTG control leading to a gradual reliance on pre-GPCR leaders, including some Doctrine Guards. Arguing that the MTG was negating the results of the GPCR, they began cautiously to criticize the latter's policies. To set an example, the MTG singled out six of the most prominent Rebels who had criticized them and subjected them to struggle. This had the effect of polarizing opinion at the school, with the large majority backing the military and a small group of Rebels remaining adamant. In April, after national policy had again shifted and MTG work had been publicly questioned, these two schools - Number 13 and Number 15 - each developed two new umbrella organizations based solely on assessment of the work of the MTG, with those favoring the MTG including more YCL members, students from lower middle school, and girls.

Military training at other secondary schools in Guangzhou was roughly comparable, although most of the MTGs were less successful than those at Numbers 13 and 15 in isolating their schools from outside influences. There were other differences as well. In many schools, particularly those in the East, the MTG arrived to find not a string of relatively small organizations among which they could choose one to use as a focus for a new alignment, but rather encountered one strong Rebel group that had achieved its dominant position in the school in the wake of the attack on the blood line theory. The primary opponents of this group, the Doctrine Guards, had simply stopped coming to school. Facing this kind of situation, the task of the MTG was more difficult. First, they persuaded all students to return to school, bringing the Rebel and Conservative organizations face-to-face. Next, they advocated the dissolution of mass organizations and instituted classes on politics, class education, and the current situation in Guangzhou. While the

results of MTG work varied from school to school, in virtually all cases the period marked a comeback for the
Doctrine Guards and a decline for the Rebels. However,
the MTG was not always successful in its aim of dissolv-
ing existing organizations. In some cases, outward compliance with the viewpoint of the MTG gained time for an
organization so that by the time the tide shifted again,
dissolution had not yet taken place.[97]

The reasons the Rebels were disadvantaged by MTG
work are not hard to find. To begin with, when the MTG
entered a school, the Rebel organization usually was in
control; therefore, a dissolution of existing organizations could only hurt them. In addition, when the military evaluated an organization or individual they used
the general standards adopted by the Provincial and Municipal Military Control Commission. The latter assessed
units on the basis of their relationship to the "four big
events," which included the power seizure and the February attack on the military region. Even though few
middle school Rebels had been involved, most organizations contained at least some members whose sympathies
had been with the perpetrators of these events. This
would often become painfully clear during the classes on
Guangzhou's current situation. Rebels were particularly
upset that value was attached only to the most recent
events; those who in their view had committed mistakes of
an equally serious character in 1966 were left untouched.
Finally, the Rebels were upset by the MTG's reliance on
those of good family origin and pre-Cultural Revolution
prominence in the schools, which they felt was a negation
of the achievements of the GPCR.[98]

Although the Rebels suffered a decline during the
"February Adverse Current" (referred to in Guangzhou as
the "March Black Wind"), particularly in terms of membership figures, their position was far from desperate.
They were, in fact, psychologically much better off than
they had been during the work team period (university
students) and the "Red Terror" (middle school students).
After all, they had recovered from these earlier setbacks.

In some schools where the Rebels had existed as the
minority faction, the loss of members who had been recruited after the successes brought about by the "January
Revolution" did not generally affect the work of the
leading backbone elements. Once again, under the sur-
veillance of their opponents, they secretly maintained
contacts, held meetings, and put up wall posters. In
addition, they had learned to read and use the official
press so that, even in late February and early March when
things were most difficult, they could find items bene-
ficial to their cause. For example, a People's Daily
report of February 24 related how a PLA officer in Shanxi
switched his support from one organization to another in

a Taiyuan factory, after becoming "enlightened."99 A
March 4 report by the Beijing Postage Stamp General Headquarters of the Revolutionary Rebels told a rather similar story.100 Rebels would take articles of this type
and copy and post them, without adding any comments of
their own.

Even those students hit hardest by the clampdown on
the SGL forces were not without encouragement and support.
The leading force in SGL, Zhongshan University Red Flag,
was able to maintain its contacts with Rebel units from
Harbin Military Engineering College and Beijing Aviation
Institute. These liaison personnel, often the sons of
military officials, analyzed for the local students the
reasons for the "March Black Wind"; in addition, they
provided detailed information on the divisions within the
Guangzhou Military Region. Moreover, their contacts with
the CCRG in Beijing furnished them with a picture of the
current situation widely at variance with the local
"official" version being propagated by the military, a
picture they were willing to share with others, much to
the consternation of the Military Region:

> Then our two comrades returned from Beijing.
> They attended several meetings held by Red
> Flag factions of the Provincial Revolutionary
> United (SGL), the Workers' United, the Pearl
> River Studio East-is-Red and some middle
> schools to explain the current situation and
> give them encouragement. On March 4, the
> Guangzhou Military Region, the Guangdong
> Provincial Military District and the Garrison
> put the Military Engineering Rebel Corps
> (Harbin) Liaison Center under their joint
> "military control" in opposition to the Cen-
> tral directive and illegally detained three
> of our comrades.101

Even this measure proved insufficient in cutting off
the ties between local Rebels and outside forces.102
Also of great importance at this time was a small organization consisting primarily of middle school students
called the Revolutionary Steel Poles (<u>Geming Ganggan</u>).
At the height of the March Black Wind they distributed
leaflets and posters in support of the SGL forces. Many
of the members of this small (around 15 members) organization were children of cadres or workers and thus their
actions were less risky than if their backgrounds had
been questionable. The influence of the Revolutionary
Steel Poles was in part due to the fact that their members included students from some of the best and most
prestigious secondary schools in the Eastern District,
such as Huafu, Number 21, August 1, and the Foreign Language School. Through their contacts with Beijing

and Guangzhou Red Guard leaders these students kept Rebel organizations at their own as well as other schools informed of events at the Center and in Guangzhou so that, when conditions did improve, rather than having been set back by the "March Black Wind," the SGL forces had vastly increased their support, particularly among middle school students.[103]

The Turn of the Tide in April

It was the events of April that brought about a sharp turn in the fortunes of the Rebels. The April 2 editorial in People's Daily entitled "Correctly Treat the Revolutionary Little Generals" was said by some informants to have had an impact similar to the October, 1966 editorial in Red Flag in that both opened up a new stage of the movement; the latter had signalled the attack on the "bourgeois reactionary line," the former marked the counter-attack on the "February Adverse Current."[104] An article carried in both People's Daily and Red Flag recounted the experiences of a PLA unit at Nanjing University, emphasizing that, in its support for the Left, the military should not necessarily try to conciliate the two factions.[105]

On April 6, the Central Military Affairs Commission issued a 10 Point Directive that severely limited the power of the PLA in its dealings with the mass organizations. Listing the problems that had arisen in "support the Left" activities, the PLA was now enjoined from declaring mass organizations reactionary, arresting the masses arbitrarily, retaliating against those who had assaulted military organs in the past, adopting a position toward a mass organization and taking action without first submitting a report to the CCRG, forcing the masses to write self-criticisms, and so forth.[106] The PLA was no longer under pressure to choose between competing mass organizations but was now to help the different organizations attain unity on their own, "through self-criticism and normal discussions and debates on the foundation of a unified main orientation...."[107]

For the first time, the MTG at Zhongshan University and the Provincial Military Commission recognized the school's Rebel units as truly revolutionary.[108] The policy changes that became known in early April had a particularly strong effect on the middle school Rebels. They took to the streets with gongs and drums to celebrate. They started ostentatiously displaying their banners and sleeve bands, forbidden when the MTG had sought to dissolve separate Red Guard organizations.

Clearly the most visible support the Rebels received at this time came from the visit of Zhou Enlai to Guangzhou from April 14-18. Although, as was typical of Zhou's style, there was something for both factions in

his talks, the main beneficiaries were the Rebels. Both
factions had eagerly awaited Zhou's words, each expecting
his support. The General (East Wind) faction felt that
the superior class backgrounds of its members and the
backing it had received from the PLA, combined with the
serious mistakes the Rebels had made, guaranteed it a
favorable hearing. The Rebels, well aware of the counter-
attacks on the "February Adverse Current" in Beijing,
were hoping Zhou's visit would lead to the rehabilitation
of Rebel units banned by the Guangzhou Military Region.[109]
    While the General faction was able to cheer Zhou's
reaffirmation of Huang Yongsheng and the PLA, the Rebels
had gotten much more. To begin with, Zhou had declared
that Zhongshan University Red Flag, South China Engineering Institute Red Flag, and Guangzhou Medical Institute
Red Flag were all Leftist organizations, as were the main
Rebel worker organizations (Workers Alliance and Red Flag
Workers). At the same time, he stated that the Red General Headquarters and the District General Headquarters
worker organizations affiliated to the General faction
leaned toward conservatism. He also listened sympatheti-
cally to Rebel complaints about the Doctrine Guards. He
defused two of the most damaging charges against the
Rebels by announcing that 1) the raid on the military
district, while a mistake, was not a big issue, and 2)
Pearl River Film Studio East is Red, one of the leaders
of SGL and banned by the PLA on March 5, was to be rehabilitated. Since the PLA had used the raid and the power
seizure by SGL as its main touchstones for determining a
revolutionary organization, the Rebels were jubilant.
One eyewitness at Zhongshan University has written of the
immediate changes which occurred there:

> At Zhongda the combined effect of the new line
> being followed by the Military Commission and
> Premier Zhou's visit was considerable, and
> showed itself clearly in relation to our Red
> Flag Commune. The Red Flag rapidly regained
> most of its old membership, including many who
> had joined the Rebellious Committee in March,
> and from being completely on the defensive, it
> once again took the offensive. The Rebels
> were jubilant and full of fight.[110]

    Of the university Rebel organizations, the greatest
beneficiary seems to have been Zhongshan University Red
Flag. Although South China Engineering Institute Red
Flag, the leader of the Third Headquarters, had also
received Zhou's approbation, by opposing SGL it had lost
its leadership status among the Rebels. Moreover, in its
own institute, it had not been relied on by the MTG.
Because of its history of rebellion and its overall orientation it had no interest in joining the General

faction; yet its opposition to SGL and support of the Conservatives in the Public Security Bureau prevented it from uniting with Zhongda Red Flag and Guangzhou Medical Institute Red Flag. The latter two organizations, flush with the victory brought about by Zhou's visit, felt that the next task was to complete the work already partially accomplished: the rehabilitation of the remaining organizations and individuals branded as counterrevolutionary because of their participation in the power seizure and the raid on the military region.

The most important of these remaining organizations was the August 1 Combat Corps, a rather complicated unit consisting of discontented workers and demobilized soldiers, a fair number of whom had problems stemming from their bad class backgrounds. The PLA, supported by the East Wind faction, was adamant in refusing to rehabilitate this organization. The SGL faction was equally determined to push for such rehabilitation. They immediately set about creating an organization that would implement these goals. On April 22, they set up the Red Rebel Headquarters (Hongsi zaofan silingbu), called Red Headquarters (Hongsi) for short. Joining the initial preparatory meetings for the Red Headquarters, in addition to the Rebels from Zhongshan University and Guangzhou Medical Institute, were the Guangzhou Regiment, Zhidian Jiangshan (A Rebel group at South China Engineering Institute opposed to the Red Flag organization there), and representatives from the Harbin Military Engineering and Beijing Aviation Institutes, among others.[111]

Although the Third Headquarters underwent some leadership changes and sent a representative to the inaugural meeting of the Red Headquarters,[112] important differences in orientation remained between these two Rebel headquarters. The Third Headquarters argued that the students would be dispersed upon graduation and that the workers would go back to their own units to concentrate on production. Therefore, the key to the success of the GPCR was the cadre question. During the period that SGL was besieged, the Center had begun to alter its position on power seizures. By early February the experience of the Rebels in seizing power in Heilongjiang province was being transmitted throughout China. Relying on the concept of a "three-way alliance," the Rebels there had sought support from within the main targets of the power seizures: the municipal and provincial Party committees.[113] The Third Headquarters had thus, relatively early, started to seek out municipal and provincial Party cadres favorable to its cause, and untarnished by ties to Tao Zhu. This had led it to support such localist cadres as Yin Linping, Zhang Yun, and Lin Jiangyun.

Those in the Red Headquarters, influenced initially by closer ties to the CCRG, and later reinforced in their beliefs by their lack of support from cadres during the dark days of the SGL period, began to entertain the notion that students or ordinary workers could occupy cadre positions and, in fact, guarantee a post-GPCR cadre force more loyal to Mao and the Party Center. They were therefore much slower in reacting to the new policy of "three-way alliance."114

The orientation of the Third Headquarters toward cadres and the Red Headquarters toward students and rehabilitation work remained throughout the GPCR and, although both were members of the Red Flag faction and were similarly opposed to the East Wind faction, at times prevented their close cooperation. The First Headquarters, at one time the strongest of the Rebel forces, had been weakened considerably by its split. The New First Headquarters remained in the Rebel camp, occupying a mid-position between the moderate Third Headquarters and the more radical Red Headquarters.

As for the middle school students, the month of April, capped by Zhou's visit and the birth of the Red Headquarters, led to several important changes. The most immediate was the decline in power of the Doctrine Guards. Rebels who had been on the defensive in March once more gained the upper hand. Even in a key stronghold of the Doctrine Guards such as Guangya, the Rebels by mid-April had, for the first time, emerged as an equal force. The ascension of the Rebels led to several important changes in their adversaries. One phenomenon many interviewees commented upon was the withdrawal, beginning in April, of many of those children of high-level cadre and military background from leading positions in the Doctrine Guards. For example, the children of military leaders such as Huang Yongsheng and Zhan Caifang, who had been prominent up to this time, now dropped out. However, this situation was generally limited to those in senior high. More than ever, the Doctrine Guards became an organization centered in junior middle sections.115 What this meant was that in many schools those who had led the old GPCR Preparatory Committees in 1966 had been replaced by students much less politically sophisticated. Although the Doctrine Guards had declined sharply in numbers, their "class hatred" for the Rebels was stronger than ever, and was almost immediately to lead to armed struggle.

In addition to the departure of those of high-level cadre and military background in senior high, the Doctrine Guards suffered other defections as well. Particularly in the Eastern District schools, a number of students of good class origin, adjusting to the comeback of the Rebels and witnessing the organizational changes in their own units, withdrew from the Doctrine Guards and established a new organization called the Red Revolutionary Alliance (Honggelian). Many of the members of this new organization were of middle-level or lower-level cadre or working class origin. They had remained with the Doctrine Guards, although they generally had not been especially politically active, and in fact had been discriminated against within the organization on the basis of blood line theory. When the Doctrine Guards began to come more and more under the control of junior high students with little discipline, they made their move. The Red Revolutionary Alliance was considered a "Rebel" organization in that its viewpoint was most similar to the Rebel faction; nevertheless, its members retained their belief that the class origins of many Rebels were too "complicated" and refused to unite with them organizationally.[116]

Even some of the stauncher members of the Doctrine Guards were unnerved by the implications of Zhou's April assessment. For example, the Doctrine Guards at Number 6 Middle School, adjacent to Zhongshan University, reacted to Zhou's visit and the birth of the Red Headquarters by organizing a series of visits to Zhongshan University in an effort to probe the response of the Zhongda Rebels to a possible alliance with them. Because of the outraged response from the Rebels at Number 6, among the largest and most loyal of the Rebel forces, the university students had to put a stop to such visits.[117]

The Factional Situation as of Late April 1967

With the establishment of the Red Headquarters on April 22, the main actors in the Guangzhou Cultural Revolution drama were all finally upon the stage. From this point on, the power of the factions would wax and wane, depending on developments in Beijing; still, given the now settled factional alignment, it may be useful to summarize the overall situation prior to looking in more detail at middle school developments.

At the summit, two factions existed; one was called the Red Flag faction (because of the presence of what Zhou Enlai called "the three red flags," (viz., Zhongshan University Red Flag, Guangzhou Medical College Red Flag, and South China Engineering Institute Red Flag) and the other called the East Wind or General faction (because of its assessment of March as a time when the "East wind prevailed over the West wind" as compared to the assessment of the same period by the Red Flag faction as the "March Black Wind" and because of the importance of the District General Headquarters and the Red General Headquarters within the faction).

Members of the Red Flag faction had arisen as "Rebels" in opposition to the control exercised over the movement in the early stages by Party committees and/or work teams (particularly at universities) or to the prevalence of the blood line theory (at secondary schools). In addition, they shared in varying degrees dissatis-

faction with the military control that had been instituted over the province beginning in March. The Red Flag
faction drew its strength primarily from university and
middle school students, although it also received support from various worker organizations, particularly the
younger, more discontented, less established ones.

The East Wind faction owed its strength to its ties
with officialdom which, by spring 1967, meant the PLA.
The East Wind found its greatest support from established,
veteran workers such as those at state factories, and
from cadres at middle-level or above.[118] Their support
in universities was strongest at Guangdong Engineering
College and Zhongshan University but, except in the former school, was no match for Flag faction strength at any
Guangzhou college.[119] Represented by the Doctrine
Guards, its strength at the middle school level was
greatest at two kinds of schools - those with many children of cadre or military origin, most notably August 1
Middle School, Guangya, and the Foreign Language School,
and those schools in factory districts in Southern Guangzhou heavily populated by those of working class origin
and strongly influenced by overall domination in these
areas by East Wind-aligned factory workers.

While the East Wind faction was for the most part
united in its goals, the Flag faction consisted more of
a loosely united congeries of groups "rebelling" for
different reasons. A moderate group was centered around
the Third Headquarters and its leader Gao Xiang; its
strength came from university students, cadres, and
workers. A more radical group was centered around the
Red Headquarters and its leader, Wu Chuanbin. Because
of its radicalism, the Red Headquarters attracted various
kinds of organizations that would have been unacceptable
to any other headquarters. For example, informal ties
were set up with educated youth who had been sent to the
countryside and were now trying to reclaim their right
to urban residency. By focusing its aims on the rehabilitation of those individuals and organizations that had
been declared counterrevolutionary during the January-
March period, the Red Headquarters quite naturally became
the hope of any group or organization that had a grievance stemming from any period of time.

This had several implications. First, it made the
Red Headquarters the prime antagonists of the East Wind
faction, since this latter organization was made up of
those most favored by the status quo. Second, it gave
the Red Headquarters a very powerful contingent during
the phase of armed struggle which began in summer 1967.
Having nowhere else to go, fringe groups established
during the GPCR hoped that loyalty and obedience to the
Red Headquarters would be rewarded by the latter's support for the redress of their grievances. On their part,
the leaders of the Headquarters felt no compunction in

146

using these forces for armed struggle engagements against
East Wind forces. Third, it meant that the class backgrounds of those in the Red Headquarters tended to be
more complicated than those in any other group. These
latter consequences in turn fed the antipathy between the
East Wind and the Red Headquarters. Finally, it also
made it sometimes difficult for the Flag faction to act
as one unit. Although the faction did set up such unified organizations as a preparatory Red Guard Congress
(June 23) and the United Committee to Criticize Tao Zhu
(piTao lianwei) (July 11), these organizations were not
much more than hollow shells rather than "unified command
structures" as one scholar has labelled them.[120] Thus,
for the purposes of armed struggle, the Red Headquarters
felt it necessary to establish and rely on a new organization, the Red Alliance (honglian) limited only to its
own members.[121]

   Diagrammatically, the factional situation is represented in Figure 3.1.

The Factional Situation in Guangzhou as of April 1967

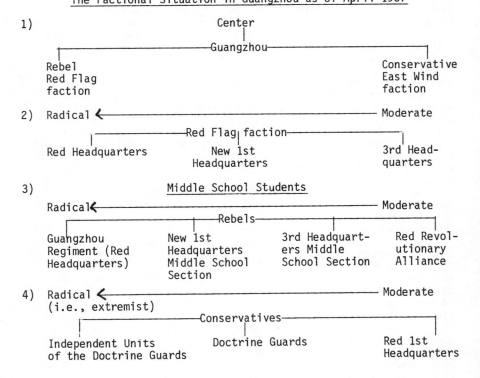

4
Middle School Factionalism in Guangzhou: The Individual Perspective

Given the general picture of the development of factions in Guangzhou drawn in Chapter Three, just which students became members and leaders of the Rebels and of the Conservatives of the Flag and General (East Wind) factions? What links were there between class origin, factional alignment, participation in the GPCR, school quality, YCL membership and leadership position? Most strikingly, as Table 4.1 shows, the conflict between the two factions was a case of "class" warfare.

Table 4.1

The "Class" Composition of Guangzhou's Two Red Guard Factions

(size of sample: 2,187 students, 50 classrooms)

	Red Class	Middle and Bad Class	Total
East Wind Red Guards (Conservatives)	81%	19%	100%
Red Flag Red Guards (Rebels)	26%	74%	100%

Source: Questionnaire remembrances of Hong Kong interviewees.

Table 4.2, below, shows in more precise terms how each of the "class" categories in the student body divided. These results are fully congruent with the picture presented in Chapter Three. The base of Conservative strength in secondary schools consisted of students of revolutionary cadre or military origin while students of middle class, particularly intellectual family origin, formed the base of Rebel strength. A student's class origin, then, tended to be a good indicator of his/her factional alignment. Some of the figures do require further elaboration, however. First, the high rates of nonparticipation by children of bad class origin.

147

Table 4.2

Red Guard Allegiances, By Class Origins[1]

Class Categorization of Father	Factional Alignments of Students				Size of Student Sample
	Red Flag (Rebel)	East Wind (Conservative)	Non-Participant	% Total	
Red-Class Family Background					
"Revolutionary cadre" (listed below by father's status, 1966)					
High-level PLA officer	10%	80%	10%	100%	62
Lower-level PLA	6%	86%	8%	100%	66
High-level civilian cadre	30%	65%	5%	100%	60
Middle-level civilian	32%	61%	7%	100%	79
Local civil-war guerrilla (still mostly rural leaders)	11%	78%	11%	100%	18
Working-class (as of Liberation)					
Industrial worker	36%	41%	23%	100%	442
Poor or lower-middle peasant	23%	36%	41%	100%	95
Middle-class Family Background (as of Liberation)					

Table 4.2 (continued)

Non-intellectual	Red Flag (Rebel)	East Wind (Conservative)	Non-Partici-pant	% total	Size of Student Sample
Peddlars and store clerks, etc.	40%	10%	50%	100%	250
Middle peasant	41%	10%	50%	101%	52
"Intelligentsia" (zhishi fenzi)					
White collar and professionals	61%	7%	32%	100%	562
High level (scientists, profes-sors, etc.)	60%	7%	33%	100%	102
Bad-class					
Overseas Chinese merchant	42%	12%	46%	100%	96
Capitalist	31%	1%	68%	100%	140
KMT official	58%	4%	38%	100%	50
Rightist	31%	4%	65%	100%	26
Rich-peasant	17%	0%	83%	100%	18
"Bad-element"	7%	0%	93%	100%	14
Landlord	33%	3%	64%	100%	39
Counterrevolutionary	31%	0%	69%	100%	16

Total number of students in sample   2,187

Source: Questionnaire remembrances of Hong Kong interviewees. (based on 50 classrooms)

Table 4.3

Cultural Revolution Participation, By Type of School

Cultural Revolution Faction	The Prestige Schools						The Middle Range of 18 Schools			The Neighborhood Junior Highs			Total Students
	1 The Top 4 Schools			2 The Next-Best 8 Schools			3			4			
No. of classrooms in sample	8			13			20			9			
	R	C	N	R	C	N	R	C	N	R	C	N	
Revolutionary Cadre N =	16% 19	76% 93	8% 10	14% 11	76% 60	10% 8	19% 9	77% 37	4% 2	33% 10	60% 18	7% 2	279
Working-class N =	32% 13	55% 22	12% 5	40% 37	35% 32	25% 23	35% 70	45% 91	19% 39	29% 59	34% 68	37% 74	533
Non-intellectual middle class N =	57% 16	7% 2	36% 10	51% 35	7% 5	41% 28	29% 35	7% 8	64% 76	40% 34	18% 15	42% 36	300
Intelligentsia middle class N =	60% 74	6% 8	34% 42	68% 137	10% 21	22% 44	58% 145	6% 14	37% 92	51% 42	5% 4	45% 37	660

Table 4.3 (continued)

	1			2			3			4			
	R	C	N	R	C	N	R	C	N	R	C	N	
Bad-Class	48% 16	6% 2	45% 15	47% 34	4% 3	49% 35	30% 68	2% 5	67% 151	26% 16	11% 7	63% 39	
N =													391
													2,163*

R = Rebels; C = Conservatives; N = Non-participants

*The total is slightly smaller than the total for Table 4.2 because of the elimination of the Provincial Experimental School in this and the following table.

Source: Questionnaire remembrances of Hong Kong interviewees.

Table 4.4

Rates of Participation in the Cultural Revolution
in Junior and Senior High School

| Senior High School | The Prestige Schools | | | | | | The Middle Range of 18 Schools | | | The Neighborhood Junior Highs | | | Total Students |
| | 1 The Top 4 Schools | | | 2 The Next-Best 8 Schools | | | 3 | | | 4 | | | |
	R	C	N	R	C	N	R	C	N	R	C	N	
Revolutionary cadre N =	18% 9	76% 37	6% 3	18% 9	76% 37	6% 3	14% 4	82% 23	4% 1				126
Working class N =	32% 7	59% 13	9% 2	56% 24	35% 15	9% 4	39% 34	45% 40	16% 14				153
Non-intelligentsia middle class N =	54% 13	4% 1	42% 10	85% 28	6% 2	9% 3	26% 24	5% 5	68% 62				148
Intelligentsia middle class N =	66% 56	5% 4	29% 25	81% 107	8% 11	11% 14	56% 101	7% 13	37% 67		None in Sample		398
Bad class and overseas Chinese N =	48% 12	0% 0	52% 13	62% 24	3% 1	36% 14	30% 49	2% 4	67% 108				225
													1,050

Table 4.4 (continued)

Junior High	1			2			3			4			Total Students
	R	C	N	R	C	N	R	C	N	R	C	N	
Revolutionary cadre N =	14% 10	77% 56	10% 7	7% 2	77% 23	17% 5	25% 5	70% 14	5% 1	33% 10	60% 18	7% 2	153
Working class N =	33% 6	50% 9	17% 3	27% 13	35% 17	39% 19	32% 36	46% 51	22% 25	29% 59	34% 68	37% 74	380
Non-intelligentsia middle class N =	75% 3	25% 1	0% 0	20% 7	9% 3	71% 25	39% 11	11% 3	50% 14	40% 34	18% 15	42% 36	152
Intelligentsia middle class N =	46% 18	10% 4	44% 17	43% 30	14% 10	43% 30	63% 44	1% 1	36% 25	51% 42	5% 4	45% 37	262
Bad class N =	50% 4	25% 2	25% 2	30% 10	6% 2	64% 21	30% 19	2% 1	68% 43	26% 16	11% 7	63% 39	166 1,113

Total in Sample =   2,163

R = Rebel; C = Conservative; N = Non-Participant

Source: Questionnaire remembrances of Hong Kong interviewees.

Although it was clear that their sympathies lay with the Rebels, students from bad family backgrounds for the most part avoided overt participation in the movement. This was due to several factors. The influence of their parents, of course, had been important in training them to avoid political controversies. The Cultural Revolution, particularly the Red Terror period, must have strongly reinforced such training. Although it is not apparent from the table, interviewees reported that even when the bad class youths participated - and they almost invariably participated on the Rebel side - they did not do so very actively. Some clearly felt it was dangerous not to participate in the movement, although the majority simply spent the GPCR years in the safety of their homes. Then, too, the Rebels were rather circumspect in their attitude toward the bad class youths, alternately encouraging and discouraging their participation, depending on the climate of the times. The relatively high percentage of youths from Overseas Chinese merchant background participating on the Conservative side can be traced to the fact that they often labelled themselves as Overseas Chinese laborer background and, by 1967 when both factions were in need of manpower, the Doctrine Guards were willing to give them the benefit of the doubt.

The figures on those of working class origin are especially interesting. These children were particularly sought after by both sides. Children of cadres grouped worker-peasant children with themselves as part of the "five reds" and distinguished students in this category from everyone else. Rebels, on the other hand, viewed their own faction as consisting primarily of "children of the laboring people" (including those of worker-peasant background) opposed to the "special privilege faction" made up of those of cadre origin. In this tug-of-war, each side claimed to represent those of worker-peasant origin against the supposed enemies of the latter. To which group did those of worker-peasant origin offer their support?

Three main patterns marked their participation. Early in the GPCR, when the blood line theory was prevalent, the overwhelming majority of those of good class origin, including those from worker-peasant backgrounds, had been supporters of this theory, but not all of them had made it into the initial Red Guard organizations. Moreover, many of those who did were denied positions of leadership by the children of revolutionary cadre and military origin. In some schools, these students of worker-peasant origin set up their own Red Guard organizations prior to the establishment of Rebel strength. By mid-1967, by which time Rebel organizations had been set up and had become firm, these early organizations of worker-peasant students had become caught in a squeeze between the Doctrine Guards led by children of cadres and

the Rebel organizations often led by children of intellectuals. More often than not, under this type of pressure, their organization suffered defections to both
sides (see Chapter Five). In this first pattern, as the
factions began polarizing in 1967, worker-peasant youth
still inclined to participate chose one or the other of
these factions and enrolled as members.

In a second pattern, however, those of worker-peasant
background moved into the Rebel camp after Zhou Enlai's
April 1967 visit to Guangzhou. In this case, recognizing the vulnerability of the Rebels on the class origin
issue and well aware that such a late "awakening" would
prevent them from gaining any leadership role, they chose
not to join any of the existing Rebel organizations but
rather established a new Rebel organization called the
Red Revolutionary Alliance. This second pattern also in
part explains the relatively high percentage of those of
revolutionary cadre origin who were affiliated with the
Rebels. In the latter case, local civilian cadre children stood in contradiction with those of military cadre
background, many of whom they saw as smug, arrogant
Northerners who had never bothered to learn Cantonese
and who generally kept to themselves. It was that assessment, fueled by further slights experienced during
the GPCR, that led to their defection. Particularly in
1967, after the PLA entered the movement, those of localist cadre background found their parents had already
been forced to stand aside and their own status had declined even further vis-a-vis those of military background. This pattern was prevalent most clearly at the
very good schools in Guangzhou's Eastern District.

A third pattern, which also helps account for the
large number of worker-peasant youth joining the Rebels,
is one which typified junior high schools in working
class neighborhoods. In these schools class background
was not the key issue in choosing a faction; indeed,
often a majority of students in the school claimed working class background. More often, Rebels and Conservatives were defined on the basis of attitude toward authority. Conservative students tended to be those who
had been activists and leaders before the GPCR, a situation which continued into the GPCR; Rebels had been less
active and less favored before the GPCR and, in fact, included many who used the signboard of "Rebel" to engage
in undisciplined, disruptive behavior (see Chapter Five).

In other words, whereas large numbers of working
class children were cleaving off from the Conservatives
in the better schools because of conflicts with the
revolutionary cadre children, almost equal proportions
of the working class children in the neighborhood junior
highs were also deserting the Conservative camp on the
basis of activists vs. nonactivists.

As for those of non-PLA cadre origin, in addition to

the reason given above, the 30-32 percent supporting the Rebels included those who had never quite fit into the mold of the typical cadre child, including those uninterested in politics and the YCL, as well as those whose parents were already under a cloud at the time of the GPCR, making them unsuitable for recruitment into the Red Guards.

Table 4.3 above shows the rates of GPCR participation by type of school. Not surprisingly, those of revolutionary cadre origin had the highest levels of participation, regardless of school quality. Even at the poorer schools, where participation rates tended to be low, the small number of cadre children were generally active participants. In fact, participation seems to have been directly related to class origin: the worse a student's background the greater the caution; middle class children declined to participate more often than working class students.

But these figures may be somewhat misleading. What tables cannot bring out, but interviews do, is that students at the less prestigious schools, including many of the working class students there, tended to be more lackluster and less consistent in their participation. Students who prior to the GPCR had been less ambitious at school - who, for example, had wanted to get manual labor jobs after graduation from junior high school - were less eager now to join very actively in the GPCR struggles.

By the same token, although only partially revealed in Table 4.4 above, in-depth interviews suggest that the junior high school students in almost every category of school tended to participate with less intense fervor than their senior high schoolmates. The senior high students had been more "achievement-oriented" before the GPCR. They had been more competitively involved in trying to get into a university, had been more eager to join the League, and had in consequence been more frustrated by the "petty deeds" of their classroom activism. They were now more eager than were the junior high students for the "big deeds" of the GPCR.

The division of classrooms along the lines of activists (Conservatives) and non-activists (Rebels), one feature distinguishing the neighborhood junior highs, was even more visible in the vocational and specialist high schools (Table 4.5). Such schools offered only terminal degrees, with jobs assured at graduation, and so, like the working class junior highs, students at such schools had not had to engage in any intense rivalry to succeed. Resenting those who had been aggressively activist, they moved toward the Rebel camp.

Competition in Chinese schools had been primarily a senior high phenomenon before the GPCR, with the contention focused on YCL membership and university admission. This competition, which had previously led to various

Table 4.5

Red Guard Allegiances at Guangzhou's
Vocational and Specialist Schools

(Sample Size: 5 Classrooms)

	Rebels	Conser-vatives	Non Partici-pants	% Total	Nos. of Students
Revolutionary cadre	29%	36%	36%	101%	14
Working class	65%	34%	1%	100%	68
Non-intelligentsia middle class	57%	9%	35%	101%	23
Intelligentsia middle class	37%	22%	41%	100%	32
Bad class	38%	9%	53%	100%	34
					171

(Note: None of these students are included in any of the other tables, which portray only the academic-track high school system).

Source: Questionnaire remembrances of Hong Kong interviewees.

types of activist behavior, continued into the GPCR. Thus, a comparison of the participation rates of YCL members with those of students in general indicates that, regardless of class background, YCL members were much more likely to participate than were ordinary masses. This finding is not unexpected, insofar as many students were merely continuing their pre-GPCR activist behavior (see Table 4.6).

SOCIAL BACKGROUND CHARACTERISTICS OF REBEL LEADERS

In addition to the aggregate figures derived from the survey questionnaire, an attempt was also made to ascertain characteristics of the leading secondary school Rebels at both school level and citywide in Guangzhou. Taking the most important Rebel leader at each school for which there is data, one finds the following situation with regard to class background:[2]

Middle Background = 22 (includes doctor, teacher, clerk, peddler, shop assistant, etc.)
Working Class Background = 18
Cadre Background = 5
Bad Class Background = 1

Further elaboration of these figures is required.

Table 4.6

League Member Affiliations in the Cultural Revolution

Sample Size: 50 classrooms

	Guangzhou Students in General					League Members				
	Size of Sample	R	C	N	% Total	Size of Sample	R	C	N	% Total
Revolutionary cadre	285	19%	73%	8%	100%	142	21%	73%	6%	100%
Working class	537	34%	40%	26%	100%	146	35%	51%	14%	100%
Non-intelli-gentsia middle class	302	40%	10%	50%	100%	25	56%	12%	32%	100%
Intelligentsia middle class	664	61%	7%	32%	100%	120	77%	11%	12%	100%
Bad class and overseas Chinese	399	36%	4%	60%	100%	37	62%	8%	30%	100%
	2,187					470				

R = Rebel; C = Conservative; N = Non-Participant

Source: Questionnaire remembrances of Hong Kong interviewees.

First, only the most important leader at each middle school has been listed, even if he/she was not the nominal leader. It was quite common for organizations to place members of good background in leadership positions and to send them outside the school as representatives. This was kept in mind during the interview process. Secondly, data on the steering committees (qinwuzu) of school-level Red Guard organizations at the various middle schools reveal an even higher proportion of middle background students than is demonstrated in the figures above. Concerning the figures themselves, many of the 22 middle background students who have been identified as leaders came from the better schools, at which there were large numbers of students of cadre background facing an even larger number of students from intellectual backgrounds. The worker background student leaders came predominantly, but not exclusively, from schools which had only junior middle sections and were considered academically inferior. For example, of the twelve schools having only junior high sections on which data is included, eight had leaders of working class origin. Two of the remaining four leaders were of non-intellectual middle class origin.

The above figures can also be broken down to determine the class background of the leaders at those schools most "active" and/or "important" during the GPCR. This category would include those schools which placed a member on the Standing Committee of the largest and most influential Rebel unit, the Guangzhou Regiment (Numbers 21, 7, 16, 13, Girls' Middle, Railroad Middle and the South China Experimental); the two "true elite" schools (Huafu and Guangya); the leading force in the New First Headquarters Middle School Section (Number 1); the leading force in the Doctrine Guards (August 1st Middle School); other schools with a strong influence on the movement, particularly during the armed struggle period (Numbers 6 and 17). The results appear in Table 4.7.

Table 4.7

The Class Backgrounds of Rebel Leaders in Guangzhou Middle Schools

	Total Schools	Active/Important Schools
Middle Class Background	22	8
Working Class Background	18	3
Cadre Background	5	2
Bad Class Background	1	0
	46	13

Source: Interviews with former Red Guards.

To bring out the importance of the leadership by those of middle background among the Rebels, it is necessary to expand on these figures. Of the two leaders of cadre origin from the active/important schools, one was from the August 1 Middle School, where all students were of high-level cadre origin. The other's father, although a high-level cadre, had already experienced problems in the pre-Cultural Revolution period. The three remaining Rebel leaders of cadre origin also had somewhat special circumstances. One was from the Foreign Language School which, having been established in 1965 when class line emphasis was strong, contained a very high percentage of students of cadre origin. Another was the child of an old Red Army soldier. Because the father had a low cultural level, he was pushed aside after 1949. A group of similarly-treated old soldiers formed a Rebel group during the Cultural Revolution called the "Old Red Army" (lao hong jun). Thus the son's behavior was not surprising. The last Rebel student leader of cadre background was also a special case. This individual, like most cadre children, had advocated the blood line theory in the early period of the Cultural Revolution. But, as soon as the theory was criticized, the student tearfully apologized to the entire student body of his school in a public speech denouncing his former attitude. This show of humility made the student famous in Guangzhou and aroused the ire of his former allies. Even so, the student was unable to extend his Rebel leadership role beyond his own school.

As noted, eight of the Rebel leaders of working class origin came from schools containing only junior high sections. Of the three who were leaders at the more important schools, one was from the Railroad Middle School, where many of the students were children of railway workers. Even at that school, however, the original leader had been of office worker (zhiyuan) background but had died during the armed struggle period. Another was from Huafu which, although it was Guangzhou's best school academically, and had been very influential early in the movement, had become rather unimportant by the time of the factional struggles of 1967.

Most of the key Rebel units were led by students of middle, usually intellectual, background. This was the case, for example, at Number 1, Number 7, and Number 21, among others. The Guangzhou Regiment was led by a student whose parents were intellectuals and four of the seven leaders of that organization were from intellectual backgrounds.[3] Of the other leaders of units which placed individuals on the Guangzhou Regiment's Steering Committee, two were of working class and one of cadre background.[4] This general pattern continued throughout the GPCR. For example, in the latter stages of the movement, when the three largest Rebel middle school units coalesced, there were six leaders, three of middle background and three of worker background. The Commander (_siling_) was of middle background as was one of the two Vice-Commanders (_fu siling_).[5]

YCL Members

When the proportion of YCL members among the Rebel leadership is examined, rather striking results appear. Of the 39 schools on which informants reported on this issue, the top leader at 29 of the schools was a member of the YCL. Of the 13 schools which have been cited as "important" schools, 11 had leaders who were YCL members. In the case of a twelfth school, every member of the steering committee Rebel leadership, except for the top leader, was a YCL member.

At every school on which reasonably detailed information was gathered, at least 50 percent of the Rebel leadership were YCL members (this includes only schools where there were senior high sections). This finding is not surprising, for League members generally were activists and the GPCR was a rare opportunity to demonstrate one's commitment. Every indication is that the large majority of Doctrine Guard leaders, particularly in the earlier part of the GPCR, were also YCL members.

A greater understanding of why so many among the Rebel leadership were YCL members requires a brief reiteration of the pre-GPCR splits in the League. Veteran League members of ordinary or bad class background were being denied cadre posts after 1964; moreover, the emphasis on class origin subjected even newly entering youths to some suspicion if their origin was less than good. When the GPCR arrived and previous emphases on academic achievement and biaoxian began to be questioned, the YCL, although still functioning, quite naturally fell under a cloud. The establishment of the Red Guards in August made the YCL superfluous but, rather than ending the debate on the League, it seemed to lead instead to an increased focus on the revisionist membership policy and character of that organization.

The "five reds," in addition to their gratuitous attacks on the hapless bad class youths, were most harsh on YCL members who were slow to acknowledge the absolute authority of the Red Guards. True, many former YCL members enthusiastically/reluctantly joined the Red Outer Circle, responding to their need for participation in officially-sanctioned activism. Many others, however, particularly those who had been most estranged from 1964-66 YCL policies, were either unwilling or were simply not permitted to join the Outer Circle. The largest number of Rebel leaders seems to have come from this latter group.

A Case Study of the Rise of a Rebel Leader

Leading positions in the Rebel faction were dominated by those of middle background and, to a much
lesser extent, by those of working class background.
Children of cadre and bad class origins were rarely able
to garner leadership positions among the Rebels. To see
why this was the case, it is helpful to examine the
experience of one individual who was later to become the
leader of the Guangzhou Regiment and subsequently the
Commander of all of Guangzhou's middle school Rebels.

In August, having seen a big character poster in
the school citing Chen Boda's advocacy of "breaking
through frames and restrictions such as one's classroom
in order to set up combat teams" and go on "exchange
experience missions" (chuanlian), he and a friend (here-
after called Wen and Chang) decided to attempt to visit
other schools in order to discover how typical the movement at their own school had been. At this time, the
individual schools were under the control of their Red
Guard units and picket squads and still semi-isolated
from each other. Wen and Chang knew that they could not
get permission from the GPCR Preparatory Committee at
their own school for their chuanlian venture; they had
not even been considered reliable enough for entrance to
the Red Outer Circle. They also knew that their class
backgrounds (one was the son of a shop assistant and the
other of an office worker) might cause them problems,
particularly at some of the Eastern District schools
where support for the blood line theory was strong.
They decided to tackle the chengfen issue head-on,
relying on the fact that their class origin was at least
not bad. Each time they visited a school and went to a
classroom they seized the initiative by "reporting their
chengfen" and delivering a set speech:

> We belong to the "sitting on the fence faction"
> (qiqiangpai); looking at things from the class
> viewpoint, we are revolutionary, but we don't
> belong to the group of those who are most revo-
> lutionary. Nevertheless, we want very much to
> do something for the revolution, therefore we
> especially come here to learn from you and hope
> to receive your support.[6]

Using this method they visited schools such as
Numbers 4, 7, 9, 16, 17, 29, 41 and Girls' Middle, among
others. Their only serious problems came, as they
expected, at some of the Eastern District schools. For
example, given the tense atmosphere at Number 7, they
were followed wherever they went in the school. Finally,
the Red Guards at Number 7 checked with their counterparts at Wen and Chang's home school (also in the Eastern

District) and discovered that they were "opportunists
who had absolutely no right to be there" (<u>yiwu shichu</u>).
At most of the schools they visited they were able to
meet, sometimes surreptitiously, with like-minded individuals, gathering information and receiving and offering
advice.

When they returned to their own school they wrote
an article entitled, "The Sitting-on-the-Fence Faction
Also Wants to Rise and Make Revolution." The purpose
of the articles was to encourage the "fence-sitters" to
rise up and take part in the GPCR. They were able to
print up the article in pamphlet form and send it to
individuals at all the schools they had visited, as well
as to all the secondary schools in the city. As a
result of this, students from some of the schools came
to see Wen and Chang for discussions. They also posted
the article at their own school, but no one at this time
came forth with a response.[7]

This early <u>chuanlian</u> experience proved invaluable
when the Rebels later began organizing on a larger scale.
Many of the students who engaged in "illicit" meetings
and discussions dating from this period subsequently
founded combat teams in their schools and became Rebel
leaders. Those of bad class background were in no
position at the time to engage in such activities; they
were under close supervision, the burden they bore because of their class background would have prevented
their successful mobilization of others, and they realized their own vulnerability.

Those of working class origin, on the other hand,
were still being swept along by the new importance being
accorded the concept of <u>chengfen</u>; their dissatisfaction
with the leadership of the children of cadres was not
yet as overt as it was to become. Thus, it was the
"sitting-on-the-fence faction" - <u>viz</u>., those of middle
class background - who organized and led the early Rebel
combat teams, particularly in the more prestigious
schools.

When students of working class origin - and some of
cadre background as well - later became disenchanted with
their own early Red Guard organizations, the growing
Rebel units welcomed their participation and some actually rose to leadership positions. Nevertheless, a Rebel
leader's prestige was based on two standards: 1) how
early he/she had rebelled; and 2) how he/she had performed when circumstances were toughest. In the case
of secondary school students, circumstances were most
difficult at the time of the blood line theory and the
Red Terror in August-September 1966, and during the
March Black Wind of 1967. Both these periods were marked
by a strong stress on class origin and a crackdown on
Rebel activity.

Having already been the earliest to rebel in August-

September 1966, students of middle class origin had become leaders of Rebel Red Guard units by early 1967.
When the March crackdown occurred, particularly with its
renewed stress on chengfen, these leaders once more became the most persistent holdouts. A fair number of
those of working class and cadre origin who had begun
drifting to the Rebel side after the January Revolution
found the reliance on chengfen by the MTG much to their
liking.[8]
  There were few changes among the Rebel leadership
during the course of the GPCR. Those who rose initially,
in the majority of cases as a result of opposition to
the blood line theory, tended to remain in leadership
positions for the remainder of the movement.

Leadership Patterns Among Conservative Middle School Students

  It has been rather more difficult to determine the
leadership of the Doctrine Guards in any great detail,
but some points seem clear. First, virtually all leaders of the Doctrine Guards seem to have been of good
class origin. This was, in fact, an important qualification for leadership. Second, the early leaders of the
Doctrine Guards were almost uniformly of cadre origin,
except in those schools having few or none from such
origins.[9] Third, as time went on, there were a number
of leadership changes in the organization. These changes
were characterized by a tendency on the part of those
of high-level cadre background in senior high to relin-
quish their leadership positions during the course of
the GPCR.
  This occurred in several stages. As early as
October 1966, Chen Boda had criticized the monopoly over
leadership positions exercised by children of cadres.
At least in Guangzhou, however, the real impetus came
with Zhou Enlai's April support for the Rebels. A number of interviewees who were Rebel leaders pointed to a
very visible modification in their opponents at this
time: those of high-level cadre background either
stopped coming to school or, when they did show up,
adopted a very low profile.
  The Rebels attributed the withdrawal of the children of military and civilian cadres to the fears of
senior military officers:

  If the children of army officers and cadres
  rise to rebel and expose their fathers'
  secrets, it would mean the end of their
  old men. So, an order was issued by the

Military Region that it should organize all
children of army officers and cadres to do
labor at the farms, and if the children
refused to go, their parents would take the
blame and be criticized.... The senior
officers of the Guangzhou Military Region
were afraid of their children and had long
let them run away. Some children have gone
to Beijing by air to take refuge while
others are recuperating in Lofou Mountain.
Thus we can see that the handful of "people in authority taking the capitalist road"
in the Party are trying to send away all
the Doctrine Guard children of army officers
and cadres to prevent them from being involved in violent struggles and ensure their
safety. But, they push the broad Doctrine
Guards from peasant-worker families to the
first line, equip them with better weapons
and encourage them to carry on violent
struggles. (They) try to bury the children
of the laboring people with themselves....10

The last stage in this process was in spring, 1968.
Many of the remaining children of cadres dropped out at
this time. Some Rebels claimed that this development
was in response to a Central directive on this issue.
In addition, the military had begun recruiting again
and many of those who entered the PLA were of cadre
background. Moreover, and related to the above phenomena, there was the increasing transformation of the
Doctrine Guards into an organization centered in lower
middle sections. With its heavy concentrations of students from good class backgrounds, junior high sections
had always been a fertile recruiting ground for the
Doctrine Guards. It was the withdrawal of much of the
senior high leadership, however, that for the first time
opened positions at the top to the secondary leaders and
rank-and-file members in junior high.

Finally, the Doctrine Guards occupied a different
position within the East Wind faction than did the middle
school Rebels in the Flag faction. This relates to the
different overall nature of the two factions. The Flag
faction tended to be a loose grouping of many different
units, encompassing a variety of viewpoints. Often,
they were at odds on goals, strategy and tactics. They
were united, however, by a general opposition to certain
aspects of the existing situation. In addition, the
major strength of the Rebels came from its student
organizations.

The East Wind faction, on the other hand, was much
less divided by internal differences; indeed, their goal

was a defense of the status quo which, by mid-1967 in
Guangzhou, meant support for the PLA's leadership of the
movement there. The source of East Wind strength was
workers and cadres, not students. This situation allowed
for much greater freedom of action among middle school
Rebels. They could choose to join one of three different
headquarters. Even within the same headquarters they
could choose to support or oppose a given action or a
given group as they deemed fit. Thus, some units within
the Red Headquarters refused to participate when the
parent group called a hunger strike in May. Thus, some
units also strongly backed certain of the sent-down youth
groups while others regarded such backing as politically
naive and damaging to the overall goals of the headquarters.

The Doctrine Guards was politically a much more
tightly controlled organization. Divisions which were
necessarily tolerated if the Flag faction was not to
break apart were not indulged within the General faction.
True, in many ways the junior high school Doctrine Guards
were rather undisciplined, but this was a matter of
personal behavior, not political stance. Southern
Guangzhou, with its large factories and rather recently
established neighborhood junior high schools, became
the major source of strength of both the East Wind
faction and the Doctrine Guards. According to informants,
the Doctrine Guards in this district spent most of their
time in the factories controlled by the District General
Headquarters (dizong), rather than at their own schools.

5
Middle School Factionalism in Guangzhou: The School Perspective

If the GPCR elicited varied reactions from Guangzhou's secondary school students, with one's class background the key determinant of behavior, the GPCR likewise varied from school to school. Although the major events of this massive movement reached all schools, the impact of the events was far from uniform. Each school had particular characteristics that made factional formation different from one school to the next. In a few schools the Party committees or outside work teams were opposed right from the start of the GPCR; in most schools, however, there was little or no opposition to these authoritative groups until much later. In some schools the blood line theory was implemented particularly forcefully; in other schools, the issue of class origin was somewhat less crucial in determining factional formation. This is not to argue, of course, that the development of factions was in any way random or unclassifiable. Quite the contrary. As was previously shown, Guangzhou's schools could be divided into four types: "true elite," "good," "ordinary," and "poor." Schools within each type shared common characteristics, such as similar student bodies, promotion rates, rankings, and so forth. In seeking to discern patterns of factional formation, it seems promising once again to treat these four types of schools separately, and to subject selected individual schools to more detailed examination.

In selecting the individual schools to be examined, a primary criterion has been the "importance" of the school. Thus, the majority of the schools chosen were among Guangzhou's best before the GPCR and/or were most prominent during the GPCR as well. The development of factional splits at true elite and good schools has been stressed not only because these schools often strongly influenced developments at ordinary and poor schools, but also because the use of these schools as examples will illustrate a major theme of this book - that the crucial factional division at the secondary schools was between

167

those of cadre origin and those of middle class origin,
and that it was on the issue of blood line theory that
the division finally became clear. Although this generalization will require qualification as a result of the
case studies introduced in this chapter, the choice of
schools containing both students of cadre and middle class
origin is a necessity. To provide some balance the GPCR
process at ordinary and poor schools will also be analyzed.

Only two schools in Guangzhou have been designated
"true elite," and both will be treated in some detail.
Huafu, in particular, is important because of its key
influence on other schools up until August 1966.

The "good" schools will be represented by Girls'
Middle, although to give some idea of the diversity of
the GPCR at these schools, shorter accounts of events at
Numbers 1, 6, and 7 are provided.

Number 7 and Girls' Middle are in Eastern Guangzhou
and had roughly similar student bodies. They both became
leading members of the Guangzhou Regiment, but there were
some interesting differences in their internal developments that are worth examining. Number 6 Middle School
in Southern Guangzhou is of interest because of its diverse student body, encompassing significant numbers of
children of cadres, workers, and intellectuals, a unique
situation for Guangzhou. Number 1 Middle School was important because its leading Rebel unit exercised uncontested control over the middle school division of the
New First Headquarters. Further, the GPCR pattern at
this school was unusual, giving the school fame/notoriety
far beyond its confines in Western Guangzhou.

Since the Red Guard newspapers that have reached the
West from Guangzhou rarely are concerned with individual
middle schools, much of the information in this chapter
is based on interviews with students from the schools sur-
veyed. In some cases many students from the same school
have been interviewed, including one or more of the
school's top Rebel leaders. In rarer cases, active members of the Conservative Red Guards have been interviewed,
although none was the top leader at school level.[1]

TRUE ELITE SCHOOLS[2]

1. Huafu: As Guangzhou's best middle school, containing a high proportion of both students of cadre origin and intellectual origin, and boasting the highest
university promotion rate of any school in the city, it
is not surprising that Huafu should have reacted to the
GPCR earliest among Guangzhou's middle schools. Although
the early student split at the school was unique in
Guangzhou, it is worth considering both because of its
importance in stimulating rebellion at other schools,
particularly in the Eastern District, and because the

nature of its student body comes closest to matching the
elite middle schools attached to Beijing's universities,
and may tell us something about those schools as well.

The earliest dazibao at the school was put up on
May 27, five days before the broadcast of Nie Yuanzi's
poster at Beijing University. The poster was written by
the son of the Vice-Governor of Guizhou province (sur-
named Li), and raised three reasons for dissatisfaction
with the school's principal/Party secretary Wang Bingshan.
First, Huafu had a school regulation which stated that
during vacation periods it was still necessary to return
to school to participate in one day's labor. Violators
were not permitted to register. During winter vacation
(1965-66), Li went to Guizhou for his vacation. When he
returned the school authorities chastised him for non-
compliance with the school regulation and at first refused to allow him to register. Li's defense was that he
had already labored in a local commune in Guizhou and
only after a lengthy argument was he allowed to register.
The poster pointed, then, to the lack of reasonableness
in school regulations and their enforcement. Li, who
brought no proof that he had actually done the required
labor, felt that his word should have been sufficient.
The second grievance brought to light by Li referred to
an incident which had occurred in a politics class.
Instead of listening to the teacher, Li openly read The
Red Flag Waves, a book containing the revolutionary
memoirs of high leaders. The book was confiscated by
the teacher; this was now condemned by Li as an example
of the school's emphasis on revisionist traditional
education. Finally, he complained that politics at the
school had for a long time taken second place to educational matters.

Li was motivated to write his poster by two external
events. Tao Zhu had spoken at Guangzhou's Zhongshan
Memorial Hall at the end of May on how to mobilize for
the Cultural Revolution. Tao had given a report criticizing Three Family Village, a newspaper column written
by Wu Han, Deng Tuo and Liao Mosha from 1961-64, criticizing Maoist policies. The storm over culture and education policy was already becoming visible. In addition,
Li had seen a copy of Mao's 1964 discussion with his
niece Wang Hairong at which Mao pointed out that school
regulations were not sacrosanct and rebellion against
unreasonable regulations was praiseworthy.[3]

Opposition to Li by other students in the school
came quickly. Posters went up accusing him of "merely
venting his own private anger and seeking revenge" as
well as opposing the school's Party committee. But Li
was not without defenders. Eventually, eleven students
of high-level cadre background, referring to themselves
as the "Huafu Eleven" supported Li's poster. These were
students from senior middle three who had transferred

from August 1st Middle School, Guangzhou's only school for children of high-level military cadres. Most were children of military cadres from outside of Guangdong province; eight of the eleven were in classroom two of senior high three. Opposed to this first group was a group centered around the children of high-level cadres affiliated to the Guangdong Provincial Party Committee. Their argument rested on the fact that the Huafu Eleven had no evidence against the Party committee, only some selfish and petty complaints. They, in turn, pointed to the school's Educational Affairs head, Mai Jiaxiang, as more closely approximating a "Three-Family-Village-type."

With the broadcast of Nie Yuanzi's poster from Beijing, coupled with the People's Daily editorials to "Sweep away all ghosts and monsters," the Party committee more actively started to try to lead the movement, focusing the spearhead squarely at Mai. In these early days, the Huafu Eleven were isolated. The students opposing Mai had detailed material to use against him, some of it gathered from the Party committee, some from their own experiences with him; those opposing the Party committee, however, had no such evidence. They, too, had no love for Mai but, having committed themselves, could not move to the anti-Mai bandwagon without abandoning their position as "rebels" and "leaders." Children of worker-peasant background, greatly under-represented at the school, quite naturally supported those defending the Party committee. Students of intellectual background, while more sympathetic with the rebellion of the Eleven, generally were non-participants. For example, when the students of Huafu wrote a letter of determination concerning the abolition of the examination system, as was common in June 1966, many children of intellectual background in senior high refused to sign their names.

On June 4, the provincial Party committee sent a work team to the school. The work team sought to unify the movement by taking over all power and suspending Mai Jiaxiang from all duties. They also organized a large-scale struggle meeting against Mai at which they hoped to set up a provisional student organization to take the place of the collapsed YCL and Student Council. Chief delegates were to be chosen for a presidium, using the Paris Commune style. Each class was to send one representative. Since the Eleven were in a small minority, they insisted that they all be elected. The work team produced a counter-proposal, offering the Eleven a proportional representative system which would guarantee them a representative on the presidium. The Eleven refused and the work team relied more and more on the group centered around the children of provincial-level cadres. In their turn, the Eleven became more open in their opposition to the work team's leadership of the movement. Opposition to the work team in Beijing University was known to them and further boosted their confidence.

The provincial committee dispatched Zhang Yun, an alternate secretary of the provincial Party committee, to the school to investigate the dispute. He supported the work team policy. Lin Liming, of the provincial Party secretariat, also made an appearance, but the Eleven maintained their defiance.[4] Zhang Yun's report to the provincial Party committee emphasized that these cadre children had a superiority complex and were easily misled by bad people. He proposed that their families order them home and help to reeducate them.

By August, however, the work teams had been ordered to withdraw. Tao Zhu, still active in the GPCR in Guangzhou, phoned the provincial committee and directed the Huafu work team to make a self-examination. Lin Liming announced that the work team had committed mistakes at the previous stage and had been "prejudiced" against the eleven Rebels. At the same time, a struggle meeting was set up to criticize the vice-head of the work team. The Huafu Eleven were able to return to the school as heroes.

On August 14, with the withdrawal of the work team and the return of the Eleven, students from August 1st Middle School went to Huafu to demonstrate their support for Huafu's Rebels. At the same time, however, they posted the couplet on the blood relationship theory (xuetong lun) previously discussed. It was at this point that the debate on the work team finally closed. Thereafter the issue which occupied the students' attention was the assessment of the couplet. Up until this point the struggle had been between the Huafu Eleven and the students led by the children of provincial-level cadres. On the issue of the couplet, however, these two groups generally found a common ground. The debates conducted at Huafu attracted students from all over Guangzhou, particularly students in the Eastern District. Given the sudden unity of the school's two leading student groups, coupled with the prestige of the Huafu Eleven as vindicated Rebels, those opposing the couplet were very much a minority. Some of the more ambitious children of intellectuals went to Guangzhou's Diesel Oil Factory and set up a forum with twenty veteran workers on the couplet. They later wrote up a lengthy investigation report documenting their visit and demonstrating the workers' opposition to the couplet.

Such investigations and reasoned debate were immediately overwhelmed by events. The establishment of Red Guard organizations as quickly as possible had become the order of the day. Two Red Guard organizations were established, again focused around the two groups of cadre children. Worker-peasant background children joined one or the other organization, but the prevalence of the blood line theory prevented those of middle or bad background from participating.

This Huafu pattern of development was later to contribute to the stagnation of the student movement at the school. When the blood line theory came under strong criticism, the organization headed by children of provincial-level cadres started to "rebel" but found their reputation as "royalists" and defenders of the Party committee, the work team and the blood line theory made it impossible for them actively to mobilize students from less favored family backgrounds.

Students from intellectual backgrounds started organizing combat teams late in 1966 but for many reasons were never able to create a firm, strong organization. First, students at Huafu from non-cadre backgrounds were excellent students, and many potential Rebels simply went home and devoted themselves to reading and studying for the duration of the GPCR. (It was commonly said that Huafu had the highest percentage of students wearing glasses in Guangzhou.) Second, the early Conservative-Rebel split at the school shifted after the criticism of the "bourgeois reactionary line" (zifanxian). The Huafu Eleven and their supporters moved to the right while their erstwhile opponents shifted to the left. This led to a situation characterized by the lack of a single focal point around which Rebels could unite. Later, when the Rebel faction in Guangzhou was under strong attack - in March, 1967 - a few of the Huafu Rebels of high-level cadre background were to play a significant role, but as individuals, not as representatives of their school. This issue of early or late rebellion remained an important factor both in keeping the two factions divided as well as in obstructing the Rebels in their attempts at intra-factional unity.

The early development of the GPCR at Huafu is noteworthy on several counts. To begin with, it presents a clear instance of one important source of rebellion: dissatisfaction by children of high-level cadres. The Huafu pattern was most likely, however, in a school with the following characteristics: a) children of high-level cadre or military background, a significant number of whom came from provinces other than Guangdong; and b) children of high-level cadre background whose parents were tied to either the municipal or provincial Party committee or to the South-Central Bureau. What seemed especially important in the Huafu case, according to interviewees, were the splits between children of military and civilian cadres and outsiders and localists. While there are indications that certain aspects of this pattern were somewhat more common in Beijing, no other school in Guangzhou had quite this situation. The Huafu Eleven were allowed to rebel because of their status. For example, they could treat the original work team

sent to Huafu in a cavalier manner because the head of
the work team was only a deputy division chief (_fu
chuzhang_) of the Central-South Bureau. The deputy head
of the team was a cadre from the Shaoguan district of
Guangdong. Since the parents of these students had higher ranks than anyone on the work team, they felt rather
secure in their activities. Even Zhao Ziyang, Tao Zhu
and Huang Yongsheng approached these Huafu Rebels very
cautiously. When word got out, early in the GPCR, that
these eleven students were going to put up a poster
saying "bombard the provincial Party committee," Zhao
Ziyang invited their leader, Cai Xiaoyan, to his office
in an attempt to persuade him to delay this action. At
that time the Party Center had an investigation group
coming to Guangzhou and Zhao was worried about the effect
this poster would have on their visit. Nevertheless,
Cai was unmoved and the students went ahead with their
poster.[5] Tao Zhu was also aware of the danger these
well-connected Rebels posed. As one Red Guard paper put
it:

> On October 4, Tao Zhu gave the Central-South
> Bureau and the Guangdong Provincial Party
> Committee his black instruction: "The Prob-
> lem of the Guangdong Provincial East-is-Red
> School (the new name of Huafu) should be
> solved internally. Don't enlarge the issue
> or make it complicated. Don't let it be
> known to the society." At the same time,
> Tao Zhu gave similar instructions to Huang
> Yongsheng at home over the long-distance
> telephone.[6]

Huang Yongsheng sought to isolate these same students not by frontal assault but by putting pressure on
other Red Guards in Guangzhou over whom he had control
not to participate in any actions with the Huafu Eleven.[7]

2. _Guangya Middle School_: Guangya superficially
shared many traits with Huafu. Some of the characteristics of Guangya's student body and its promotion system
and the consequences of these characteristics on GPCR
factionalism have already been discussed in Chapter One.
For example, like Huafu the school included many of high-
level cadre background and many of intellectual background. There was a high promotion rate to the university, although it was clearly lower than the Huafu rate.
Some important differences between the two best schools
in Guangzhou did exist, however, and these contributed
to making the movement at the two schools rather
different.

To begin with, as noted in Chapter One, Guangya
seems to have promoted the class line policy after 1964

rather more strongly than Huafu. With over 75% of the
students entering in 1964 and 1965 of cadre background
(many from military families), there was a ready-made
constituency among those in first and second year junior
high for the most extreme forms of the blood line theory.
A number of interviewees from the two schools advanced
the view that Guangya, which had been universally recognized as the top middle school in Guangzhou throughout
the 1950s, had lost its leading role to Huafu in the
1960s and so, by recruiting almost exclusively children
of cadres, sought to ride the class line policy back to
the top. Another difference between the schools was
their geographical location. Because Guangya is in the
northwest of Guangzhou, in an area not heavily populated
by high-level cadres or intellectuals, and containing no
other schools with heavy concentrations of children from
the aforementioned two groups, the GPCR could be carried
out there in a more controlled fashion. Whereas Huafu,
in addition to being situated in the university district
of Guangzhou, early in the GPCR served as a focal point
for other schools in Eastern Guangzhou, Guangya was most
heavily influenced by the extremist United Action Red
Guards from Beijing, who in their turn received their
warmest welcome from the cadre children in lower middle
school at Guangya.

Soon after the start of the GPCR, the children of
high-level cadres at Guangya set up an organization
called the "Committee of the Children of High-level
Cadres." They assumed the leadership over school affairs
as a matter of course, limiting the committee's membership to those students whose fathers held the cadre rank
of 13-level or above. In each class this committee
established a small group based on similar principles.
With the arrival of the work team, the committee was
altered to become a "Cultural Revolution Preparatory
Committee" and its membership was expanded to include
children whose parents were of cadre rank below the 13-
level, as well as some of worker-peasant background.
High-level cadre children still controlled the movement,
however. With the establishment of Red Guard organizations, the high-level cadre children set up an organization called the Mao Zedong Thought Red Guards (sixiang
bing), again limited only to those whose parents were of
13-level or above. Because there were many of good class
origin who objected to this monopolization of power,
another organization called the Maoism Red Guards (zhuyi
bing) was set up, on the basis of the five red categories.
With the establishment of this latter organization, not
wishing to be outflanked, the Mao Thought Red Guards
decided to set up an auxiliary subordinate organization
for those not of five red category origin who had good
biaoxian.[8]

Due to the influence of the chuanlian movement, students of ordinary class background started participating more directly and set up many small combat teams. They drew their membership generally from those who had been in auxiliary organizations (which began folding in December, 1966), those who had not previously participated, and some who had come over from the Maoism Red Guards or the Mao Thought Red Guards after the blood line theory had begun to be criticized. Complicating matters was the arrival at this same time of Red Guards from Beijing who were members of the notorious United Action Committee; having moved to the defensive as the Beijing Red Guard movement took a more radical turn, they sought to escape the pressure they faced in the capital by fanning out to the provinces.

By January, 1967, there were four organizations at the school. One group (the Mao Thought Red Guards) was still centered around those whose parents were high-level cadres. A second group (the Independent Brigade), based among students in lower middle, was set up with the help of the United Action Red Guards. They promoted the blood line policy even more strongly than the first group, doling out either velvet or silk sleeve badges depending on whether the father's rank was eleven-level or below. This group was to remain active at the school throughout the GPCR, refusing to accept the authority of the Conservative faction either at the school or the citywide level. The third organization (the Maoism Red Guards) was made up mostly of students of worker-peasant background. In 1966, these students had been the main opposition to the children of cadres, but in 1967, with the rise of the Rebels, mainly on the issue of opposition to the blood line theory, this group became progressively weaker. Some of its members eventually joined the Rebels, some moved to the aforementioned Mao Thought Red Guards when, as most organizations were forced to do, the latter revised its strict entrance requirements. In any event, given the relatively small numbers of worker-peasant students at the school, it is not surprising that this organization was not a strong one. The fourth organization was really nothing more than a series of combat teams, with very loose ties. It was only by mid-April, 1967 that the Rebel faction was able to set up a relatively unified organization, and even then only because of a concerted attack on the school by other Rebel organizations from Guangzhou's Western District.

The delayed development of a firm Rebel unit at Guangya had certain consequences for the movement at the school. First, it meant that when the Military Training Group (MTG) arrived at the school in March, 1967 there were only two reasonably firm organizations - the Mao

Thought Red Guards and the Maoism Red Guards; both were
Conservative and both recruited almost exclusively those
who were of good class origin. The Rebel combat teams,
having no firm organization, had already collapsed by
the time of the March Black Wind. This made the job of
the MTG much easier. Unlike the situation at most
schools, there were no Rebel units which had seized power
during the January Revolution or had developed sympathies
for SGL and now had to be convinced to dissolve their
organizations in the interests of unity. Therefore, at
Guangya the assessment of the MTG, which played such a
big part at so many Guangzhou secondary schools, was not
a key issue.

Second, it meant that when the Rebels finally did
set up a unified organization (on April 10), the leadership included a surprising number of children of cadre
origin. As has been shown, Rebel units at most of the
good schools traced their origins to the anti-blood line
theory movement. Those who became leaders at that time
generally remained so for the remainder of the GPCR. At
Guangya, however, this counter-movement was retarded by
the control of those of good class background. When the
Rebels came together after the tide had turned in April,
there were few whose revolutionary merits were conspic-
uous or long-standing. The united organization (called
Guangya April 10th Red Rebel Regiment) took into its
"service group" (qinwuzu) those who were leading prominent combat teams. By this time some children of cadres
had split off from the two Conservative organizations and
were leading their own "Rebel" combat teams, generally
supporting the Flag faction. They therefore were in-
corporated into Guangya's overall Rebel command. In
fact, of the nine members of "April 10th's" service
group, four were of cadre origin, three of intellectual
origin, one of working class origin and one of bad class
origin, a very untypical situation for Guangzhou.

Third, because "April 10th" was an umbrella organization consisting essentially of a melange of independent
combat teams, it remained independent of the different
Rebel headquarters which existed at the citywide level.
Nevertheless, some of its subordinate units freely joined
one or another of the headquarters.

At the school level, April 10th was the main opposition for the Mao Thought Red Guards, who were affiliated
to the Doctrine Guards citywide. Guangya's Rebels, however, were generally much more concerned with issues
relating to their own school than they were with the
overall municipal factional struggle. Indeed, the newspapers printed by April 10th which are available to us
deal primarily with internal issues, particularly the
elitism of education at Guangya.[9]

Summarizing then, neither of Guangzhou's two best

schools were an important source of Rebel strength. In both schools it was the children of cadre origin who dominated the movement. Children of middle class origin, so important to the Rebel cause in many schools, were unable or unwilling to exert such influence at Huafu or Guangya. For one thing, their numbers were smaller at these two schools. One Rebel from Guangya estimated that children of high-level cadre background occupied 70% of the places in junior high and 25% in senior high.

One of the Guangzhou Regiment's top leaders claimed that this was only part of the problem. In explaining why Huafu and Guangya did not produce strong Rebel contingents he argued that the students at these two schools were "aloof" (qinggao) in their dealings with others attending less prestigious schools and preferred to act independently. Indeed, Guangya Rebels explicitly recognized the validity of this criticism. As they wrote in their newspaper in 1968:

> Under the influence of feudal, capitalist and revisionist education, among not a few of our Guangya classmates there has flourished a kind of "Guangya chauvinism" (da Guangya zhuyi), and a disparagement of other schools. Some schoolmates even go to the point of cursing other schools as "schools for the mean people in society," "low-class vulgar types" (diji shikui). When comrades in arms from some schools have heart-to-heart talks with us they say: "As soon as we talk with you people from Guangya we immediately feel a bit fearful and restrained."10

The Good Schools

It is to those schools we have categorized as "good" rather than the two elite schools that we must look for Rebel strength. The reasons for this seem rooted in the social class backgrounds of the students in these schools as well as in the quality of the schools themselves. Guangya and Huafu were the cream of the cream. One found children with the most favored chengfen and students with the best academic records. One also found high promotion rates to the university. There was something of a modus vivendi between these two groups, however, particularly in senior high. One's entrance to either of these schools was a cause for celebration; chances for continuation to the university were very good indeed. Thus, the disparagement of other schools indicated by the quote above is not surprising.

Although YCL membership in these two schools was rather high, part of the reason for this was the number of students in the schools of cadre origin (of whom a

high percentage were members), and part was due to recruitment to the League of those of outstanding academic
achievement prior to 1964. I interviewed a fair number
of students at Huafu, however, who felt that academic
achievement and the benefits of a Huafu education would
obviate the need for intense political activism. Hence,
they spent most of their time studying, content to let
others achieve activist status.

At the "good" schools, however, a different atmosphere prevailed. Students of middle class origin at
these schools were, like their counterparts at Guangya
and Huafu, relying on academic achievement for university
entrance. In addition, though, they generally seemed
to realize the importance of biaoxian. Rejected by (or
in many cases not daring to apply to) the two top schools,
students at the good schools who relied on academic
achievement had less reason to feel their grades alone
would be sufficient to carry them through. Judging from
reports of interviewees, activist competition and competition to join the YCL at these schools was more intense
than at Huafu or Guangya. It was of more significance
for their future prospects. In these schools there was
less of the "unity" which derived from merely being a
student at Guangya or Huafu and partaking of its great
tradition, particularly as school officials and teachers
at these latter two schools continually stressed the
"Guangya (or Huafu) reputation" and "one's fortune in
being chosen for this school."[11]

1. The Girls' Middle School:[12] Girls' Middle is,
in several ways, typical of other "good" schools. To
begin with, it is located in Guangzhou's Eastern District,
which has been the favored residential area for Guangzhou's elite since the 1930s and, in keeping with that
tradition, contained a high percentage of Guangzhou's
leading cadres, both military and civilian. In addition
to location, Girls' Middle, like a number of other good
schools, had a pre-Liberation tradition of educational
quality, having been set up as far back as the early
1930s.

What characterized Girls' Middle as a good school,
however, was the nature of its student body and its
promotion rate to the university. While all schools, of
course, attempted to enroll the most promising students,
it was the schools which had high promotion rates that
were most successful. By maintaining a promotion rate of
30-50%, Girls' Middle was able to recruit many children
of intellectuals along with a somewhat smaller number
whose parents were cadres. In line with the increasing
emphasis given to class origin beginning in 1964, students from intellectual family backgrounds were most
heavily represented in the higher years, particularly in
senior high three, while those from cadre origins were to

be found in largest numbers in senior high one and in junior high. For example, while senior high three contained only eight girls out of 160 of high-level cadre origin (5%), senior high two had around 15 out of 150 (10%), and senior high one had over 30 out of 180 (16.7%). The percentages were even higher in lower middle school.

Before discussing Girls' Middle in any detail, some general observations can be made which hold not just for this school, but for many of Guangzhou's secondary schools with similar student bodies. First, Rebel leadership was strongest in senior high 3. Conservative leadership, while also initially strong in senior high 3, increasingly became centered in the lower years of senior high and also in junior high. Further, Rebel rank-and-file support generally came from the higher years of senior high while Conservative support was concentrated in senior high 1 and junior high. Second, and related to the first point, is the fact that the lower the year in school, the better the class origins of the students. Thus, students in senior high 1 had much better class origins than their counterparts in senior high 2, who had better chengfen than those in senior high 3. Third, Rebel leadership frequently was centered in one classroom in a school. At Girls' Middle it was senior high three, class two, which was to supply the Rebels with most of its leadership strength.

The initial split at the school was to some extent tied to a recent personnel shift made by the municipal committee. Zhu Zhaoxiang had been principal/Party secretary until Fall 1965. At that time, Zhang Ke arrived at the school to become Party secretary with Zhu retaining the position of principal. In the spring, Zhu moved on to Number 8 Middle School and Zhang became principal as well as Party secretary of Girls' Middle. This was one of several shifts made concerning leading cadres at middle schools during the Socialist Education Movement. In addition to Girls' Middle, changes were made at Numbers 5, 7, and 10, among others, although only in the case of Number 5, which was a keypoint in the campaign, were the changes clearly seen as disciplinary. Most of the new arrivals, such as Zhang Ke, were old revolutionaries. In Zhang's case, her revolutionary history dated back to Yanan in the late 1930s; she had been a graduate of Kangda (Resist Japan University). This was of some significance because when, in imitation of Beijing University, the first posters went up against Zhang on June 6, criticizing her for her "revisionist educational line," her defenders claimed that the real culprit had been Zhu.[13] Apportioning the blame for this "revisionist educational line" which all recognized as a feature of education in the pre-GPCR period was an issue which was to resurface again and again at various times, whenever

the movement reverted to questions of educational reform
(see Chapter Six).

The arrival of a work team quickly reduced some of
the conflict by focusing the attacks on selected teachers,
particularly those who were vulnerable because of class
background, overseas experience, previous political mistakes, etc. This tactic was of course not unique to this
particular work team, but was common at those schools
which the Municipal Education Bureau had singled out as
"well-run," particularly those in which reliable personnel had recently been installed.

The work team arrived on June 12 and remained until
the end of July. While in residence they had divided up
the students into three categories on the basis of chengfen and biaoxian and set up a Preparatory Committee to
lead the GPCR. The work team chose the majority of the
Preparatory Committee's leadership from class 2 of senior
high 3 and this class then became the focal point in the
GPCR, with many of the leaders of the two main factions
originally coming out of this class.

The prominence of class two of senior high three can
be traced to several factors. First, a majority of the
eight girls of high-level cadre background were in this
class, including the YCL secretary. Second, many of the
school's pre-GPCR leaders were in this class. Third, the
YCL was split over the issue of how to implement the concept of "stress on deeds" (zhongzai biaoxian) and there
had already been intense debates before the Cultural
Revolution over YCL recruitment policies. Nine of the
eleven students in the class from good class background
were already in the League at the time of the GPCR, as
were seven of the 23 students from middle class backgrounds. None of the six students of bad class origin
had been admitted to the League.

The withdrawal of the work team in late July led a
number of students in this class to begin to question
some of its policies, as well as its choices of some
members of the Preparatory Committee. The small number
of dissident students held a meeting on August 9 to
criticize the work team but events were already making
this issue less important.

Ten days later there was a debate on the role of the
Preparatory Committee; by this time, however, many of the
students had become preoccupied with the increasingly
prominent issue of class origin. All other issues were
beginning to be seen merely as reflections of this central concern. This change was perhaps best symbolized on
August 25 when the Preparatory Committee issued books of
Mao quotations for the first time. Because the number of
copies received from the municipal committee was small,
only those of five red categories were issued books.
Given the climate of the time, no one complained openly

about this method of distribution. After the distribution ceremony, however, those from five red category origins mounted the stage to express their gratitude, and used the occasion to vent their contempt for those of bad class origin and even, to a certain extent, those of petty bourgeois origin. After the meeting had broken up, individual classes held meetings for the same purpose. Once again, it was only class 2 of senior high 3 that offered any resistance to these verbal assaults. Although one of the leading resisters was of high-level cadre background, the others were of middle class origin.[14]

From this point on, the development of factionalism at Girls' Middle was rather standard. Relying on the types of illicit chuanlian described in Chapter Three, these early Rebels slowly increased their strength. A Rebel organization - called Jinggangshan - was finally set up on November 3, although only by January were they able to gain mass support. In January, a second Rebel Red Guard organization, Red Flag, was established. Finally, in April, a third Rebel organization, the Red Revolutionary Alliance, was set up.

It is in the date of birth and the membership of these three separate Rebel organizations that one sees the relevance of our brief examination of the different years of senior high. Jinggangshan was established by a small number of students who had begun their rebellion early in August. Their organization was set up at a time when the Doctrine Guards were still the major force at the school, when it was still dangerous openly to oppose them. Jinggangshan had just over ten members in its key leadership, almost all of whom came from senior high 3. They had five leaders, however, who were most important. All came from class number 2. Most of their leadership was of middle class origin. Red Flag, on the other hand, was set up only after the blood line theory began to be criticized officially in the press, in January. Although the two organizations began collaborating in 1967, a feeling remained on the part of the Jinggangshan leadership that Red Flag's revolutionary credentials were to a certain extent unconfirmed because they had begun rebelling during a period of ascension of the radical line.

There were other important differences between the two organizations. Whereas Jinggangshan was a senior high 3 organization, Red Flag drew its support from senior high 2 and, to a lesser extent, from senior high 1. Three of its top five leaders were from class 1 of senior high 2, the other two leaders were from separate classes in senior high 1. More significant, however, was the different policy toward class origin followed by the two organizations. Jinggangshan accepted students from all class backgrounds into their organization al-

though they were not completely unconcerned with the
issue of class origin.

During 1967, when the Party's division of chengfen
categories was no longer so distinct, Jinggangshan simply
redefined the categories as they saw fit. Having arisen
as an organization on the basis of opposition to the
leadership of those of five red categories, they now
defined category one - those of good class background -
to include the five red categories, plus such other categories as peddler, shop assistant, office worker and
teacher. In category two were children of "other laboring people's families" and here were included those
of small merchant (xiaoshang), higher intellectual, overseas Chinese laborer, free professional, and middle
peasant. Moreover, they took categories one and two as
including together those of good or comparatively good
background. They called their category three "children
from families of non-laboring people."[15] This of course
referred to those of bad class origin.[16]

In the case of the Red Flag organization, class was
treated as a much more important factor in determining
membership. Their top five leaders, for example, included four of working class and one of peddler background. Most of their members were of working class
origin. A major reason they set up a separate Red Guard
organization, in fact, was because they felt that Jinggangshan was too liberal in its class line policy.

The third Rebel unit at the school was the Red
Revolutionary Alliance. As has been pointed out, this
organization was set up by those who had previously been
members of a Conservative group but, recognizing the
error of their ways after Zhou Enlai's April visit to
Guangzhou, withdrew and established a separate Red Guard
unit which generally took "Rebel" positions. At Girls'
Middle, as was the case at many of the better Eastern
District schools, this organization contained between
20-30 active members, none coming from senior high three
or two. The organization was centered in senior high one
and junior high two and three; all members were of good
class origin.[17]

Girls' Middle had two Conservative Red Guard organizations, the Doctrine Guards and the Red First Headquarters, the former by far the more important. The
development of the Doctrine Guards at the school was
broadly similar to the pattern at other good schools in
Eastern Guangzhou. The original leaders were all either
of military or civilian cadre background from senior
high. All were YCL members. As time went on and these
students started relinquishing posts under pressure from
parents, central leaders, and so forth, they were increasingly replaced by junior high students who generally
were not YCL members.

Whereas the Doctrine Guards were the main opponents

of the Rebels, particularly of Jinggangshan, the Red
First Headquarters tried to be more "neutral" Conservatives. The organization was set up in March, 1967 after
the citywide split in the First Headquarters. Their
members were primarily of working class origin, although
some were from middle class families; none were from
cadre backgrounds. Many had originally been in the Red
Outer Circle of the Doctrine Guards and had not advanced
to the parent organization; some simply were not considered qualified by the Doctrine Guards for full Red
Guard status, but others, realizing the decline in fortune of the organization after the criticism of blood
line theory, were wary of boarding a sinking ship.
     The Red First Headquarters was looked upon with
undisguised contempt by many Rebels and even by many
committed Conservatives because of their caution and
refusal to take a strong stand. For example, when the
Flag faction began its bombardment of Huang Yongsheng in
1967, the Doctrine Guards responded by launching a campaign to defend Huang against the attacks of the Rebels.
The Red First Headquarters refused to take a position
on this issue. In speeches they generally defended the
PLA but whenever it was a question of their attitude
toward a specific individual or a controversial issue,
they preferred to remain silent. In retrospect, they
might have had the right idea. In the senior high class
that has been examined most closely - senior high 3,
class 2 - there were seven students allowed to remain in
Guangzhou after the GPCR, to be allocated to jobs in
factories. Four were of good class background and were
members of the Doctrine Guards. The remaining three were
of middle class origin; not coincidentally, they were
also the only Red First Headquarters members in the class.
     While the proliferation of Red Guard organizations
at Girls' Middle (three Rebel, two Conservative) was not
dissimilar to factional splits at many of Guangzhou's
secondary schools, what was typical by and large of only
the "good" schools was the fact that the organizations
were so clearly differentiated by the social class origins of their members and the date of birth of the organizations. It was only at schools which contained sufficient numbers of students from cadre/military, middle
class and worker/peasant backgrounds that such a pattern
was likely. The initial split would generally pit those
of cadre background, more or less supported by those of
working class origin, against those of middle class background, dividing over the issue of the importance of
family origin as a key to behavior, most specifically
represented by one's position on the blood line couplet.
     As the movement developed, this initial split soon
was transformed by two tendencies: on the one hand,
students of worker-peasant background began to chafe
under the monopoly children of cadre background exercised

over the Red Guards; on the other hand, the increasing
respectability accorded to those taking a critical view
of the couplet, as first the visiting university students
and then official policy (in the form of speeches by CCRG
leaders) questioned the couplet's conclusions, strenth-
ened those of middle class origin opposed to the couplet's implications.

In a number of schools, as has been noted in Chapter
Three, particularly those in which children of intellectual background did not constitute a formidable force, a
second Red Guard unit, still cognizant of the importance
of class origin and seeking pre-GPCR activists as members, had been set up by October.

In "good" schools like Girls' Middle, however, where
those from intellectual family origins did possess
strength and unity, the more likely pattern saw the
second Red Guard unit emerging out of those of middle
class origin who had set up a "minority faction"
(shaoshu pai) on the basis of their opposition to the
blood line theory, with other, less important, Rebel
organizations developing at a later period.

Hence, by January 1967, Girls' Middle had two Rebel
organizations, one consisting primarily of students of
middle class origin which had been set up in October and
another containing mostly worker-peasant background students and only organized in January. The opposition
consisted of the original Red Guards, still led by children of cadres. Although two additional Red Guard organizations (one Rebel, one Conservative) were set up in
March-April, 1967, these first three organizations remained the most important ones throughout the GPCR.

While the above analysis provides a general picture
of the nature of the Cultural Revolution splits at
schools containing student bodies similar to Girls'
Middle, to give a more accurate measure of the complexity
of GPCR factional formation, it is necessary to consider
in briefer form a few of the idiosyncratic variations
from this general pattern which some "good" schools
exhibited.

2. Number 6 Middle School: Factional developments
at Number 6 deserve a brief mention because Number 6's
geographical location made it perhaps the only school in
Guangzhou to contain substantial numbers of children of
cadres, intellectuals, workers and peasants. Because of
the relatively large number of students of working class
origin combined with the exclusivity practiced by the
children of military cadres from the nearby naval base,
of whom there were more than 50 at the school, the Rebels
won over many of worker-peasant background to their side
early on. In fact, by December 1966 the nucleaus for
four Red Guard organizations had already been established,

two Rebel and two Conservative. The larger of the Rebel units - East is Red - by mid-1967 had expanded to include around 800 of the school's 1,400 students. Although an important member of the Red Headquarters and a strong opponent of blood line theory, 90% of the leadership of this organization was of working class origin. The main opposition to East is Red was the Doctrine Guards which, as at most schools, was headed by children of cadre origin. In the special circumstances of Number 6 Middle School, the organization was controlled by children of officers from the naval base.

The other two Red Guard organizations should perhaps be considered together; both were centered in class 3 of senior high 2. This particular classroom was interesting because it was one of the few at the school that was very united politically before the GPCR. For example, there were already 28 YCL members by senior high 2. In addition, there was only one student in the class of military cadre background and he was isolated.[18] The class had always been characterized by a high level of obedience and conformity to school authority, hence the large number of League members. When the GPCR began this class staunchly defended the Party committee and the work team. But they quickly realized their inability to co-exist with the military cadre children in the Doctrine Guards. When the class did split, along with everyone else on the blood line issue, rather than follow the trend in other classes and gravitate toward East is Red or the Doctrine Guards, they set up two separate organizations, one having those of worker-peasant background as a basis, the other oriented toward those of middle background. These two organizations then began attracting adherents from other classrooms who wanted to avoid the increasingly harsh East is Red-Doctrine Guards division. Both these new organizations attracted many YCL members. In fact, the more conservative of the two had most of the school's pre-GPCR YCL leadership among its membership. 80% of its members were in the YCL. They affiliated citywide with the Red First Headquarters. YCL members made up approximately 60% of the second of these organizations, which affiliated citywide with the New First Headquarters.

Another rather special feature of the factionalism at Number 6 was the insularity of the Doctrine Guards. Number 6 was the only one of the good schools not to have a Red Outer Circle early in the movement. In addition, the Doctrine Guards were actively hostile to the school's other Conservative organization, vilifying that organization's top leader for his bad class origin. Actually, the student in question was the son of a worker who was also a Party member; extensive investigation by the Doctrine Guards had uncovered, however, the disturbing fact that the lad's mother had once been married to a landlord.

3. <u>Number 1 Middle School</u>: Number 1 should be
noted briefly because of several characteristics which
made it very well-known in the GPCR. First, except for
Huafu, it had been the earliest middle school in the city
to stage a rebellion against its Party committee, on June
13. At the opposite end of the city from Huafu, Number
1 was not influenced at all by the rebellion of a few
children of high-level cadres at the former school. In
fact, it was because of the complicated class backgrounds
of the early Rebels at Number 1 that the school became so
well-known in Guangzhou. Of the six senior high 3 students who opposed the school's Party committee, three
were of capitalist background and three of intellectual
background. All were YCL members and most were YCL
cadres; five of the six were from one classroom, including the YCL branch secretary. Particularly in senior
high 3, class 2 the opposition to the Party committee
could be said to be opposition by the class YCL branch,
something unprecedented in other Guangzhou schools, and
it is interesting to speculate just why this was the
case.

Interviews with two former Rebel leaders from senior
high 3 (neither was one of the original six, however)
provided somewhat contrasting pictures of the motivation
of these early Rebels. One interviewee argued that the
six had risen up against the Party committee out of self-
interest, in imitation of the situation at Beijing University. As important YCL members, the school's Party
committee had in fact been relying on them as activists
up until that point. This interviewee felt that they
were opportunists concerned only with their future job
allocations.

A second interviewee argued, on the contrary, that
the six were not really considered so reliable by the
school's leadership. In fact, they had been shrewd
enough to notice that the increasing emphasis on class
line after 1964 had begun to affect their status. In
spite of their positions within the League and, because
they had access to League and other documents, they
recognized the handwriting on the wall and rebelled
before they lost all their power and influence. After
all, this interviewee argued, the Party secretary of
Number 1, Chen Ping, had visibly begun recruiting students of cadre background from Eastern Guangzhou after
1964 and had spoken in favor of emphasizing class line
policies on several occasions. In addition, the six
Rebels felt that they had been only superficially relied
upon during the criticism of <u>Three Family Village</u>, Wu Han
and Deng Tuo, but even that had stopped with the early
June attacks on "cow-ghosts and snake-demons."[19]

Regardless of their motivations, the early Rebels
immediately came into conflict with the municipal committee and its work team. In fact, they later followed up

their rebellion at Number 1 by organizing a group to investigate relations between the school's Party committee, its work team and the Guangzhou municipal committee. This brought them in contact with university students similarly engaged, and they became the earliest middle school unit to join the First Headquarters, remaining leaders of the middle school section of this headquarters for the remainder of the movement.

Given its location in Western Guangzhou, and its rather limited number of children of cadre background, Number 1 never had a strong Doctrine Guards organization. There was no strong opposition to the Rebels, who called themselves the July 1st Rebel Team. What opposition there was came from a rather inactive Red First Headquarters organization which had split off from the July 1st Rebel Team. There was also a small Red Headquarters unit at the school. These latter two organizations had initially been sympathetic to the July 1st Rebel Team but, under the influence of the blood line theory, decided it was unwise to unite organizationally with a group whose leadership was top-heavy with youths from bad class origins.

Number 1 Middle School was important because of its influence on other Rebel groups in Western Guangzhou. Its pattern of rebellion provided an alternate model for schools with few cadre children. Unlike the Eastern District schools, whose Rebels owed their rise to their opposition to the blood line theory and the privileges of children of cadres, those in the West faced different questions. While Eastern schools of necessity banded together in 1967 to resist their common enemy - the Doctrine Guards - this kind of unity was not an imperative for those in the West. Other schools followed the example of Number 1 in joining the New 1st Headquarters middle school section but, lacking strong pressure from the Conservatives, they had less need to coordinate their activities. Moreover, the early rebellion highlighted by the leadership of students of bad class background remained unique, even among schools in Guangzhou's Western District.[20]

4. Number 7 Middle School:[21] As one of Guangzhou's better schools, located in the Eastern District, Number 7 had a fair percentage of cadre children as well as many of ordinary and even bad class background as students. Because it was located just opposite the Guangzhou Military Region headquarters, many of the cadre children there were from military families. It had been a Protestant-run school before 1949 and its facilities remained outstanding.[22]

At Number 7 the first GPCR split occurred very early. This school was heavily influenced by the "Letter from Beijing Incident" at South China Engineering

Institute and by the Huafu situation.[23] The first student organization to be set up at the school was called
the Revolutionary Rebel Committee and was made up of students from various class backgrounds, although children
of high-level cadres and of intellectuals were perhaps
most heavily represented. The organization made its
appearance in July, 1966 and was established by those who
were opposed to the school's Party committee and work
team. The opposing organization consisted mostly of students of ordinary cadre and worker-peasant backgrounds
and was called The First Brigade.[24] This split continued
until the spread of the blood line theory, at which time
a second split occurred. At this time, the Revolutionary
Rebel Committee split into two branches, one called the
Red Intruding Generals and the other called the Red Flag
Commune. The former organization consisted of those on
the Revolutionary Rebel Committee who were of high-level
cadre background. The latter group was an umbrella
organization consisting of many different combat teams,
albeit with broadly similar views with regard to the main
issues of the GPCR at this time.

By August, 1966, there were three basic groups at
the school: 1) those who were still in favor of supporting the Party committee and the work team (The First
Brigade); 2) those of high-level cadre background, small
in number, who opposed the Party committee and the work
team, but had formed a separate group at the time of the
blood line theory (Red Intruding Generals); and 3) another group, consisting of sets of combat teams, who had
opposed the Party committee and the work team, but containing members from all backgrounds (Red Flag Commune).

Even this, however, is an oversimplication. Within
the Red Flag Commune, for example, one could find the
Red Flag Red Guards, an organization of Rebels who were
still not prepared to unite directly with those of middle,
much less of bad class origin. With the establishment
of Red Guard organizations, both the Red Intruding Generals and The First Brigade took the name Doctrine Guards,
the former taking the name Independent Brigade of the
Doctrine Guards, the latter the name First Brigade of the
Doctrine Guards.

Interestingly enough, when the Beijing middle school
Red Guards arrived in Guangzhou, they linked up with the
children of cadres to carry out the Destroy Four Olds
movement. The Conservative-Rebel split over assessment
of school authorities at Number 7 was not of importance
to them; on the basis of the blood line theory, they
rapidly allied with the children of high-level cadre background who had been the school's early "Rebels." Even
after the blood line theory had been officially repu-
diated, children of high-level cadres made no self-
criticisms. On the other hand, the members of The First
Brigade were willing to undergo some self-criticism and

sought, albeit unsuccessfully, to win over some of the students they had rejected in the prior stage of the movement. As the GPCR developed, in what was a general pattern in Guangzhou, the children of high-level cadre background increasingly became less active. By 1967, the two organizations left facing each other were the Red Flag Commune and the First Brigade although, after Zhou Enlai's visit in April, between twenty and thirty members left The First Brigade to join the Red Revolutionary Alliance.

There are some surface similarities between the Huafu case and the Number 7 case. For example, in both instances we see children of high-level cadres rising up as early Rebels. Secondly, there was a two-step process of rebellion. The initial rebellion divided the students on the basis of their attitudes toward the Party committee and the work team. The second stage produced a different alignment on the basis of family origin. Thirdly, children of high-level cadre background became less active beginning in late 1966.

There were, however, important differences which help explain why Rebel strength at Number 7 developed into a formidable force while the Rebels at Huafu remained weak. For one thing, there were many more students of middle class origin at Number 7 than there were at Huafu. Moreover, these students had become Rebels very early in the GPCR. Huafu's early Rebels, on the other hand, were all of high-level cadre or military background and there were only eleven of them at that. Students at Huafu who were not of cadre background, therefore, were not able to play any role until much later; their logical role, that of Rebels, had been preempted by the Huafu Eleven, who neither asked for nor required any help in their rebellion.

The early rebellion of the middle class students at Number 7 had gained legitimacy precisely because they had as allies those of high-level cadre origin. In addition, their early rebellion meant that when a second division developed along the axis of class origin, they were able to retain a fair number of students of good class origin (primarily worker-peasant background, plus some of ordinary-level cadre background) who felt that the original issues were more important than class origin differences. Still later, in 1967, the Red Flag Commune expanded and at its height had approximately 1,000 members, around five times the number of its opponents.

Finally, the geographical location of the school also contributed to the strength of the Number 7 Rebels. Located in the heart of the Eastern District, they were in frequent contact with nearby schools such as Numbers 16 and 21, the Railroad Middle School, the Girls' Middle School and the South China Experimental School. It was these five schools, with the addition of Number 7, that became the six most important members of the Guangzhou Regiment. The rather complete control exercised over their own school gave the Number 7 Rebels a great deal of independence and influence within the citywide Guangzhou Regiment.

But the Number 7 pattern was not really typical of Guangzhou's "good" middle schools. In fact, with its early rebellion of students of all class backgrounds, the pattern had certain similarities to the situation at some of Guangzhou's universities. The more familiar pattern was one in which children of cadres and intellectuals, revealing differences right from the start of the GPCR, became firm opponents in August.

ORDINARY SCHOOLS[25]

A prominent feature of the schools which have been examined thus far has been the role of the children of cadres early in the GPCR; except in the special case of Number 1, at all the other schools that have been considered the Rebels were only able to rise up after the criticism of the blood line theory had begun in earnest. Rebel units owed their strength to their repudiation of the blood line theory and those who had pushed it most strongly. The most powerful middle school Rebel organizations in Guangzhou - those making up the leadership of the Guangzhou Regiment - all fit this pattern.

To a certain extent, this pattern also holds for what we have called the ordinary schools. Nevertheless, as one moves from the better quality schools to those of lesser quality, some noticeable differences appear. First, one finds that both Rebels and Conservatives at these schools tended to be a step behind the movement at the better schools. The important factor here seems to be the nature of their student bodies. As was discussed in Chapter One, these schools had few children of cadres in residence. Particularly in the early stages of the GPCR, information on the latest events in Beijing reached the ears of cadre children quickest and were then spread by them, usually through their contacts with others of similar class backgrounds. This is why the movement in Eastern Guangzhou, as the primary residential area for cadres and the location of many of the best schools, developed most quickly.

Second, schools that fall into the category of "ordinary" did not produce any of the key leaders of the Rebel faction. To become an influential Rebel leader at citywide level required that one represent a powerful Rebel force at one's home school. Few of the ordinary schools had such powerful forces, either Rebel or Conservative. The situation could be viewed as links in a chain. Having low promotion rates to the university

these schools were unable to recruit large numbers of
children of cadres or middle class intellectuals. The
low promotion rates to the university and the absence of
these two major competing groups of students meant that
the issue of "class line" was less salient at these
schools than it was at the better schools. Nor were the
strivings for activist status and YCL membership as pronounced at these schools. Hence, when the GPCR arrived,
neither the initial attack on university entrance exams
nor the subsequent stress in August on the blood line
theory had quite the impact that it achieved at the
better schools. Having few children of cadres to rely
on, the work teams paid more attention to biaoxian at
these schools and, when the Red Guards were set up, unlike the situation at the better schools in which one's
father's rank was most important as a criterion for membership, in these schools one's pre-GPCR position, it
seems, was given equal weight. Thus, the original Red
Guards at Numbers 4 and 29 Middle Schools all were YCL
cadres of good class origin. Nor did the Beijing Red
Guards, so important in spreading blood line policies,
devote much time to these schools, preferring to visit
those schools blessed by the presence of children of high-
level cadres. In the absence of a strong enforcement of
the blood line theory, there was no forceful counter-
reaction by those whose activism had been denied during
that period. The above is not to deny, of course, that
such universal phenomena as the blood line theory existed
at these schools; attacks on teachers and students of bad
class origin were common at all schools. The point being
made, however, is that for all the reasons given above,
the extremes of the the GPCR impacted much less forcefully at the ordinary schools.[26]

POOR SCHOOLS [27]

When we move down the scale to poor schools - almost
exclusively neigborhood junior high schools - we see certain aspects of the situation which prevailed at the
ordinary schools, combined with behavioral patterns
common to junior high students even at the better schools.
For example, even more than in the case of the ordinary
schools, the movement at the neighborhood junior highs
lagged behind. This was particularly the case for many
that had been set up relatively recently, in outlying or
newly industrialized areas, such as those in the Number
40-50 range. Because the majority of their student
bodies consisted of children of laboring people (mostly
working class origin), the blood line theory was not the
major determinant of factional participation as it had
been at the good, and even the ordinary schools.[28] Even
in schools where it had initially been important, it

diminished greatly as time went on. Ironically, however,
even though both sides often contained majorities of good
class origin, interviewees report that there was less of
an attempt to win over one's enemy at these schools than
was the case at the better schools, where the factions
were divided more clearly by class origin and other prominent issues. Members of Rebel organizations at many of
these schools, for example, vowed to fight the Doctrine
Guards to the death. Indeed, in late 1968, after the
most prominent Rebel organizations had been disbanded,
a "United Statement" was issued by 47 of Guangzhou's
Rebel units still functioning, vowing to continue the
struggle. Of the 36 middle school organizations signing
this statement, 19 were from neighborhood schools, 9 were
from work-study schools and most of the remaining 8 were
from ordinary schools.[29]

As might be expected, junior high students generally
were more enthusiastic about the large-scale, more physical activities of the GPCR. They tended to be eager
participants in armed struggle, hunger strikes, demon-
strations, marches and so forth. Conversely, they were
less interested in the more painstaking but rewarding
(in the long run) activities such as investigating a
cadre's history to determine whether or not to support
him/her, working on educational reform, and so forth.
They also had severe problems when it came to establishing a firm organizational structure with a division of
labor and a chain of command. Frequently, Rebel enthu-
siasts assigned to desk jobs would see others embarking
to participate in a demonstration or a hunger strike and,
more often than not, would rush to the scene and join in,
rather than miss out on any of the "action." While this
tendency existed among middle school students even in
schools with senior highs, the older, more mature students at these latter schools were to a large extent able
to control the situation through their prestige. At the
neighborhood junior highs there was frequently no one in
control.

Another striking characteristic at the junior highs
was the fact that organizational participation often was
more dependent on friendship groups than on issues. For
example, one interviewee from Number 42 Middle School
reported that although many of working class background
in his class had been Doctrine Guards initially, after
the Red Headquarters had been set up, between 10-20 students shifted over to this organization because they were
on very good terms with the class leader of that group.
Generally, at schools of this type, chengfen was less a
barrier to organizational participation than at any other
type of school being considered. As many expressed it,
if a leader was your friend, you could enter any Red
Guard group. It is not surprising, therefore, that we
find the largest percentage of bad class youths joining

Conservative organizations in these types of schools (see Table 4.3, Chapter Four).

One more difference between the neighborhood junior highs and other schools is that organizations at the former schools usually had no Red Guard newspaper of their own, further limiting intra-school communication.

To highlight the situation at these neighborhood junior highs, Number 42 Middle School will be briefly examined. The school was in the southern part of Guangzhou (Henan) and had been set up in the wake of the Great Leap Forward. According to several informants, it had been set up so quickly that the first class of students had dubbed it "perilous building" (weilou), implying that it might collapse at any time because of poor workmanship. Subsequent classes continued the usage of the school's nickname; those attending the school primarily were children who lived nearby who had not done well enough on the citywide entrance exams to attend better schools. Since it was located in a heavily working class district with many factories and worker's dormitories, a majority of the students were of working class origin. Some, however, had parents working at Zhongshan University, which was not very far away.

The first Red Guard organization to be established was the Doctrine Guards which, following the citywide situation, was limited to those of good class origin. The organization came to include not just those who had been class or League cadres but also those good background students who had been undisciplined before the GPCR, a not inconsiderable number. There was also a Red Outer Circle, but relatively few students were members. With the criticism of the blood line theory, the Doctrine Guards split. A substantial number who, as children of workers, had joined the Guards because they felt the blood line theory to be in their best interests, now rebelled.[30]

The Flag faction at the school by 1967 came to include two types of students: the first type included the school's best students who had been very obedient toward school authority in the pre-GPCR period. They were from both good and middle class origins, although the leadership was of good class origin. They formed the wendou (struggle by words) group, made up of three separate organizations at the school. The second type of student joining the Rebels had had very poor grades before the GPCR; in addition, they were the most disobedient students in the school. They formed the wudou (struggle by force) group, and set up an organization called the Iron Cavalry.[31] This latter group had been staunch Conservatives early in the GPCR during the height of the blood line theory. They had not hesitated in abusing teachers who they felt had discriminated against them in pre-GPCR days simply because they had not been obedient or studious. They rebelled against their former unit, the Doctrine Guards, because such rebellion offered them even greater opportunities for unrestrained behavior. Those remaining in the Conservative organization tended to include the pre-GPCR activists and YCL members of good class origin and this unit had closer ties with authority. By splitting off from this faction the wudou group was able to retaliate freely against activists, with whom they had never been on good terms.

An interesting relationship developed between the wendou and wudou wings of the Flag faction at this school. Because Number 42 was in a working class factory district, the surrounding areas were under the control of the worker-dominated East Wind faction. At most of the junior highs in the area (for example, Numbers 41, 45 and 49) the Doctrine Guards, in alliance with the Conservative workers, were very strong. Number 42, because of the Iron Cavalry, was something of an exception. Although its relationship with the wendou units was less than cordial, the latter realized that the fighting power of the Iron Cavalry was necessary to their own survival and so the two groups had a modus vivendi, particularly during armed struggle periods. The wendou groups did try to tone down some of the more outrageous behavior of the Iron Cavalry, finding it something of an embarrassment, but were able to exercise little or no control over that group.

CONCLUSION

Patterns of factional formation among Guangzhou's middle schools during the Cultural Revolution varied in largest part on the basis of whether a school was "true elite," "good," "ordinary" or "poor." Each of the four categories of schools had a rather distinct student body which in turn seemed to be the most important factor determining the nature of factional formation at that category of school.

Moreover, the major battleground between Conservatives and Rebels was the "good" schools. In a sense, Guangzhou's "true elite" schools had too many children from cadre backgrounds while ordinary and poor schools had too few. The balance between children of cadres and those from middle class origins at the good schools intensified factional politics at these schools. At Huafu and Guangya, early dominance by those from high-level cadre backgrounds relegated other students to supporting roles at best. At Huafu the early Rebel-Conservative split among children of high-level cadre background in effect denied other students an opportunity to play a leading role, while at Guangya the early solidarity among these same favored children had similar consequences. More conventional Rebel organizations were not set up until much later at these two schools and by then Rebel units at the "good" schools had already become sufficiently strong and unified to occupy the leading positions in citywide alliances, the primary example being the case of the Guangzhou Regiment.

6
The Cultural Revolution Winds Down: Rebels and Conservatives in Guangzhou After April 1967

After Zhou Enlai's visit to Guangzhou in mid-April 1967, few important changes occurred in the overall Rebel-Conservative configuration. Nevertheless, despite the relative stability of the Red Flag and East Wind factions, the period from May 1967 to autumn 1968 was marked by several shifts in the balance of power between the two factions as those leading the Cultural Revolution in Beijing lurched to the Left and Right in their policy decisions. The antagonists in Guangzhou were continually being confronted with the problem of reacting to these policy alternations. Several turning points can be distinguished in this process. The first came in September 1967.

Between May and September the factional struggle in Guangzhou developed, to use the language of a leading participant, from one of cold war (lengzhan) to one of armed confrontation.[1] By the end of August, however, the Center had apparently become firmly committed to a policy of consolidation and demobilization. The issues of immediate concern to the two factions in the summer - the Rebels were seeking to topple Huang Yongsheng and the Conservatives were defending him; both sides seemed intent on establishing their own "turf" and driving their "enemies" away, and so forth - had shifted dramatically by the autumn. The beginning of September saw a return to center stage of a number of issues that had temporarily been left unattended while concerns with "seizing power" and "toppling capitalist roaders in authority" had been paramount. These issues included, inter alia, cadre assessment, the establishment of revolutionary committees, the reform of the educational system, and the allocation of the present student population onto the job market.

The politics of consolidation and demobilization of the post-September period in many ways was to provide a sterner test for the Rebels of the Flag faction than had the politics of armed confrontation. The exigencies of the summer had combined to produce at least a semblance of unity among Rebels representing the various headquarters as a means of coping with their external environment. However, simultaneous with the increasing cooperation of the Rebels on one level, the necessities of armed struggle brought forth the makings of a new split, between those who felt that victory could be won only by force and those who felt that the armed confrontation was merely a passing phase.

These coexisting countertendencies were brought into direct conflict as a result of a series of "peace talks" organized in Beijing by Zhou Enlai. Zhou's aim was to end the armed struggle and bring the Rebels and Conservatives closer together. The Flag faction leadership, recognizing the indispensability of the support of central leaders, dutifully shifted the focus of their aims to accommodate the moderate policies being pursued in Beijing. As a result of this shift in priorities, a significant and vocal minority of the Rebels, including many who had been active during the armed struggle period, began to question both the central leadership and their own leaders in Guangzhou. As the politics of moderation continued throughout autumn and winter, these dissidents - in effect the real "radicals" in the GPCR - began to take the initial steps toward formulating a heterodox analysis of Chinese society, complete with an explanation of the successes and failures of the GPCR to date that was far removed from official accounts.

This particular division in Rebel ranks was most pronounced between September 1967 and late March 1968. By April 1968 it had become clear - both to Rebels in Guangzhou as well as their backers in Beijing - that policies of moderation only served to consolidate the control of the Conservatives at the local level. Thus in late March, when the GPCR pendulum again took a swing to the Left in Beijing, Guangzhou's Rebels were once more brought closer together for the final struggle.

Rather than merely summarizing the latter part of the GPCR and Red Guard movement, this chapter will also highlight a number of issues on which there was interfactional or, in some cases, intrafactional contention.

FACTIONAL DIVISIONS: MAY 1967 TO LATE MARCH 1968

At the beginning of May 1967 the Rebels had reason to be optimistic; by the end of March 1968, the Rebels were about to begin what was to be their last counterattack on their opponents. In the space of these eleven months the Rebels were to rise, albeit briefly, to the zenith of their power, and then sink, once again, almost to their nadir.

May to September 1967: Prelude to Peace. At the be-

ginning of May 1967, the factional situation in Guangzhou
was as follows: 1) Premier Zhou Enlai had just left the
city after affirming that the general orientation of the
organizations known as the "three red flags" (South China
Engineering Institute Red Flag, Zhongshan University Red
Flag, and Guangzhou Medical Institute Red Flag) had been
correct while their opponents had generally been too conservative; 2)The Red Headquarters had been set up by the
Red Flag units of Zhongshan University and Guangzhou Medical Institute and were joined by the majority of the
middle school Rebels and many other groups that had participated in the January power seizure led by the Provincial Revolutionary Alliance (SGL). The immediate aim of
this organization was to seek to bring about the rehabilitation of individuals and groups suppressed by the military because of their participation in SGL-related activities; 3)The Third Headquarters, headed by South China
Engineering Institute Red Flag, had been at odds with the
SGL units over the power seizure and other issues and
therefore was not especially concerned about the question
of rehabilitation. They instead directed their energies
toward the issue of cadre assessment with the objective
of selecting reliable officials to join them as part of
a "three-way alliance" (mass organizations, cadres, and
PLA), which had replaced direct power seizure as the preferred method of distributing power at the provincial level and below. Initially, they considered most worthy
of support those "localist cadres" (difang ganbu) who had
been pushed aside or discriminated against during the
reign of the now-disgraced Tao Zhu; 4)The "victory" obtained by the Rebels as a result of Zhou's visit had not
been a complete one, however. Zhou's reaffirmation of
the work of Huang Yongsheng and the PLA had given the
Conservatives a rallying point around which to regroup.
If it had not been clear before, the situation at the
time of Zhou's departure from Guangzhou had made the attentive public in both the Flag and East Wind factions
aware that the power of the Flag faction was tied in no
small part to the ability of the Center to intervene in
the local Guangzhou situation while East Wind's power was
likely to increase in direct proportion to the independence the Center permitted the Guangdong Provincial Military District Command.

    To a great extent, therefore, it is possible to look
upon political outcomes in the post-April 1967 period in
Guangzhou in terms of the effectiveness of central leaders (i.e. the CCRG and Zhou Enlai) to induce a recalcitrant military to adopt an even-handed approach to the
Flag and East Wind factions in place of a pro-East Wind
orientation. For its part, the Red Headquarters did not
hesitate to use its "Beijing Connection" in its effort to
realize its goal of rehabilitation. Thus, in times of

radical ascendance - generally between May and August
1967 - Guangzhou's Rebels were able to achieve some of
their immediate aims. Somewhat ironically, it was largely due to the limited gains the Rebels attained through
the intervention of central leaders in the summer that
prevented all but a radical minority within the Flag faction from reacting negatively when the Center shifted
from a policy of struggle leading to a unity of the revolutionary Left to a policy of moderation and unity
through a "great alliance" of all factions.

The Partial Success of the Red Headquarters. Zhou
Enlai's visit to Guangzhou in April had the effect of re-
suscitating the SGL forces. Among other things, he had
managed to persuade the military to order the rehabilitation of one of the key participants in the January power
seizure: Pearl River Film Studio's "East is Red," which
had been labeled a counterrevolutionary organization in
March. The manner of the "rehabilitation," however, was
such that the SGL forces were far from satisfied. The
military's "Rehabilitation Notice" made it clear that,
far from being a case of the PLA's lack of understanding
of "East is Red's" correct orientation, it was merely an
overreaction by the PLA to the incorrect policies of
"East is Red" that had led to the military clampdown.
The language used in Point 5 of the "Notice" was unequi-
vocal on that score:

> We viewed Pearl River Film Studio "East is
> Red's" attack of the Military District as
> well as some of their defects and errors
> in an excessively severe manner. Because
> of this it is reasonable to rehabilitate
> them, permit them to restore their organiza-
> tion, their reputation and their activities.[2]

Moreover, those in the organization released from
jail were given a certificate saying that their release
was due to the "recognition of their mistakes, their
self-confession, and their good attitude."[3] It was this
style of "rehabilitation" that convinced the Rebels that
despite Zhou's visit the military had changed neither its
negative assessment of the power seizure nor its support
for those organizations Zhou had labeled conservative-
leaning.

Given the absence of support from the military, the
Red Headquarters sought to provoke the Center into more
direct intervention into affairs in Guangzhou. The immediate goal was the complete rehabilitation of all individuals and organizations suppressed by the military as a
result of SGL-related activities. Foremost among these
organizations was the August 1 Combat Corps, an organiza-

tion consisting primarily of dissatisfied factory workers, many of whom were demobilized soldiers. The Guangdong Provincial Military District Command had banned the Corps as a counterrevolutionary organization on March 1, 1967 on the basis of ten charges. Most significantly, the Corps had been cited for the bad class origins of its members, the attempt to carry out class revenge by "striking down all Party members, YCL members and activists...," and its anti-PLA stance and seeming desire to pose itself as an alternative to the PLA (which included donning military uniforms and maintaining contacts with similar groups of demobilized soldiers in other provinces, some of which had earlier been declared counterrevolutionary by the Center).[4] The above charges, concentrating on the question of class origin and criticism of Party officials and the PLA had of course become key issues dividing the Red Headquarters (and to a lesser extent other groups in the Flag faction) from the East Wind Conservatives. In April, Zhou Enlai had ruled that because of the complicated membership and activities of this organization, rehabilitation could not be considered without deeper investigation.[5]

Rebuffed on the issue of the Combat Corps, the Red Headquarters chose instead as their first object for rehabilitation an individual named Xiang Ming. Xiang Ming was a cadre from a provincial-level bureau who had played an important part in the January power seizure and had been arrested during the "March Black Wind." On May 2, the Red Headquarters organized a hunger strike outside the main public security offices to demand Xiang's release hoping, according to one of the strike's leaders, "to force the Center to express an opinion." The Rebels organized two detachments; one detachment was to present its case to the military and persuade them to release the prisoner while at the same time maintaining liaison with Beijing and keeping officials at the Center aware of developments. The second detachment was in charge of propaganda among Guangzhou's citizenry.

The military remained adamant in refusing to release Xiang Ming, arguing that the question of whom to release would only be discussed if the hunger strikers began eating again. On May 6, Zhou Enlai sent telegrams to the military and the Red Headquarters, stating: 1) you should fill up your stomachs to make revolution; 2) those people wrongly "arrested" (zhua) should be released; and 3) if the masses have opinions and objections, they can send representatives to negotiate with the military authorities. Xiang Ming was immediately released and appeared before the hunger strikers as a hero. As the first action of the new headquarters, it confirmed their belief that rehabilitation of Rebels was of major importance to the success of their aims and that success against the military could be achieved only with the support of the

Center.[6]

The Xiang Ming case was only one instance of intervention from the Center on behalf of the Rebels. In mid-May both Mao Zedong and Kang Sheng sought to induce the PLA to recognize its errors. Mao's intervention came in the form of a comment he made on a report submitted by the Guangzhou Military District Command to the Center on its "support the Left" work; in his comment, Mao warned that its mistakes should be corrected early.[7] Kang Sheng's intervention was more direct. He flew into Guangzhou just for an evening, bringing "important instructions from the Center" to Guangzhou's military leaders.[8]

These initiatives from the Center were beginning to bear fruit. The PLA, at least on the surface and through measures that would be visible to leaders in Beijing, seemingly had begun to make an effort to treat the factions more equally. Thus, the PLA-controlled Guangzhou radio station began to report the activities of the Red Flag faction, and PLA personnel, including Huang Yongsheng, appeared at meetings convened by Red Flag units, speaking in a conciliatory manner.[9]

Nevertheless, Guangzhou's Rebels remained wary of Huang's intentions, arguing that his speeches were "self-contradictory...saying one thing to this organization and another thing to that organization."[10] Nor were they any more favorably disposed by his actions. Throughout May and June, Guangdong's PLA issued a series of notices that the Flag faction interpreted as directed against its interests. The most important of these notices was issued on May 30 and hinted broadly that the responsibility for the current confusion in the GPCR in Guangzhou was due to some of the organizations affiliated with the Flag faction. More specifically, the notice affirmed that it was necessary for the Military Control Commission to continue to engage in investigatory work and the collection of materials against any organization considered a threat to public order or representing an "unhealthy social tendency." Moreover, the notice went on, the materials collected must of necessity remain secret. The Flag faction looked upon notices of this sort as an open invitation for the continued suppression of organizations banned during the "March Black Wind," in particular the August 1 Combat Corps.[11]

Ideologically, East Wind was also active at this time, producing a set of "theories" that sought to negate Zhou Enlai's April assessment of the two factions. The title of some of East Wind's writings in this period are sufficient to gauge their intent: "The Theory of the New Stage"; "The Theory of Assessing the Situation Anew."[12]

Given this state of affairs, the Flag faction was

becoming more and more openly opposed to the Military
Control Commission (MCC) and Huang Yongsheng. The bold-
er units began referring to Huang as "Guangzhou's Tan
Zhenlin" (after the leader most closely associated with
the "February Adverse Current" in Beijing). Flag faction
leaders began to hold meetings to develop a strategy of
opposition to the Military District and to compile a collection of "black materials" against Huang and his subordinates.[13]

In spite of their continuing differences, the various headquarters within the Flag faction began, at the
urging of outside Red Guard units with close ties to the
CCRG in Beijing, to draw somewhat closer together. On
June 30, for example, the Red Guard Congress (Preparatory)
of Universities and Colleges in Guangzhou was established.[14] East Wind's university students, not to be outdone,
set up their own unified organization on July 6.[15]

From time to time in the May-June period, the tensions between the two factions boiled over into armed
struggle, as on May 8 and 10 and June 15 and 18. Although the Center issued a series of national directives
prohibiting armed struggle and enjoining the PLA to arrest and punish all those "who start trouble," Guangdong's PLA, still under strong pressure from Beijing not
to suppress the Rebels, tended to "look the other way"
when armed confrontations occurred.[16]

Armed confrontation reached its high tide, however,
after the so-called "Wuhan Incident," beginning July
20.[17] The kidnapping of two representatives from Beijing
by the Conservative mass organizations with the collusion
of the local military had a tremendous impact throughout
the country, most particularly in those areas where Rebels had been searching for the proper cudgel with which
to do combat with their own regional military commands
and the Conservative mass organizations which these commands backed. Guangzhou was no exception.

The CCRG in Beijing, in its handling of the Wuhan
Incident, provided the cudgel the Rebels needed. On July
22, Jiang Qing delivered a speech to a delegation from
Henan Province in which she advocated "attacking with
words and defending with force" (wengong wuwei) when
Rebels were confronted by armed Conservatives.[18]

The influence of this slogan cannot be overesti-
mated. One Rebel leader described to me the excitement
with which the Wuhan Incident and the Center's reaction
were greeted by Rebels in Guangzhou. They immediately
organized a demonstration march through the streets during which the marchers shouted over and over: wengong
wuwei.[19]

Almost immediately the scale of armed struggle increased dramatically throughout China.[20] Adding fuel to
the fire, the August 1 issue of Red Flag carried an edi-

torial entitled "The Proletariat Must Take Firm Hold of the Gun," which advocated a power seizure from "the handful of power-holders in the army" and immediately stimulated Rebels throughout the country to seize power from the PLA.[21]

The radical wing of Guangzhou's Rebels was beside itself with joy and began to reinterpret the entire history of the GPCR in light of the present circumstances. For example, the SGL assault on the Guangzhou Military District in February, which until this time had remained as a black mark against Guangzhou's Rebels, was now declared to have been "a magnificent, heroic, and greatly revolutionary action."[22] The Rebels also demanded a reversal of verdicts on the "four big incidents" (in addition to the attack on the Military District Command, the incidents refer to the attack on the Public Security Bureau in January, and on Radio Guangzhou, as well as the SGL question).[23]

Perhaps the atmosphere of early August can best be conveyed by the sudden shift in the behavior of the Conservative mass organizations. East Wind groups in a massive aboutface began to find it necessary to criticize both the Wuhan Conservatives and "Guangzhou's Tan Zhenlin." The radicals scorned such a volte-face by their opponents, however. Indeed, the radicals in the Red Headquarters even balked at cooperating very closely with more moderate Rebels at this time, accusing the latter of opportunism. The following quote from early August is typical of their point of view:

> Those people who hold that agreement can be reached through negotiation and that struggle by violence can be stopped by disarming both parties, are actually upholding Khrushchev's theory of disarmament. They can only betray the interests of the proletarian revolutionary Rebels!
> It must be pointed out that the overflow of opportunist ideas among the Rebels is the internal cause of the missing of opportunity in the struggle. Opportunism is characterized by its high affinity. They do not have a stable political target. They often betray the revolution in meeting other people![24]

Although this point will be considered further when examining the intrafactional splits in Red Flag, here it might briefly be noted that the Red Headquarters set up an organization apart from other Flag faction units at this time. The organization - called the Red Alliance (honglian) - was established to coordinate policy for the headquarters in the chaotic days of early-mid-August.

One of the Red Alliance's first acts was to set up an organization called the Red Garrison Headquarters (hongzhansi), an armed detachment whose function was to preserve social order. In effect, this organization initially attempted to take over power from the Public Security Bureau and eventually from the Military Control Commission itself. Moreover, it apparently sought to gain control of key industrial and mining enterprises in Guangzhou.[25]

The Beijing Peace Talks (Beijing Tanpan) and the Role of Zhou Enlai (Stage 1). In mid-August as well, the painstaking liaison work Flag faction members had long been conducting in Beijing - viz., maintaining close ties to the CCRG and Zhou Enlai by providing detailed information to them with regard to the Guangzhou situation - was bearing fruit. On August 14 and again on August 16, Zhou Enlai received representatives of Flag faction units in Beijing and reviewed various GPCR issues with them. These meetings were to set the stage for what became known as the "Beijing Peace Talks" which, beginning in late August and lasting until mid-November, consisted of a series of meetings between representatives of the Red Flag and East Wind factions, with Zhou presiding.

The published accounts of these meetings provide a fascinating glimpse of Zhou's style of subtle persuasion and reveal the reasons his diplomacy was so successful. The preliminary meetings in which only Flag faction representatives participated are a case in point. In these meetings Zhou was able to gain the complete confidence of the Rebels by endorsing a number of their views. First, he reaffirmed his April assessment that they were indeed revolutionary while their opponents tended to be conservative-leaning. Second, when informed that the August 1 Combat Corps was still considered a counterrevolutionary organization by the Military Control Commission, he immediately announced its rehabilitation, accomplishing in an instant what Red Headquarters partisans had been striving to achieve for months. Following Zhou's statement, several Flag faction units undertook a month-long investigation of the August 1 Combat Corps, concentrating on its "organization, development, and activities" as well as on the persecution its members suffered after the organization was banned.[26] The Military District Command maintained its reluctance to completely exonerate the Corps, however, issuing partial rehabilitation notices in mid-August and mid-September before finally agreeing to a "thorough-going" rehabilitation on October 14.[27]

In addition to giving support to positions espoused by the Flag faction, Zhou made it clear that the key to success in the GPCR in Guangzhou lay with them. The task of maintaining revolutionary order and public safety was to be placed in large part in the hands of the Rebels. In carrying out these important responsibilities, Zhou argued, the Rebels should solve the differences that had divided them into subfactional units. As he put it:

> At present your form does not lead to a position of superiority; you're too scattered, in separate parts rather than one body. How will that do? You need to unite on the basis of factories and schools. When the Left occupies the superior position, then things can be done well.[28]

Another reason for unity, according to Zhou, was the necessity to set up a preparatory small group prior to the formation of the Guangdong Provincial Revolutionary Committee. The Rebels were expected to occupy the majority of places in this small group. Moreover, Zhou asked the CCRG to organize a liaison station in Guangzhou to solve personally the problem of Guangdong.

The Rebels had every reason to feel elated by the turn events were taking. As the first stage of the peace talks with East Wind began in Beijing on August 17, Red Flag leaders voiced their confidence in the talks. The entire first stage of the talks, which lasted until September 5, saw East Wind and their PLA backers on the defensive. On August 20, for example, the Party committee of the Guangzhou Military District Command issued a written self-criticism. Entitled "An Examination of Mistakes Made in the Work of Supporting the Left in the Guangzhou Area," this document makes abundantly clear the pressure the Center had been putting on the military to adopt a more even-handed approach toward the Rebels.[29]

In this "self-examination" the Military District Command admitted its mistakes in denouncing SGL and excluding all mass organizations that had participated in the January power seizure from the PLA-sponsored "production command headquarters" set up in February; recognized that its ban of the August 1 Combat Corps was an error; and agreed that it was unreponsive to central initiatives to balance its policy and correct its mistakes.[30]

There were other visible indications at this time that the Center was devoting its attention to events in Guangzhou, and tempering its support for the local military leadership. For example, Huang Yongsheng had been called to Beijing and was to remain there until November.[31] At the end of August, a Central Investigation Team arrived in Guangzhou and, as interviewees pointed out, served as an alternate source of authority to the Military Control Commission.[32] Units of the 47th Army were sent into Guangzhou at this time and supported the

Rebels in organizations they entered.33
        Even local PLA units suddenly began to support Rebel
organizations at this time. For example, when Red Flag
worker organizations united at the end of August to form
the Workers Revolutionary Alliance (gonggelian), the
Guangzhou Military District expressed its support. When
the East Wind workers so united eleven days later, the
PLA decided not even to offer congratulations.34 Many of
the most radical Red Flag units - such as Zhongshan University Red Flag and Pearl River Film Studio East is Red
- began to publicly express their appreciation to the
local PLA and to Huang Yongsheng in particular.
        Local East Wind forces reacted strongly to the pre-
vailing trend, blaming Zhou Enlai and posting wall posters questioning his authority.35 In addition to attacks
on Zhou, East Wind forces obstructed the work of the Central Investigation Team, particularly in areas of the
city which remained under their control, such as Southern
Guangzhou.36
        It was in this atmosphere that the first agreement
between the two factions was signed on September 1 in
Beijing. In keeping with the emphasis in the first stage
of the negotiations, the four-point agreement stressed
the cessation of armed struggle and the sealing of weapons, declared opposition to further seizure of weapons
from the PLA, and supported the PLA in maintaining order
and the release of all arrested personnel.37 On September 5, the two factions in Guangzhou's Railway Bureau
signed a similar agreement.38

        September, 1967 to March, 1968: The Decline of the
        Rebels

        The Beijing Peace Talks (Stage 2). The second stage
of the Beijing Peace Talks lasted from September 5 to
November 14, but in a far different atmosphere than had
been the case in August. Although some of the initial
decisions to deradicalize the GPCR appear to have been
taken in August, it was only in September that the new
policy became evident.39 Decisions taken at an important
meeting of the Beijing Revoluionary Committee on September 1 specifically pointed to the new focus. For example, Chen Boda ordered all Beijing Red Guards doing liaison work in other areas of the country to return to the
capital by the 11th of the month.40 As a result of this
order, the Fighting Guangzhou Corps, made up of 123 organizations from 21 provinces and municipalities and a
major force in Guangzhou's anti-PLA movement since the
Corps' founding on August 9, announced its dissolution on
September 6.41
        Jiang Qing, in her speech to the Beijing Revolu-
tionary Committee, stressed the dual themes of support
for the PLA and emphasis on unity:

Of the several millions in the armed forces
very few are bad. And the slogan of going
everywhere to pluck out a small group of
individuals within the army is mistaken.
Making trouble among our own army is just
like tearing down the Great Wall. The important thing is for Beijing to get on with
the struggle, criticism and transformation,
the great unity and the triple alliance, and
to stop violent struggle.[42]

This emphasis continued throughout the month. On
September 5, a Central Committee Order prohibited the
seizure of military supplies from the PLA; perhaps even
more significant, in terms of its impact on recalcitrant
Rebels, Jiang Qing was "dragged" (her own term) to a conference of Anhui representatives specifically to defend
the PLA and the revolutionary committees then being formed;
moreover, at this same meeting she unequivocally rejected
her own slogan "attack with words and defend with force"
as unnecessary in the present situation.[43] Jiang's
speech was immediately transmitted to Guangzhou and given
wide publicity there.[44]
        Finally, Mao Zedong had recently returned from a
two-month tour of China's provinces convinced that the
split among the mass organizations was unnecessary. A
series of instructions, eventually to be called Mao's
"great strategic plan," began to be issued in the press.
The first instruction appeared on September 14 in a People's Daily editorial, as follows:

There is no conflict of fundamental interests
in the ranks of the working class. Under the
dictatorship of the proletariat, there is no
reason whatsoever for the working class to
split into organizations belonging to two opposing sides.[45]

It is not surprising, therefore, that when Zhou
Enlai next addressed Guangzhou's two factions, on September 27, his tone had changed completely. He began by
making it clear that the previous meetings had been geared to dealing with immediate, urgent problems, such as
armed struggle. Now, however, the "...more important
question...is how to move forward the revolutionary great
alliance through revolutionary criticism and repudiation...."[46] Citing Mao's recent directives, Zhou urged
an alliance between Guangzhou's factions be formed on the
basis of the slogan: "Fight self, repudiate revisionism"
(dousi pixiu). In the context of Guangzhou, repudiating
revisionism meant directing one's venom toward Tao Zhu
and Zhao Ziyang, rather than against the military. Zhou
made it clear that it was the Flag faction that would

have to prove itself on this point:

> For all the rebellious spirit shown in the
> past, you will have to be judged by whether
> you now direct the spearhead against revision-
> ism and the capitalist-roaders or whether you
> drag out the small handful within the army
> and old Tan of Guangdong.[47]

"Fight self" as well was directed at the Flag faction which, according to Zhou, was "laden with internal
contradictions." The faction was enjoined to unite its
own members quickly and then to unite with East Wind.
More ominously, in sharp contrast to his comments in August when he told Flag faction representatives that they
would occupy the majority of places in the preparatory
group for the Guangdong Provincial Revolutionary Committee, Zhou now warned the Rebels:

> Even if you rebelled earlier, have performed
> a great service and are large in number, that
> does not necessarily mean you must form the
> core of the alliance. Those who rebelled late
> and have performed less service have the right
> to repudiate revisionism.
>   There is no need to divide people into
> Flag faction and East Wind faction. Your Flag
> faction and East Wind faction are man-made.[48]

Zhou also insisted on the strengthening of military
control over public security organs, airports, railways,
warehouses, wharves and ports, on the return of weapons
still in the hands of factional forces, and on the effective (as distinct from the nominal) abolition of the
various headquarters. Each of these demands tended to
favor East Wind over Red Flag and were opposed by a vocal
minority of radicals in Flag faction units.

Throughout the autumn and into the winter, as the
consolidation and demobilization gathered momentum, the
East Wind faction, particularly in the schools, began to
recover its strength. As students returned to the
schools to work out, under PLA auspices, the establishment of revolutionary committees, as Mao Zedong Thought
Study Classes were set up to break down factional thinking,[49] and as the students were told to abandon their
links with the working class in order to return to their
schools to concern themselves with the task of educational reform, the Rebels had clearly lost the initiative.

The press began to contrast the "petty bourgeois
mentality" of student Rebels, who are able to stand firm
against oppression (such as that suffered under the work
teams) but cannot adjust to the dictates of "proletarian
discipline," with the virtues of the "true proletarian" -

the working class. The time had come for the students,
who had been instrumental in fanning the flames of the
GPCR to other sectors of society, once again to return to
their schools.

Zhou spoke again to Guangzhou representatives on October 19 (to five representatives of the Flag faction),
on October 31 (to representatives of the East Wind faction), on November 3 (to ten representatives of the Flag
faction), on November 8 (to representatives of both factions), and again on November 14 (to representatives of
both factions in the morning and again in the evening).[50]

The emphasis in each of these talks was on unity. On
October 19, Zhou told Flag faction representatives that
politically they were in a superior position to that of
their opponents. Nevertheless, Zhou continued, the question was whether they could turn this political advantage
into an advantage organizationally. Zhou strongly hinted
that if the Flag faction wished to maintain this advantage it would have to comply with the policies emanating
from the Center:

> Your general orientation is correct. If you
> grasp policy well, your opponents won't be
> able to catch up to you; of course, if you're
> backward, they'll catch up and we will welcome
> them and unite with them. The standard of
> being Left is to follow Mao Zedong Thought
> forever forward! Even if an organization
> originally was Rebel (zaofan), if you make
> mistakes of direction and moreover don't cor-
> rect them, can we protect you?[51]

In the same speech Zhou made clear some of the "cor-
rections" the Flag faction needed to make. For example,
he alluded to the rebellion of the sent-down youth, making it clear that they should obey the recent Central
directive to return to the countryside. In his later
speeches, Zhou kept returning to this theme. For example, on November 3 he warned Guangzhou's Rebels not to
follow the example of their counterparts in Hunan, who
had maintained close ties with the sent-down youth.
Guangzhou's Rebels, he argued, needed actively to convince these youth to return to the countryside. As he
put it to them: "You must express your attitude and put
out a statement to this effect."[52] But relations between
the Flag faction and the sent-down youth were somewhat
delicate. Many sent-down youth had made use of the opportunity provided by the GPCR to return to Guangzhou in
the hope that they could reestablish their urban residences, arguing that their enforced departure for the
countryside was due primarily to the erroneous policies
of power-holders such as Liu Shaoqi and Tao Zhu. Since
the Flag faction was also oriented toward an opposition

to powerholders, and to the status quo, a number of the sent-down youth groups - as well as other groups with grievances they wanted redressed - sought to win support from the Flag faction or, failing that, from some of the more radical consituent units within that faction. Nor was the relationship a one-way street. These "under-privileged" groups, such as the sent-down youth, were able to provide substantial support to the Rebels at cru-cial periods of the GPCR when many of the more "orthodox" members of the Flag faction found it discreet to withdraw from active participation. For instance, they remained active during the "March Black Wind" and provided man-power for the Rebels during the days of armed struggle in July and August. Nevertheless, following Zhou's com-ments, Flag faction leaders, always somewhat sensitive about their ties to "unorthodox" groups, began to sever even informal ties to these groups.

In spite of their attempts to accommodate themselves to the Center's new emphasis on unity, many Rebels re-mained apprehensive about the course the GPCR was taking. They realized that the Rebels had always been at a dis-advantage during periods of consolidation. It was pre-cisely in such periods that the forces representing "or-der" and "construction" - the PLA, the working class, the cadres - came to the fore, as indeed was the case in au-tumn 1967. And it was equally clear that, given the orientation of these forces for order, their return to center stage with the blessings of Mao and the central leadership meant that a revival in the fortunes of the East Wind faction would inevitably follow.

Throughout the GPCR the Rebels had insisted that they were the Left while their opponents had consistently been guilty of "defending the capitalist-roaders holding pow-er." Moreover, the Rebels had been backed in this as-sessment by the CCRG and Zhou Enlai on numerous occa-sions. It was because of such firm beliefs in their own "glorious" history of having been correct and vindicated at each key stage in the GPCR that they refused to consi-der East Wind as a revolutionary organization and were willing to put their trust in the central authorities leading the movement.

By early November, however, the emphasis on uni-ty and the formation of a great alliance made Zhou and the Center less willing to make invidious distinctions among mass organizations in their desire to unite the Left:

> In the past we said that we should take the
> Left as the core. Now ours all are revolu-
> tionary mass organizations. We sometimes say
> mass organizations and sometimes say revolu-
> tionary mass organizations. All the masses
> are determined to make revolution. Can it be

that under the conditions of proletarian
dictatorship the masses do not want to make
revolution? There is no strict distinction
between revolutionary organizations and
mass organizations.

The leadership, too, should be subject
to analysis. Some organizations were controlled by capitalist roaders last year;
this year they have changed because the capitalist roaders are no longer in power.[53]

Nor was Zhou willing to entertain any more discussion concerning "grievances" or reversal of cases from
the Rebels. In his last reception of Guangzhou's mass
organizations he made the point very clear:

On the question of reversing the judgement
passed on the "August 1 Corps," don't bring
up the issue any more because the wrong
done to the whole organization has been redressed while the examination report of the
military district command has also mentioned
it. No more reversal of cases, and this also
applies to factories, since they have formed
an alliance.[54] (emphasis added).

Radicals vs. Moderates Within the Flag Faction

In spite of misgivings, most of the Flag faction
leadership dutifully went along with the official policy.
Upon returning to Guangzhou, they pushed strongly for the
realization of student, worker, and peasant alliances
with their East Wind counterparts. On December 30, 1967,
a citywide alliance representing Guangzhou's university
and college students was set up and by January 1 more
than 80 percent of the city's universities and colleges
had achieved successful alliances. A citywide alliance
of workers took a bit longer, but was established by late
January. By February 17 there was a peasant alliance as
well.

Support for the new policies was far from uniform
within the Flag faction, however. Opposition had been
building since September but only crystallized in late
December as a result of two related events: an important
conference held by the Flag faction in the city of Foshan
from December 9 to 19, to which most of its consituent
units sent delegates; and a meeting of the preparatory
committee of the Provincial Revolutionary Committee on
December 12, at which Huang Yongsheng delivered an important speech. Representatives from both factions attended the December 12 meeting, including some Rebel
leaders who were also attending the meetings in Foshan.

The impact of these two events can be appreciated most fully only if one is clear as to the atmosphere prevailing among Rebel units at that time. Under pressure from the Center, the Beijing Peace Talks had turned what had been an armed struggle between two factions into a quest for unity. At the same time Huang Yongsheng, the regional military commander who had long been supported by one faction and vilified by the other, had been put in charge of the preparatory committee of the Guangdong Provincial Revolutionary Committee small group. Needless to say, there were many Rebels who remained unconvinced that Huang had suddenly developed an understanding of the purpose of the GPCR or would now be able to distinguish "revolutionaries" from "conservatives." Moreover, many of these same people questioned some of the decisions agreed to in Beijing by their representatives, or interpreted these decisions in a far different manner than their leaders.

The Foshan meeting, then, was called to sum up the situation as Flag faction leaders viewed it at that time, and to arrive at a unified policy for the future. The conclusions reached at the meeting reaffirmed Flag faction support for Huang Yongsheng and the politics of consolidation. Under the slogan, "the general situation has already become fixed and power has been grasped" (dazhu yiding, daquan zaiwo), Flag leaders supported Huang Yongsheng and the other members of the newly established Provincial Revolutionary Preparatory Small Group; agreed that Tao Zhu, Zhao Ziyang, and their supporters had already completely collapsed; and made a self-criticism concerning their previous antagonistic attitude and erroneous slogans against the Military District Command.55

However, rather than develop a unified policy for the Flag faction, the Foshan meeting only exacerbated the split between moderates and radicals within the faction. Not surprisingly, most of the radicals were from units affiliated to the Red Headquarters, such as the August 1 Combat Corps; in this instance, however, much of the Red Headquarters leadership supported the moderate position.

Huang Yongsheng's speech on December 12, coming at precisely the same time that the Flag faction moderates had acknowledged Huang's leading role in Guangzhou's future, clearly revealed the dilemma Flag faction leaders faced in trying to adhere to central policy, support Huang Yongsheng, and still maintain some control over their increasingly recalcitrant basic-level units. Huang, for example, made the following points in summing up the situation in Guangzhou:

Some organizations and some people have a debate of principle on the question of who

should be the core of the alliance.... Ours
are revolutionary mass organizations. It is
incorrect to appoint any of our organizations
to be the core.... (It is) necessary to eagerly and patiently help those comrades who
had been influenced by "ultra-Left" ideas.

Recently the atmosphere in Guangzhou has
become tense and factionalism is serious.
Some people do not act according to Chairman
Mao's instructions and yet they accuse other
organizations of being "Right" and "conservative" and hinder them by all possible means.
Some people demolish the mountain strongholds
while some others establish new mountain strongholds. Some organizations fight self-interest
and repudiate revisionism, while some others
prepare for violent struggle and scheme big-
scale disturbances....[56]

In his speech, Huang cited the three greatest dangers
to Guangzhou as: 1) demons and monsters; 2) reactionary
influence and Japanese and Soviet secret agents; and 3)
attempted vindication of provincialism. Moreover, Huang
also called for the return to their own provinces of all
those still in Guangzhou on chuanlian, in particular
singling out the "3,200 men of Hunan Xiangjiang Fenglei,"
that province's most radical organization. And, he
insisted that youth from rural areas should quickly return to those areas, telling mass organizations in the
cities not to accept or support them in their activities
in Guangzhou.[57]

The juxtaposition of Huang's speech - unequivocally
pointing to elements within the Flag faction as the principal stumbling blocks in the GPCR - with what Flag faction radicals regarded as the toadying behavior of their
own leadership led to open opposition to the latter's
"reformism" (gailiang zhuyi). Essentially, the issue was
the assessment of the GPCR at the current stage and the
requirements necessary to carry the movement to a successful conclusion. More specifically, the issues in
dispute between moderates and radicals covered the following points: a) Was power already in the hands of the
revolutionaries or was it still in dispute? b) What
should be the role of the provincial preparatory group
headed by Huang Yongsheng? c) How should one interpret
Zhou Enlai's instructions as delivered during the Beijing
Peace Talks and how should one go about implementing
Mao's "great strategic plan"? d) What was the nature of
the Conservative mass organizations and the leadership of
those organizations? Could they be allied with at present? e) Could one still legitimately speak of a distinction between "Left" and "Right" in the movement, or

had all mass organizations become revolutionary? f) Had
the relationship between leaders and masses within the
Flag faction changed since the period of consolidation
had begun? g) Had Tao Zhu, Zhao Ziyang, and their "sworn
partners" really collapsed and was it clear which cadres
could be trusted and which should be opposed? h) Had
those victimized during the early stages of the GPCR been
fully rehabilitated?

Flag faction radicals rejected completely the spirit
of the Foshan meeting with its emphasis on self-criticism
and the speedy realization of a "great alliance" and
pointed instead to the struggle that still lay ahead. In
place of the slogan "the general situation has already
become fixed and power has been grasped" they substituted
"the general situation is still undecided and power is
still in dispute" (dazhu weiding, daquan zaizheng).58

The split between moderates and radicals in the Flag
faction dominated Guangzhou's GPCR politics between January and March 1968, with the dispute almost immediately
drawing the attention of all the competing elements in
Guangzhou's political struggle. The position of the radicals was diametrically opposed to the decisions reached
at the Foshan meeting. For example, on the crucial issue
of power, the radicals argued as follows:

> Some of the heads said that "the power is now
> in our hands" and "the founding of the Guang-
> dong Provincial Preparatory Group for the Rev-
> olutionary Committee has announced the complete
> collapse of the black headquarters of Tao and
> Zhao and announced that the proletarian head-
> quarters has held firmly the political power
> in Guangdong." First of all, let us see whether
> or not the power is in our hand! The Provincial
> Preparatory Group is trusted by the Central
> Committee, and of that there should be no
> doubt. However, it is still a preparatory
> group. What is there to prepare? To prepare
> a leadership team, is it enough to rely on only
> two responsible comrades of the Central-South
> Bureau and five from the military region?
> Exceedingly few of the provincial and munic-
> ipal leading cadres have been outstanding,
> and none of the principal leaders' character
> can be confirmed! Furthermore, power cannot
> be an empty framework. It should include the
> power of all districts and units at the basic
> levels and all the departments. This power
> should be seized from the bottom up. It is
> impossible for the Provincial Preparatory
> Group to give power to them one by one from
> the top down. Is power now entirely in the
> hands of proletarian revolutionaries in all

units? You may count the great number of
factories from the People's Brigade onward.
Can you point out any one of them "holding
power in its hand?!"[59]

Nor were the radicals willing to accept Zhou Enlai's
admonition to forego any further attmepts at rehabilitation work:

In the early stage of the great cultural revolution movement in Guangzhou, the revolutionary
masses of many factories, enterprises, schools
and literary and art departments were branded
as "counterrevolutionary." Thus far, these
people have not been completely rehabilitated,
let alone certain leading cadres at the intermediate level. This shows the widespread and
deep-rooted poison spread by the bourgeois
reactionary line in Guangzhou.[60]

In fact, it was precisely the kinds of people the
radicals felt should be rehabilitated that Huang Yongsheng had labelled stumbling blocks to the movement in
his December speech, i.e., those he referred to as
"ghosts and monsters."[61]
The radicals were particularly critical of those who
rushed to implement Zhou's instructions on forming alliances as quickly as possible:

In uniting all the mass organizations at the
present moment, we should of course forge alliances on the basis of Mao Zedong's Thought
and through extensive consultations, not alliances on the orders issued and time set by
certain authorities....[62]

Moreover, they deliberately ignored Zhou's clear-cut
statements in November that mass organizations hence-
forth were to be treated equally, with previous distinctions favoring "Leftists" as the core no longer necessary. And, they played down the importance of alliances
between the factions at the present stage:

The present alliance between the two major
factions is in fact merely a union for con-
sultative and liaison purposes, far from
playing the part of unified leadership. Only
when the "Left" faction has greater superiority
in the relative strength between the two major
factions (not merely in the relative number
of places in the united organ) can the members
of that faction play the role of unified leadership. Therefore, even if the two major

factions have now formed an alliance, they
should not immediately abandon their "mountain strongholds." This is because if the
Rebels do so, in a certain sense they will
be abandoning the struggle in the course
of forming an alliance and abandoning their
responsibility for leading the great cultural revolution movement.63

As to the nature of the mass organizations, the radicals ridiculed the notion that they should be treated
equally:

Talking nonsense (some people) said: "After
Chairman Mao's latest instructions have been
transmitted to the lower levels, it is no
longer necessary to make an analysis of the
historical backgrounds and lines of the mass
organizations. Since there is no distinction
between the revolutionaries and the conservatives, we are all members of the "Left." As
such, all should be treated on an equal footing and should form alliances unconditionally."64

Some uncompromisingly and ominously suggested that
the "peaceful transformation" of Conservatives into
Rebels was an impossibility:

In short, it is impossible for the Conservative masses to "peacefully grow" to be Rebels!
    The bad heads of the Conservatives were
black henchmen of the capitalist roaders!
They hoodwinked others, and are not to be included with those who "were hoodwinked but
guiltless!" Those reactionary fellows should
definitely be attacked and thoroughly exposed
before we can win over the broad hookwinked
masses.
They are the victims, but they are different
from the Rebels. One is the victim, the other
is the persecuted. The former was obsessed
with self-interest either to keep certain advantages already gained or because of having
been hoodwinked and, thus, poisoned. Therefore, it was basically impossible that they
could have offered the same resistance as the
Rebels against the persecution of the bourgeois
reactionary line.65

Finally, the radicals felt that their erstwhile leaders had become self-satisfied and opportunistic, no longer deigning to consult with those at the basic levels.66

It was not long before these radicals - dubbed
"ultra-Leftists" by their opponents - were informally
united organizationally in a group called the "August 5
Commune." Rejecting the orthodox leadership of the Flag
faction because of what it regarded as the latter's all-
consuming interest in striving for seats on the Provincial Revolutionary Committee (set up on February 21,
1968), the August 5 Commune in a similar manner to the
more well-known Provincial Proletarian Alliance (Shengwulian) of Hunan province began to devote its attention
to an examination of the causes of the present adverse
current in the GPCR. And, as Shengwulian had, it concluded that the official delineation of classes in China
was no longer relevant. The main contradiction in
Chinese society was now embodied in the struggle of those
most underprivileged - such as sent-down youth and con-
tract workers - against those who had usurped the power
of the working class.[67]

This internecine split within the Flag faction provided the East Wind faction with a golden opportunity to
seize the initiative in defense of the instructions of
the Party Center and the soon-to-be-established Provincial Revolutionary Committee. Hunan's Shengwulian
had been publicly labelled a counterrevolutionary organization by the CCRG leadership on January 24, and a
movement was immediately launched throughout the country
to combat the "'ultra-Left' trend of thought" then prevalent in many areas. Although the Flag faction leaders
of necessity joined the attack on the "ultra-Leftists,"
they were unavoidably caught in a very uncomfortable
squeeze. Whereas the East Wind Conservatives could
freely oppose everything the August 5 Commune had espoused, for the Flag faction the issue was more complex.
To begin with, the radicals being attacked all had been
and, in many cases, still were members of units within
the ever-decentralized Flag faction. In spite of their
disagreements with the Flag leadership they were still
attempting to convince those within their own faction to
alter their assessment of the current situation. Moreover, in tracing the development of the GPCR to date, the
radicals offered effusive praise for such previous epi-
sodes as the January power seizure by the SGL forces, the
resistance to the "March Black Wind," and so forth, all
of which were a part of the shared experiences of the
Flag faction and/or the Red Headquarters as a whole.
Although the faction's leaders, as part of the agreement
worked out at the Center to facilitate the establishment
of great alliances and revolutionary committees, had re-
frained from referring to such past glories, they could
do little when radical elements organized celebrations to
commemorate the anniversaries of these events. The ob-
servance of the first anniversary of the SGL power sei-

zure in particular drew strong support even from some moderate elements in the Flag faction, much to the distaste of the East Wind forces and the PLA.[68]

East Wind propagandists hammered hard on the theme of the dangers of ultra-Leftism, focusing their attacks not only on the most vulnerable targets such as the August 5 Commune, but also broadening their offensive to include cadres who were being supported by the Flag faction. They concentrated much of their fire on the Central-South Bureau, a stronghold of Flag faction support, in particular singling out those cadres who had publicly taken a stand criticizing the PLA's role in the GPCR during the heady days of August 1967.[69]

The balancing act attempted by the Flag faction leaders as they tried to follow closely Mao's "great strategic plan," support the local power structure headed by Huang Yongsheng and Guangzhou's military authorities, and defend themselves against East Wind's charges of "ultra-Leftism" while at the same time retaining the support of the rank-and-file at the basic levels, was becoming more and more difficult by March. All along Flag leaders had recognized that their fortunes rested on the ability and willingness of central leaders to intervene in the local situation in Guangzhou. Whenever Huang Yongsheng had a relatively free hand, the Rebels had been suppressed; whenever Huang faced constraints from Beijing, the local PLA had adopted a more even-handed policy. For this reason, Flag leaders had urged their subordinate organizations to accede to central wishes and accept Huang's leadership as unavoidable.

In late February, when the Guangdong Provincial and Guangzhou Municipal Revolutionary Committees were finally set up, the Flag faction had one more instance of the differing perspectives of central and local authorities. The provincial committee was set up under the auspices of central leaders in Beijing; the Guangzhou Municipal Revolutionary Committee, on the other hand, was arranged directly by the provincial revolutionary preparatory small group and the Municipal Military Control Commission. The personnel differences between the two committees are instructive.

Inevitably, the most important posts on the provincial committee were occupied by military figures, including the chairman (Huang Yongsheng) and the first vice-chairman (Kong Shiquan). In addition, three of the remaining seven vice-chairmen were also military figures.[70] Nevertheless, below the top level, mass organizations in general and the Flag faction in particular did well. For example, on the standing committee, around 40% of the 33 members were mass organization representatives. Of the 180 members of the provincial committee, only 15% were cadres or PLA men.

In terms of factional representation on the standing committee, the Flag faction had five representatives, including a vice-chairman; the East Wind had four representatives, with no vice-chairman. Moreover, Flag-nominated cadres outnumbered East Wind-nominated cadres five to three.[71]

The municipal committee, however, although set up at the same time, revealed a different pattern. Once again, the PLA dominated at the top level, with the chairman and two of the five vice-chairmen representing the military. On the standing committee, East Wind prevailed as well. Four of the five cadres chosen were supported by East Wind, while three of the five mass representatives who can be identified also were East Wind supporters. None of the cadres from the Central-South Bureau who had been nominated by the Flag faction was given a position; at the same time, the cadre opposed most strongly by them - Jiao Linyi - was chosen as one of the committee's vice-chairmen.[72] The Rebels were later to complain that "'80% of the working personnel of the Guangzhou Municipal Revolutionary Committee was pro-East Wind' and, at the lower level, 'almost all working personnel of the revolutionary committee were the same groups of the old political department.'"[73]

Perhaps the most important lesson the Rebels learned from the allocation of seats on these committees was that even after the Center had given a clear signal, through its approval of the choices for the provincial committee, the Guangzhou Military District had felt under no compulsion to follow that lead in its choices for lower-level committees. In other words, it seemed clear that the fate of the Rebels once more was in the hands of the PLA.

Events following the establishment of the revolutionary committees soon confirmed that the Rebels were correct. Both military leaders and East Wind began increasingly to attack the "factionalism" practiced by the Flag faction, which was held to be obstructing the formation of "great alliances." Moreover, they began once again to reinterpret previous GPCR developments. For example, the attack on the Guangzhou Military District by the Rebels back in February 1967 was now said to have been a manifestation of the "February Adverse Current" and was indicative of the consistent anti-PLA bias the Rebels had demonstrated.

The Conservative forces continued to press for immediate alliances. The results of alliances set up on the basis of systems (xitong) and trades (hangye) decimated what limited strength the Rebels had possessed among workers and peasants. With their far greater strength in the factories and suburban communes, the Conservative East Wind forces quickly took over control of the Guangzhou Worker and Peasant Representative Committees (gongdaihui and nongdaihui), leaving the Flag faction in a superior position only among the Red Guard Representative Committee (hongdaihui). The latter committee remained in an adversary relationship with the worker and peasant committees for many months, constantly under great pressure from the PLA and the East Wind forces. Finally, in August 1968, when the Rebels were in the process of being completely suppressed, a revolt in the hongdaihui brought that organization back into line as well.

One of the first acts of the new provincial revolutionary committee was an attempt to reinstate order in Guangzhou. To accomplish this, a Workers' Picket Team (gongren jiuchadui) was set up early in March. Not surprisingly, since the basic-level worker organizations were controlled by the East Wind and the PLA, very few workers who had been affiliated with the Flag faction found their way onto these teams. Originally an appendage of the gongdaihui, by the end of the GPCR these armed worker organizations were to become the instruments used by the military in their final suppression of the Flag faction.[74]

ISSUES DIVIDING GUANGZHOU'S MIDDLE SCHOOL STUDENTS

The above account, tracing factionalism in Guangzhou down to spring 1968, is generally applicable to developments at both university and middle school levels. Indeed, during this period there was a good deal of cooperation between factional adherents at the two levels. Nevertheless, not all issues arising in this period were equally important to university and middle school students. For example, educational reform seems to have concerned middle school students much more than their university counterparts. Nor did students at the two levels react to the events of 1967-68 in quite the same way. The present section examines the responses of Guangzhou's middle school students to some of the key developments in this period, such as the tension within factional units during times of change, the debate over educational reform, and the formation of revolutionary committees.

Wendou, Wudou, and Jin'gen: Rebels vs. Rebels and Conservatives vs. Conservatives in the Middle Schools

The division of school-level factions into wendou and wudou units, while by no means entirely absent among university students, was repeatedly brought up by interviewees as a particularly prominent feature at the middle school level, especially in the better schools containing both children of cadres and children of intellectuals. Moreover, this division was common in both Rebel and Conservative units.

The split can be traced directly to the rather chaotic days of armed struggle in summer 1967, although the roots of the split go back to an even earlier period. Essentially, what separated those who favored armed struggle from those who did not - among both the Rebels and the Conservatives - was the question of the nature of the 'enemy' and the proper method to deal with him. Among the Doctrine Guards, for example, the wudou elements accused the Rebels of engaging in an attempt to "overturn the proletarian dictatorship and restore the bourgeoisie to power." The wendou elements were sanguine about the possibilities of winning over the majority of the Rebels. Wudou elements often displayed contempt for their wendou counterparts, looking upon the latter as bookworms. As one interviewee who led the Rebel wendou faction at his school put it: "The wudou group would constantly ask us: 'Where has your broadcasting equipment come from? Your paper to print newspapers? If not for us, how could you people ever be successful?'"[75]

As the conflict in Guangzhou escalated, the wudou groups, ostensibly a subordinate unit under the faction's steering committee, began to act more and more independently. After the Wuhan Incident in July, armed struggle departments of many Rebel units felt their view of the contradictions dividing the factions had been vindicated and split off almost completely from the overall command structure of their school's faction. In some schools in the Eastern District - Number 7 is a prime example - the Rebels had been able to chase the Conservatives away from the school during the armed struggle period but the latter, whose homes were nearby, were periodically able to launch surprise attacks on the school. In this type of situation, the influence of wudou elements became stronger than ever as they turned the school into an armed fortress. The wendou policy of trying to organize triangular talks among the Rebels, Conservatives, and the Military Training Group (MTG) had little chance of success in this atmosphere of mutual suspicion.

In many schools, however, wudou units, being quite small, had a more limited influence on the overall faction. Steering committees had a number of methods they could use to keep wudou groups under at least a minimum of control. For example, they made certain that a key member of the wudou unit would have a seat on the steering committee so that communication lines would remain open at all times. Moreover, some steering committees set up an "acrobatic skills squad" which often was larger and had a greater combat strength than the wudou unit. If the wudou group became too estranged from the parent organization and refused to recognize the authority of the latter, these "acrobatic skill squads" could take on some of the functions the wudou groups had performed. Ultimately, since both wudou and wendou elements needed each other, estrangement seldom reached these outer limits. The Eastern District's wudou Rebel units came closest when they joined together, during the height of armed struggle, to set up the Guangzhou Regiment Garrison Headquarters. Even in this instance, however, and in spite of their relative independence, they retained the name of their parent organization: the Guangzhou Regiment.

With the arrival of the "Beijing Peace Talks" and the new emphasis on consolidation and unity in September 1967, the strict division between wendou and wudou groupings became less salient. The publication in late September of a series of comments made by Mao during a tour of North, Central, and East China was soon to lead to a new division, particularly within the ranks of the Rebels. Chairman Mao's "Great Strategic Plan" stressed unity and consolidation. Among other things, Mao stressed that too many cadres had been overthrown; that the Left-wing must be educated to prevent it from becoming ultra-Left; that chaos must be avoided in the army and the latter's prestige must be safeguarded; that the presence of two factions in an organization did not mean that one was leftist and the other rightist.[76]

Almost immediately the call went out to "closely follow Chairman Mao's Great Strategic Plan."[77] At first, of course, all GPCR participants, regardless of factional alignment, claimed to be "closely following" (jin'gen) Mao's plan. Rather quickly, however, as it was clear that this plan strongly favored their East Wind opponents, a fair number of Rebels began to resist the new orientation. Leaders of the Red Headquarters, for example, held a series of meetings to which they invited representatives from their subordinate units in order to explain the new central policy, but their efforts were far from a complete success.[78]

The first issue which revealed the recalcitrance of a segment of the Rebels was the question of turning over weapons (jiaoqiang) to the military. One former Rebel leader described the atmosphere at these September meetings:

> The question of turning over weapons surfaced
> after the September 5 Order. The headquarters
> held a meeting. The policy of the Center was
> now very clear and could no longer be fudged.
> Some leaders at this meeting actually were
> in tears. They said that they did not under-
> stand what was happening or why. In the
> secondary schools, among rank-and-file, there

was also this feeling. Even though leaders
like Wu Chuanbin told them to turn in weapons,
the masses and some leaders as well were not
convinced. Many weapons were hidden.[79]

In spite of the existence of such feelings among
some of the Rebels, it seems clear that the majority of
the Rebels rallied behind the jin'gen slogan. Indeed,
the pressure on them to do so was quite strong. For
example, a Red Flag editorial on September 17 tied the
policy of "great alliance" to Mao's comment that there
was no fundamental split within the working class. A
People's Daily editorial on the 22nd, entitled "The Great
Historical Current," reiterated this theme. This emphasis continued throughout September; in early October,
"fight self and criticize revisionism" became the key
slogan of the GPCR.[80]
    Interviewees in leadership positions reported on the
pressure they felt to adapt to this "great alliance
tide." Some among them began to feel that their own assessment of the situation had been erroneous and that
they were in danger of being "washed away by history";
others felt that whatever their "subjective hopes," ac-
commodation with the new policy was essential.[81] It
became very fashionable at this time to become jin'gen
and to criticize those responding with less alacrity as
"imbued with selfishness." The Central Investigation
Team, arriving from Beijing at the end of August, adopted
a "neutral" policy toward the factions and was succeeding
where the MTGs had failed. The wudou elements, so strong
in July and August, had little support in September and
October.[82]
    The Municipal Military Control Commission and the
Central Investigation Team sought to take advantage of
this surging tide by bringing leaders of the two factions
together to discuss implementation of the policy of
"great alliance." On October 12, a People's Daily editorial promoted the establishment of "Mao Zedong Thought
Study Classes" throughout the country and the Military
Control Commission began to organize classes for Guangzhou's middle school Red Guards. In general, the Central
Investigation Team forums, at which Rebel and Conservative middle school leaders met and exchanged views for
the first time, were much more successful than the Mao
Study classes sponsored by the Military Control Commission. For example, the top leaders of the Doctrine
Guards and the Guangzhou Regiment finally met for the
first time under Investigation Team auspices. The Control Commission, recognizing that it was still viewed
with some suspicion by a significant percentage of the
leading Rebels, changed its strategy in November. It
began subtly to shift the format of the Mao Study classes
from one in which leaders of the two factions would meet

to develop a common outlook on unity to one in which factional members who had participated most openly in armed struggle met for thinly-disguised classes in proletarian discipline.[83]

But the Control Commission organized more legitimate study classes as well. As "great alliances" were beginning to be realized in a number of secondary schools in Guangzhou - by December 23 over 60 of Guangzhou's middle schools had formed such alliances - with a corresponding weakness in the strength of the mass organizations, the Control Commission decided to set up study classes in each of Guangzhou's four districts.

The Eastern District class at August 1 Middle School was typical. Classes were conducted over a two week period after which those most successful in "struggling against selfishness and criticizing revisionism" became "models" and were sent on a tour of all the Eastern District schools to report on the success of the class. To build up support for the program, the first two classes were made up solely of those who were jin'gen elements and, because of this, were quite successful. By the third class - which lasted for three weeks in January 1968 - there was an attempt once again to bring together leaders of the two factions. Under the slogan that "there is no fundamental difference between the factions," the familiar method of forming "red pairs" was utilized. It worked fairly well until the "red pair" left the isolation of the class and became involved once more in the factional issues still current in society.

Once outside the class, leaders were frequently under pressure from their subordinates to demonstrate factional solidarity. For example, on January 21, the anniversary of the establishment of the Guangzhou Regiment, some of the organization's members made preparations for an anniversary celebration, marching to the study class to inform their leaders and to get their support. Several thousand of the organization's members attended the celebrations and the leaders, far from opposing this example of factional behavior, ended up writing the anniversary speech. Not surpisingly, the Doctrine Guards registered a strong protest with the Military Control Commission. The anniversary of the establishment of SGL on January 22 produced an even larger demonstration of support and a correspondingly larger protest as well.

But with central leaders and the Military Control Commission both pushing strongly for unity and the "levelling of mountain-tops," Guangzhou's middle school Rebels knew that they would have to move quickly in the direction of unity or risk being overtaken by events. It was with this in mind that most of the middle school Rebel organizations united together at the end of 1967 to form the "Middle School Revolutionary Alliance" (zhong-

xue gelian). With the constituent members - including
the Guangzhou Regiment, the New First Headquarters and
the Third Headquarters Middle School Departments and the
Red Combat Regiment - more concerned about the units
within their command structure, however, this "Alliance"
was never much more than an empty shell.

The movement toward unity seems to have been strongest in November and December, with the Foshan meeting in
December representing the movement's peak. The Foshan
meeting and Huang Yongsheng's December 12 speech also
mark the beginning of the decline of the jin'gen forces.
As it became clear to many Rebels that the ultimate consequences of the policy being pursued by Huang and the
military would be the permanent subordination of the Flag
faction, "closely following," which had been a term of
approbation at first, now began to take on a different
connotation, one closer to naivete at best or opportunism
at worst.

According to one former top leader who had considered himself to be jin'gen in October and November, by January he would no longer have used this term to describe
his attitude.[84] Making a somewhat self-serving distinction, he argued that by winter 1968 there were at least
three competing forces within the ranks of middle school
Rebels: the closely following faction (jin'gen pai); the
realistic faction (shixian pai); and the ultra-left faction (jizuo pai). Placing himself in the second of these
categories, he felt that the realists were those whose
ideology was close to the ultra-Left, but whose actions
tended to be closer to those followed by the jin'gen
forces. As he put it, there were basically two kinds of
people who remained firmly in the jin'gen camp:

> One was those whose backgrounds were question-
> able because of bad class origin or because
> of family problems and who had been politically
> active up to that point. Perhaps they feared
> the consequences. Another group was mostly
> worker kids, especially YCL members, who had
> favored such things as turning in weapons, etc.[85]

"Ultra-Leftism" had begun as a reaction against the
jin'gen group. Leaving Guangzhou for the more congenial
atmosphere of Wuhan or Changsha, those opposed to such
developments as the Foshan meeting returned with glowing
reports of the radical activities carried out by Rebel
units in Hubei and Hunan. It was these "radicals," whose
articles have been cited earlier in this chapter, who
sought to convince the mainstream of the Rebel faction to
resist what they called unprincipled unity.[86]

Educational Reform: Rebels vs. Conservatives in the Middle Schools

If university students, to judge from the Red Guard newspapers they published, seemed primarily concerned with the larger societal issues of the GPCR, beyond the confines of their schools, middle school students on the contrary devoted proportionally much more time to questions of education. When one does find discussions of educational reform in newspapers issued by university groups, they tend to be in specialized newspapers devoted only to this subject.[87]

Although there seem to be several reasons for this phenomenon, perhaps the primary reason can be traced to the fact that one of the key values to be achieved in Chinese society is entrance to a university. Because of the scarcity of places open at that level, the competition to enter a university - particularly a good university - was extremely keen. Those who had already succeeded in this competition had, in a real sense, surmounted the major hurdle in the system. Indeed, one of the key debates presented in middle school newspapers, that of the proper criteria for university entrance, was no longer directly relevant to university students.

It was educational reform that had been the first issue to galvanize China's middle school students into action back in June 1966. As the movement expanded, however, involving the students in broader societal issues outside the school, a concern with educational reform had seemed to many to be too parochial and even selfish an issue to consider while the Manichean struggle between capitalism and socialism was raging.[88] It was precisely because of this attitude on the part of the students that periodic attempts - the most sustained one having occurred with much fanfare in spring 1967 - to return the students to the schools to deal with the question of educational reform had been notably unsuccessful. Moreover, Rebels in particular saw this issue as something of a red herring that would only divert the GPCR from its more essential concerns, such as the organization of power in Chinese society. Once these more crucial, primary questions were solved, secondary issues such as the reform of the school system could be addressed.

By fall 1967, however, the issue of educational reform could no longer be so cavalierly slighted as secondary in nature. The cessation of armed struggle and the call to break up organizations cutting across functional lines had the consequence once more of turning the attention of the students inward toward the problems of their own schools. For the first time in many months, the Center's new policies had brought the two factions face to face with each other. The Doctrine Guards, who had been chased away from many schools during the armed struggle phase because of the superior strength of the Rebels,[89] were again able to return to their schools in force.[89] Central directives and People's Daily editorials emphasized the need to reopen the schools and criticize "the bourgeois system of education."[90] The MTGs again began to play an active role in leading the resumption of classes and the criticism of the old educational system.

Not surprisingly, the issue of educational reform, as was the case with most issues surfacing during the GPCR, immediately became entangled in factional politics. Initially, it was the Doctrine Guards who enthusiastically embraced the new role assigned to the students. Criticism of the "bourgeois educational system" that "discriminated against children of working class and peasant families" had, after all, been the key theme at the beginning of the GPCR. It was only after the movement had expanded that the Rebels, capitalizing on the mistakes committed by the "overzealous" Doctrine Guards, had seized the initiative. A return to this early issue, the Conservatives felt, negated many of the merits the Rebels had subsequently accumulated. The Rebels were noticeably less enthusiastic about the issue of educational reform, but when they saw it as irresistable, they too moved quickly to stake out a position.

Basically, the differences between the Conservative Doctrine Guards and the Flag faction Rebels came down to their answers to a series of interrelated questions: 1) What should be the purpose of the educational revolution? 2) What was the relationship between the issue of educational reform and other issues that had surfaced during the GPCR? 3) Who were to be the main targets of the proposed revolution in education? Who were to be the main beneficiaries of this revolution? Put another way, who was to blame for the old educational system, who had benefitted from it, and who had been disadvantaged by it? 4) Could the educational revolution be isolated from the other issues concurrently under discussion both inside and outside the schools?

On each of these questions, Rebels and Conservatives offered divergent views. Although one of the few points on which the two sides partially agreed was the need for some sort of educational revolution, the first contentious issue they faced was a disagreement over the nature of the old educational system that had to be changed. The Doctrine Guards, repeatedly quoting Mao to buttress their case, maintained that the major problem in the schools was one of teachers. If these "bourgeois educational authorities" - routinely referred to as "bastards" (wangba) in the accounts of the Doctrine Guards - could be eliminated,[91] then the schools could be put back on the right track.[91] It had been the control of the schools by these "authorities" that had produced both the revisionist educational content and the enrollment and cultivation of children from bourgeois and petty bourgeois class origin, to be molded into clones of their mentors. To the Doctrine Guards, the schools needed to be reclaimed by Party cadres who would transform the content of the curriculum as well as change the social base of recruitment by eliminating the children of bourgeois and petty bourgeois intellectuals and replacing them with children of workers, peasants, and cadres. In this regard, they felt that the early thrust of the GPCR in the secondary schools - to focus attacks on teachers, particularly those of bad class background - had been correct. Thus, the Doctrine Guards saw the educational revolution as a straightforward question concerned with the control of the schools, which could be handled simply by removing power from the hands of the teachers.

While this argument had been a powerful one during the early stages of the GPCR and, in fact, had been generally supported by the large majority of secondary school students, much had happened in the interim to cast doubt on the veracity of this rather simplistic account of the power structure of the schools. Moreover, unlike the period at the beginning of the GPCR, the Rebels - the majority of whom were of middle class origin - were no longer intimidated by the good class origin of their opponents. The twists and turns of the GPCR had provided them with a great deal of ammunition with which to challenge the position taken by the Conservatives.

By fall 1967 the Rebels had at least two advantages that they had not possessed earlier. First, the earlier educational reform campaign had occurred before the children of cadres had become infected by blood line theory and before the venality of Party cadres at all levels of the hierarchy had been revealed. Therefore, when the Conservatives once again set out after teachers of bad class origin as the prime culprits responsible for the ills of the educational system, the Rebels could accuse them of attempting to peddle the officially discredited blood line theory and shielding the real villians: the capitalist-roaders within the Party.

Second, as a result of the Cultural Revolution, a great deal of material concerning the pre-GPCR educational system had been selectively leaked by various factions in the education bureau sympathetic to one or another of the antagonists. The Rebels had discovered, for example, that the best schools in Guangzhou - most notably Guangya and Huafu - had refocused their enrollment policies in 1964 and 1965 to favor children of cadres over all other categories of students. Although they had been more or less aware of such a phenomenon on the basis of their own experience or that of their friends, they now had some hard statistical data to publish to document this point. Guangya's Rebel newspapers in 1968, for example, began publishing enrollment figures for the 1964 and 1965 classes (see Chapter One for details on these figures). These figures resonated strongly with Rebel charges that children of cadres formed a special stratum in society with the socialization that prepared them for taking their place in this stratum beginning first in their homes under the tutelage of their parents (the GPCR's capitalist-roaders) and then continuing in the schools (where they were set apart from more "ordinary" students).

Pressing these advantages, the Rebel challenge to the Conservatives was based on the following two points: 1) It was the leadership of the Party committees in the schools and, through the chain of command, Party leaders all the way up to Liu Shaoqi at the top, who were the cause of the revisionist educational system; teachers were simply pawns taking orders. 2) The social base of recruitment indeed needed to be changed; however, the problem there was not that children of bourgeois and petty bourgeois intellectuals were disproportionately represented in the better schools, but that children of cadres and military officers had, in the name of the workers and peasants, usurped the latter's places in the schools.

Further, once in the schools, children of cadres and military officers had set themselves up as a separate privileged stratum (tequan jieceng) apart from the rest of the student body. The Rebels concluded, on the basis of the situation described above, that the revolution in education could fully be realized only by an expansion and redirection of those to be targeted. They maintained that it was ridiculous to view the problems in education as an isolated issue. Getting rid of some so-called "counterrevolutionary teachers" would not really alter anything. The educational system, as a reflection of society, could not be transformed without first dealing with more fundamental societal problems.[92] The spearhead, therefore, would have to be directed vertically, through the Party institution itself, to show the links between local power-holders and the revisionists like Liu Shaoqi near the apex of the Party hierarchy.

In spite of some differences of viewpoint separating those more radical from the mainstream Rebels, both groups were unanimous in this view that the main problem came not from such relatively powerless groups as teachers, but rather from power-holders at higher levels:

> They (Doctrine Guards)...forget this wise
> judgment: "Among those making reckless attempts
> to subvert our country's proletarian dictator-
> ship through counterrevolutionary activities
> are those at the upper as well as the lower
> levels, and the upper levels are the most im-

portant. The greatest danger comes from the
upper levels."
   "...the greatest danger of a capitalist
restoration is not from the capitalist class
itself or from some counterrevolutionary intellectuals subordinate to them, but rather from
the capitalist roaders who have wormed their
way into the Party."   "It is the same way with
the schools."[93]

To buttress this point, the Rebels brought out in their
newspapers many examples of attempts at subversion of the
aims of the GPCR by Party officials in the schools.[94]
   The basis of their second challenge to the Conservatives - their accusation that it was the children of
cadres who had been favored for admission to the better
schools over those of worker-peasant background - was
documented much more fully. The Rebels provided lurid
pictures of life in schools set up for the children of
cadres. August 1 Middle School was particularly singled
out for criticism. To begin with, these schools were
excoriated for their opulence, both in terms of physical
facilities and administrative personnel. August 1 Middle
School, for example, had one teacher for every six students and also one worker for every six students. Unlike
other schools, at which academic achievement and class
origin were both important as admissions criteria, August
1 slighted the former in favor of the latter. Once admitted to the school, cadre children were allowed to
maintain a rather grand style of life with regard to
food, clothing, entertainment, and so forth. Even during
the period of economic difficulties in the early 1960s,
they were provided with a special subsidy to maintain
their high standard of living. Moreover, unlike ordinary
students, the influence of their parents shielded them
from the increasingly intense rustication movement which
had begun by 1964. Finally, in spite of the "redness" of
their occupants, schools like August 1 did not emphasize
the study of Mao's works, hence even politically they
were said to be backward.[95]
   Reading the Red Guard newspapers published by each
side in the debate over education, one gets the impression that the advocates are writing about two completely
different educational systems. The Conservatives provided rather detailed lists of teachers who came from bad
class backgrounds and/or had been classified as rightists
in the past, provided figures on those of good class origin who had been held back, and castigated the YCL for
its undue emphasis on admitting students of high academic
achievement over those of good class origin who were more
concerned with political activism.[96]
   The Rebels, in their turn, complained that children
of cadres had monopolized places in the best schools even

though their grades did not warrant their admittance to these schools, had been automatically recruited into the YCL because of their parents' influence, and had not condescended to associate with children of worker-peasant background.

In a real sense, the two groups were indeed writing about two different educational systems. The Conservative newspapers were referring to the educational system from 1961-1963 and the Rebels were describing the educational system as it was from 1964-1966. The emphasis on the earlier period by newspapers affiliated to the Conservative faction becomes very clear when one examines the set of articles entitled "How Bourgeois Intellectuals Control Guangzhou's Middle Schools."[97] Ironically, these articles unwittingly provided a picture which, if anything, indicated a lack of control by intellectuals in the schools since in many cases the villain being vilified is listed as, for example, former principal rather than current principal. The guilty parties had already lost their jobs before the GPCR. Moreover, the school singled out for the most severe and detailed criticism in terms of personnel is Number 5 Middle School. In fact, this school had been made the keypoint school in Guangzhou during the Socialist Education Movement in 1964 and 1965 so that, once again, the problems had been discovered and cleared up (through dismissals and personnel transfers) before the GPCR.[98]

It must of course be remembered that the debate over the evils of the educational system was not being held in a vacuum. Concurrent with this debate were the ongoing attempts - in winter 1967 and spring 1968 - to set up three-way alliances and revolutionary committees in the schools. Predictably, the issue of educational reform quickly became entangled in the alliance issue as the two sides made their positions clear. To the Conservatives, the highest priority was given to the establishment of three-way alliances, under whose leadership the educational system of the past 17 years could be criticized. As this was a period of retrenchment in the ebb and flow of the GPCR, setting up a power organ in the schools at this time would have clearly favored them. The Rebels, needless to say, opposed such precipitate action. Arguing that the atmosphere within some schools with regard to teachers at present was reminiscent of the early days of the GPCR, they pushed for an investigation of that early period that would lead to the rehabilitation of those teachers and students unjustly criticized back in the summer of 1966. Until this sort of investigation occurred, it would be impossible to determine just who was qualified to participate in the new power structure to be set up. It was in fact this failure to pinpoint those responsible for the "bourgeois reactionary line" of 1966 that had doomed all previous attempts to return to classes.[99]

The Rebels monitored rehabilitation work at the various schools very closely. For example, they pointed out that Number 4 Middle School had criticized the "bourgeois reactionary line" on two separate occasions, but more than 20 teachers who had been labelled "ghosts and monsters" had not yet been rehabilitated.[100] More satisfying, they felt, was the situation at Number 37. In this latter school, the repudiation of the "bourgeois reactionary line" had included the burning of black materials, the public rehabilitation of victimized teachers, and the concurrent self-criticism of the powerholders responsible for the suppression of these teachers. This "revolutionary" atmosphere, the Rebels reported, marked the ideal time to commence the formation of a revolutionary committee for the school.[101]

The Formation of Revolutionary Committees in the Middle Schools: The Beginning of the End for the Rebels

The high tide in the debate on educational reform, to judge from the distribution of articles in the Red Guard newspapers, appears to have lasted from November 1967 to February 1968. Although no definitive conclusion had been reached, and in fact the debate continued, albeit at a lower level of visibility, already by February the more urgent question of reestablishing organs of political power in the schools had superimposed itself on all other issues. This represented a victory for the Conservative forces. The Rebels, after all, had been arguing that the reestablishment of organs of power such as three-way alliances and revolutionary committees should await a thorough investigation of the "bourgeois reactionary line" which had been followed during the GPCR. Until a reassessment of the proportionate guilt to be borne by various cadres and teachers in the schools had been determined, all moves toward "construction," they had argued, were premature.

Having been rebuffed on that issue, the Rebels next sought to gain representation on the new revolutionary committees being set up commensurate with their numerical strength. The Conservatives, not unexpectedly, opposed the method of awarding seats on the committees on the basis of sheer numbers. They argued that mere numbers could not be a substitute for correct thought and correct political line. Moreover, they rather self-servingly objected that for the Flag faction even to mention its dominance of the middle schools was in itself to promote factionalism.[102]

Two separate issues had to be decided. First, which cadres should be chosen to join the committees? Second, how should the available seats be divided up among the mass organizations? As the Rebels were later to complain, they were disadvantaged in both selections.

As was the case with all other issues, criteria for the selection of suitable cadres was inseparable from factional politics. Consistent with their position on other questions, the Rebels argued that cadres should be selected on the basis of their performance during the GPCR, particularly during those periods that the Rebels regarded as the "crucial moments," viz., the criticism of the "bourgeois reactionary line," the January power seizure, and the "March Black Wind."[103] The Conservatives, supported by the MTGs that had the responsibility for making the final decisions, also tended to be consistent in their criteria. In contradistinction to the Rebels, the Conservatives emphasized the pre-GPCR performance of the cadre being considered; in other words, what had that individual done in the 17 years from 1949-1966? They did not, however, completely ignore the GPCR record. They, too, looked at performance during the "crucial moments" of the movement. The discrepancy, of course, arose in the different "moments" the two sides considered crucial. The Conservatives and their PLA backers investigated a cadre to determine whether he/she had in any way supported the "dragging out of Guangzhou's Tan Zhenlin," had been chosen as targets by Party committees and work teams early in the movement, and so forth.[104]

In addition, the Conservatives placed great emphasis on family background and the rank of the cadre being considered. For example, the Conservatives usually supported the school's Party secretary and/or principal to head the revolutionary committee, arguing that "a cadre of the intermediate level cannot be made the No. 1 man," while the Rebels were more likely to support cadres who had held such positions as deputy Party secretary, supervisor of studies, or personnel secretary.[105]

The choice of mass representatives for the revolutionary committees also found each faction leading with its strength. Superficially, the Rebels seemed to be in a strong position to dominate these committees. Even the Doctrine Guards had to admit that their opponents in the middle schools had more members, more power, and an earlier history of rebellion; still, this was held to be unimportant because the Rebels lacked the proper "class feelings." As the Conservatives explained it, "Mao's proletarian class line" was not a "reliance on those people of strong rebel spirit," and was not a "reliance on a faction that temporarily seemed to have more people and greater power." The most important point to remember about the class line policy, they averred, was its emphasis on "taking the children of the laboring people as its basis."[106] In fact, the Conservatives attributed their self-confessed earlier GPCR mistakes precisely to "an excess of proletarian class feelings, which temporarily caused them to see things too one-sidedly."107

The Rebels, on the other hand, had allegedly performed their "merits" for all the wrong reasons. As the Doctrine Guards put it:

> ...when they were oppressed, to effect their own liberation, they displayed a definite quality of resistance, objectively a definite revolutionary quality. But they rebelled out of selfishness (even to the point of acting to benefit the interests of their own reactionary class). As their starting point was the advantage or disadvantage to be gained individually or for their faction...they observed the situation, weighed what might be gained or lost, and decided on their tactics.108

The Conservatives constantly accused the Rebels of trying to negate or transform the Party's class line. For example, they accused the latter of arguing that "after the GPCR a new division between revolutionary and counterrevolutionary class chengfen will be made according to the categories Rebel and Conservative."109 Even when ostensibly engaged in self-criticism, Conservative middle school students commonly redirected the spearhead of attack away from themselves by describing their own shortcomings as, for example, not putting up a stronger defense of the PLA when the Rebels, "influenced by the ultra-Left trend of thought," put forward the slogan of "dragging out a handful within the Army."110

As had happened with the selection of cadres, the MTGs adopted policies that favored the Conservative masses. Perhaps the most important decision was the adoption of what was called the "principle of coordination and political equality." Under this principle, Rebels and Conservatives were considered equal in strength, regardless of their actual numbers. In some places, like Number 5 Middle School, the Rebel-Conservative balance was 10:1 in favor of the Rebels. The principle of coordination also limited the overall number of students to be chosen on the committee because of the necessity to include teachers, "militia representatives," "freedom fighters," workers, and so forth. In this manner, the Rebels claimed, the municipal committee could insure that the Rebels remained a minority on the organs of political power being set up.

Another method the Rebels claimed discriminated against their interests was the employment of a series of tactics designed to limit their power of selection. One way this was done was to exclude representatives chosen by the Rebels from participating in the nomination process for the revolutionary committees. In addition, some of the more activist Rebels who had been chosen for the revolutionary committees were not allowed to take their seats; instead, the MTGs carefully selected less controversial "Rebels" (those who had already become inactive or had never really taken a strong stand) and elevated them to important positions. In some cases the MTGs went further and selected the most conservative members of the Rebels, even if they had little support within their own organizations.

These tactics, the Rebels claimed, were part of a larger "conspiracy" to divide Rebel leaders from rank-and-file members. Claiming that "the masses were good and only the Rebel leaders had problems," the MTGs urged the former to "drag out" the latter. Even when leading Rebels were not excluded from the revolutionary committees, they were seldom permitted to become members of the nucleus group or to assume important posts. Moreover, the Rebels charged, in those cases in which they overcame all of the above obstacles and were able to obtain leading posts for their nominees, the municipal revolutionary committee might well refuse to assign any duties to that person. The Rebels published statistics from various schools to show the extent of Conservative domination within key departments or offices under the revolutionary committees. Using their majority position within these departments, the East Wind forces were able to exclude the Rebels from any real decision-making power.

The Rebels, whose backers were far away in Beijing, had little chance to prevail against their Conservative opponents who were being backed by the MTGs in the schools. As if the odds were not already strongly against them, even in those cases in which the MTG at a particular school adopted a more even-handed policy toward the Rebels, all decisions were subject to veto by MTG units at higher levels (there was an MTG office for each of Guangzhou's four districts) or by the municipal revolutionary committee, on which the Flag faction was in a minority. These PLA-dominated groups at higher levels, unaware of the details of the schools about which they were making authoritative decisions, generally emphasized such issues as class background, cadre rank, and support for the PLA even more than did the local MTGs, which at least had direct contact with the individuals being evaluated.[111]

Finally, all of these developments were occurring concurrently with the "Campaign to Clean Up Class Ranks" and this, too, favored the Conservatives. As part of this campaign, the Red Guards were once again to be reconstituted. In place of the existing separate organizations, a unified Red Guard organization was to be established. Once again, the Rebels pointed to their performance in the GPCR as evidence that they, as the true "revolutionary Left," should form the core of this new organization. Given the character of the times, however, class origin was taken as the prime qualification for Red Guard membership and large numbers of Rebels were excluded. Furthermore, what rankled the Rebels additionally was the fact that organizations that had collapsed or been discredited long before and had contributed virtually nothing to the GPCR were now revived and, because their members had good class backgrounds, were absorbed into the "unified Red Guards."

One other event in this period, according to many interviewees, contributed to the growing feelings of exasperation and despair among the Rebels. It was at this time - spring 1968 - that the PLA began once again to recruit. As there had been a two-year hiatus in recruiting, a larger number than usual would have to be chosen. Thus, many students in both factions were hopeful they would be selected. The results of the recruitment drive, however, were not dissimilar to the results for the reconstitution of the Red Guards or for the allocation of seats on the revolutionary committees. If anything, the PLA on this issue was even stricter in insisting on the importance of a good class origin and a "proper attitude" toward the military. Therefore, the Conservatives generally were much more successful than the Rebels; and, the Conservatives took their success as added proof that Rebel ascendance was at an end.

Taken in conjunction with the other events favoring them at this time, some Conservatives developed an interpretation of the GPCR that explained their success by dividing the movement into stages. At its most simplistic, this interpretation suggested that the high tide of Rebel strength occurred early on, during the period of "destruction," when it was necessary to break through the shackles imposed by the "bourgeois reactionary line." However, the fall of Liu Shaoqi and his minions had long made such "heroic resistance" passe. The present and future stages of "construction" required those most imbued with proletarian spirit, discipline, and reliability. For this reason, the Conservatives argued, it had been eminently reasonable to deny all but a small number of Rebels access to military service.[112]

Ironically, in the period from December 1967 to late March 1968, during which time these decisions were being made, even the official line in Beijing favored the Conservatives. As part of the Campaign to Clean Up Class Ranks, CCRG leaders such as Jiang Qing stressed the importance of good class origin as a prerequisite for mass organization leadership, so that the Rebels, in effect, had no strong authority that would champion their cause.[113]

THE LAST HURRAH AND THE FINAL DEMOBILIZATION

The denial of seats on the revolutionary committees being set up in middle schools can be taken as a microcosm of Rebel fortunes during the entire demobilization phase of the GPCR. Their relationship to the local PLA authorities - one long marked by a degree of mutual suspicion - left them exposed and vulnerable whenever their supporters in Beijing were unable to intervene on their behalf. The remainder of the GPCR - except for one last effort by the CCRG to push the movement leftward - witnessed a steady decline in the fortunes of the Rebels.

This last period of the GPCR can be divided into two stages: the period from late March to early June when the Rebels, followiing the shift in direction at the Center, once more actively opposed what was called the "rightist reversal of verdicts," and the period beginning in June when the Center once again reoriented itself and strongly advocated a return to order, leaving the final disposition of Rebels to the discretion of the PLA.

The Counterattack Against the Rightist Reversal of Verdicts

Events in Beijing in March provided Guangzhou's Rebels the opportunity to protest openly against provincial and municipal decisions that had gone against their interests. The key event was the purge of Yang Chengwu, acting chief of staff of the PLA, along with two other military figures. Since a detailed explanation of the reasons behind this purge are not of immediate concern to the argument, suffice it to say that Yang and his cohorts were dismissed for their open opposition to the CCRG.

The purge of Yang enabled the CCRG to argue that the main danger the country faced at present emanated from the "Right," in the form of "four rightist trends" - rightist reversal of verdicts, rightist splittism, rightist capitulationism and rightist opportunism.[114]

Jiang Qing led the attack on these "dangerous trends," calling on the PLA to protect and support the Rebels. Official policy, as transmitted through the media, reflected the new orientation. For example, Red Flag resumed publication in April and declared, in its first issue, that the criterion for determining who was to be considered a proletarian revolutionalry was not social origin, but rather was support for Chairman Mao's line. Factionalism, which had previously been uniformly condemned, was also re-analyzed so that "proletarian factionalism" was now distinguished from "bourgeois factionalism."[115]

The Rebels in Guangzhou were not long in applying these new interpretations to their own situation. They

had already formed a united organization - Guangzhou Red
Flag - by early April 1968, in order to coordinate their
resistance to the rightist trends.[116]

After the shift in central policy had become clear,
a leading Rebel from Zhongshan University Red Flag,
Huang Yijian, was sent to Beijing to investigate how the
new anti-rightist campaign could be used by the Rebels in
Guangzhou. Upon his return, he journeyed throughout the
city presenting reports on his findings. His message was
clear: leading military officials in the provincial revolutionary committee were guilty of implementing a
"rightist reversal of verdicts." The main targets of
Huang's attacks, which were soon picked up by other
Rebels, were Kong Shiquan and Liu Xingyuan, two officials
of the Guangdong Provincial Revolutionary Committee.
Kong, for example, was said to be "Guangzhou's Yang
Chengwu" and was alleged to have been sent to Guangzhou
by Yang.[117] Flag faction leaders extended their criticisms to denounce the provincial committee's nucleus
group as a product of the "new February (1968) Adverse
Current" and called for a "Second October Revolution" to
replace it.

Moreover, the transmission to Guangzhou of Mao's
latest directive in May further fueled Rebel hopes. Mao
likened the present struggle to a great political revolution being fought between socialism and capitalism, between the CCP and the Guomindang. The thrust of the
directive, taken in conjunction with the support of "proletarian factionalism," was indeed a far cry from previous injunctions that had argued that there was no necessity for dividing into factions.

The Flag faction once again became active throughout
the province. Although still maintaining their separate
headquarters, independent units within the faction drew
closer together than ever before. The formation of
Guangzhou Red Flag as a unit of coordination is one example of this. In addition, middle school units representing different organizations within the Red Headquarters
united together in early May to form the Three Red
Regiment (Hongsantuan) to synchronize their activities.[118]

The provincial committee and its backers representing the PLA and the Conservative mass organizations
were far from quiescent during the period of the Rebel
renascence. Seeking to turn the centrally-endorsed
campaign against the rightist reversal of verdicts to
their own advantage, they launched an attack on "ultra-
Leftism," mountain-topism, and factionalism, equating all
three deviations with rightism.[119]

In the secondary schools, Rebels who sought to maintain reasonably good relations with the MTG at their
school were faced with a crucial decision. In early May
these students began meeting in study classes devoted to

combating "the four rightist trends." The scope of these
discussions quickly expanded and soon included a general
airing of grievances by the representatives attending,
concentrating primarily on their dissatisfaction with
their exclusion from positions of power on the new revolutionary committees.[120]
    The MTGs, attempting to maintain control over the
situation, warned the Rebels against becoming involved in
the "unhealthy currents" swirling about outside the
school. Typical was the situation at Number 21. The
revolutionary committee had been established at the
school on March 7, 1968, with the Rebels, although under-
represented in proportion to their numerical strength,
occupying some important positions. When the struggle
to oppose the four rightist trends reached Guangzhou,
the Rebels at Number 21 organized a conference of representatives of activists in the study of Mao's Thought
(on April 15) and then began participating in the aforementioned citywide study classes of early May. Urged
by the MTG not to abandon the GPCR at the school, the
leading Rebels nevertheless found it impossible to avoid
being drawn back into society.[121] The departure of the
school's Rebel leadership, including several who were in
positions of responsibility on the revolutionary committee, prevented the committee from performing its work.
The MTG later traced the problems of the revolutionary
committee to this period and placed the blame solely on
the Flag faction.[122]
    The military authorities in Guangzhou began, by mid-
May, to adopt stronger measures aimed at preventing the
Flag faction from using the nationwide movement against
rightism to undermine the "order" they were painstakingly
establishing. For example, using the justification of
"clearing up rumors," they moved to arrest Huang Yijian
on May 13. This incident further poisoned relations between the Flag faction and the provincial revolutionary
committee.[123]
    On May 31 an important meeting of the provincial
committee was held at which the differing viewpoints separating the Flag faction leadership from the committee
were aired. Kong Shiquan gave the main speech, admonish-
ing the Flag leadership not to isolate itself from the
mainstream of the movement.[124]
    But events were moving too quickly for reasoned dis-
cussion to prevail. May and June brought a recurrence of
armed struggle incidents not just in Guangzhou, but
throughout the country. East Wind, spearheaded by the
Doctrine Guards, launched a series of attacks aimed at
"liberating" the entire Southern Guangzhou area. By mid-
June they had scored notable successes in restricting the
influence of the Flag faction in Guangzhou's main factory
district.[125]
    Even more ominous for Rebel fortunes, their erst-

while backers in Beijing, alarmed by the splits developing within the PLA, had decided by mid-June to stabilize the situation and impose military control over China.[126] Without strong backing from the Center, Guangzhou's Rebels would have little leverage against their opponents.

Under these increasingly trying circumstances, from June 22 to June 25, the Flag faction held its first comprehensive meeting since the Foshan Conference. All wings of the faction were represented, with more than 20 leaders present. At the close of the meeting, the participants summarized their conclusions and published and circulated them. Among other things, they argued that the "rightist reversal of verdicts" remained the greatest danger at present. Moreover, in a pointed remark, they stressed that this phenomenon had appeared <u>after</u> the establishment of the provincial and municipal revolutionary committees. They further complained that such catchphrases as "oppose the ultra-Left," "level mountaintops," "exterminate factionalism," and "clean up class ranks" were being used as justifications for attacking and dispersing the Flag faction. Finally, they protested that at the same time as cadres supported by the Flag faction were being accused of being "black hands" and their mass representatives were being eased out, cadres and masses loyal to East Wind were consolidating their strength.[127]

Such meetings could not really alter the Rebels' circumstances. The suppression of the Flag faction had already become part of the larger picture nationwide. This development had been brought home to Guangzhou's Rebels most forcefully by the mass exodus, from April to June, of the Rebels from the neighboring province of Guangxi. As they poured into Guangzhou to escape suppression by the military and the Conservative mass organizations, it gradually became clear that the suppression of the Left was taking place on a national scale and that only an appeal directly to Beijing could once again stem the tide.

Therefore, armed with the appropriate documentation to be presented to the central leaders, Wu Chuanbin, the leader of the Red Headquarters, left Guangzhou with more than one hundred other Rebels on June 30, arriving in Beijing on July 4 with the dual purpose of turning over his evidence of the suppression of Rebels to central leaders and organizing a national conference of Rebels. The conference, in spite of various setbacks, was finally held at Beijing Aviation Institute on July 17 and included Rebels from Beijing, Guangzhou, Guangxi, Heilongjiang, and Liaoning, among other places, with more than 20 organizations participating.[128]

The conference sought to establish a nationwide communications network for Rebels and to fortify the ties between Rebels in the various provinces and the central authorities. But it was too late. Far from desiring a set of expanded relationships with the Rebels, by July the Center was even willing to scrap its previous insistence on negotiated settlements, which had been a means of protecting the Rebels in the provinces. Ending armed struggle had become the top priority. On July 3 and again on July 24, the Center issued notices which, although directed at specific provinces (Guangxi and Shaanxi respectively), were meant to apply to the nation as a whole. In these notices armed struggle, no matter what the justification, was prohibited.[129]

The reaction in Guangzhou was swift. On July 10 the standing committees of the Guangdong Provincial and Guangzhou Municipal Revolutionary Committees held a joint meeting from which members of the Flag faction were excluded. On July 12, as a result of this meeting, two notices were published. One notice concerned the implementation of the Center's July 3 Notice; the other notice was addressed to those persons from other areas still remaining in Guangzhou. These notices, in essence, called for 1) an end to all armed struggle, 2) a return to their original units by those, such as sent-down youth, who were illegally remaining in Guangzhou, and 3) a call for absolute support for the PLA and the worker picket teams.[130]

Beginning on July 13 the Guangzhou Military District began to take action against the Flag faction and to restore order. Military control was exercised over the Central-South Bureau, which had been an important base for the Rebels. Worker picket teams and public safety committees, both under East Wind control, were used to restore order. Several bases set up by the Flag faction were destroyed by the military.[131]

The Flag faction continued holding meetings throughout July, but to little effect. Some units still clung to the hope that they could make distinctions between the PLA and the worker organizations set up to police the return to public order. For example, in mid-July the Three Red Regiment convened a meeting to discuss its response to the notices of July 12. The result was a directive containing four points: 1) A Mao Thought study class would be convened to study the two notices; 2) In view of the fact that the worker picket teams were made up of members representing only the East Wind faction, the Three Red Regiment would not recognize this organization nor would it permit the organization to carry out investigative work among the Regiment's subordinate units; 3) The PLA, on the other hand, was welcome to carry out such investigative work; 4) Two days after the end of the study class, they would meet again to discuss what further actions to take.[132]

Following the Center's July 24 Notice, demobilization of the Red Guards was accelerated. On July 31, a

Mao Thought Workers Propaganda Team, drawn from the worker picket teams, entered Zhongshan University to aid in demobilization work. In August, worker propaganda teams entered Guangzhou's other colleges as well.[133]

The Second Enlarged Meeting of the Guangdong Provincial Revolutionary Committee convened on July 30 and 31 and was devoted to criticizing and struggling against the Rebels' top leader, Wu Chuanbin.[134] Following this meeting, there were struggle meetings at Zhongshan University in early August to which other leaders of the Red Headquarters were dragged. On August 7 and 8, at a continuation of the second session of the Guangdong Provincial Revolutionary Committee, the Flag faction suffered further reverses. Most of the leading individuals and organizations within the faction were criticized by name, with the heaviest criticism reserved for the August 1 Combat Corps. Even moderate leaders, such as Gao Xiang of the Third Headquarters, were made to undergo self-examinations.[135]

By mid-August, the Flag faction-controlled Red Guard Congress had expelled Wu Chuanbin, among other Rebels, and the Congress then issued a self-examination detailing the crimes of "Wu Chuanbin and his gang" in leading the Congress astray.[136]

By late August, therefore, the dismantling of the Flag faction was well under way. After the units cutting across functional lines, such as Guangzhou Red Flag, were broken up, top leaders - called "bad heads" (huai toutou) - of individual units in schools, factories, offices, and so forth were dragged out for struggle meetings and, in many cases, placed under arrest.[137]

With the demise of the Rebels the class line policies stressed during each of the previous periods of retrenchment in the GPCR once again were put into effect. Teachers once more were targeted for criticism and struggle. A series of "anti-Maoist" organizations were discovered during the Campaign to Clean Up Class Ranks. According to the allegations made, these organizations had managed to carry out their subversive activities under the guise of pretending to be revolutionary mass organizations. Common features of these "counterrevolutionary organizations" were the bad class origins of their leaders and their ties, either present or past, to the Guomindang. All had been in some way or other supportive of the Flag faction.[138]

The Rustication of the Red Guards

The Red Guards were brought back to their schools to be disciplined and allocated to job posts. Once again, by turning to the middle schools and making use of questionnaire data, a suggestive picture of which students were rusticated at the close of the GPCR emerges.

Allocation of job posts was an important issue for the young students. There were four possible allocations a student could obtain. First, the student could be chosen to enter the PLA. Second, a number of urban jobs, mostly in factories, had become available over the past two years. Third, some students would be chosen to continue their studies. Fourth, a large percentage - those not chosen for any of the other allocations - would be compelled to rusticate.

It had become clear that, aside from some very young first and second year junior high students who would be allowed to continue their studies for one more year, the majority of the students could not expect to remain at school; it was necessary to make room for those moving up from primary school. In addition, there had been no expansion of industry in Guangzhou from 1966-68 so that urban jobs were at a premium. Finally, the experience of the Rebels during the first wave of recruitment for the PLA in spring, combined with the events of the past 4-5 months, had convinced them that their prospects for becoming soldiers were minimal. Thus, it was clear that avoidance of a rural assignment would be the preserve of only a chosen few.

Important differences distinguished this 1968 rustication from the pre-GPCR program. First, while the pre-GPCR program had been voluntary, the present rustication was compulsory. Moreover, avoidance of one's assignment was not a real possibility. Second, whereas in the earlier period the mobilization of students to participate in the rustication program had been assigned to school officials, teachers, and municipal cadres, rustication decisions now were to be taken by the MTGs and the worker propaganda teams that had recently entered the schools, with less time to be devoted to the niceties of persuasion typical of pre-GPCR mobilization.

Just as the earlier recruitment by the military had been viewed as a contest by the two factions, the allocation decisions of September 1968, coming at the end of the GPCR, were also construed in terms of "victory" or "defeat" by the antagonists, with a forced rural assignment clearly serving as an indicator of defeat.

With this in mind, the results of our questionnaire survey can be examined. First, as can be seen from Table 6.1 below, the allocation of a choice assignment depended largely on one's class background.

Moreover, our questionnaire survey revealed that those who were able to avoid a rural posting were much more likely to have participated on the Conservative side in the GPCR, and were also more likely to have been Youth League members. But, although certain categories of students were clearly favored by the allocation decisions, Table 6.1 also makes clear - and data from interviews strongly confirm these findings - that the first phase

Table 6.1

Postings of Former Red Guards, 1968-69
(Size of Sample: 55 Classrooms)

Class Origin	Entered PLA	Urban Jobs	Con-tinued Studies	Total % Not Going to Country-side	% Going to Country-side
Revolutionary Cadre	26%	12%	4%	42%	58%
N =	100	47	16	163	
Working Class	3%	20%	8%	31%	69%
N =	20	133	55	208	
Non-Intellectual Middle Class	0%	5%	0%	5%	95%
N =	1	19	1	21	
Intellectual Middle Class	0%	3%	1%	4%	96%
N =	0	22	4	26	
Overseas Chinese	0%	1%	2%	3%	97%
N =	0	1	2	3	
Bad Class	0%	1%	0%	1%	99%
N =	0	2	0	2	
Total N =	121	224	78	423	

Source: Remembrances of Hong Kong interviewees

of the GPCR in Guangzhou ended with the forced rustication of most of Guangzhou's secondary school students.

7
Epilogue

The mobilization phase of the Cultural Revolution
ended in autumn 1968 with the forcible dispatch of a majority of the Red Guards to the countryside. In Guangzhou, those Red Guards dealt with most harshly were members of the Rebel faction who were not of good class
origin. But the rustication program was by no means
limited to these students. According to newspaper reports from Guangzhou, almost 75 percent of the city's
former high school students were assigned to the countryside in the winter of 1968-69. These new rusticants
constituted more than twice the total number that had
been mobilized during the ten years prior to the GPCR.
It was an exodus of more than 5 percent of Guangzhou's
total population, and the better part of an entire
generation.[1]
There are strong indications that for many Red
Guards the immediate fruit of the GPCR was a sense of
disillusionment. This seems particularly to have been
the case for the major antagonists: children of intellectuals and children of cadres. Ironically, it has been
reported that in the immediate aftermath of the GPCR, a
fair number of these erstwhile antagonists were actually
drawn close together by their common fate. One Red Guard
leader recalled that it was not unusual in those days to
see children of cadres in the company of children of
intellectuals.[2]
For those still in school, the period up to 1970
marked a time of transition. According to one interviewee, factionalism remained a disruptive factor in his
secondary school as the Doctrine Guards were still
strong. For this reason, when monitors or leaders were
to be chosen from among the students, almost all of those
so chosen were from worker-peasant backgrounds. Neither
children of cadres nor those from non-red background
homes were favored with such posts.[3]
As the new educational structure began to take shape
beginning in 1970-71, it became clear that the radicals

supervising national educational policy sought to eliminate the old system that had favored the offspring of
intellectuals and cadres. The new educational system
abolished the university and middle school entrance examinations that had favored middle class youth. At the
same time, middle school graduates were no longer to move
directly on to the university upon graduation; they were
now expected to engage in productive labor for a minimum
of two years. After completing this labor obligation,
the decision as to their further schooling was to be made
jointly by their work units, higher political authorities, and the university.

This new educational structure reflected the victory
of those Party leaders who had argued that higher education should not become the preserve of those who would
turn themselves into "intellectual aristocrats"; rather,
it was to train the children of the working people who,
upon graduation, would return to their original work
units with enhanced practical skills.

But the victory was not an uncontested or complete
one. Throughout the 1970's - until the elimination of
the radicals in October, 1976 - there was a strong coun-
tercurrent to the prevailing radical line in education.
"Moderates" who were concerned with rapid economic development and "modernization" had at various times during
the period in question sought to reintroduce elements
of the pre-GPCR educational system. On several occasions
this radical-moderate struggle over higher education
spilled onto the front pages of People's Daily.

One issue of particular concern to both sides was
the question of academic criteria. The debate on this
issue, centered around the question of entrance examinations, was perhaps most heated in 1972 and 1973. In
1972, Guangdong province had restored rather rudimentary
examinations at the final county-level stage to screen
prospective university applicants. In April 1973 the
State Council decided to institute similar examinations
in all provinces. Although opposed to such "back-
sliding," the radicals were insufficiently strong to
prevent it. They were, however, poised to use the mass
media under their control should an opportunity present
itself.

Fortuitously, in 1973 a university applicant from
Liaoning province named Zhang Tiesheng provided the radicals with the opening they had been seeking. Zhang had
been a junior high school student at the time of the GPCR
and had gone to the countryside in 1968. He had applied
for the university and had gotten as far as the examination stage but found himself at a loss when faced with
the questions on science and math. Rather than attempt
to answer them, he instead used the back of the exam
paper to complain that as a production team cadre he had

been engaged in agricultural labor and had not had the
time to prepare for such questions.

Zhang's essay was quickly reprinted in <u>Liaoning
Daily</u> and within a month was headlined in <u>People's Daily</u>
as well. An extensive media campaign was organized by
the radicals, compelling many of China's other provinces
to follow Liaoning's example and rescind their entrance
examinations.[4] The victory of the radicals did not, however, mark the end of the debate. By 1975 universities
were once again using entrance examinations as an important part of the enrollment process.

THE STRUCTURE OF EDUCATION TODAY

The death of Mao Zedong in September 1976 and the
subsequent political demise of the radicals in October
cleared the way for those stressing the importance of
China's modernization once again to alter the Chinese
educational system. In effect, the consequence of their
alteration has been to revive many of the practices that
prevailed during the early 1960's. On a number of the
most controversial issues that had divided the two factions during the GPCR, present policy has come down
strongly in favor of the Rebel position.

The starting point for the present leadership is a
reevaluation of the pre-GPCR educational system and the
role of the intellectuals within that system. Somewhat
ironically, whereas both factions during the GPCR were in
agreement that the educational system as it existed from
1949-66 was "revisionist," and that intellectuals were
indeed insufficiently transformed "bourgeois academic
authorities,"[5] the present leaders have determined that
the dominant aspect of education and of intellectuals in
that period was positive, even revolutionary.[6]

In fact, taking up the cudgels for an argument that
the Rebels had only suggested during the GPCR, Party
leaders have now acclaimed the intellectuals as a section
of the laboring people.[7] No longer are the differences
between mental and manual labor to be emphasized as a key
division within Chinese society. This new designation
has already had a profound impact in many areas of life.
Of most interest to the concerns of this study are the
new university enrollment practices.

Post-Cultural Revolution reports on university enrollment have begun to offer statistics containing the
combined totals of <u>all</u> laboring people, rather than providing separate figures for students of worker-peasant
background. For example, 97.4% of the students admitted
to the university in the 1977-78 school year were children of workers, poor and lower middle peasants, and other
laboring people.[8] Further, given this book's analysis
of Red Guard factionalism at the middle school level as

class-based, it is interesting to note that "other laboring people" have now specifically been defined to include in the same category the prime antagonists in the GPCR: revolutionary armymen, cadres, and intellectuals.

There has been no attempt to deny that under this new system the children of intellectuals have become the most favored group. It has been openly admitted that in 1977-78 "the number of students from families of intellectuals was greater in proportion to the total population than in previous years," while "students of worker and peasant origin were proportionately fewer than before."[9] More recent reports have noted the continuation of this phenomenon.[10]

Predictably, a number of people in China have voiced opposition to this trend. At a national conference on enrollment held in May 1978 there were charges that matriculating the best examinees was "putting marks in command," "widening the differences between town and country, worker and peasant, and between mental and manual labor," and "would lead to deviation from the Party's class line."[11]

Interestingly, the response to these charges has been that the present system is actually in the long-range interest of worker-peasant children. The argument is two-pronged: First, it is alleged that under the system prevailing from 1970-76, worker-peasant children had no chance at all to attend a university. Relying on the method of "recommendation" in place of examination, ordinary people were not able to compete against those who abused their power and influence to obtain university slots for their children by "back-door deals." The present system is seen as an improvement because all can now participate in the entrance examinations.

Second, it is argued, enrolling the best students will lead to the earliest realization of socialist modernization. As a consequence of modernization, the quality of primary and secondary education will be universally raised, even in backward areas. Thus, a larger proportion of students of worker and peasant origin will be able to advance their education and the "three major differences" will be narrowed.[12]

Another major feature of the new educational system is a reintroduction of the concept of elite, key-point schools. Once again, the new policy is unabashedly straightforward. There is little of the defensiveness that marked discussion of such schools in the mid-1960s. These key schools have been provided with better teachers, bigger budgets, and better equipment. They are expected to enroll the best students.[13] Within these schools, students in the same year are divided into "quick" and "slow" classes, with the very best students forming a special class.

In an effort to make it crystal clear that running such key schools is not a deviation, those schools that became most notorious during the GPCR for their educational elitism now seem to be getting the most favorable publicity. One obvious case in point is Beijing's Jingshan school, which had set up a model ten-year experimental program in 1960. Vilified during the GPCR as "a place for training intellectual aristocrats" and "an experimental plot for the revisionist line in education," those same experiments (such as dividing senior high classes into those stressing either liberal arts or natural sciences, attempting to produce graduates who had attained the level of first-year college students, allowing students to receive double promotions, to take their college entrance exams before graduation, and so forth) are now considered to have been absolutely correct and have resumed.[14]

The reinstitution of the key schools seemed certain to produce once again the phenomenon of competition by the secondary schools to raise their university promotion rates. Indeed, schools at first were actually being urged to compete with each other. While the pre-GPCR key primary and middle schools were being restored and developed, others in 1978 had been promised:

> Ordinary schools should be run according to
> the requirements set for key schools, and the
> really good ones will later also be classified
> as key schools.[15]

At present, however, the determination of key schools has been finalized. Far from encouraging ordinary schools to seek keypoint status, many mediocre secondary schools are in the process of being transformed into technical or vocational schools.[16] Moreover, the pre-Cultural Revolution deviationist tendency of paying attention only to key schools and high promotion rates seems to have returned stronger than ever.[17]

Local newspapers from Guangzhou confirm these trends. For example, results from the 1980 university entrance examinations once again found the city's three best secondary schools occupying pride of place. Huafu's promotion rate was back to 75.69 percent, Number 2 Middle School reached 63.05 percent, and Guangya was third at 61.77 percent.[18] When "Huafu Day" was celebrated in August 1980, over 5,000 visitors showed up, leading to appropriate newspaper coverage.[19] Perhaps most revealing of the present disparity between the favored and the unfashionable schools, and the emphasis on promotion rate, was the juxtaposition of three articles on page one of Guangzhou Daily on June 19, 1980. The first article lauded Guangya for preparing its students for the coming

university entrance examinations. The second article
examined the situation at a second-rate middle school -
Number 14 (see Chapter One for Number 14's attempt to
increase its promotion rate before the Cultural Revolution). At Number 14, only 40 percent of the graduating
class had signed up to take the university examination.
The other students there were being organized into technical training classes. The third article reported on a
recent investigation by the Municipal Education Bureau
which found that Guangzhou's middle schools paid attention only to those students preparing to take the university entrance examinations. This was the case not only
at the municipal and district keypoint schools, but was
also true for the keypoint class at each of the non-key-
point schools. Finally, Guangzhou secondary schools
currently accorded keypoint status follow the pre-GPCR
rankings closely. The two "true elite" schools - Huafu
and Guangya - are provincial keypoints, as is the Provincial Experimental School. Municipal keypoints include
the Girls' Middle School (now co-educational and referred
to as Zhixin Middle School), Numbers 2 and 6. District
keypoints are Numbers 1, 3, 5, and 7.[20]

Classroom Relationships: Thus far there have been
far fewer reports on the impact of the new educational
structure on student relationships than on the new structure itself. Some things seem clear, however. First, in
keeping with the new emphasis on expertise, class origin
is again being downplayed as an indicator of political
performance. The current line was put succinctly by Han
Ying, Chairman of the Preparatory Committee for the Tenth
National Congress of the YCL:

> Whether or not a youth is revolutionary should
> be judged by his own social practice. We should
> not hand on the problems of the parents to their
> children, still less should we let second and
> third generations inherit the class status of
> their ancestors.[21]

Second, once again a key measure of the "redness" of
the student "is to see if he or she delves into his or
her own field of work and diligently studies to master
science and culture for the revolution."[22] Moreover,
intellectuals are not expected to attain the same high
standards of redness as others. Their support for
socialism can be demonstrated through their professional
work.[23] In like manner, membership in the YCL in middle
schools seems to be based once more on academic achievement. Promoting "study" has become a central task -
perhaps the central task - of the League[24] and complaints have been made that marks are now the standard
for League entrance.[25] More ominously, some students

have joined the YCL simply because it enhances one's application to university.[26]   Ideological and political education have suffered neglect.[27]   Therefore, the fact that a large percentage of university students in recent years have been YCL members may not be particularly significant.[28]

New Sources of Discontent: Winners and Losers Under the New System

The new reforms cannot have pleased everyone engaged in the debate on education. An undetermined number of administrators had complained that the extreme emphasis put on entrance examination scores was a violation of the Party's class line policies. Most likely to have been upset would be those of good class origin and their children. In particular, cadres and their children who, by all accounts, had been most advantaged by the Cultural Revolution enrollment policies, would seem to have obvious grounds for dissatisfaction.

Another group likely to be somewhat bitter are students who graduated from secondary school during the Cultural Revolution years and therefore never had much opportunity to compete for university entrance. Present enrollment regulations do not, under normal circumstances, permit those over twenty-five years of age to participate in the entrance examinations.[29]   Even when age requirements were more relaxed - from 1977 to 1979 - there were reports from some provinces that students over the age of twenty-five who had entered middle school after the GPCR had begun were barred from the examinations on the grounds that such schooling could not have sufficiently prepared them for the university.[30]   Moreover, the present policy is to encourage only those students with outstanding grades to participate in the entrance examinations.[31]   Even among those allowed to compete, however, the overwhelming majority of current secondary school students will have little chance to obtain a university education. Only 3-4 percent of China's secondary school graduates in recent years have been able to gain entrance to a university.[32]   Ironically, given the emphasis in Part One on the competition among senior high graduates to enter a university, recent statistics from China suggest that one reason the competition may have been intense is because students recognized that university entrance was a reasonable possibility, particularly for those at good high schools. As Table 7.1 shows, that possibility has all but vanished for today's senior high students, and with it, reportedly, much of their motivation.[33]

Table 7.1

New University Students
and Senior High Graduates 1965-1979

	1965	1976	1979
New Students Recruited for Higher Education	164,000	217,000	275,000
Graduating Students from Senior High Schools	360,000	5,172,000	7,265,000
Ratio of Senior High Graduates to Incoming College Freshmen Expressed as a Percentage	45.56%	4.20%	3.79%

Source: Zhongguo Baike Nianjian 1980, p. 538.

Guangzhou's Rebels: The Real Winners?

For many of Guangzhou's Rebels the demobilization of 1968 resulted in their forcible rustication, ostensibly for life. Nevertheless, there is some evidence that, in the final assessment, Guangzhou's Rebels may not be among the foremost victims of the GPCR. Both the political changes that rocked Guangzhou in the 1970s and the revival of much of the pre-GPCR educational system have redounded to the benefit of the Rebels.

The most important political development after the GPCR was the purge of Lin Biao and his followers beginning in late 1971. Guangzhou had been one of Lin's strongholds; there were even reports that, upon the failure of his "coup" against Mao, he had planned to set up a base area in that city. The demise of Lin Biao led to a purge of those closely associated with him. Among the first to go was Huang Yongsheng, former commander of the Guangzhou Military District and later chief of staff of the army. Huang had been the key backer of the East Wind faction in its struggle with Red Flag. In fact, at the time of Huang's disappearance, Rebel leaders were still undergoing extensive criticism; some were in prison or under house arrest.

By 1974, Guangzhou's new leadership, headed by military commander Xu Shiyou and Party secretary Zhao Ziyang were meeting with Rebel leaders to gather materials on

Huang and other Lin Biao supporters in the Guangzhou Military District. For example, Mo Jingwei, one of the most severely criticized of the Rebels because of his leadership of the August 1 Combat Corps, was appointed vice-director of the "Criticize Lin Biao, Criticize Confucius" staff office.[34] Wu Chuanbin was also meeting with Zhao at this time.

But Rebel attacks were not limited to Lin Biao and his followers. By 1973-74, many of the Rebels had begun to adopt political perspectives antagonistic to the radical wing of the Party. The post-GPCR policies of the "Maoists" had hardly favored them. Most were still in the countryside; their parents - as middle-class intellectuals - were looked upon suspiciously; their younger brothers and sisters had little opportunity to further their education.

It was understandable, then, that former Rebel leaders would be willing to forge a tactical alliance with the very people whom they had helped topple during the GPCR. Perhaps the most famous case of an alliance of this type was the one that united Zhao Ziyang with one of the most "radical" of the Rebels, Li Zhengtian. Li, together with two comrades (collectively known as "Li Yizhe") had posted a wall poster in November 1974 that was critical of the "Lin Biao system" and, less explicitly, of the radicals around Mao.

The Li Yizhe poster created a sensation and led to Li's arrest. Li was taken from unit to unit in Guangzhou, ostensibly to be criticized for his views. At these "criticism meetings," however, Li was allowed to make use of his well-known oratorical skills to refute his critics. At the end of 1978, Li and his comrades described the earlier situation and their relationship to Zhao Ziyang:

> (Zhao) permitted us to put up wall posters, permitted us to raise criticisms, permitted us to answer and defend ourselves. At that time, Zhao Ziyang's group was butting heads with the gang of four. By then we had already made it known to the Party organization that in addition to being directed against Lin Biao, our poster was also directed against Jiang Qing's bunch. Under these circumstances Zhao did not brand us as counterrevolutionaries. On the contrary, he gave repeated orders that we be allowed to sit on benches during the criticism meeting, that we be given a hot water thermos for drinking, that people be sent to protect us, and so forth.[35]

Those forced to rusticate in the wake of the post-GPCR demobilization also received good news in 1975. In the spring, Guangdong's provincial Party committee passed a decree that terminated the "rustication for life" policy; the same decree stated that all the youths who had been sent to the countryside in 1968-69, as well as all of the pre-GPCR rusticants, were to be recalled from the villages. Altogether, almost 400,000 young people were "rescued."[36]

The death of Mao and the defeat of the Party radicals led to the adoption of policies most in accord with the interests of middle-class Rebels. Academic achievement once again was the dominant criterion for university entrance; intellectuals were now included as members of the laboring people; redness for intellectuals again was defined in terms of expertise. Moreover, as suggested earlier, the renewed university entrance examination system initially provided a clear advantage to those who had attended high schools in the 1960s over those who had been students in the 1970s.

Plus ça change, plus c'est la même chose!

Notes

Chapter 1. Mission and Structure of the Educational
System

1. See, for example, Joint Publications Research
Service (JPRS), #17, 601, February 12, 1963 for a
translation of the Japanese language edition of People's
China (Jinmin Chugoku) in which a Qinghua University
student says almost every high school graduate in
China thinks of entering a university.

2. There has been some confusion, inside as well as
outside China, over the terms chengfen and chushen. In
the present context we are concerned only with chengfen
as a concept referring to family origin. A person's
family origin is hereditary on the father's side. The
best discussion of the concept of chengfen is found in
Richard Kraus, The Evolving Concept of Class in Post-
Liberation China (unpublished Ph.D. dissertation,
Columbia University, 1974).

3. At times the class category "shop assistant" was
considered to be almost equivalent to a "worker" chengfen.
See, for example, the report in Renmin Ribao (RMRB),
May 4, 1966, telling young people to "go to factories,
villages, shops and army units to become workers,
peasants, shop assistants, and soldiers." Translated
in China Notes #164, May 19, 1966.

4. Most students were knowledgeable only about a small
part of this process. Much of my information in this
section comes from interviews carried out in Hong Kong
from 1972-76. I was fortunate to meet a number of
students who, because they were graduating seniors in
middle school at the time of the Cultural Revolution,
expended a great deal of energy during this movement in
trying to ascertain just how the process of university
enrollment was carried out. This was done because they
felt that with the inevitable dying down of the movement and the reopening of the schools they would stand
a better chance of being promoted if they had an intimate
knowledge of exactly how university students were chosen.

5. The best schools in Beijing seemed to recruit primarily from a rather limited geographical area. Of the Qinghua University entering classes between 1962 and 1965 for example, 52% to 61% of the students were from Beijing, Shanghai, or Jiangsu province. See Qinghua Jinggangshan November 24, 1967. There was apparently also a tendency for some schools to give preference to those coming from their attached middle schools. See Jinggangshan October 12, 1967.

6. At least in part because of these considerations of strategy, many students did not list the top schools like Qinghua University among their choices. For periodic appeals for more middle school graduates to apply to the key universities see Guangming Ribao (GMRB), June 22, 1962 and Zhongguo Qingnian Bao (ZGQNB), June 16, 1964.

7. Zhongguo Xinwen (ZGXW), December 16, 1964. From an interview with the head of the provincial Higher Education Bureau.

8. Interview with C.R.T., June 19, 1976.

9. Ibid.

10. C.R.T. August 31, 1976.

11. The process of application had changed by 1963 so that most schools were now listed in category one. A student listed four choices regardless of school category and generally only had to sit for one exam. There was, however, a second exam for minban schools. One Red Guard source says that Guangzhou middle schools were originally divided into four categories (perhaps including the schools for dependents of workers mentioned above), based on academic standards. See Tiaozhan, mid-March, 1968, p. 2.

12. I interviewed one person who, because of failure on all three examinations, had attended a school for children of factory workers. He commented at length on the low standard of both students and teachers at his school. There seem to have been rather few of this type of school in Guangzhou.

13. Although some information on Guangya was available in Yangcheng Wanbao (YCWB), most information in this section was provided in a series of interviews with former students from that school, such as Y.H., L.N.Z., and Z.D.K.

14. There were three purely experimental schools in
Guangzhou which continued the program up until the Cultural Revolution. These schools had a ten-year overall
program, encompassing primary school as well.

15. Another exception was the middle school attached to
South China Normal Institute (Huafu). The students there
took an internal examination to decide whether or not
they could continue at the school for senior middle.
Only those failing Huafu's own exam would have to take
their chances with the rest of the city's students, the
argument being that Huafu's own exam was tougher than the
citywide exam anyway.

16. Information on Number 21 was provided primarily by
L.X.P., W.C., and H.X.P.

17. Traditionally, wealthy merchants and the official
class made their residences in the Western suburbs
(Xiguan) of Guangzhou, and even up to the Cultural Revolution the social origin of students at schools in this
district tended to be worse than in other districts. The
"foreignized" returned students, however, chose to make
their homes in Guangzhou's Eastern District (Dongshan qu)
and this area became fashionable for intellectuals and
officials. On the characterization of Guangzhou's different districts before 1949, see Dr. Kerr, A Guide to the
City and Suburbs of Canton (Hong Kong, 1904) and Edward
Bingshuey Lee, Modern Canton (Shanghai, 1936), especially
pp. 25 and 29. Interviewees recited several slogans popular in pre-Liberation Guangzhou about the different districts. For example: "If you have money and you have
influence, you live in the East; if you have money without influence, you live in the Western suburbs" (youqian
youshi zhu dongshan, youqian meishi zhu xiguan); "In the
East are the nobles, in the West are the rich, the poor
are at the small North gate" (dong gui xi fu, qiong zai
xiao bei men). They also said that, at least in the East
the situation is still true. When many capitalists left
Guangzhou for Hong Kong, they left their homes in the
Western suburbs for their family and relatives to live
in.

18. There were numerous cases reported to me in interviews, as well as documented in the Red Guard press, as
to how children of cadres, given sufficiently high rank,
could gain admittance to superior middle schools above
and beyond the advantages gained because of good class
background. For example, these would include personal
appearances at the school by the parent of the student or
the parent's secretary to appeal on his child's behalf;
either the Central-South Bureau, or the provincial or

municipal committee staff offices would issue a namelist
of cadre children and ask the schools in question to admit them; originally Guangzhou middle schools were divided into four categories and one's score on the citywide
entrance exam determined which category school one could
enter. To attend Guangya, for instance, your entrance
exam score had to be within the parameters of category
one. Cadre children, however, could be accepted at
Guangya (among other schools) if they could pass the entrance examination at a category three level. It was also quite common to lower the admittance standard by 10-20
points in the case of recruitment of those of revolutionary cadre background. See, for example, Tiaozhan, mid-
March 1968, p. 2; Xin Sizhong, June 14, 1967, p. 6; Zhi
Ba Chunlai Bao, February 26, 1967, pp. 3-4 and March 12,
1967, p. 4.

19. On the small number of students of worker-peasant
background at Guangya and Huafu, see Xiaobing, December
24, 1967; Tiaozhan, mid-March 1968; and Xiaobing, November 9, 1967.

20. This section is a generalized account based on interviews with students from many different "average" schools.

21. Once again, a large number of informants have been
consulted.

22. See Zhongxue Doupigai #1, June 19, 1967 in Survey of
the China Mainland Press (Supplement) #200, August 31,
1967, pp. 26-27; Guangya 831, mid-March 1968, p. 2; Xiaobing, November 9, 1967; Jiaoyu Geming (JYGM), November
30, 1967, p. 2.

23. Information from this section came from interviews
with former students from these schools. In addition,
some data presented here as well as in the sections on
YCL membership and Cultural Revolution factionalism comes
from the aforementioned questionnaire.

24. Tiaozhan, mid-March 1968, p. 2.

25. Xiaobing, November 9, 1967, p. 2.

26. Ibid.

27. Bingtuan Zhanbao (BTZB), August 18, 1967, p. 3.

28. See interviews with L.X.P. and C.R.T.

29. China Reconstructs, January 1963, p. 37.

30. Shanghai Wenhui Bao (WHB), November 17, 1965.

31. Shandong Jiaoyu #2, February 20, 1965, p. 27, translated in JPRS #30, 222, May 24, 1965, p. 53.

32. Ibid., p. 55.

33. Ibid.

34. GMRB, November 12, 1964, translated in SCMP #3346.

35. Beijing Ribao (BJRB), October 12, 1964, translated in SCMP(S) #133, February 12, 1965.

36. Zhinong Hongqi, January, 1968, translated in China Topics, May 27, 1968.

37. See, for example, YCWB, November 7, 1963, for a report on Guangya's 75th anniversary.

38. JYGM, June 9, 1967, p. 4.

39. Interview with S.S.P, May 18, 1976.

40. Shanghai Hongweibing Zhanbao, December 24, 1968.

41. Nanfang Ribao (NFRB), June 22, 1964, p. 1.

42. ZGQNB editorial, June 12, 1965, in SCMP #3504. See also GMRB editorial, June 11, 1965.

43. This example is from the first chapter of a 400-page (Chinese) manuscript provided by my research assistant. See L.X.P. Account. L.X.P. had been the leader of the middle school Rebel Red Guards in Guangzhou during the Cultural Revolution.

44. The information on Number 6 Middle School was provided primarily by H.W.C., with additional material supplied by Y.U., Z.Z.C., X.A.X., and S.S.M.

45. Guangya 831, early March, 1968, p. 2.

46. Based on interviews with W.C.J.

47. Interview with W.J.C., #4. I later brought up this particular case to quite a number of interviewees. While those who graduated senior middle school after 1963 found it unusual, those who graduated in 1963 said the same policy of dividing the classes after senior middle two was followed in their school and, they argued, this was rather common in the best schools at that time. For a

262

discussion of whether "the level of the rate of students
proceeding to higher studies should be considered one of
the standards for the evaluation of the quality of the
work of a school" see Shandong Jiaoyu No. 2, February 20,
1965 in JPRS #30, 222 (May 24, 1965), pp. 53-55. On the
"basic correction of the erroneous methods adopted by
some schools in the past for the purpose of seeking a
higher percentage of students admitted to advanced studies" see GMRB April 14, 1965 in JPRS 29,931 (May 4, 1965)
pp. 54-56.

48. Interview with L.X.Y.

49. Interview with T.W.X.

50. Interview with T.W.X. #1 and L.X.X. #1. Although
skeptical that a year of mathematics teaching could have
such an impact on the promotion rate to the university,
there is an account in the Red Guard press confirming
that this particular teacher was hired by Number 5 Middle
School with the sole aim of teaching senior middle three
classes and reversing the promotion rate which had
fallen. See Xiaobing, December 9, 1967, p. 4. In addition, Number 5 Middle School was particularly singled out
for criticism by the "Conservative" Red Guard press.
During the Socialist Education Movement in 1965, its
principal, Hu Yong, was replaced by Shen Wuhua, who had
been a teacher at "Resist Japan University" (Kangda).

51. Interviews with L.Z.Q., #1 and #2.

52. Huaqiao Middle School moved to Eastern Guangzhou in
1965.

53. S.B.F., October 3, 1976. Even minban schools scout-
ed around for students who were unsuccessful in gaining
a place in the school of their choice. One interviewee
who was of middle class background, with good grades, and
a member of the YCL, described how she had confidently
applied to Guangzhou's best schools for senior high and
had been turned down by all of them. Upon receiving the
news, she immediately volunteered to go to the countryside. She continues the story:

     ...just before I was to go to the countryside,
     a minban...suddenly informed me that they had
     accepted me...it was a government-controlled
     school, but it was a minban and so charged a
     lot: 50 yuan a term, 100 yuan a year. I didn't
     apply to it, but they'd taken a look at my
     dossier and my exam results and sought me out.

Whether the <u>minban</u> school was seeking to recruit good
students to raise its reputation or perhaps just to earn
some money, it is interesting that they too had access to
the files of the Education Bureau to determine who was
unable to get into a school. Interview with W.W., August
28, 1975, supplied by Jonathan Unger.

54. Hong Yung Lee, "The Radical Students in Kwangtung
During the Cultural Revolution," The China Quarterly #64,
December 1975, p. 676 (hereinafter cited as Lee, Radical)

55. BTZB, August 18, 1967, p. 3.

56. Xiaobing, December 24, 1967, p. 2.

57. L.L.X., July 11, 1976. Number 2 Middle School, in
fact, has recently been made a key-point school once
again and has been proudly telling foreign visitors that
its promotion rate before the Cultural Revolution was as
high as 70%. Interview notes of Susan Gruneberg who visited the school as part of a delegation in Mav, 1978.
See also Ezra Vogel's interview notes, August, 1980.

58. Zhongxue Doupigai #1, June 19, 1967, in SCMP (S)
#200, August 31, 1967.

59. Nahan Zhanbao #4, April 1968, p. 1. For similar
complaints by suburban schools in Wuhan against schools
being ranked, the keypoint system, and so forth, see
Wuqianli Kuanglan #2, November 29, 1967, p. 1.

60. See the table covering the years 1951-1962 in Hong
Yung Lee, The Politics of the Chinese Cultural Revolut-
ion (Berkeley, 1978), p. 79; Donald Munro, "Egalitarian
Ideal and Educational Fact in Communist China" in John
Lindbeck, China: Management of a Revolutionary Society,
(Seattle, 1971), pp. 256-301; K. S. Karol, China: The
Other Communism, (New York 1968), second edition, p. 300.

61. Chinese Sociology and Anthropology, Fall-Winter,
1969-1970, p. 40. The translation is from Jiaoxue Pipan
(Pedagogical Critique), August 20, 1967.

62. Ibid., p. 59.

63. JYGM, November 30, 1967, p. 2.

64. L.H.S., September 22, 1976.

65. JYGM, November 30, 1967, p. 2.

66. Ibid.

67. Sha referred to those who had been executed (qiangbi). The first guan referred to those who had been imprisoned (jianjin). The second guan referred to those who had been under close supervision (guanzhi).

68. JYGM, November 30, 1967, p. 2.

69. Collier, China's Socialist Revolution, p. 137.

70. Interestingly, this decline in the enrollment of students of worker-peasant background during the early 1960s, which peaked in 1962, was not readily apparent until the revelations of the GPCR. Reports in the media and briefings by officials to foreigners stressed the steady increase in the number of students of proletarian origin in the nation's universities and colleges. For example, one visitor to China was given the following figures by an official in the Ministry of Education:

Year	% of Students of Working-Class or Peasant Origin in Universities
1952	20.46%
1958	36.42%
1962	42.34%
1965	49.65%

See Karol, p. 300.

71. New China News Agency (NCNA), English, Beijing, September 5, 1964, in SCMP #3296. The category of "families of working people" would normally include those of revolutionary cadre or military background.

72. This example is from an interview conducted by Jonathan Unger, which has been made available to me. My own interviews with students who applied for the university in 1964 or 1965 (some got in, most did not) and with those who were applying in 1966, confirm that indeed there was a sharp decline in the success of those of exploiting class origin. No longer was political activism or Youth League membership enough to compensate for an unfortunate family background.

73. Cited in Lee, Politics, p. 79.

74. BJRB, May 4, 1962, in SCMP(S), #97, July 9, 1962. Overall, the percentage of students of good class background at Beijing University fluctuated as follows:

Year	% of Good Class Origin
1952	15% (Beijing Daily, May 4, 1962)
May, 1962	48% (Ibid.)
Fall, 1962	37.7% (BTZB, August 18, 1967, p. 3.)
Eve of GPCR (1966)	52% (Lee, p. 79)

75. For Mao's Spring Festival talk see Stuart Schram, Chairman Mao Talks to the People, (New York, 1974), pp. 197-211.

76. Collier, China's Socialist Revolution, p. 131.

77. The first exam group actually included engineering, science, certain specializations within the fields of agriculture and forestry, and biochemistry and biophysics in medicine. The second group included medicine, agriculture and forestry, biology, physical culture, and psychology. The third group included arts and music, philosophy and economic geography. See Joseph C. Kun, "Higher Education: Selection and Enrollment," The China Quarterly, #8, October-December, 1961, pp. 143-146.

78. Enrollment regulations for 1964 and 1965 are in SCMP, #3234 and #3492, respectively. On the changing entrance exam requirements, see Robert Taylor, Education and University Enrollment Policies in China, 1949-71, (Contemporary China Papers No. 6, Australian National University, Canberra, 1973). Joseph C. Kun, "Higher Education Selection and Enrollment," The China Quarterly, #8 October-December 1961, pp. 143-144. K. Hsu, Chinese Communist Education: The Cultural Revolution, (unpublished Ph.D. dissertation, George Peabody College for Teachers, 1972), p. 234.

79. Hsu, Chinese Communist Education, p. 234.

80. Interview with L.Z.I., February 29, 1976.

81. Xiaobing, November 9, 1967.

82. Peking Review, February 3, 1978, p. 17.

83. WHB, Hong Kong, April 2, 1965. Of the 89,000 in lower middle school in 1965, 35,000 were in junior middle one.

84. The figures for 1963 are from YCWB, June 19, 1963 and July 12, 1963.

85. NFRB, September 16, 1964; YCWB, September 10, 1964.

86. <u>YCWB</u>, August 31, 1965. Several of the 25 vocational schools set up in 1964 had already folded by this time, so the total number of such schools as of September, 1965 seems to have been 29.

87. Interviews with L.I. and X.I.E., June 25, 1976 and with T.J.X., March 14, 1976.

88. The characterization of the work-study school as a dumping ground is common in the Red Guard press. See (Beijing Normal Institute) <u>Dongfanghong</u>, May 12, 1967, pp. 3-4, for a particular kind of work-study school similar to a Western reform school. For more standard work-study schools see <u>Kangda Zhanbao</u>, May 13, 1967 and April 1, 1967; <u>Weidong</u> April 22, 1967; Joel Glassman, <u>The Implementation of Education Policy in Communist China</u>, (unpublished Ph.D. dissertation, Michigan, 1974.), p. 255. A revealing case is also provided by a young man who became a YCL cadre. Because of his atrocious, undisciplined behavior, he was expelled from primary school. Only a work-study school run by the Party would accept him as a student. See <u>ZGQNB</u>, September 18, 1965 in <u>SCMP</u> #3551. On the opening of new work-study schools in Guangdong of the <u>jigong</u> type, see <u>NFRB</u>, September 14, 1964, p. 1. For schools of the <u>zhiye</u> type, see <u>YCWB</u>, July 16, 1964. L.D.H., October 8, 1976, presents a vivid picture of the vocational school attached to the Commercial Bureau which he attended.

89. For material on the case of the 600 students and their rebellion in the Cultural Revolution, see Stanley Rosen, <u>The Role of the Sent-Down Youth in the Chinese Cultural Revolution: The Case of Guangzhou</u> (Berkeley: Center for Chinese Studies, forthcoming).

90. Guangzhou radio, August 29, 1964.

91. Ibid., December 12, 1965 and <u>YCWB</u>, January 14, 1965.

92. From material supplied by Jonathan Unger.

93. Karol, <u>China</u>, p. 300.

94. <u>JYGM</u>, November 30, 1967, p. 2. There is some limited evidence that students of worker-peasant background might have fared better in Shanghai in these years. Ray Wylie, a Canadian who taught English at the Shanghai Foreign Languages Institute from 1965 until 1967, has stated that in his institute there were a considerable number of first and second year students of worker-peasant background at the time of the Cultural Revolution. Third and fourth year students, on the other hand,

tended to be from bourgeois and cadre families. Interview conducted by Fred Teiwes in Hong Kong in July and
August, 1967 (supplied to me by Richard Baum). Neale
Hunter, teaching at the same institute, says that children of cadres put up a wall poster early in the GPCR
seeking to show that, contrary to common belief, students
of working class origin received no real benefits in
terms of increased recruitment, even after 1964. See
Neale Hunter, Shanghai Journal, (New York, 1969), pp. 55ff

95. G.L., January 1, 1976.

96. Xiaobing, December 24, 1967, p. 2.

97. G.L., February 1, 1976.

98. JYGM, November 30, 1967, p. 4. The relevant article
is entitled "Piercing the Lie that 'Everyone is Equal
Before Marks'." This particular article includes other
instances of similar behavior by children of high-level
cadres and their parents.

99. Regrettably, we have few accurate figures for individual universities in Guangzhou. The closest we come are
approximate figures for Zhongshan University which reveal
the following variations in enrollment:

Year	Enrollment	Source
1959	3,200+	WHB, Hong Kong, June 5, 1959.
1961	4,000+	WHB, March 12, 1961.
1963	4,800	ZGXW, March 16, 1963.
1964	4,300+	YCWB, November 12, 1964.
1965	4,500+	Xingdao Ribao, Hong Kong, February 16, 1965.
1966	4,000+	ZGXW, March 11, 1966.
1966 (eve of the Cultural Revolution)	"perhaps 5,000"	Collier, p. 72.

100. Recently published data reveals that, nationally,
China produced only 360,000 senior high graduates in 1965,
while recruiting 164,000 students for higher education
that year. See Zhongguo Baike Nianjian 1980 (Beijing,
Shanghai, 1980), p. 538.

101. The 1959-60 figures were given to Edgar Snow in 1960 by a Chinese vice-minister of education. The 1964-65 figures were given to Charles Lynch, a Canadian journalist, by the director of industrial education of the Chinese Ministry of Higher Education in 1965. See Richman, pp. 140-141. Recently published figures, however, reveal that there were only 1,308,000 students in regular senior highs and 8,030,000 in regular junior highs in 1965. See Zhongguo Baike Nianjian 1980, p. 536.

102. NFRB, June 25, 1964 and June 27, 1964. See SCMP, #3270, July 31, 1964, for a translation of the first of these articles.

103. Ken Ling, The Revenge of Heaven, (New York, 1972), p. 4.

Chapter 2. Student Relationships Prior to the Cultural Revolution

1. Susan Shirk, The Middle School Experience in China, (unpublished Ph.D. dissertation, M.I.T., 1974).

2. Communist China Yearbook: 1962 (Hong Kong, 1963), p. 431. Originally in ZGQNB, September 2, 1961.

3. Xiaobing, November 9, 1967.

4. Ibid.

5. Current Background, July 30, 1964.

6. ZGQNB, December 24, 1964, editorial.

7. Zhongguo Qingnian (ZGQN), September 16, 1964, p. 30.

8. GMRB, February 5, 1965, in SCMP #3399.

9. RMRB, August 4, 1964. In Training Successors for the Revolution is the Party's Strategic Task, (Beijing, 1965), pp. 36-40.

10. Ibid., pp. 41-42.

11. Shirk, Middle School, p. 284.

12. Interview with C.H.J., February 5, 1976, p. 2.

13. K.H.J., May 2, 1976, p. 1.

14. K.H.J., May 2, 1976; Y.U., May 10, 1976. This con-

ceit was manifested in such ways as showing off in class by raising difficult questions which diverted the teacher and the class from the lesson at hand.

15. In addition to my own interviews, Martin Whyte makes the same point in Small Groups and Political Rituals in China, (Berkeley, 1974), p. 121.

16. C.H.J., February 5, 1976, p. 1.

17. By "non-good background" I mean students who were not of revolutionary cadre, revolutionary military, revolutionary martyr, worker or poor and lower-middle peasant background. In other words "non-five red" background. On opposing the entrance of students of worker-peasant background to the YCL because of poor grades and study habits and the preference in the early 1960s for students of bourgeois origin who had good grades see GMRB, February 5, 1965, in SCMP #3399, pp. 8-12. For the emphasis on recruitment of children of workers and poor and lower-middle peasants into the YCL as part of the new class line policy see ZGQNB editorial of December 24, 1964.

18. On the emphasis on behavior as a more important factor than class origin, see "The Party's Class Policy Lays Stress on Deeds" in ZGQNB, September 9, 1965, in SCMP #3554. Also see Yike Hongxin Xiangzhe Dang (A Red Heart Towards the Party), excerpts from the diary of Tan Jianhua, (Beijing, 1966).

19. ZGQNB, July 27, 1965.

20. ZGQNB, August 10, 1965, in SCMP #3523.

21. ZGQN, August 16, 1965, pp. 18-21.

22. Y.U., May 10, 1976, and W.S.B., June 16, 1976.

23. For reports of these special tutorials see "Guangya Middle School Helps Children of Workers and Peasants Review Their Lessons," in NFRB, June 27, 1964. Also see "Warmly Help the Children of Poor and Lower-Middle Peasants and Workers to Study Well," in RMRB, July 23, 1964, in SCMP #3275, and also GMRB, February 5, 1965, op cit.

24. BJRB, May 26, 1962, in SCMP (S) #97, and Shanghai WHB, December 9, 1962, in SCMP (S) #108.

25. BJRB, November 26, 1964, in SCMP (S), #133.

26. YCWB, February 11, 1963. For another report on children of working class background studying their family histories see YCWB, September 18, 1963, on the Guangzhou Railroad Middle School; for children of cadres studying the models presented by their parents, see YCWB, September 19, 1963, a report of Guangzhou Number 16 Middle School.

27. Zhongxue Luntan, March 11, 1967, p. 3.

28. Ibid.

29. Tiaozhan, mid-March, 1968, p. 2.

30. Ibid.

31. Z.Z.B., March 25, 1976, p. 3.

32. Ibid.

33. "Does a Good Family Background Obviate the Need of Ideological Remolding?," in ZGQNB, March 28, 1963, in SCMP #2968. On a similar point expressed more theoretically, see "On the Formation of Communist Morality" in Shanghai WHB, December 19, 1963, translated in URS, Vol. 34, p. 383.

34. RMRB, June 1, 1963.

35. Ibid. Also see ZGQN, #7, April 1, 1963, pp. 8-9.

36. Judging from interviews with several former university students who had participated in the four cleans movement in the countryside, this feeling of wastefulness with regard to academic study was particularly prevalent among social science and humanities students. Students of economics, for example, no longer wanted to study foreign languages or Western economics; they even felt that Marx's Das Kapital, previously treated almost like a bible, should be somewhat de-emphasized, to be replaced by readings more relevant to Chinese society, such as Mao's works.

37. For these slogans, among others, see "Study Eagerly for the Revolution" in ZGQN #8, April 16, 1965, pp. 12-13. Also see Shanghai WHB, June 3, 1964, p. 4.

38. NFRB, June 27, 1964; RMRB, July 23, 1964; GMRB, February 5, 1965.

39. See Peng's report at the 2nd session of the 4th National Committee of the All-China Youth Federation and the

18th National Student Representative Conference (January, 1965) in RMRB, January 31, 1965, translated in SCMP #3395, February 11, 1965, pp. 1-4.

40.   ZGQNB, September 9, 1965.

41.   Ibid.

42.   RMRB, May 4, 1965; ZGQNB, October 5, 1965; Shirk, Middle School, pp. 195-96.   In addition to these sources, stories had previously appeared in the press describing how students of good class background could be led astray by those from exploiting class or petty bourgeois background.   One described a senior middle student of cadre origin who, influenced by her non-good background friends, looked down on students with less money than she had.   See ZGQN, August 1, 1964 in Selections from China Mainland Magazines #440.   Also see Tiaozhan, mid-March 1968, p. 1.

43.   ZGQNB, October 5, 1965.

44.   Shanghai WHB, May 5, 1966, in SCMP (S) #152.

45.   NCNA, Peking, February 18, 1966, in SCMP #3646.

46.   Ibid.   The phenomenon of students of bad class origin "giving up and not trying" had become common and was commented upon in the press on several occasions.   See, for example, ZGQNB, June 3, 1965, in SCMP #3478.   Shirk reports on this attitude among her informants and I found it common among my interviewees as well.

47.   The Diary of Wang Jie (Beijing: Foreign Language Press, 1967), p. 6.   For Wang Jie's comments on his class background see especially p. 59 and pp. 81-82.

48.   For an attempt by a Red Guard group to put Wang Jie on the samp plane   as Lei Feng see "Origin Theory" in Gordon White, Class Background in Modern Chinese Politics: The Case of the Cultural Revolution (Australian National Press monograph, 1975), p. 81.   One former YCL student cadre said there were at least three models for students to learn from: Lei Feng, Wang Jie, and Tan Jianhua, ranked in descending order.   Lei Feng was the earliest, had his impeccable class background, and Mao's own imprimatur to recommend him for study; Wang Jie was of middle peasant background but lacked Mao's direct stamp of approval.   Tan Jianhua was of landlord background and was studied mostly in YCL meetings rather than by all students.   During the Cultural Revolution, Tan was posthumously accused of having feigned his activism (he had drowned in 1965).   Interview with L.X.Y., August 28,

1976, p. 2.

49. White, <u>Class Background</u>, p. 81.

50. On the opposition to the view that experts should
be "politically passable, professionally proficient, and
materially well off" which had become prevalent since
1961, see <u>NFRB</u>, March 14, 1965; <u>ZGQNB</u> forum from December
24, 1964 to January 23, 1965; and Guangzhou radio, March
20, 1966.

51. W.C.J., August 1976.

52. Susan Shirk, "Political Culture in the People's Republic of China: The Strategies of Chinese Students,"
paper presented at the University of Michigan, August,
1977, p. 14.

53. <u>NFRB</u>, January 17, 1959, p. 3.

54. <u>GMRB</u>, November 12, 1964, in <u>SCMP</u> #3346. See Chapter
One for details on the elite status of this Harbin
school. In schools for cadre children the interest in
YCL membership would be even greater. One Red Guard
newspaper reported that 95% of the lower middle school
graduates at August 1 Middle School in Beijing became
YCL members. See <u>Chinese Sociology and Anthropology</u>,
Summer 1969, p. 15.

55. H.R.J., July 28, 1976, and L.J.S., June 8, 1976.
On the Yucai example, see ZGQNB, September 7, 1965, in
<u>SCMP</u> #3551 and <u>GMRB</u> in <u>SCMP</u> #3560. Also see <u>ZGQNB</u>,
September 18, 1965. Shirk (Michigan paper), p. 9,
provides an example of the phenomenon of students "giving
up hope" at <u>minban</u> schools.

Part 2:   The Cultural Revolution

1. For the best analysis of these differences see Hong
Yung Lee, "The Radical Students in Kwangtung During the
Cultural Revolution," in <u>The China Quarterly</u> (<u>CQ</u>), #64,
December, 1975, pp. 645-683.

2. From material found in Livio Maitan, <u>Party, Army, and
Masses in China</u>, New Left Books, (London, 1976), pp. 362-
363.

Chapter 3.   <u>The Cultural Revolution in Guangzhou: The
            Initial Division Into Factions (June 1966-
            April 1967)</u>

1. Wenhui Bao (WHB), (Shanghai), November 10, 1965. For an English translation see Current Background (CB), #783. Also see Byung-joon Ahn, Chinese Politics and the Cultural Revolution, (Seattle, 1976), pp. 195 ff.

2. Ahn, Chinese Politics, p. 196.

3. Renmin Ribao (RMRB), May 4, 1966, in China Notes, #164, May 19, 1966.

4. For contents of Nie's poster see RMRB, June 2, 1966 in SCMP #3719, June 16, 1966.

5. RMRB, June 1, 1966, in SCMP #3712, June 6, 1966. The influence of this editorial can be seen from the fact that it was singled out as evidence in the recent trial of Chen Boda. The prosecution alleged that the editorial was written to prepare public opinion for "the framing and persecution of cadres and ordinary people" which followed. See Beijing Review (BR), No. 5, February 2, 1981, p. 26.

6. Liberation Army Daily (LAD) editorial, June 7, 1966, in SCMP #3716, June 10, 1966.

7. For the material on Number 10 Middle School see YCWB, June 24, 1966, in SCMP #3740 and GMRB, June 14, 1966. For Number 45 Middle School see the reports in RMRB, June 24, 1966, in SCMP #3735; ZGQNB editorial and article, June 25, 1966; YCWB, June 25, and July 9, 1966. Also see Hai Feng, Guangzhou, pp. 33-34. In addition, some of my material on these two schools has been supplied by refugee informants who were either students at these schools, or were familiar with the situation.

8. On Cai Sanjian's past history, see Mingbao (daily), July 15, 1966.

9. Qin Mu was a Guangdong writer who had already been singled out for criticism.

10. Gordon Bennett and Ronald Montaperto, Red Guard: The Political Biography of Dai Hsiao-ai (New York, 1971), pp. 39-41.

11. Ibid., pp. 46-49.

12. Guangzhou Ribao (GZRB), June 14, 1966, p. 1.

13. Beijing radio, June 18, 1966; NCNA, June 18, 1966.

14. Interview with C.W.D., October, 1974. Until this directive, at a number of schools it was students at

senior high two level, who did not need to study for
university entrance exams, who had taken the lead in the
GPCR.

15. Guangzhou radio, July 7, 1966.

16. Red Flag editorial, #8, July 8, 1966, entitled "Long
Live the Great Proletarian Cultural Revolution!"

17. Several schools, such as Huafu, Guangya, and the
Provincial Experimental School were provincially run, and
so work teams were sent out by the provincial Party
committee.

18. Pitao Zhanbao, March 14, 1967, p. 2, quotes Tao as
saying that the "rightists" among university students
should not exceed 1%. Also see Ahn, Chinese Politics, who
cites another source in arguing that 3% of the university
students and 1% of the middle school students were to be
singled out as rightists. For material on the CCRG, see
Ding Wang, Zhonggong Wenge Yundongzhong de Zuzhi yu
Renshi Wenti, Contemporary China Research Institute, Hong
Kong, 1970, pp. 55-70.

19. Zhongbao Zhoukan. The quote is from a series of
articles entitled "Hongweibing shouji," by Zhuang Yi,
issues #53-127, 1968-69.

20. Interview with L.I., May, 1976.

21. See, for example, L.X.P.'s account of the GPCR,
Chapter 2. L.X.P., who was to become the leader of
Guangzhou's middle school Rebels, has written out more
than 400 pages (in Chinese) on his GPCR experiences.
Hereinafter cited as Account.

22. Interview with S.H.J. and J.B.F.

23. Bennett and Montaperto, Red Guard, pp. 73-77.

24. See Lee, Politics, op. cit. for an excellent analysis of these differences.

25. L.X.P., Account, Chapter 2. Also see Bennett and
Montaperto, Red Guard, p. 65.

26. See, for example, RMRB, August 1, 1966, "The Whole
Country Should Become a Great School in Mao Tse-tung
Thought" in SCMP #3754.

27. RMRB, June 24, 1966, "The Sunlight of the Party
Illuminates the Road of the Great Cultural Revolution,"
in SCMP #3728.

28. <u>URI Documents</u>, pp. 42-70.

29. Ibid., p. 46.

30. An exception to this lack of understanding would appear to be Ken Ling and his Red Guard group at Xiamen Number 8 Middle School in Fujian. After reading the 16 Articles it became clear to them:

> that the Cultural Revolution was actually directed against the "power faction within the Party that followed the capitalist road." After lengthy discussion we reached the general conclusion that persons such as mayors, municipal Party secretaries, provincial governors and provincial party secretaries could be regarded as among the "power faction" to be tested during the Cultural Revolution to determine whether or not they stood on Mao's side. The communique set a new task for the Red Guards. We now understood that the previous movement to destroy the four olds in society had been a mere tempering and a trial of Red Guard courage. The Cultural Revolution had only now begun.

While Ling's journal - <u>The Revenge of Heaven</u> - appears to contain several obvious mistakes and exaggerations, on this point there is some evidence that his account may be reasonably accurate. There is a twelve-page mimeographed Red Guard document dated September 6, 1966 which deals with Xiamen Number 8 Middle School and substantiates several of Ling's points. For example, the mimeographed report does say that 300 students from this middle school went to the Xiamen Municipal Party committee on August 12 and demanded, among other things, that the head of the Education Department, Wang Yugeng, who was also the wife of the provincial first Party secretary Ye Fei, be grabbed and returned to Xiamen.
    The school, however, was unusual in several ways. First, according to the report, students of good class background made up less than 10% of the student body. Second, the work team, even during the height of the emphasis on "blood line," refused to allow outside students with different views into the school to exchange experiences. This was particularly the case when the issue of class background became most prominent in August-September, 1966. Third, the work team was against forming a Red Guard unit in the school because it would undermine unity. Finally, events forced the establishment of a Red Guard unit on September 1. While some of the above points from the report are congruent with Ling's own account, others are not. For example, in

Ling's account the Red Guards were formed in his school
on July 16, 1966; moreover, we are told that his school
was the first in Xiamen to form such an organization.
Ling generally seems to have a problem with chronology
as well. For example, in Ling's account the work team
left his school on June 12, 1966 on orders of the provincial Party committee. But the order for work teams to
withdraw from schools did not come until late July. His
participation in the "Destroy the Four Olds" campaign in
early July also pre-dated the nationwide movement which
developed in mid-August. Thus, one must read the book
with care.

On the formation of the Red Guards at his school
see Ken Ling, The Revenge of Heaven, (New York, 1974),
p. 28. For the mimeographed document report see Diaocha
Baogao, September 6, 1966. In addition, interviews conducted with Red Guards from Xiamen and Fuzhou turned up
several incidences of exaggeration of actual events on
Ken Ling's part.

31. For a somewhat different assessment of the role of
the 16 Articles see Lee, Politics, pp. 64-67 and 118-125.

32. Bennett and Montaperto, Red Guard, pp. 69-77.

33. Ling, The Revenge of Heaven, pp. 24-35.

34. Bennett and Montaperto, Red Guard, pp. 69-77.

35. Diaocha Baogao, September 6, 1966; Ling, The Revenge
of Heaven, pp. 24-35.

36. A good discussion of the couplet's influence can be
found in White, Class Origin.

37. See, for example, interview with L.I., a YCL member
of bad class background at Number 5 Middle School. He
described the rebellion of those of non-five red background at the first two school-wide debates. When he
spoke at the third debate on August 23, however, he was
silenced and beaten for the first time.

38. NCNA, August 18, 1966, in SCMP#3766, August 23,
1966, p. 6.

39. C.R.T., August 31, 1976.

40. W.S.B., June 11, 1976.

41. L.S.P., July 18, 1975.

42. See Chapter One for a brief discussion of the process of self-classification by middle school students

before the GPCR.

43. The example from Number 21 was provided by H.X.P., April 21, 1976, a student in third year junior high at that time.

44. For some of the new restrictions the Red Guards placed on those in Guangzhou with bourgeois habits, see Sunday-Herald, (Hong Kong), September 4, 1966; China Mail, (Hong Kong), September 6, 1966.

45. The future leader of the Guangzhou middle school Rebels had led an unauthorized group in the "Destroy Four Olds" movement until the Red Guards in his school discovered his group and ordered it to return to the campus. He, of course, had not been an Outer Circle member. He later recalled his anger at being denied the chance to take part in this activity. See L.X.P., Account, Chapter 2.

46. Hai Feng, Guangzhou, p. 54; "Who Led the Ism Guards Astray" in Hongqi Bao, September 10, 1967, translated in URS, Vol. 48, #24, September 22, 1967, p. 338. The First Congress of Guangzhou's Red Guards was held at Zhongshan Memorial Hall with 4,000 Red Guards and many provincial and military leaders in attendance. See Guangzhou radio, September 3, 1966 and Hongwei Bao editorial, September 3, 1966 in SCMP #3780 and JPRS (Communist China Digest), #177. On Red Guard organization at this time see Xingdao Ribao (Hong Kong), October 3, 1966 and November 2, 1966.

47. URS, Vol. 48, #24, p. 339.

48. C.H.M., June, 1975.

49. Hongwei Bao (Guangzhou), September 14, 1966 provides an eyewitness account of this rally by a representative of Guangzhou's Number 4 Middle School.

50. See The China Quarterly #28, 1966, p. 182.

51. L.X.P., Account, Chapter 2.

52. See Guangzhou radio, September 18, 1966 and Hongwei Bao, September 18, 1966 in SCMP #3790.

53. Ibid. and Bennett and Montaperto, Red Guard, pp. 93-94.

54. L.X.P., Account, Chapter 2.

55. Ibid.

56. "Who Led the Ism Guards Astray?," pp. 338-339.

57. The "23 Points" can be found in Documents of the Chinese Communist Party Central Committee September 1956-April 1969, Vol. I, (URI, Hong Kong, 1971), pp. 823-836. The material on Zhongshan University comes from many interviews with S.S.P., a member of the school's August 31st Rebel organization (Zhongda Basanyi). In addition, two other former students were interviewed on the situation at that university. Also see Collier, China's Socialist Revolution, pp. 84-92.

58. See Hai Feng, Guangzhou, pp. 30-33 and Hongqi Bao, June 24, 1967. My account of the incident at this institute and its influence also comes from interviews with C.R.T., S.S.P., L.X.P., and L.N.Z.

59. Hongqi Bao, June 24, 1967, p. 3 in SCMP #4026, pp. 13-16.

60. L.X.P., February, 1975.

61. L.X.P., Account, Chapter 2.

62. F.W.M., March 16, 1976.

63. W,S.B., June 11, 1976 and June 16, 1976. Also see Mao Tse-tung, An Analysis of the Classes in Chinese Society, (Beijing, 1956), p. 6. This phenomenon was reported by other interviewees from Guangzhou and Beijing.

64. Wuchan Jieji Wenhua Dageming Dashiji (The Great Proletarian Cultural Revolution -- A Record of Major Events), (Beijing, February 1967). Translated in JPRS, #420, pp. 1-61, at pp. 47-48.

65. Kuai was declared innocent by Zhou Enlai on August 4 at a meeting attended by CCRG leaders and 10,000 people. Major Events, p. 35.

66. The Doctrine Guards had a strong case. Song, for example, while declaiming his belief in the freedom of the masses to make revolution, at the same time defended the "cow cages" used at Qinghua University to house bourgeois academic authorities as required by the necessities of proletarian dictatorship. On Song's visit see C.W.D., June 3, 1974 and L.X.P., June, 1975 and Account. Song's message to the students at Dai Hsiao-ai's school was not limited to advice on the formation of a Red Guard organization; he also dealt with the rehabilitation of students who had been denied freedom by the school's work team, although because of obedience to the work team,

this had not been an important issue at the school.
Interview with Dai, June 27, 1974.

67. "Who Led The Ism Guards Astray?" There were also
Red Guards from Beijing who were attacking the municipal
committee at this time, such as those from the elite
Number 101 Middle School. They accused the Guangzhou Red
Guards of weakness because of the latter's support for
the municipal committee. Guangzhou Red Guards, in turn,
accused their Beijing counterparts of violating the 16
Points.   See China News Items from the Press (CNIFP),
September 27, 1966 (original report in Tian Tian Daily,
(Hong Kong), September 23.) On the acknowledgement of
differences between local and outside Red Guards see
Hongwei Bao, September 27, 1966 in SCMP #3795, October 6,
1966 and CNIFP, #142, October 20, 1966, which is a report
of an article in Tian Tian Daily, October 14, 1966.

68. Lin Biao, in a November 3 speech, advocated exchanging revolutionary experiences on foot. See URI Documents, p. 110.
     As in Beijing, the university students in Guangzhou
had disposed of the blood line theory earlier than the
middle school students. For example, in October, a
Japanese delegation visited Zhongshan University and
asked the Red Guards who were their hosts: "Among the
students, what are the sons of wealthy men and landowners
doing?" The reply was as follows:

     Together with us they are taking part in
     the Great Proletarian Cultural Revolution.
     I think this is a question of the class
     system chengfen argument. "Chengfen" means
     family standing. It means what class a
     person belongs to. We embrace even those
     coming from such families as our comrades...
     We look at the individual's political
     expressions and action. Since they have
     received the influence of their families,
     they appear in some aspects. They must
     make greater efforts than others. Whether
     they can unite with us or not is judged
     from their own political activities.

This approach seems little different from the Party's
class line policy which the CCRG was supporting at the
time. See DSJP (Magazines), October 24, 1966, p. 70.
     Indeed, foreign instructors at Zhongshan University
divided Rebels and Conservatives at that school on the
basis of issues other than class origin. The following
quote describes the situation in September, 1966:

From the beginning, the Red Guard groups started
to polarize into two opposed sides, mainly on the
basis of their assessment of the events of the
summer. Those who had rebelled against the Party
committee and those who now sympathized   with
the Rebels formed one side...;and those who had
rallied to the support of the Party committee
in June and had been sympathetic to the work team
and most critical of the Rebels formed the other
side (...the Conservatives).

Collier, China's Socialist Revolution, pp. 91-92.

69. Red Flag, January 1, 1967. Also see China News
Summary (CNS), #152, January 5, 1967.

70. See the series of interviews with H.W.C., beginning
July, 1975, but especially the March 6, 1976 interview.

71. Collier, China's Socialist Revolution, p. 94 and
interviews with S.S.P. and C.R.T.

72. Lin Yun's letter to the Guangzhou Military Region
Command in URS, Vol. 52, #7-8, July 26, 1968, pp. 86-87.

73. "Hongweibing shouji," op. cit.

74. Hongwei Bao Chuandan, February 18, 1967 in SCMM
#574, May 1, 1967, p. 26.

75. "Hongweibing shouji," op. cit.

76. On the Red Guard News incident, also see Leaflet No.
1 of the Red Guard News Revolutionary Rebel Regiment,
January 16, 1967; Red Guard News Leaflet, February 18,
1967 in SCMM #547, May 1, 1967; Guangzhou Hongweibing
Baofeng Yizhounian Zhuankan, December 13, 1967 and
"Yangcheng Wanbao bei fengji" in Zhongbao Zhoukan, September 19, 1969.

77. The units represented were from Number 21, Number 7,
Number 16, Number 13, the Railroad Middle School, the
Girls' Middle School, and South China Experimental School.
All were Eastern District schools, except Number 13 which
was a borderline case. See L.X.P., Account, Chapters
4 and 5, for details on the origin and development of
the Guangzhou Regiment. On the New First Headquarters
Middle School Department see Account as well as interviews with Z.Z.B., S.H.J., J.B.F., Z.T.R., and H.W.C.

78. For details of the power seizure and the positions
taken by various Red Guard groups see Guangdong Zhanbao,

February 22, 1967, translated in SCMP #3921, April 18, 1967, pp. 9-17; Guangzhou Hongweibing, February 10, 1967, translated in SCMP #3929, May 1, 1967, pp. 1-19; Hai Feng, Guangzhou, pp. 79-84. For details supplied by observers and participants see L.X.P. Account; interviews with S.S.P.; and Wang Chao, Guangzhou Dianyingjie de Zaofanzhe (Hong Kong, 1969), pp. 76-83. This latter book deals with the rise and fall of the Rebel faction at Pearl River Film Studio in Guangzhou. Hai Feng, Haifeng Wenhua Geming Jishu (Hong Kong, 1969), pp. 53-55 describes the power seizure period in Haifeng county, Guangdong province.

79. Hai Feng, Guangzhou, p. 75.

80. See, for example, Lin Yun's Letter. The outside Red Guards became closely tied to the Zhongda Rebels after November 30. Until November the Rebel movement in Guangzhou had centered on South China Engineering Institute Red Flag but, over the issue of recovering "black materials" Zhongda became the center of Rebel activity. The first raid of Party offices there had taken place on November 10. On November 24, Zhongda Red Flag was formally set up, but the main event occurred on November 30. The provincial Party committee had stored a good many of these "black materials" in the library at Zhongshan University where they were heavily defended. Soon the attackers and defenders both called reinforcements, with the two sides now separated by more than 1,000 PLA soldiers. Eventually, the Rebels were able to break through and make off with some (10%) of these "black materials." The incident is important because the participants attacking the library (including, for example, Pearl River Film Studio East is Red and the August 1st Combat Corps) were soon to become the leaders in the January power seizure. The defenders, including Conservative workers and the Doctrine Guards, were later to become the nucleus of the East Wind faction. On the seizure of the black materials, see Guangzhou Dianyingjie de Zaofanzhe, pp. 71-76; Lin Yun's Letter, p. 86; and Collier, China's Socialist Revolution, p. 94.

81. See SCMP #3921, April 18, 1967, pp. 9-17.

82. Interviews with S.S.P., 1975-1976.

83. On this whole period, see Hai Feng, Guangzhou, pp. 74-117.

84. See, for example, Lin Yun's Letter.

85. The Central Military Affairs Commission (CMAC) had condemned the February 8 raid, strengthening Huang's

hand. An open letter to the Guangzhou Daily publicly
announced that "the PLA fighters in Guangzhou did not and
do not express support to SGL." Huang also was able to
use the occasion to dispose of those in the Military
Region who had favored the Rebels. See URI Documents,
pp. 249-250 for the CMAC order and Jurgen Domes, "General
and the Red Guards" in The Asia Quarterly (1971), pp. 3-
31; 123-159.

86. Hai Feng, Guangzhou, p. 97.

87. Ibid. An earlier criticism of SGL published by Xin
Beida (New Beijing University Commune) on February 9 is
reprinted in Ming Bao (Daily), March 2, 1967, p. 5.
Also see interviews with Z.Z.C. and S.S.P.

88. See, for example, Guangzhou radio, February 25, 1967
and March 5, 1967.

89. In setting up its organization, the Guangzhou Regiment received advice and support from Beijing Aviation
Red Flag and Harbin Military Engineering Red Rebel Regiment. While Rebels representing Guangzhou's universities
did send people to do liaison work, the Regiment made it
clear that they did not want to be an "attached" unit
of any headquarters. Information on the Guangzhou Regiment comes mainly from L.X.P., Account, plus interviews
with C.R.T., L.X., and W.C.

90. L.X.P., Account, Chapter 3.

91. Guangdong Zhanbao, February 22, 1967 in SCMP #3921,
April 18, 1967, p. 13. The parentheses are in the original.

92. See, for example, Jinggangshan (Qinghua University),
January 11, 1967, in SCMP #3913, April 6, 1967.

93. URI Documents, pp. 321-324.

94. Ibid., p. 356.

95. See interviews with Z.R.T., June, 1975 and C.H.G.,
May 2, 1976, both students from Number 13 Middle School.

96. URI Documents, pp. 351-360.

97. L.X.P., Account, Chapter 4.

98. This was the case, for example, at Huafu, where the
MTG relied upon Tao Zhu's nephew and Ou Mengjue's daughter. The fact that these two high-level cadres had al-

ready fallen apparently did not influence the MTG to any great extent. See interview with G.L., January 1, 1976. For details of MTG work at two Guangzhou middle schools, see Red Guard, pp. 166-80 and L.X.P., Account, Chapter 4.

99. RMRB, February 24, 1967 in CNIFP, March 23, 1967.

100. RMRB, March 4, 1967.

101. Lin Yun's Letter, p. 92.

102. For example, on the eve of the March 5 order calling on the five leaders of Zhongshan University Red Flag to give themselves up within five days, Lin Yun (of Harbin Military Engineering Institute) spoke at an emergency meeting of Zhongshan University's Rebels. According to one member who attended, this speech was instrumental in overcoming irresolution and apprehension in the organization. See S.S.P. interview, December 1975. In mid-March, Dong Daozhu of Beijing Geology East is Red addressed around ten of Guangzhou's leading Rebels at a secret meeting at which he reported on Tan Zhenlin's "adverse current" in the Agriculture and Forestry Bureau and on a meeting then being held at the Center to combat such tendencies. See L.X.P. Account, Chapter 3, section 3.

103. On the Revolutionary Steel Poles, see L.X.P., Account, Chapter 3; H.W.C., and Lin Yun's Letter.

104. See, for example, L.X.P., Account, Chapters 4-5.

105. NCNA, English, April 4, 1967 or Red Flag #5, March 30, 1967 in SCMM #572, pp. 1-5. On the importance of this and other articles to the spirit of the Rebels, see L.X.P., Account, Chapter 5.

106. URI Documents, pp. 407-411.

107. LAD, April 10, 1967, reprinted in RMRB, April 10, 1967, in SCMP #3922, April 19, 1967.

108. Collier, China's Socialist Revolution, p. 112.

109. "Hongweibing shouji," January 23, 1970.

110. Collier, China's Socialist Revolution, pp. 155-56. Zhou's speeches are dealt with most fully in Collier, pp. 147-154; Hai Feng, Guangzhou, pp. 121-124; and "Hongweibing shouji," January 23, 1970. The latter account is interesting because it reveals the mood of both factions at the meetings with Zhou and how their spirits rose or fell sentence by sentence. For the impact of Zhou's visit on Pearl River Film Studio's Rebels, see Guangzhou

Dianyingjie de Zaofanzhe, pp. 106-137.

111. Several articles on the establishment of the Red Headquarters, including the latter's manifesto, appear in <u>Zhidian Jiangshan</u>, April 23, 1967, pp. 2-4.

112. See <u>Lin Yun's Letter</u>, p. 93 and <u>Zhidian Jiangshan</u>, April 23, 1967, p. 2.

113. On the Heilongjiang power seizure, see Jean Esmein, <u>The Chinese Cultural Revolution</u>, (New York, 1970), p. 222; <u>RMRB</u> editorial, February 10, 1967 in <u>SCMP</u> #3880, February 15, 1967 and <u>Peking Review</u> #8, February 17, 1967, pp. 15-17.

114. There were other reasons as well for the ties between the Third Headquarters and the provincial Party committee. The two main leaders from South China Engineering Institute Red Flag were Gao Xiang and Meng Yufei. Gao was the son of Gao Lifu, a leading cadre (14-level) in the foreign trade field. Gao Lifu had joined the revolution before Liberation and was well educated. Because of his high position he had frequent contact with provincial-level cadres, often participating in meetings at that level. In addition, Gao Xiang was rumored to be the boyfriend of Yin Linping's daughter. While most Rebels I interviewed had heard this rumor and some claimed that it was definitely the case, one interviewee who worked closely with Gao on the cadre question insisted that there was no basis to the rumor. Rather, she said, Yin Linping's daughter, a student at Huafu, would often go to meetings held by the Third Headquarters to plead her father's case. She knew that the Third Headquarters was in the process of investigating the provincial Party committee and heard that Yin was being favorably considered. My informant argued that the rumor was spread in part by the immaturity of Yin's daughter. She would return from one of these meetings and inform her friends that she had just been talking to Gao Xiang. Since Gao was an important Rebel leader and was well-known in Guangzhou ever since the "Letter from Beijing" incident, she was basically name-dropping. In addition, she did it in a rather coquettish way, as a high school student might in referring to a famous university "big man on campus." The rumors were then spread by opponents of Gao and Yin, including those affiliated to the Red Headquarters. While this informant's account rings true, this particular rumor nevertheless had a negative influence on relations between the Third and the Red Headquarters. One informant, a member of Zhongshan University's August 31st. Regiment, a key organization in the Red Headquarters, claimed that Wu Chuanbin, the leader

of the Red Headquarters, never felt comfortable sharing
secret material with Gao Xiang because the material would
always find its way to some members of the provincial
Party committee.
Meng Yufei's father was a member of the provincial Party
committee in Hunan province. See interviews with C.R.T.,
June 2, 1976 and S.S.P. for the differences between the
Third and the Red Headquarters.

115. See, for example, L.X.P., Account, Chapter 5, and
interviews with C.R.T., June 26, 1976, and Y.H., January
28, 1976.

116. C.R.T., June 24, 1976; L.X.P., Account, Chapter 5;
and W.C., October 8, 1976.

117. Z.Z.C., August 10, 1975 and H.W.C., March 10, 1976.
The latter interviewee stated that the Doctrine Guards
from Guangya Middle School also sent representatives to
visit Zhongda Rebels at this time. Also see L.X.P.,
Account which argues that other Doctrine Guard units as
well sought out the Zhongda Rebels.

118. One interviewee, L.I.A., a mid-level cadre and
Party member at a factory in northern Guangzhou described
how, although he was sympathetic generally to the Flag
faction, the pressures of Party discipline from his
superiors made certain that he joined the East Wind
group.

119. One former Red Guard leader estimated that the
Rebels outnumbered the Conservatives in Guangzhou's
universities by a ratio of 20:1. See Livio Maitan,
Party, Army and Masses in China, (London, 1976), pp. 362-
363. I have also interviewed this particular Red Guard
and can vouch for his veracity and knowledgability.

120. I take issue on this point with Hong Yung Lee. My
information is derived from interviews with members of
these organizations such as S.S.P. and L.X.P. For
example, Guangzhou's "United Committee to Criticize Tao
Zhu," according to S.S.P., "was only a liaison station
with no leadership authority. Its task was simply to
criticize Tao by, among other things, investigating
cadres, exchanging materials, organizing united actions
for criticizing Tao, and so forth. In the GPCR in
Guangdong, the criticize Tao organization from beginning
to end was weak and powerless, limited to the tasks above.
This essential nature of the United Committee to Criticize Tao Zhu meant that in the armed struggle period it
was without use or power." S.S.P., October, 1975.

121. S.S.P. interview. For differences between the United Committee to Criticize Tao Zhu and the Red Alliance, as well as the differences between the Red Headquarters and the Third Headquarters, see Hai Feng, Guangzhou, pp. 193-200.

Chapter 4 Middle School Factionalism in Guangzhou: The Individual Perspective

1. Methodological Note: In filling out the questionnaire, the students were asked to assess a person's faction as of mid-1967, when the two factions had become stabilized. This was crucial because if the factions had been assessed before April 1967 there would have been many more non-participants listed. For example, Rebel strength was particularly weak during the "March Black Wind" while Conservative strength, after waning in many schools during the "January Revolution," had recovered by May 1967. Another problem raised by informants was how to determine the meaning of factional alignment. Was it to be an ideological term, viz., the faction toward which each student was most sympathetic or an organizational term, viz., the faction in which a student actively participated. Had the first been chosen the column on non-participation would have been empty; had the second been chosen, the result would have tended in the opposite direction. In literally hours of discussion with many of those filling out the questionnaire, a balance was struck between the possible meanings of factional alignment. At a minimum, to be factionally aligned a person had to publicly "put up a sign-board" (gua yige pai) even if he/she were not particularly active in the organization. Rebels included those affiliated to the Red Headquarters (the large majority), the New First Headquarters, the Third Headquarters, or the independent Red Revolutionary Alliance. Conservatives were affiliated either to the Doctrine Guards, the Red First Headquarters or, in rare cases, a separate unit such as the Independent Brigade at Guangya.

2. Methodological Note: The data in this and the following table was collected in the following way. First, I interviewed one of the top Rebel leaders at the middle school level about the GPCR and its leadership at all schools with which he was familiar. Since he was not just the leader at his own school but also had important responsibilities at the municipal level, including liaison work with Rebel units at other schools, his knowledge was considerable. Because he was a member of the Red Headquarters, I independently interviewed two leaders of the New First Headquarters Middle School Section in

order to gather data on the leading Rebels at schools
which had units affiliated with that Headquarters. Next,
I checked the responses I had received with individuals
from as many of the schools in question as I could
locate. Concordance was over 95%. At schools in which
my informants had been unclear about Rebel leadership
(i.e., at those schools where the Rebels were exception-
ally weak or unimportant in the overall factional picture, primarily the neighborhood junior high schools), I
relied directly on students from those schools, if
knowledgeable respondents could be found. I then re-
checked the results with other Rebel leaders. In cases
of doubt or ambiguity, I did not include the school in
the survey. In a few instances difficulties were presented by the presence of two leaders of equal stature
at a school, the death of one leader and his replacement
by another midway through the GPCR, and so forth, but
these instances were rare. Because the leading Rebel
unit at most secondary schools was affiliated to the Red
Headquarters, most of the leaders cited in the table were
members of that organization. In schools where the New
First Headquarters was the stronger, I have taken their
leader for inclusion in the table.

3. In the case of one of them, his parents were low-
ranking Party members who had spent long years working
outside China, with his father an artist and his mother
the principal of a patriotic school in Hong Kong. He
himself was not actually a student, but had been assigned
to teach and lead YCL work at his school. In a previous
account I had included him under the rubric of cadre
origin, but further consultations with individuals who
knew his situation convinced me to change his status to
middle background. For the previous account, see The
China Quarterly #70, 1977, p. 395.

4. Six of the seven leaders of the Guangzhou Regiment
were also the number one leaders at their own schools.
In the case of the Girls' Middle School, the number one
leader was of cadre origin, but the person sent to represent the school on the standing committee of the
Guangzhou Regiment was of overseas worker origin. Still,
she was one of the top five Rebel leaders at the school,
albeit the only one of working class origin.

5. The China Quarterly #70, 1977, p. 396.

6. L.X.P., Account, Chapter 2, Part I.

7. For more details on this period, including the
differing situations Wen and Chang encountered at the
various schools, see L.X.P., Account.

8. The most prominent exceptions, of course, were those Rebels who got together to form the Revolutionary Steel Poles. The majority of this group came from impeccable family backgrounds. Even here, however, there were special circumstances. Those of cadre origin from Huafu who joined the group, for example, had originally been defenders of the school's Party committee. When they later tried to switch and become "Rebels" in the school, the Rebels, remembering their earlier stand, were reluctant to accept them. Thus, most of their activity on behalf of the citywide Rebel faction took place outside their own school. Later in 1967, when Central and local authorities were trying to unite the factions, this "middle class" tendency to resist authority was specifically brought up in both official and factional criticism of those who displayed the "petty-bourgeois" quality of rebellion. It was said that these people were able to withstand pressure from work teams but at the same time they could not distinguish between resistance to bourgeois authority and the revolutionary discipline which must necessarily be accorded to proletarian authority.

9. A listing of the early leadership of the Doctrine Guards was published in a Hong Kong newspaper that employed many former Red Guards as correspondents. The list included the following individuals:

  a. Yang Qiuyuan of August 1 Middle School (the son of Yang Meisheng, the deputy commander of the Guangzhou Military Region).
  b. Huang Chunming of Number 21 Middle School (the son of Huang Yongsheng).
  c. Zhan Heping of Number 21 Middle School (the son of Zhan Caifang).
  d. Bai Shaohua of the Railroad Middle School (the son of Bai Yule).
  e. Zeng Kenan of Number 2 Middle School (the daughter of Zeng Sheng, the mayor of Guangzhou).
  f. Wang Xixiao of Number 2 Middle School (the son of Wang De).

Other leaders listed were the children of various military officials. The newspaper account did not list the schools from which these leaders came. This information has been supplied by my informants. In addition, the newspaper article erroneously listed Wang Xixiao as Wang Xiou and identified him as a daughter rather than a son of Wang De. See Zhongbao Zhoukan #32, April 26, 1968.

10. "Who Led the Ism (Doctrine) Guards Astray?" in Hongqi Bao, September 10, 1967. Translated in URS, Vol. 48, September 22, 1967, p. 349.

Chapter 5   Middle School Factionalism in Guangzhou: The
            School Perspective

1. Interviewees who supported Conservative factions
tended to be from ordinary schools (such as Number 3 and
Number 18) and poor schools (such as Number 42); however,
one of the more informative interviewees was a Doctrine
Guard from Number 6 Middle School.

2. For characteristics of these schools, see Table 1.1
and maps.

3. Mao Zedong Sixiang Wansui, 1969, pp. 526-531.

4. One reason for the concern of the provincial Party
committee was the suicide of Mai Jiaxiang.

5. See Stanley Rosen, Comment: "The Radical Students
in Kwangtung During the Cultural Revolution," The China
Quarterly #70, June, 1977, p. 394.

6. "Who Led the Doctrine Guards Astray?" p. 340.

7. Ibid., pp. 340-341. Information on the Huafu case
has come from: 1) An investigation report prepared by
L.X.P., based on interviews with L.S.P.; 2) "Who Led the
Doctrine Guards Astray?"; and 3) interviews with G.L.,
H.R.J., C.H.E., L.J.S., and L.I.
    The degeneration of the Huafu 11 as a Rebel force
was described in the following way by later Huafu Rebels:

> At the beginning of the campaign, the Doc-
> trine Guards in our school were really a rebel
> force; they opposed the black Party committee
> of the school, opposed the work teams, opposed
> the black CCP Guangdong Provincial Committee
> and opposed Tao Zhu. They had done their
> part in the cultural revolution in Guangdong.
> But, they also had certain shortcomings. The
> Doctrine Guards of our school had been poisoned
> by the reactionary theory of "blood relations."
> After the large-scale "exchange of revolution-
> ary experience" in November last year, the
> Doctrine Guard organization had been basically
> paralyzed. Many of the Doctrine Guards alienat-
> ed themselves from the political struggle for
> a long time while some of them accepted the
> ideas of the United Action and believed them-
> selves of noble blood. When their fathers be-
> came the targets of revolution, they could not
> understand the actions of the Rebels and
> sought to protect their old men.

This quote is from "Who Led the Doctrine Guards Astray?" at p. 346.

8. It should be noted that the Maoism Red Guards (zhuyi bing) at Guangya were not affiliated to the Doctrine Guards (zhuyi bing) citywide. In fact, it was the Mao Thought Red Guards (sixiang bing) that made up the Guangya chapter of the Doctrine Guards. At all other schools with which I am familiar, the Doctrine Guards at the school level were affiliated with the citywide organization of the same name. I have therefore chosen to call Guangya's zhuyi bing the "Maoism Red Guards" to avoid confusion.

9. See Guangya 831, early March 1968; April-May 1968; and May 1968. Guangya June 8 Counterrevolutionary Incident Special Issue, June 1968; Tiaozhan, mid-March 1968 and July 1968. In addition to these newspaper reports, much of the detail has been provided by a series of interviews with Y.H. and Z.D.K., both of whom were members of the Rebel faction at Guangya during the Cultural Revolution.

10. Guangya 831, early March 1968, p. 2.

11. Interview with Y.H.

12. Although I have access to no Red Guard newspapers published at Girls' Middle, I have interviewed more former students from this school than from any other. The material below comes primarily from C.R.T., C.W.D., and C.B.H.

13. When Zhu was transferred to Number 8 during the Socialist Education Movement other leading cadres at the school were also transferred, although they were sent to different schools. The work team sent to Number 8 Middle School early in the GPCR opposed Zhu for not carrying out the educational revolution. He was also accused of favoritism toward those of bad class origin and of not really putting the class line of the Party into effect. The Flag faction at the school later took a position in support of Zhu. Zhu was liberated in 1970 and became a member of the standing committee of what had been one of Guangzhou's mediocre schools in the pre-GPCR period, in charge of educational reform work. See interview with C.R.T., July 17, 1976.

14. The Rebel from a high-level cadre background was something of a special case in that her father had already come under a cloud in the pre-GPCR period and so was treated on less than an equal footing by other cadre children. Nevertheless, her mother still held an im-

portant Party position. Although a YCL member, she had
always been something of a maverick, not just in her
relations with other cadre children, but more generally
in terms of viewpoint. For example, before the GPCR,
she argued that anyone who strove for entrance to a
university that prepared one for a role in industry
rather than agriculture was in the final analysis doing
it for selfish reasons, no matter what the ideological
rationalization might be. She therefore looked down on
many of those eagerly preparing for university entrance
exams. Her outspokenness, independence, and cadre origin
were all important factors contributing to her willingness to "go against the tide" when the GPCR arrived.

15. This term appears frequently in the Red Guard press
as a euphemism used by the Rebels when talking about
those of their members whose backgrounds were bad.

16. Jinggangshan made one other concession on the issue
of class. They set up two leadership groups, one called
the steering committee (qinwuzu) and the other the
nucleus group (hexinzu). The former group was the one
visible to those outside the organization and included
three students of good background out of five (once
again, four of the five were from senior high 3, class
2). It was the nucleus group, however, that was the more
important group, having the responsibility for the actual
work tasks. For example, like most Red Guard organizations, Jinggangshan was divided into sections (bu),
including propaganda, organization, warmaking, and log-
istics. It was the nucleus group, rather than the steering committee, that contained the leader of each section.
Whereas students of bad class background could not hold
leadership positions in the steering committee, they
could and did hold leadership positions in the more important nucleus group (although this, too, was rare).
Ironically, this "tactical hypocrisy" was criticized on
numerous occasions by other leading organizations in the
Guangzhou Regiment who were unaware of the functions of
the nucleus group. Having only a steering committee
themselves, they assumed that Jinggangshan's steering
committee was its key leadership organ and accused
Jinggangshan of not being "true Rebels" because of the
overreliance on changfen, rather than on ability.

17. The members of the Red Revolutionary Alliance formed a subgroup. In 1965, Girls' Middle had specifically
recruited ten students of poor and lower-middle peasant
background from suburban areas. These students had
attended lower middle at schools in either Hua or Conghua
counties and had very poor academic records. Most, however, were YCL members and had turned up at Girls' Middle

because of the latter's designation as a test point by the municipal committee. These ten students had all originally joined the Doctrine Guards but, because they had never really been well-treated within that organization, left to join the Red Revolutionary Alliance in 1967.

18. The importance of the pre-GPCR unity of a classroom in explaining subsequent behavior should not be underestimated. At another senior high two class at this same school, again in which there was only one student of military cadre origin, the class had acted as a unit (50:2) in questioning some of the tactics of the work team in July 1966. The class was quickly surrounded by almost everyone else in the school and the nascent rebellion was crushed.

19. It is useful to give some background information about these two interviewees. The skeptic is of cadre background and remained with the Rebels until January 1967. He later tried to convince his erstwhile comrades to join him as a member of the Red First Headquarters, arguing that they would later suffer because of their complicated class origins. They ignored his advice. On the other hand, the second interviewee remained with the Rebels until the end of the movement and became active in the middle school department of the New First Headquarters as well as an editor for the Number 1 Middle School Rebel newspaper.

20. This is not to say that other schools in Western Guangzhou did not have students of bad class background among its Rebel leadership. Number 29 Middle School, for example, had such leadership. No other school, however, developed and maintained such leadership from such an early date.

21. Although I interviewed several students from this school, most of the information came from L.X., a Rebel leader there.

22. It is one of the schools in Guangzhou to which foreign visitors are taken.

23. For details on the influence of the "Letter from Beijing" incident see Chapter Three.

24. This alliance between those of high-level cadre and those of middle class origin is perhaps less incomprehensible when one considers some of the findings of one recent study. Susan Shirk, based on interviews with former high school students from Guangzhou has argued as follows:

...unlike many other activists, the sons and daughters of cadres do not worry about being seen with classmates of bad family origin. Apparently many children of cadres are drawn to the achievers, the athletic stars, and the valedictorians, regardless of class background. Several respondents of bad class origin remarked that whereas most of their classmates, anxious about their futures, avoided any association with them, the children of cadres freely offered their friendship.

See Susan Shirk, "Political Culture in the People's Republic of China: The Strategies of Chinese Students," p. 13.

25. This section is based on interviews with students from many different schools including, among others, Numbers 3, 4, 9, 13, 18, 22, 24, 28, 29, and 30.

26. It is interesting that two schools which contained a fair number of children of cadre origin and had very high promotion rates to the university seemed to fit the pattern of ordinary rather than good schools when it came to GPCR activism. The schools were the Provincial Experimental School and Number 2 Middle School. The reasons for the deviation from expections are not hard to find. Most important, according to interviewees from these schools, was the fact that neither of the two schools contained more than a negligible number of students who were Northerners and/or from military cadre backgrounds. Those of cadre background at the Provincial Experimental School were predominantly of middle or low-level localist cadre origin and therefore were not much different in outlook and behavior from many children of intellectual background. In addition, they needed to maintain average grades or better to enter and remain at the school, so the academic achievement issue did not really divide them from their classmates.

Those of cadre origin at Number 2 Middle School included a fair number from high-level cadre families, most notably those affiliated to the provincial and municipal Party committees, whose offices were nearby the school; but again, there were few from military origins or from the North and so the pre-GPCR atmosphere had been much less tense than was the case in the Eastern District schools. When the Beijing Red Guards descended upon Guangzhou, these two schools were not important targets to them. Interviewees who attended Number 2 Middle School include L.H.S., L.Z.I., E.L.I.M., and L.X.X. Those from the Provincial Experimental School include L.N.G.

and H.U.A.

27. Those interviewed included students from Numbers 25, 32, 33, 42, 45, and 46.

28. This phenomenon is hidden when one looks at the statistics of GPCR participation by those of working class origin provided in Table 4.4, but was repeatedly stressed by interviewees. Moreover, when children of intellectual middle class background at these schools participated, they seem to have been drawn overwhelmingly to the Rebel side.

29. Xianggang Shibao, September 14, 1968, p. 3. Also see Ming Bao, November 13, 1968 for a report on worker propaganda team personnel being attacked by students at Number 32 Middle School, another neighborhood junior high.

30. Two interviewees of working class origin from this school said that they and most of those they knew had joined the Doctrine Guards solely because its emphasis on class line favored them. When the Doctrine Guards' association with the blood line theory had become a burden, one of the two became a Rebel; the other remained in the Guards, mostly because his friends were members.

31. The names wendou and wudou were of course unofficial since no group would claim openly to be solely a wudou organization. Nevertheless, the groups were generally known by these names.

Chapter 6   The Cultural Revolution Winds Down: Rebels
             and Conservatives in Guangzhou After April
             1967.

1. L.X.P., Account, Chapter 6.

2. Wang Chao, Zhuying, p. 115.

3. Ibid., p. 116.

4. The ten charges appear in a handbill translated in SCMP #3905, March 23, 1967, pp. 1-4.

5. Wang Chao, Zhuying, pp. 111-112.

6. On the Xiang Ming case see L.X.P. Account, Chapter 5; Zhongbao Zhoukan #127, March 6, 1969; and Hai Feng, Guangzhou, p. 121.

7. Hai Feng, Guangzhou, p. 124.

8. Ibid. Also see Wang Chao, Zhuying, p. 105.

9. Lee, Politics, p. 238.

10. Liuyue Tianbing, June 29, 1967 in SCMP #4075, p. 10; Hai Feng, Guangzhou, pp. 140-143.

11. For material on the May 30 notice see L.X.P., Account, Chapter 6; Guangyi Hongi, June 16, 1967, pp. 1-4; Hai Feng, Guangzhou, p. 143.

12. Hai Feng, Guangzhou, p. 143.

13. L.X.P., Account, Chapter 6. According to L.X.P. and others, there were only two kinds of charges that would have been acceptable to the Center as a justification for the Rebels openly to attack the Guangdong military. The first was to argue that the military had committed mistakes similar to those of Zhao Yongfu in Qinghai province. Zhao, the deputy commander of the Qinghai Provinvial Military District, had been cited in a Central Committee document in March for staging a counterrevolutionary coup and usurping military power in the province. The second line of attack was to discover clear-cut material that would implicate leading members of the military district as followers of Liu Shaoqi or others already denounced as "capitalist roaders" and send these materials to the Center. The first of these possibilities was not applicable to the situation in Guangdong. The second approach could only be carried out with utmost secrecy so that, for a period following the first appearance of the code-name "Guangzhou's Tan," leaders in the Red Headquarters, when asked by rank-and-file members which individuals should be targeted as "Guangzhou's Tan" gave rather ambiguous responses. The Central Committee document on Zhao Yongfu can be found in URI Documents, pp. 383-387. Interestingly enough, by August the Rebels were able publicly to use both lines of attack (the comparison with Zhao Yongfu and the charge that the Guangdong military had been infiltrated by "capitalist roaders" who had staged a coup) in their assault of the PLA.

14. Lin Yun's Letter, p. 96.

15. Hai Feng, Guangzhou, p. 202.

16. Some of these directives prohibiting armed struggle can be found in URI Documents, pp. 461-476. Also see L.X.P., Account, Chapter 6.

17. See Thomas W. Robinson, "The Wuhan Incident: Local Strife and Provincial Rebellion During the Cultural Revolution," in The China Quarterly #47, July-September, 1971, pp. 413-438.

18. For Jiang's speech see SCMP (S) #198, August 16, 1967. Other statements by central leaders on "attacking with words and defending with force" can be found in SCMP (S) #220, March 8, 1968. For excerpts of speeches by central leaders attacking the Wuhan conservatives that were printed in Guangzhou's Red Guard newspapers see, for example, Zhuying Dongfanghong, August 8, 1967, in SCMP #4023, pp. 20-22.

19. Interview with C.W.D., October, 1974. The influence of Jiang's slogan is described in China News Summary (CNS) #189, September 28, 1967.

20. For an account of the various armed struggle incidents in Guangzhou see Hai Feng, Guangzhou, pp. 150-175.

21. Some of the units in the Red Headquarters quickly wrote theoretical articles to justify their attacks on the military. See "On Military Power" in Hongse Baodong #16, August 16, 1967, p. 1, translated in SCMP #4071, pp. 13-17. The article argued, among other things, that political and military power could not be separated, that the Guangzhou Military Region had been taken over earlier by Tao Zhu's henchmen and that the leaders of the Guangzhou Military Region were similar to Zhao Yongfu of Qinghai and Chen Zaidao of Wuhan.

22. "Long Live the Revolutionary Rebel Spirit of the 'February 8' Incident" in Zhuying Dongfanghong, August 8, 1967, translated in SCMP #4022, September 15, 1967, pp. 7-9.

23. "Tightly Grasp the Opportunity to Launch a General Attack on Tan Zhenlin of Guangzhou" in Zhuying Dongfanghong, August 8, 1967, translated in SCMP #4020, September 13, 1967, pp. 1-6. The above analysis was written by Hongsi Nahan, one of the most radical groups in the Red Headquarters. Li Zhengtian, the leader of this group, became the moving force behind the famous "Li Yizhe poster" that appeared on the Guangzhou streets in 1974. Li Zhengtian had been the vice-head of propaganda in the Red Headquarters but, in opposition to what he and other radicals considered to be "rightist tendencies," in the summer of 1967 he withdrew from the propaganda department and together with some members of the Revolutionary Steel Poles, set up an organization called "Outcry Battalion" (Nahan Zhantuan), which was not restricted in its activ-

ities by the Red Headquarters. According to an informant familiar with this group, Li and his followers would take the lead during periods of disorder, but at times of peace their provocative words and acts caused the Red Headquarters and the Flag faction numerous headaches. See L.X.P., Account, Chapter 8. For contents of the Li Yizhe poster, see Issues and Studies (Taiwan), January and February, 1976.

24. "Tightly Grasp....." op. cit., p. 3.

25. Information on the establishment of the Red Alliance and the Red Garrison Headquarters can be found in Yiyue Fengbao, August 28, 1967, p. 3; Hai Feng, Guangzhou, p. 196; interviews with S.S.P. and L.X.P. The charges that the Red Garrison Headquarters sought to replace the regular public security and military control organs can be found in the newspaper Sanjun Lianwei Zhanbao, September 3, September 13, and September 24, 1968. Some of these charges were confirmed as basically correct by Rebel leaders that I interviewed. On the other hand, they insisted that the above newspaper was a notoriously unreliable source with regard to Flag faction activities because it was put out in a hurried manner by the military at the end of the GPCR as part of a general suppression campaign against the Rebels. These interviewees charged that factual accuracy was unimportant to those publishing this paper and often names and events that appeared were incorrect. Even when there was truth to the charges printed, it was often exaggerated out of all proportion.

26. Gangbayi, October 15, 1967, p. 2, translated in URS, Vol. 49, #21, December 12, 1967, p. 281.

27. Gangbayi, October 15, 1967, in SCMP #4096, pp. 9-12. Also see Bayi Zhanbao #3, October 14, 1967.

28. Sansi Zhanbao, August 24, 1967, p. 1.

29. This document appears in Ziliao Zhuanji, November 17, 1967 and is translated in SCMP #4082, December 18, 1967, pp. 1-5.

30. Ibid.

31. China Topics, YB 519, March 13, 1969, p. 10.

32. Lin Yun's Letter, p. 98; some of the acts of the Central Investigation Team can be found in L.X.P., Account, Chapter 8.

33. Letter, op. cit.

34. Hai Feng, Guangzhou, p. 24.

35. For contents of these posters see Hai Feng, Guang-zhou, p. 249. Also see Zhuying Dongfanghong #11, September 13, 1967, p. 2.

36. SCMP #4028, p. 17.

37. This circular is translated in SCMP #4036, p. 8. The September 1 Agreement was actually a reiteration of an agreement which had been signed on August 22, but had not been effective.

38. Ibid., pp. 7-8.

39. On August 11 the existence of the May 16 Group opposed to Zhou Enlai was first revealed; on August 20, a Red Flag editorial, later published in issue #14 (on September 17) was published in People's Daily.

40. Letter, p. 100 and Xingdao Ribao, September 22, 1967.

41. Letter, p. 99.

42. China Topics, Appendix E (date unknown), pp. 1-4. Also see Jean Esmein, The Chinese Cultural Revolution, p. 280ff; NCNA (Beijing), English, September 2, 1967, in SCMP #4015 and DSJP Mainichi, September 5, 1967.

43. See URI Documents, pp. 507-533. Jiang Qing's opening statement is worth reprinting here: "I have come rather hurriedly, and I have no idea of what is going on here. Old Kang [Kang Sheng] just dragged me here. Nor have I prepared for the few words which I shall say here. If what I am going to say is right, you may use it for reference; if not, you may criticize me. You may even bombard me or burn me!," p. 521.

44. Ibid., p. 520.

45. RMRB, September 14, 1967, in SCMP #4024, September 20, 1967. A later Red Guard account traced this instruction of Mao's to July 18, 1967, when the Chairman was in Wuhan negotiating with military commander Chen Zaidao. See Wenge Tongxun #14, April 1968, in SCMP #4172, May 7, 1968, p. 11. Some of the directives Mao issued during his inspection tour can be found in URI Documents, pp. 545-556.

46. SCMP (S)#215, p. 1.

47. Ibid.

48. Ibid., p. 2.

49. L.X.P., Account, Chapter 8; Rice, Mao's Way, p. 427;
Guangzhou Radio, October 12, 1967 and October 21, 1967.

50. Most of Zhou's speeches can be found reprinted in
Hai Feng, Guangzhou, pp. 263-301. For English translations see the following sources: the October 19 speech
is in SCMP #4091, January 3, 1968, pp. 1-6; the November
3 speech is in SCMM #611, January 22, 1968, pp. 12-18;
the November 8 speech is in JPRS #438 (44, 414), February
19, 1968, pp. 13-22; the speech on the morning of November 14 is in SCMP #4085, December 21, 1967, pp. 1-12.
The October 31 speech seems to be untranslated and can
be found in Beijing Laidian (no date).

51. Hai Feng, Guangzhou, p. 269.

52. SCMM #611, p. 15. Relations between the sent-down
youth and the Flag faction are explored in detail in
Rosen, Sent-Down Youth.

53. Gongnongbing Zhanbao #18, November 14, 1967 in SCMP
#4078, December 12, 1967, p. 3.

54. See either Ziliao Zhuanji, November 17, 1967 or
Dongfeng Bao, November 18, 1967; a translation appears
in SCMP #4085, December 21, 1967, p. 11.

55. NFRB, December 21, 1967 and Hai Feng, Guangzhou, pp.
323-325.

56. SCMP #4098, pp. 5-6.

57. Ibid., p. 6.

58. Zhongda Hongqi #60, March 15, 1967, p. 4.

59. URS, Vol. 50, p. 150.

60. Bayi Zhanbao #4, January 1968, p. 3. A translation
appears in SCMP #4121, pp. 5-14, at p. 12.

61. "Ghosts and monsters" was a codeword for those of
bad class origin, primarily intellectuals, who had been
the earliest struggle objects in the GPCR.

62. Bayi Zhanbao, January, 1968, p. 2, in SCMP #4121,

p. 11.

63. Ibid.

64. <u>SCMP</u> #4115, p. 6.

65. <u>URS</u>, Vol. 50, p. 154. I have altered the translation in two places based on the original Chinese text.
Other Rebels were less harsh, accepting the fact that
both factions were indeed revolutionary:

> ...certain people have completely ignored the
> objective fact and its historical development
> relative to the struggle between the two lines
> which is inherent in the two big factions in
> Guangzhou. They had disregarded the fact that
> while both factions constitute revolutionary
> mass organizations, one is different from another
> as the revolutionary and advanced is different
> from the conservative and backward.

<u>SCMP</u> #4115, p. 8.

66. <u>URS</u>, Vol. 50, pp. 159-160.

67. <u>Zhongda Hongqi</u>, March 15, 1968, p. 4.

68. L.X.P., <u>Account</u>, Chapter 8.

69. <u>Zhongda Hongqi</u>, March 2, 1968 and Hai Feng, <u>Guang-
zhou</u>, pp. 332-334.

70. Chien Yu-shen, <u>China's Fading Revolution</u>, (Hong
Kong, 1969), pp. 308-309.

71. Hai Feng, <u>Guangzhou</u>, pp. 348-349.

72. Ibid., p. 352.

73. Lee, <u>Politics</u>, p. 270.

74. Hai Feng, <u>Guangzhou</u>, pp. 360-364.

75. L.X.P., <u>Account</u>, Chapter 6.

76. For Mao's comments see <u>Wenge Tongxun</u> #1, October 9,
1967 in <u>SCMP</u> #4060, November 15, 1967, pp. 1-2; <u>Zhengfa
Hongqi</u> #3-4, October 17, 1967.

77. Actually, this call had gone out even earlier. An
editorial, with this exact title, had been printed in the
<u>LAD</u> on September 7 and was reprinted in <u>RMRB</u> on the same

day.

78. L.X.P., Account, Chapter 8.

79. Interview with H.W.C., March 10, 1976.

80. See Red Flag #15, October 15, 1967; RMRB, October 6, 1967; and LAD, October 4, 1967.

81. L.X.P., Account, Chapter 8.

82. It is interesting that the accounts of L.X.P. and H.W.C., two of the three most important Rebel leaders at the secondary school level in Guangzhou differ somewhat on the atmosphere at this time. While L.X.P., in both his Account and in my interviews with him emphasized the strength of the jin'gen forces in September and October, H.W.C. tended to focus on the opposition within the Head-quarters to this current. Their divergent perspectives can be explained most clearly by the fact that H.W.C.'s leadership position stemmed from his very early rebellion and continuing support for radical causes. For example, he had been an important member of the "Revolutionary Steel Poles" and was very active during the period of the March Black Wind. He was well known in the city as a de-bater and spent much of his time moving back and forth between Rebel units at many of Guangzhou's middle schools doing liaison work. Thus, he was well attuned to the attitudes prevalent among the rank-and-file.
     L.X.P., on the other hand, as the leader of the Guangzhou Regiment, devoted much of his energy to deal-ings with other leaders and the university and middle school levels, with members of the Central Investigation Team and with the MTG at his school. A born bureaucrat and organization man, he moved smoothly in the corridors of power. Whereas H.W.C. was perpetually attempting to move the Rebels toward a more radical posture and was oriented toward the lower levels of the faction, L.X.P. was less consciously concerned with ideology and more concerned with the consolidation of the faction's power, and thus oriented himself toward the higher levels.

83. Although many of those taking part initially viewed it as participation in a study class - indeed, they were referred to as "study members" (xueyuan) - it became clear, especially to outsiders, that these "study mem-bers" were actually in a detention class run by the mil-itary. There were more than 80 members of this class by March, 1968. L.X.P., Account, Chapter 8.

84. Ibid.

85. L.X.P., interview, May 7, 1976.

86. L.X.P. argues that these radicals came from weak organizations. For example, he argues that reactions to the Foshan Meeting varied directly with the strength of the organization. If an organization was strong, such as the Guangzhou Regiment, they supported the Foshan Meeting. Weak organizations tended to oppose the meeting. "Red Outcry," headed by Li Zhengtian, could oppose the attempts of the Rebels to work with the MCC and the Conservatives because they were "mere ideologists" with no real organizational responsibilities. According to L.X.P., such organizations had nothing to gain from consolidation and order since they did not represent any power bloc.

87. A prime example is Jiaoyu Geming, put out by Beijing Normal University.

88. This point was brought out to me by many interviewees.

89. In factory districts, such as Southern Guangzhou, it was the Rebels who had been chased away; they, too, were now able to return.

90. These documents would include the October 14 Notice for all students to return to classes, People's Daily editorials on October 25 and November 26, and Mao directives of November and December in People's Daily, November 2, 1967 and URI Documents, pp. 635-638.

91. See, for example, Xiaobing, December 24, 1967, p. 4.

92. Hongqi Pinglun/Gangbayi Zhanqi, January 1968, p. 2; Guangya Basanyi, early March 1968, p. 1; Hong Zhantuan, November 1967, p. 3; Gangbayi Zhanbao/Zhongjiao Hongqi, January 1968, p. 1.

93. Hong Zhantuan, November 1967, p. 3.

94. A representative sample of the various forms of subversion can be found in Hongse Zaofanzhe, new #2, late June 1968, translated in Current Background #861, September 3, 1968, pp. 1-19.

95. Bayi Fengbao, March 1968.

96. See, for example, Xiaobing, November 9, 1967, p. 4, and interviews with T.W.X. and L.I. This emphasis on using the early 1960's to criticize the control of the schools by bourgeois academic authorities and the advantages of those of bad class background was also prevalent in Beijing Red Guard newspapers.

97. Xiaobing, December 9 and 24, 1967.

98. On Number 5 Middle School see Xiaobing, December 9, 1967, p. 4, and interviews with T.W.X. and L.I.

99. Gangbayi Zhanbao/Zhongjiao Hongqi #2, January 1968, p. 1.

100. Ibid., p. 4. Hong Zhantuan makes a similar point about Number 4 Middle School.

101. Ibid., p. 3. Also see Hongqi Pinglun/Gangbayi Zhanqi, February 1968, p. 2.

102. In like manner, the Conservatives favored the allocation of positions in the Red Guard Congress on the basis of correct political line and class origin rather than on the basis of overall numerical strength or proportionally on a school-by-school basis. See Xiaobing, February 17, 1968, p. 4.

103. "The 'Right Deviation Trend of Trying to Reverse Correct Decisions' in Some Middle Schools in Canton" in Current Background (CB) #861, September 3, 1968, p. 5.

104. Ibid., pp. 5-6.

105. Ibid., pp. 2-7.

106. Xiaobing, December 24, 1967, p. 3.

107. Ibid.

108. Xiaobing, December 9, 1967, p. 3.

109. Xiaobing, December 24, 1967, p. 3.

110. CB #861, p. 10.

111. Ibid.

112. There were many "theories" dividing the GPCR into stages at this time. Perhaps the most prevalent was one that originated with the April 14 Regiment at Qinghua University in Beijing. Entitled "The April 14 Tide of Thought is Bound to Win," it was used by that unit as a means to counter the great popularity their opponents at Qinghua - under the direction of Kuai Dafu - had built up because of their early rebellion. For material on this slogan and on the military recruitment drive of spring, 1968, see L.X.P., Account, Chapter 9.

113. CB #861, pp. 1-18; see L.X.P., Account, Chaps. 8-10

for details on one particular middle school.

114. CNS #217, April 25, 1968.

115. Lee, Politics, pp. 279-280. The article on factionalism appears in RMRB, April 20, 1968.

116. Zhan Zhongnan #4, August 23, 1968.

117. Hai Feng, Guangzhou, pp. 364-365. For the impact
of Huang Yijian's reports on Guangzhou's Rebels see
L.X.P., Account, Chapter 10.

118. L.X.P., Account, Chapter 10. The units involved
were the Guangzhou Regiment, the Red Combat Regiment and
the Half-work Half-study Regiment.

119. NFRB, April 4, 1968.

120. See, for example, the reports cited in CB #861.

121. L.X.P., Account, Chapter 10.

122. Ibid.

123. On Huang's Beijing trip and his subsequent arrest,
see Basanyi #21, May 31, 1968, translated in SCMP #4208,
pp. 3-6.

124. Hong Dianxun, July 1968, in Hai Feng, Guangzhou,
pp. 366-369.

125. For an account of the various armed incidents in
Guangzhou at this time, see Hai Feng, Guangzhou, pp. 369-
380. On the situation in Southern Guangzhou, see Gongyedadaoqu Hongqi #1, July 1968.

126. Lee, Politics, p. 283.

127. The summary can be found in Zhan Guangdong, July 10,
1968, translated in SCMM #629, pp. 13-23. Also see Hai
Feng, Guangzhou, pp. 383-384 and for a personal account
of the meeting, L.X.P., Account, Chapter 10.

128. Gongren Pinglun, early August 1968; Hai Feng,
Guangzhou, pp. 384-386.

129. The contents of the July 3 and July 24 Notices are
in Hai Feng, Guangzhou, pp. 414-415 and 420-422.

130. These two notices can be found in Hai Feng,
Guangzhou, pp. 416-420.

131. Hai Feng, Guangzhou, p. 399.

132. L.X.P., <u>Account,</u> Chapter 11. This chapter also contains an account of the suppression of the Flag faction after July 10, along with the inadequate responses of that faction.

133. Hai Feng, <u>Guangzhou</u>, p. 399.

134. <u>Zhongda Zhanbao,</u> August 4, 1968, translated in <u>SCMP</u> #4257, September 13, 1968, pp. 1-5.

135. <u>Zhan Zhongnan,</u> August 23, 1968, pp. 1-2, translated in <u>SCMP</u> #4262, September 20, 1968, pp. 1-8. Also see the report in <u>Xingdao Ribao,</u> September 20, 1968. Criticism of the August 1 Combat Corps and its leader, Mo Jingwei, can also be found in <u>Guangzhou Gongdaihui,</u> August 11, 1968, reprinted in <u>Xingdao Ribao,</u> November 18, 1968.

136. <u>Guangzhou Hongdaihui</u> #11, August 29, 1968, translated in <u>SCMP</u> #4303, November 21, 1968, pp. 1-10.

137. L.X.P., <u>Account,</u> Chapter 11.

138. For details on six of these organizations see Hai Feng, <u>Guangzhou</u>, pp. 407-412.

Chapter 7   Epilogue

1. See "Students and Class Warfare: The Social Roots of The Red Guard Conflict in Guangzhou" by Anita Chan, Stanley Rosen and Jonathan Unger, <u>The China Quarterly</u>, No. 83, September 1980, pp. 397-446.

2. Interviews with L.X.P., 1976.

3. Interview with L.Y.P., September 11, 1976. Students of worker-peasant origin were favored at this time through their appointment as class cadres and as members of the schools' "security force" (<u>qingwei fendui</u>). They also took the lead in "struggle-criticism-transformation" work and in going to the countryside to labor. Jonathan Unger, in his interviews, found a somewhat different pattern. He found the class line policies of the 1968-70 period still strongly favored children of cadre origin over all others.

4. Zhang's essay was reprinted in <u>Liaoning Daily</u> on July 19, 1973 and in <u>People's Daily</u> on August 10, 1973. For a good analysis of the debate over higher education, see Jonathan Unger, "The Chinese Controversy Over Higher Education," <u>Pacific Affairs,</u> Vol. 53, No. 1, Spring 1980, pp. 29-47.

5.   They did, however, differ as to who was primarily at
fault for allowing such a situation to develop, who benefitted from such a situation, and the actual power such
untransformed intellectuals really had in the schools.

6.   Beijing Review (BR) #51, December 16, 1977, pp. 4-9.

7.   GMRB, August 12, 1977 in Survey of the People's
Republic of China Press #6411, August 26, 1977, pp. 155-
158.

8.   BR #30, July 28, 1978, p. 18.

9.   Ibid.

10.   Monsoon, Vol. 3, No. 7, August, 1980, pp. 30-32.

11.   BR #30, pp. 18-19.

12.   Ibid., pp. 19 and 22.

13.   BR #20 May 18, 1979, p. 6. For details on the new
keypoint system, see Stanley Rosen, "The Influence of
Structure on Behavior: Recent Changes in China's Secondary School Structure," Modern China (forthcoming).

14.   BR #5, February 3, 1978, pp. 18-19; ZGQNB, April 3,
1980, p. 1; RMRB, May 5, 1980, p. 1.

15.   BR #8, February 24, 1978, p. 15.

16.   There have been many reports in the press on this
transformation. See, for example, Renmin Jiaoyu, February, 1980, pp. 7-10; Guangzhou Ribao, June 19, 1980,
p. 1.; Changchun Radio, in FBIS, May 9, 1980, p. S3.

17.   BR #20, p. 6; BR #28, July 13, 1979, p. 7; ZGQNB,
November 13, 1980, p. 2; Jiaoyu Yanjiu, No. 4, 1980,
pp. 36-38; Renmin Jiaoyu No. 10, 1980, pp. 12-15; Nanfang
Ribao, July 21, 1980, p. 2.

18.   YCWB, August 12, 1980, p. 1.

19.   YCWB, August 16, 1980, p. 1.

20.   This information comes from an interview conducted
in Guangzhou the summer of 1980 by Professor Ezra Vogel.

21.   BR #46, November 17, 1978, p. 12.

22.   Ibid., p. 9.

23. BR #43, October 27, 1978, pp. 15-17.

24. Guiyang Radio, April 5, 1979, in JPRS No. 73316 (April 26, 1979); BR #30, July 28, 1978, p. 19.

25. ZGQNB, April 12, 1980, p. 2.

26. New York Times Magazine, December 28, 1980, pp. 22-26, 30, 35.

27. Fujian Ribao, April 21, 1979, in FBIS, April 23, 1979, pp. O2-3.

28. For reports on YCL membership among new university students, see BR #30, July 28, 1978, p. 19; NCNA, April 14, 1980, in FBIS, April 18, 1980, pp. L5-6.

29. NCNA, May 9, 1980, in FBIS, May 13, 1980, p. L2.

30. The above information comes from a letter received from a recent visitor to China with familial ties to education officials. The letter reported on a number of sources of student discontent.

31. NCNA, May 9, 1980, in FBIS, May 13, 1980, p. L2.

32. BR #30, July 28, 1980, p. 19.

33. It seems clear that the tremendous increase in senior high enrollment must include large numbers of students from working class and peasant backgrounds who would not have made it to senior high in the 1960's. Moreover, given the current importance of academic achievement as a criterion for university enrollment, these students are still not serious competitors. Nevertheless, judging from reports in the Chinese press, the large number of students in senior high, combined with the small number of those gaining acceptance to the university, has dampened the enthusiasm and motivation of students from all class backgrounds. For details on the readjustment of China's secondary school system, see Rosen, "The Influence of Structure on Behavior," Modern China, forthcoming.

34. See interviews with H.W.C. and L.X.P.

35. Dongxiang, (Hong Kong), #5, February, 1979, p. 19. For more recent developments on the Li Yizhe case, see Stanley Rosen, introduction to "The Rehabilitation and Dissolution of 'Li Yizhe'" in Chinese Law and Government, forthcoming.

308

36.   Jonathan Unger, "China's Troubled Down-to-the-Countryside Campaign," <u>Contemporary China,</u> Vol. 3, No. 2 (1979), pp. 79-92.

Bibliography

I. English Language Materials

    A. Books and Pamphlets (Authored)

Ahn, Byung-joon. <u>Chinese Politics and the Cultural Rev-</u>
<u>olution</u>. Seattle: University of Washington Press,
1976.

Baum, Richard. <u>Prelude to Revolution</u>. New York: Columbia University Press, 1975.

Bennett, Gordon and Montaperto, Ronald. <u>Red Guard: The</u>
<u>Political Biography of Dai Hsiao-ai.</u> New York: Double-
day, 1971.

Bernstein, Thomas. <u>Up to the Mountains and Down to the</u>
<u>Villages</u>. New Haven: Yale University Press, 1977.

Chien Yu-shen. <u>China's Fading Revolution</u>. Hong Kong:
Center of Contemporary Chinese Studies, 1969.

Chung Hua-min and Miller, Arthur C. <u>Madame Mao: A Pro-</u>
<u>file of Chiang Ch'ing</u>. Hong Kong: Union Research In-
stitute, 1968.

Collier, John and Elsie. <u>China's Socialist Revolution</u>.
New York: Monthly Review Press, 1973.

Esmein, Jean. <u>The Chinese Cultural Revolution</u>. New
York: Doubleday, 1970.

Hinton, William. <u>Hundred Day War.</u> New York: Monthly
Review Press, 1972.

Hunter, Neale. <u>Shanghai Journal</u>. New York: Praeger, 1969

Karol, K.S. <u>China: The Other Communism,</u> 2nd edition.
New York: Hill and Wang, 1968.

Kerr, Dr. J.G. <u>A Guide to the City and Suburbs of Canton</u>.
Hong Kong: Kelly and Walsh, 1904.

Lee, Edward Bing-shuey. <u>Modern Canton</u>. Shanghai: Shanghai Mercury Press, 1936.

Lee, Hong Yung. <u>The Politics of the Chinese Cultural</u>
<u>Revolution: A Case Study</u>. Berkeley: University of
California Press, 1978.

310

Leys, Simon. _Chinese Shadows_. New York: Viking, 1977.

Ling, Ken. _The Revenge of Heaven_. New York: Putnam, 1972.

Maitan, Livio. _Party, Army and Masses in China._ London: New Left Books, 1976.

Mao Tse-tung. _An Analysis of the Classes in Chinese Society_. Beijing: Foreign Language Press, 1956.

Mehnert, Klaus. _Peking and the New Left: At Home and Abroad_. Berkeley: Center for Chinese Studies, 1970.

Milton, David and Nancy Dall. _The Wind Will Not Subside._ New York: Pantheon, 1976.

Rice, Edward. _Mao's Way_. Berkeley: University of California Press, 1972.

Richman, Barry. _Industrial Society in Communist China._ New York: Random House, 1969.

Robinson, Thomas (ed.). _The Cultural Revolution in China_ Berkeley: University of California Press, 1971.

Rosen, Stanley. _The Role of the Sent-down Youth in the Chinese Cultural Revolution: The Case of Guangzhou._ Center for Chinese Studies, University of California, Berkeley, forthcoming.

Schram, Stuart (ed.). _The Political Thought of Mao Tsetung_. New York: Pantheon, 1974.

Taylor, Robert. _Education and University Enrollment Policies in China, 1949-1971_. Canberra: Australian National University, 1973.

Vogel, Ezra. _Canton Under Communism_. Cambridge: Harvard University Press, 1969.

Wang Jie. _The Diary of Wang Jie._ Beijing Foreign Language Press, 1967.

White, D. Gordon. _Class Background in Modern Chinese Politics: The Case of the Cultural Revolution._ Canberra: Australian National University, 1975.

Whyte, Martin K. _Small Groups and Political Rituals in China_. Berkeley: University of California Press, 1974

B. Translations of Chinese Documents or Articles in Book Form.

CCP Documents of the Great Proletarian Cultural Revolution 1966-67. Hong Kong: Union Research Institute, 1968.

Documents of the Chinese Communist Party Central Committee, September, 1956-April, 1968, Volume I. Hong Kong: Union Research Institute, 1971.

On the Proletarian Revolutionaries' Struggle to Seize Power. Beijing: Foreign Language Press, 1968.

On the Revolutionary "Three-in-One" Combination. Beijing: Foreign Language Press, 1968.

Training Successors for the Revolution is the Party's Strategic Task. Beijing: Foreign Language Press, 1965

C. Articles

Baum, Richard. "Elite Behavior Under Conditions of Stress: The Lesson of the 'Tang-ch'uan p'ai' in the Cultural Revolution" in Robert A. Scalapino, Elites in the People's Republic of China. Seattle: University of Washington Press, 1972.

Chan, Anita, Stanley Rosen and Jonathan Unger. "Students and Class Warfare: The Social Roots of the Red Guard Conflict in Guangzhou," The China Quarterly, #83, September 1980, pp. 397-446.

Chen, Pi-chao. "Overurbanization, Rustication of Urban-educated Youths, and Politics of Rural Transformation: The Case of China" in Comparative Politics, Volume 4, Number 3, April, 1972.

Cheng Chu-yuan. "Scientific and Engineering Manpower in Communist China" in An Economic Profile of Mainland China. New York: Praeger, 1968.

Crook, David. "Who Goes to College in China Now?" in Eastern Horizon, Volume 15, Number 3, 1976.

Domes, Jurgen. "Generals and Red Guards - The Role of Huang Yung-sheng and the Canton Military Area Command in the Kwangtung Cultural Revolution" in The Asia Quarterly (1971), pp. 3-31; 123-159.

Emerson, John Philip. "Employment in Mainland China: Problems and Prospects" in An Economic Profile of Mainland China. New York: Praeger, 1968.

312

"The Great Proletarian Cultural Revolution -- a Record of Major Events" in Chingkangshan, February, 1967. Translated in JPRS Translations on Communist China #420, August 25, 1967.

Kun, Joseph C. "Higher Education: Some Problems of Selection and Enrollment" in The China Quarterly, #8, October-December, 1961.

Lee, Hong Yung. "The Radical Students in Kwangtung During the Cultural Revolution" in The China Quarterly, #64, December, 1975.

"Lin Yun's Letter to the Canton Military Region Command," translated in Union Research Service (Hong Kong), Volume 52, #7-8, July 26, 1968.

Munro, Donald. "Egalitarian Ideal and Educational Fact in Communist China" in John M.H. Lindbeck, China: Management of a Revolutionary Society. Seattle: University of Washington Press, 1971.

Orleans, Leo. "Communist China's Education Policies, Problems and Prospects" in An Economic Profile of Mainland China. New York: Praeger, 1968.

"The 'Right Deviation Trend of Trying to Reverse Correct Decisions' in Some Middle Schools in Canton" in Current Background, #861, September 3, 1968.

Robinson, Thomas, "The Wuhan Incident: Local Strife and Provincial Rebellion During the Cultural Revolution" in The China Quarterly, #47, July-September, 1971.

Rosen, Stanley. "Comment: The Radical Students in Kwangtung During the Cultural Revolution" in The China Quarterly, #70, June, 1977.

Rosen, Stanley. "The Influence of Structure on Behavior: Recent Changes in China's Secondary School Structure in Pre-Cultural Revolution and Cultural Revolution Perspective," Modern China, forthcoming.

Rosen, Stanley. "The Rehabilitation and Dissolution of 'Li Yizhe,'" Chinese Law and Government, forthcoming.

Salaff, Janet W. "Urban Residential Communities in the Wake of the Cultural Revolution" in John Lewis, ed. The City in Communist China. Palo Alto: Stanford University Press, 1971.

Shirk, Susan. "Political Culture in the People's Republic of China: The Strategies of Chinese Students" (unpublished paper presented at the University of Michigan on August 10, 1977).

Unger, Jonathan. "China's Troubled Down-to-the-Country-side Campaign," Contemporary China, Vol. 31, No. 2 (1979), pp. 79-92.

Unger, Jonathan. "The Chinese Controversy Over Higher Education," Pacific Affairs, Vol. 53, No. 1, Spring 1980, pp. 24-47.

White, Lynn. "Shanghai's Polity in the Cultural Revolution" in John Lewis, ed. The City in Communist China. Palo Alto: Stanford University Press, 1971.

          D. Ph.D. Dissertations

Glassman, Joel. The Implementation of Education Policy in Communist China. University of Michigan, 1974.

Hsu, K. Chinese Communist Education: The Cultural Revolution. George Peabody College for Teachers, 1972.

Kraus, Richard Curt. The Evolving Concept of Class in Post-Liberation China. Columbia University, 1974.

Shirk, Susan L. The Middle School Experience in China. Massachusetts Institute of Technology, 1974.

Chinese Language Materials

          A. Books, Manuscripts, Pamphlets and Serialized Articles.

Ding Wang. Zhonggong Wenge Yundongzhong de Zuzhi yu Renshi Wenti. [The Question of Organizational and Personal Affairs in the Chinese Cultural Revolution]. Hong Kong: Contemporary China Research Institute, 1970.

Hai Feng. Haifeng Wenhua Geming Jishu. [An Account of the Cultural Revolution in Haifeng County]. Hong Kong: Zhongbao Zhoukan, 1969.

Hai Feng. Guangzhou Diqu Wenge Licheng Shulue. [An Account of the Cultural Revolution in the Guangzhou Area] Hong Kong: Union Research Institute, 1971.

Li Yizhe. Guanyu Shehui Zhuyi de Minzhu yu Fazhi. [Concerning Socialist Democracy and the Legal System]. Notes by Qi Hao. Hong Kong: Bibliotheque Asistique Series, 1976.

L.X.P. An Account of the Great Proletarian Cultural Revolution (handwritten unpublished). Hong Kong: 1975-76.

Mao Zedong. Mao Zedong Sixiang Wansui. [Long Live the Thought of Mao Zedong]. Tokyo: No publisher listed, 1967, 1969.

Tan Jianhua. Yike Hongxin Xiangzhe Dang. [A Red Heart Towards the Party]. Beijing: Renmin Chubanshe, 1966.

Union Research Institute. Collection of Red Guard Materials, Volume I. Hong Kong: No Date.

Wang Chao. Guangzhou Dianyingjie de Zaofanzhe. [The Rebels in Guangzhou Film Circles]. Hong Kong: Zhongbao Zhoukan, 1969.

Zhuang Yi. "Hongweibing Shouji" [Notes of a Red Guard]. In Zhongbao Zhoukan, issues #53-127 (1968-69).

Zhongguo Baike Nianjian 1980. [Encyclopedia Yearbook of China]. Beijing, Shanghai: China Encyclopedia Publishing House, 1980.

B. Newspapers and Periodicals

Beijing Ribao (Beijing)
Dagong Bao (Beijing)
Dagong Bao (Hong Kong)
Dongxiang (Hong Kong)
Guangming Ribao (Beijing)
Guangzhou Ribao (Guangzhou)
Hongqi (Beijing)
Hongwei Bao (Guangzhou)
Jiaoyu Yanjiu (Beijing)
Jiefang Junbao (Beijing)
Jinri Dalu (Taibei)
Ming Bao (Hong Kong)
Nanfang Ribao (Guangzhou)
Renmin Jiaoyu (Beijing)
Renmin Ribao (Beijing)
Wenhui Bao (Hong Kong)
Wenhui Bao (Shanghai)
Xianggang Shibao (Hong Kong)
Xingdao Ribao (Hong Kong)
Yangcheng Wanbao (Guangzhou)
Zhongbao Zhoukan (Hong Kong)
Zhongguo Qingnian (Beijing)
Zhongguo Qingnian Bao (Beijing)
Zhongguo Xinwen (Guangzhou)

C. Red Guard Newspapers

1. From Guangzhou

Basanyi
Bayi Fengbao
Beijing Laidian
Dongfeng Zhanbao
Fanyou Tekan
Gangbayi
Cangbayi Zhanbao/ Jiaogai Haojiao
Gongnongbing Zhanbao
Gongren Pinglun
Gongyedadaoqu Hongqi
Guangdong Zhanbao
Guangya Basanyi
Guangya 6.8 Fangeming Shijian Junkan
Guangyi Hongqi

Guangyin Hongqi
Guangzhou Gongdaihui
Guangzhou Hongdaihui
Guangzhou Hongweibing
Hong Dianxun
Hongse Baodong
Hongse Zaofanzhe
Hongqi Bao
Hongqi Pinglun/Gangbayi
  Zhanqi
Hongzhan Bao
Hongzhan Tuan
Liuyue Tianbing
Nahan Zhanbao
Sanjun Lianwei Zhanbao

Sansi Zhanbao
Tiaozhan
Wenge Pinglun
Wenge Tongxun
Xiaobing
Yiyue Fengbao
Zhan Guangdong
Zhan Zhongnan
Zhidian Jiangshan
Zhongda Hongqi
Zhongda Zhanbao
Zhongxue Hongweibing
Zhuying Dongfanghong
Ziliao Zhuanji
831

2. From Beijing and Other Cities

Bingtuan Zhanbao (Beijing)
Chunlei (Beijing)
Dongfanghong(Beijing)
Dongfeng Bao (Beijing)
Hongweibing Zhanbao (Shanghai)
Jiaoyu Geming (Beijing)
Jinggangshan (Beijing)

Kangda Zhanbao (Beijing)
Pitao Zhanbao (Beijing)
Weidong (Nanjing)
Wuqianli Kuanglan (Wuhan)
Xin Beida (Beijing)
Zhengfa Hongqi (Beijing)
Zhiba Chunlai Bao (Beijing)
Zhongxue Doupigai (Beijing)
Zhongxue Luntan (Beijing)

Index